Imperial Co-operation and Transfer, 1870–1930

Imperial Co-operation and Transfer, 1870–1930

Empires and Encounters

Edited by
Volker Barth and Roland Cvetkovski

Bloomsbury Academic
An imprint of Bloomsbury Publishing Plc

BLOOMSBURY
LONDON • OXFORD • NEW YORK • NEW DELHI • SYDNEY

Bloomsbury Academic
An imprint of Bloomsbury Publishing Plc

50 Bedford Square	1385 Broadway
London	New York
WC1B 3DP	NY 10018
UK	USA

www.bloomsbury.com

BLOOMSBURY and the Diana logo are trademarks of Bloomsbury Publishing Plc

First published 2015
Paperback edition first published 2017

© Volker Barth, Roland Cvetkovski and Contributors, 2015

All rights reserved. No part of this publication may be reproduced or transmitted in any form or by any means, electronic or mechanical, including photocopying, recording, or any information storage or retrieval system, without prior permission in writing from the publishers.

No responsibility for loss caused to any individual or organization acting on or refraining from action as a result of the material in this publication can be accepted by Bloomsbury or the authors.

British Library Cataloguing-in-Publication Data
A catalogue record for this book is available from the British Library.

ISBN: HB: 978-1-4725-9213-2
PB: 978-1-3500-2477-9
ePDF: 978-1-4725-9214-9
ePub: 978-1-4725-9215-6

Library of Congress Cataloging-in-Publication Data
Imperial co-operation and transfer, 1870-1930 : empires and encounters / edited by Volker Barth and Roland Cvetkovski.
pages cm
ISBN 978-1-4725-9213-2 (hardback) – ISBN 978-1-4725-9214-9 (ePDF) – ISBN 978-1-4725-9215-6 (ePub) 1. History, Modern--19th century 2. History, Modern–20th century. 3. Imperialism–History–19th century. 4. Imperialism–History–20th century. 5. International cooperation–History–19th century. 6. International cooperation–History–20th century. 7. Cultural relations–History–19th century. 8. Cultural relations–History–20th century. 9. World politics–19th century. 10. World politics–1900–1945. I. Barth, Volker, 1974– II. Cvetkovski, Roland. III. Title: Imperial cooperation and transfer, 1870–1930.
D359.7.I56 2015
909.81–dc23
2015005075

Typeset by RefineCatch Ltd, Bungay, Suffolk

Contents

List of Illustrations	vii
Notes on Contributors	viii
Acknowledgments	xi

Part One   Conceptual Horizons

Introduction – Encounters of Empires: Methodological Approaches
Volker Barth and Roland Cvetkovski   3

1 European Imperialism: A Zone of Co-operation Rather than Competition? *John M. MacKenzie*   35

Part Two   Connecting Colonialisms

2 New Forms of Knowledge Exchange Between Imperial Powers: The Development of the Institut Colonial International (ICI) Since the End of the Nineteenth Century *Ulrike Lindner*   57

3 Private Colonialism and International Co-operation in Europe, 1870–1914 *Florian Wagner*   79

Part Three   Law Transfers

4 Riparian Rights in Lower Canada and Canada East: Inter-imperial Legal Influences *David Schorr*   107

5 Creating a Colonial *Shariʿa* for Russian Turkestan: Count Pahlen, the *Hidaya* and Anglo-Muhammadan Law *Alexander Morrison*   127

Part Four   Adaptation and Counterbalance

6 Same Race, Same Fate? Theories of Asian Commonality and the Shift of Regional Hegemony in East Asia After the First Sino-Japanese War (1894/5) *Torsten Weber*   153

7 The Origins of Trans-imperial Policing: British-French Government Co-operation in the Surveillance of Anti-colonialists in Europe, 1905–25   *Daniel Brückenhaus*   171

Part Five   Military and Violence

8 Co-operation Between German and French Troops During the Boxer War in China, 1900/1: The Punitive Expedition to Baoding
   Susanne Kuss   197

9 Deadly Learning? Concentration Camps in Colonial Wars Around 1900   *Jonas Kreienbaum*   219

Index   237

List of Illustrations

Figure 4.1	View of the Miner's Dam, Granby, QC, about 1910	108
Figure 4.2	Sitting of a Judicial Committee of the Privy Council	109
Figure 6.1	White Peril cartoon (*Yomiuri Shinbun*, 1900)	164

Notes on Contributors

Volker Barth is assistant professor of modern history at the University of Cologne. He was educated in Germany and France. In 2004 he received a co-tutelle PhD from the Ludwig-Maximilians-University (LMU), Munich, and the École des Hautes Études en Sciences Sociales (EHESS), Paris. Further teaching and research positions include the Université Paris VII-Denis Diderot, the German Academic Exchange Service (DAAD) and the Bureau International des Expositions (BIE), Paris. His current research project focuses on the co-operation of globally operating news agencies between the mid-nineteenth century and the interwar period.

Daniel Brückenhaus received his PhD from Yale University in 2011. After a year as a post-doctoral fellow at the Max Planck Institute for Human Development, Center for the History of Emotions, in Berlin, he is now an assistant professor of modern European history at Beloit College. Research interests include the history of the European colonial empires, the history of government surveillance and the history of emotions. Daniel Brückenhaus has published articles on the history of trust, and on European memories. He is currently finishing a book manuscript on the transnational surveillance of anti-colonialists in early twentieth-century Europe, and he is working on a research project on the history of dignity, honour and shame under colonialism.

Roland Cvetkovski is assistant professor in the Department of Eastern European History at the University of Cologne, where he completed his doctoral degree in 2005. He is the author of *Modernisierung durch Beschleunigung. Raum und Mobilität im Zarenreich* (*Modernization through acceleration. Space and mobility in the Tsarist Empire*) (Frankfurt, M.: Campus, 2006) and has worked on several topics of Russian, Ottoman and French cultural and imperial history from the eighteenth to the twentieth century. Currently he is writing a book on the revolutionary museum culture in early Soviet Russia.

Jonas Kreienbaum is assistant professor at the Historical Institute of the University of Rostock. He studied history, philosophy and political science at the Humboldt University Berlin and the University of Nottingham. In 2013 he was awarded a PhD at the Humboldt University for his thesis 'A sad fiasco. Colonial concentration camps around 1900'. He is specialized in colonial and genocide studies as well as North-South relations in the post-colonial world. Currently he is working on a post-doc project scrutinizing the effects of the 1970s oil crises on the negotiations for a New International Economic Order.

Susanne Kuss is *Privatdozentin* in modern history at the University of Bern (Switzerland). Following her study of history and philosophy in Berlin and Freiburg

(Germany), she obtained a PhD in history from the University of Freiburg. Having taught at the Universities of Freiburg and Kassel, she now lectures at the University of Bern. One focus of her research is the German colonial wars in Africa and China. Her most recent book, also focusing on this topic, was awarded a prize from the German Publishers and Booksellers Association together with the Thyssen endowment.

Ulrike Lindner is a professor in modern history at the University of Cologne. She first worked on comparative European social policy after World War II and published a book on health policy in West Germany and Great Britain. Afterwards she concentrated on colonial and global history, publishing a book and many articles on encounters and transfers between British and German African colonies before World War I. She is currently involved in research on knowledge exchange between European colonial powers until the 1940s, on colonial social policy and in an interdisciplinary project 'From slave to coolie: migrations, work, and coolie culture' at the Global South Studies Centre, Cologne.

John M. MacKenzie is Emeritus Professor of Imperial History at Lancaster University. He also holds honorary professorships of the Universities of Aberdeen and St Andrews and is an honorary professorial fellow at the University of Edinburgh. He is a Fellow of the Royal Society of Edinburgh and of the Royal Historical Society. Among his publications are *Propaganda and Empire*, *The Empire of Nature*, *Orientalism: History, Theory and the Arts*, *The Scots in South Africa* and *Museums and Empire*. He is the editor and co-editor of many books, including *European Empires and the People*, *Scotland and the British Empire*, *Exhibiting the Empire* and *Scotland, Empire and Decolonisation*. He has edited the Manchester University Press *Studies in Imperialism* series for thirty years and is currently editor-in-chief of the Wiley-Blackwell *Encyclopedia of Empire*, which will cover empires in human history in four volumes and 1.2 million words.

Alexander Morrison is professor of history at Nazarbayev University in Astana, Kazakhstan. Between 2007 and 2013 he was lecturer in imperial history at the University of Liverpool, and between 2000 and 2007 a Prize Fellow of All Souls College, Oxford. He is the author of *Russian Rule in Samarkand 1868–1910: A Comparison with British India* (Oxford University Press, 2008), and is currently writing a history of the Russian conquest of Central Asia. In 2012 he won a Philip Leverhulme Prize.

David Schorr is a senior lecturer at Tel Aviv University, Buchmann Faculty of Law, where he teaches environmental law and legal history. His book on the development of water law in the western United States, *The Colorado Doctrine: Water Rights, Corporations, and Distributive Justice on the American Frontier* was published by Yale University Press in 2012, and he is currently at work on a book on the history of water law in the British Empire. He blogs at *Environment, Law, and History* (environmentlawhistory.blogspot.com).

Florian Wagner is a PhD candidate at the University of Freiburg and at the European University Institute in Florence. In his dissertation, he analyses colonial internationalism and the transfers of expert knowledge in institutions like the *Institut Colonial International*. His case studies include colonial interest groups in Germany, France, Spain and Belgium, with reference made to British, Dutch and Argentine colonialism.

Torsten Weber is a senior research fellow at the German Institute for Japanese Studies (DIJ) in Tokyo. He received his PhD in Japanese studies from Heidelberg University and an MA in Chinese studies from the School of Oriental and African Studies (University of London). His research in the fields of modern and contemporary East Asian history focuses on Asianism, history politics, historical reconciliation and regional integration. His latest project studies sociopolitical discourse on happiness in Imperial Japan.

Acknowledgments

The contributions of this volume are the result of a conference held in January 2013 at the Center for Advanced Studies *Morphomata* at the University of Cologne. We are particularly indebted to its director Prof. Dr Dietrich Boschung as well as to Dr Larissa Förster for their vivid interest in our project and for funding, advertising and co-organizing the conference. The warm reception at the Morphomata Center and its inspiring atmosphere made us feel at home and stimulated our discussions. We were also thrilled about the participants' commitment, and we especially appreciate their patience in the editing process. The comments of Bloomsbury's anonymous referees undoubtedly improved our project and made us think more thoroughly about some aspects of inter-imperial co-operations and encounters of empires. Finally, we could not imagine a more uncomplicated and easy communication than that we had with Claire Lipscomb and Emma Goode of Bloomsbury's editorial team.

Volker Barth and Roland Cvetkovski

Part One

Conceptual Horizons

INTRODUCTION

Encounters of Empires: Methodological Approaches

Volker Barth and Roland Cvetkovski

Empires were always considered as decisive agents of historical development. From the very beginning of recorded history, Mesopotamian, Roman and Chinese imperial state formations proved to have long lasting impacts on entire continents. Later, the founding of empires in the so-called New World by Spain and Portugal marked the beginning of what European historians labelled the modern era. From the sixteenth century onwards new empires like the Dutch and the British followed in their footsteps and along with the Russian, Habsburg, German and also the Ottoman Empires became key actors of European expansion which until quite recently was regarded by many historians as nothing less than the driving force of history as such.[1] The significance of this historical idea can be observed even in political debates today. In the last few years the traces of empire and its effect on contemporary politics came into the picture most impressively in the United States, as its intervention in Iraq was accompanied by a public revival of 'empire talk' scrutinizing America's hegemonic role in the world.[2] The persistence of the imperial concept to describe the implications of modern foreign policy even after the 'classical' empires had disappeared from the historical scene is striking.

In common understanding, the period from the mid-nineteenth century until the beginning of World War II marked the climax of the imperial impact on world history and has therefore been labelled the age of European high imperialism for many decades. In most instances this term referred to power struggles between European empires for colonial territories which were later joined by Western or Westernized imperial newcomers such as the United States and Japan. Their relations, it has been often argued, were above all competitive, and thus characterized by specific efforts of outdoing the other. To be sure, constant rivalry and opposition was a crucial part of imperialism. The present volume, however, attempts to complement this approach by assuming another starting point. By underlining first the global dimensions of imperialism in the period under consideration and second by providing analytic case studies that highlight the multiple collaborations between empires, we argue that despite continuous competition, empires also interacted in a considerable number of fields. The analysis of imperialism as both a set of ideas and a set of practices bound to identifiable sites has to take account of diverse inter-imperial encounters.

While the first argument is rather easy to substantiate, the second requires explanation, and a thorough examination of the historiography of imperialism. Between 1870 and 1930 the influence of empires obviously reached far beyond the already impressive confines of European high imperialism. In Africa, older empires like the British, the French, the Spanish and the Portuguese not only intensified their conquests and exploitations but were challenged by newcomer empires such as Germany, Italy and Belgium. While Latin America had become largely independent from imperial rule in the first decades of the nineteenth century, the entire American continent was heavily affected by the coming of age of the United States. In Asia, a continent that had been object and subject of imperial rule for centuries, Chinese imperial rule declined, Dutch imperialism persisted in the Indonesian archipelago, all while the wider region experienced the spectacular establishment of the Japanese Empire. As far as the Ottoman, Habsburg and Russian Empires on the Eurasian continent were concerned, their constantly predicted dissolution did not happen any sooner than at the end of World War I.

Even if the concept of empire was and still is omnipresent in academic as well as public debate, a clear-cut definition remains controversial, although, or perhaps precisely because, most historians, at least according to Jürgen Osterhammel, agree that empires were 'on a global level the dominant territorial form of the organization of power'.[3] For all their heterogeneity in the nineteenth and early twentieth centuries they still shared a certain number of common features such as multi-ethnicity, asymmetrical and repressive power structures, authoritarian forms of government, inherent universalistic ideologies as well as the constant threat and repeated exercise of violence.[4] Diachronically, they could be described as moving along trajectories of military expansion and conquest abroad and intensification of authoritarian governance at home. But expansionism is only one characteristic of empires. More significantly, empires display a certain set of institutional features identifying them as a recognizable form of political organization in which the ruling class of the dominant state establishes networks of associated local elites who accept subordination in order to preserve their social and political position. In this sense empires represent a specific 'system of rule' that, in the end, stabilized social as well as political inequalities.[5] In the most general way, as Frederick Cooper puts it, an empire is a 'political unit that is large, expansionist (or with memories of an expansionist past), and which reproduces differentiation and inequality among people it incorporates'.[6]

General characterizations of colonial conditions and practices certainly do offer tools of analysis for specific empires. Most studies, however, continue to examine empires as 'clearly bounded geopolities', as one critic recently observed. 'Historical evidence', she continues, actually 'points in another direction – not at fixed boundaries, but at fluid, ill-defined ones'.[7] Therefore, the present volume does not focus on unambiguously delimited entities, but investigates the permeability of boundaries, cross-border exchanges by identifiable actors, the networks and channels in which these transgressions occurred and, finally, the effects they produced. In order to do so, we first address the historiography of empires, turn then to the lacunae in research concerning inter-imperial co-operation and delineate the contact zones in which these inter-imperial encounters emerged. Finally, we provide methodological and conceptual considerations necessary to distinguish inter-imperial transfers from other forms of contact and attempt a research design for inter-imperial exchanges.

I. Histories of empire

For many decades, historians – many of whom had personally participated in imperialist movements – described empires almost exclusively from a white, male, upper-class, European perspective. Mostly praising imperial accomplishments and sometimes criticizing insufficient realizations of imperial potentials, these authors hardly ever questioned the righteousness of imperialism.[8] The huge decolonization processes in Africa and Asia from the 1940s onward, however, brought voices to the forefront – most prominently those of Frantz Fanon and Aimé Césaire – that proposed a radically different perspective on the apparent blessings of imperial conquests. Almost simultaneously and with regards to the British case, John Gallagher and Ronald Robinson established yet another but equally influential analysis of the intensification of imperialism from the 1870s onwards. They identified informal empires and especially the idea of free trade which supposedly reduced commitment while maximizing financial benefits as the genuine ideal of British imperialism. In the mindset of most British officials actual territorial occupation, i.e. formal empire, was most of all a reluctantly undertaken remedy to cure serious crises of informal rule. They ultimately argued that, 'far from staging a forward march from the bastions of mid-Victorian imperialism, the British were condemned by secular change to run faster to stay in the same place. [...] Britain was a *status quo* power drawn into reluctant expansion by the crises in her spheres of influence.'[9]

Gallagher's and Robinson's analysis of imperialism was based on the 'official mind': powerful white men residing in European metropoles who decided, even though increasingly hesitantly, desperately, and in a disillusioned way, the fate of imperial endeavours. Thus, empires appeared to be conceptualized, designed and established by a confined circle of high-ranking military and administrative officials who reacted to crisis situations in the so-called periphery.[10] That point of view came under scrutiny in the 1990s when P.J. Cain and A.G. Hopkins published influential accounts of the British Empire in which the City of London's financial district was described as the driving force of imperial expansion. Motivated by the prospect of enormous benefits triggered by the constant exploitation of virtually limitless colonial resources, 'gentlemen capitalists' pushed the London government towards the conquest of more and more colonial spaces.[11]

Despite important differences both models shared an analytical framework that, firstly, highlighted a selected number of European metropolitan protagonists and, secondly, challenged the idea that imperialism was limited to the territorial frontiers of state government. Consequently, both analyses contributed to an increasing scepticism regarding the analytical potential of histories of imperialism that addressed only one isolated empire. Historians were increasingly convinced that imperialism only reveals itself when placed in a much wider and ultimately global context.

Over the last few decades, however, authors from former European colonies and especially from India, have continued to criticize the predominantly European perspective of these studies. By focusing on local and regional levels within the colonies, Dipesh Chakrabarty, Partha Chatterjee, Gayatri Chakravorty Spivak and others threw both the practical and the analytical difference between imperialism and colonialism into sharp relief. They perceived empire predominantly as an expansionist, largely territorially defined entity whose heterogeneous institutions were held together by a universalistic programme and by various forms of violence. Colonialism, by contrast, referred to a hierarchical relationship in which colonial rulers decided on the lifestyle of colonized peoples.[12] The resolute appeal of these authors to investigate the so-called subaltern groups prompted their colleagues to rewrite colonial subjects back into imperial narratives.[13] By that they contested established divisions between colonizers/colonized and metropole/periphery that they regarded as part of the ideological framework and not as the actual outcome of imperialism.

As a result, the search for a single fundamental *movens* of empire has been challenged. In this process the emerging 'new imperial history' underlined the complexity of imperial rule and concentrated on competing visions of empire as formulated by a large variety of imperial actors that can be found not only within single empires but also across different imperial units.[14] Such studies retraced overlapping, partly connected, partly competing networks of people and ideas that bound imperial rule together. They looked on the 'macrosystem' of empires and focused on the interaction between different imperial protagonists.[15] The idea was to 'identify multiple, and often contestatory, "projects" of colonialism, rather than try to isolate the single driving force behind imperial expansion'.[16]

In augmenting the degree of complexity, these approaches challenged established definitions. Imperialism now appeared as 'a common framework for the mutual constitution of metropole and colony' as well as 'the aggregate of actions for the conquest and preservation of an empire'.[17] Remarkably, such a definition implicitly eclipses an aspect that had been a cornerstone for the conceptualization of empires for decades: empires as competing power structures. Paul Kennedy, for example, focusing on the Anglo-German antagonism on the eve of World War I, found hardly any examples of collaboration between the two empires. He judged 'the issues agreed upon (or nearly agreed upon) by 1914 in comparison to the more fundamental causes of disharmony' as almost negligible.[18] Without relativizing the obvious conflicts between the two states it is striking how Kennedy's approach tacitly blanked out all kinds of established forms of interaction – diplomatic, scientific, cultural etc. – and thus excludes all cooperative activities from the outset. In contrast, the idea of informal imperialism, postcolonial studies and the wider field of new imperial history have paved the way for investigating inter-imperial encounters. Empires were no longer addressed as blindly obeying to the principles of *realpolitik*, leading them almost automatically into the 'scramble for Africa' or the 'great game' in Asia. Instead, an empire appeared as a specific framework for related political, economic, and cultural practices within and across state formations.

Apart from the overall scarcity of empirical studies of inter-imperial collaboration, the principal challenge consists of finding an analytical position that allows us to investigate encounters of empires over time while simultaneously interrelating their history and historiography.[19] This is what the chapters of this volume try to tackle. They share a common scepticism towards earlier conceptualizations limiting empires to fragile but expanding power formations that were automatically and continuously involved in political, economic and military competition over territories, peoples and resources. Instead, the contributions address various forms of collaboration between empires, comprising the coexistence of different and sometimes contradictory practices as well as specific regimes of imperial rule. This does not mean, however, that all empires are considered as equals in the first place, nor that their similarities outweigh their differences. It does assume, though, that they did share common assumptions, challenges and techniques regarding the conquest, administration and exploitation of their respective colonies. The coexistence of separate imperial formations was, as we argue, also significantly characterized by co-operation, inasmuch as various groups of imperial actors formed inter-imperial networks through which empires could openly display mutual willingness to interact with each other.

Thus, the main purpose of the present volume is to show that circulation and transfers of specific knowledge orders and power practices were crucial for the implementation as well as the durability of empires. Even though scholars time and again mention that empires constantly learned from each other, we know surprisingly little of how, when and where these processes took place, who initiated them and how they impinged on or even created different imperial narratives.[20] In orchestrating inter-imperial encounters, imperial elites from various fields generated a substantial interest in common techniques of effective imperial rule. These experts forged distinct knowledge patterns of imperial governance, which were made available and, by consequence, applicable to diverse imperial settings, and which could give to single empires a cutting edge within the concert of imperial competition. So shedding light on inter-imperial encounters as well as their imperial repercussions and spin-offs can contribute far more to imperial research agendas than merely filling empirical gaps.

II. Fields of encounters

Surprisingly, historians have found a considerable amount of evidence for inter-imperial exchanges while hardly ever including their findings into wider definitions or theories of imperialism. After all, exchanges between empires 'in fields as diverse as the military, administration, trade, and religion' are by no means restricted to the years between 1870 and 1930.[21] Therefore it might be no coincidence that political scientists picked up on that issue, stating a 'new imperial dynamic in the development of transnational relations' from the nineteenth century onward.[22]

Within historical accounts of single empires the relationships between metropoles and colonies, just as between colonizers and colonized, remain prevailing, even though these terms and the concepts emerging from them have undergone dramatic changes. Without necessarily weakening these familiar antagonisms, the focus on inner-imperial relationships illuminates how colonial encounters produced a specific 'culture of imperial rule' and how governance originated from the specific dynamics initiated by the collaboration between colonizers and colonized. In his brilliant book about the encounter of the British and the Xhosa in South Africa, Richard Price demonstrates how the collaboration between colonizers and colonized led to distinguishable techniques of domination.[23] Nevertheless, scholars hesitate to apply such bold approaches to inter-imperial relationships where questions of state sovereignty are likely to join features of cultural amalgamation.

Recent imperial histories have underlined that the very notion of state sovereignty was critical to justify, mobilize and legitimate colonial rule. They stress that 'colonial state construction derived from European international legal notions'.[24] Sometimes colonial collaboration based on ideas of international law even led to the joint governance of occupied territories. This was the case in the Danubian principalities in the eighteenth and nineteenth centuries, in territories administered within the League of Nations' mandate system in the early twentieth century and even in the French-British condominium of the New Hebrides (Vanuatu) after World War II.[25]

All the same, historical studies of collaboration mostly remain at the level of well-known diplomatic coalitions.[26] For example, Lutz Raphael's recent account of European history between 1914 and 1945 explicitly focuses on the imperial context but stresses yet again the imperial confrontation that led to World War I. This thoughtful study, although very carefully avoiding limiting European interwar history solely to the European continent, interprets the various inter-imperial relations at the turn of the century as anticipations of future war alliances.[27] But were these specific and intricate political relations not also responsible for preventing an earlier implosion of Europe? Isn't it revealing that neither 'the scramble for Africa', nor the 'great game' in Asia led to large scale military clashes between empires before World War II? One may wonder why the perpetual inner-European tensions hardly ever resulted in open inter-imperial clashes within the colonies. Even the notable exception of the wars between the Japanese and Chinese Empires, as Torsten Weber discusses in his contribution, led to new efforts in inter-imperial collaboration.

From an imperial perspective it makes little sense to view Europe exclusively as a set of competing state entities disregarding a whole range of transfer processes between them. It is equally unconvincing to simply transpose European rivalries into the colonial setting, assuming that their colonies were merely additional arenas for competition. Just like nation-states, empires never were hermetical structures that can be analytically isolated from territorial neighbours, economic challengers or ideological counterparts. Grant, Levine and Trentmann are certainly right when they point out that 'transnational forces and ideas were also an intrinsic part of the way in which many of these states operated as empires'.[28] Furthermore, recent publications show that strictly comparative studies of empires run the risk of artificially separating highly intertwined units. They tend to deepen cleavages between Western and Eastern empires by reproducing apparently typical patterns of occidental and oriental government as well as essentializing differences between continental and maritime empires.[29] Alexei Miller and Alfred J. Rieber questioned such artificial antagonisms and instead emphasized intertwined spheres of imperial action. With regard to Austria-Hungary, Russia, the Ottoman Empire and Germany they argued that the empires' actions and reactions only become explainable when investigated as part of a much wider system of power relations throwing the mutual dependence of the neighbouring empires into sharp relief.[30]

It is therefore crucial to include specific contact zones in the study of imperial relationships in particular and imperialism in general, as they were likely to produce temporary co-operation. Empires faced similar tasks when implementing imperial rule. Among them were the recruitment of workforces, the establishment of allegiances within heterogeneous colonial societies, and the general demonstration of cultural and economic superiority. Observing how other empires managed to do this and exchanging related experiences was a common pattern of imperial rule and able to stabilize colonialism within one country, as Alexander Morrison shows in his contribution about the attempt of the Russian Empire to regulate Islamic law in Central Asia by borrowing from the experiences of the British in India. These 'international connections' and means of 'inter-imperial "lesson-learning"' impinged heavily on imperial policies.[31]

There are plenty of examples of inter-imperial contacts, collaboration and exchanges. Some authors have even tried to compile the various fields and practices which characterize encounters of empires. According to Miller and Rieber, these embrace the 'interaction of ideological, national, religious, population and frontier policies among empires; interaction of imperial and national ideologies within empires; interaction of different forms of legitimacy (*translatio imperii*); interaction of pragmatic and dogmatic methods of rule; interaction of core and periphery within and between empires'.[32] This list, however, obviously requires not only a more thorough selection but also more careful analytical differentiation between instances of the mere influence of imperial relations within a global setting, and genuine cases of imperial policies resulting from a deliberate engagement of one empire with the way colonial issues were handled by another.

Translatio imperii, for example, i.e. the way empires designed their policies by referring to imperial predecessors, provided a reliable method to prevent 'the provincialism of each empire prevailing'[33] on the one hand, and to legitimize imperial policies on the other. Referring to an apparent historical tradition helped to mould a coherent imperial ideology which made empires visible, recognizable and ultimately capable of acting.[34] In Britain, the idea of an empire understood as related parts forming an ideological unit emerged at the end of the eighteenth century. Only then did metropolitan elites start elaborating solutions for colonial problems which they considered universally applicable. From now on colonies were imagined less as singular territories than as interchangeable elements requiring similar actions.[35] Consequently, in 1849 Edward Gibbon Wakefield could publish a study entitled *A View of the Art of Colonization* that while dealing with the specific example of Britain's colony in New Zealand, outlined a theory of administering and developing overseas colonies in general.

Even if the limits of such meta-theories quickly became apparent, Wakefield's manual reflected the extent to which specific techniques and knowledge patterns became central to imperial rule.[36] In the long run, however, the colonizers' physical appropriation of new territories was actually undermined as imperial protagonists in the metropoles did not so much try to gain knowledge from, but rather produce it for, the colonies.[37] As Saul Dubow has pointed out with regard to the British Cape Colony, white colonial settlers in Africa and elsewhere put much emphasis on constructing explanations of colonialism 'so as to fit in with, and inform, universal western schemes of knowledge. Theirs was the knowledge *about* Africans rather than the knowledge *of* Africans themselves.'[38] Working on the wider region including present day Namibia, the former colony of German South-West Africa, Ulrike Lindner goes one step further and stresses the colonizer's 'need for developing a common imperial archive'.[39] French imperial authorities in particular made many efforts to elaborate overall theories of *mise en valeur* supposed to serve as guidelines for administering French colonies all over the globe. The colony that all European empires regarded as a model of *mise en valeur* and, by consequence, studied intensively was the Dutch controlled archipelago of present day Indonesia. Between 1891 and 1904 the French sent no fewer than twenty-five study delegations to Dutch East India and the British used their observations of the Dutch to inform policies in their colony in Malaya.[40]

Apparently, shared values motivated actors from various empires to participate in common endeavours. As Ulrike Kirchberger has convincingly shown, many German scientists contributed decisively to British imperialism by consciously putting their work into the service of British displays of power. For these German scientists British conquests not only opened up new career opportunities but also provided new spaces to put their conviction of the overall benefits of imperialism into practice. In fact, they can be regarded as 'precursors of British overseas expansion'.[41] Furthermore, they were eager to instrumentalize the research results obtained in British colonies for German imperial endeavours.[42]

Science was one of the shared values, not least because colonial theory itself was meant to be scientific. It played a significant role in inscribing colonial conquests and imperial administration practices into the general 'language of progress' as well as into the 'chain of civilization'.[43] In *Colonialism and Its Forms of Knowledge*, Bernard S. Cohn distinguishes six fields of knowledge production. Among these cartography, anthropology and medicine proved to be particularly influential for imperial expansion,[44] and scientists from various empires collaborated along the lines of these 'investigative modalities'.[45] French agricultural scientists, for example, carefully studied the success of their British colleagues in Australia. As early as the late 1860s, by planting trees such as the Australian eucalyptus that helped drain swamps, the French had considerably improved the sanitary conditions of their Algerian colony. The British for their part despatched study commissions to Algeria in order to work out blueprints for hygiene improvements in India.[46] Within the colonial context, science served as a platform for exchanging ideological resources and became a powerful instrument to theorize and legitimate imperial rule. Generally, in the period between 1870 and 1930 scientists acted as 'techniciens de la colonisation'.[47]

For many of them, colonies provided huge and largely unexplored fields for all kinds of activities. Small, influential and strongly connected communities of leading experts from several empires soon seized these opportunities. The results of their investigations were carefully studied by their colleagues back home and quickly made their way to other colonies. There, they could be tested, adapted and put into the service of specific imperial requirements. Deborah J. Neill has shown this for the domain of tropical medicine, one of the paradigmatic disciplines of colonial science:

> They [the tropical physicians] benefited from the expansion of European empires that offered them new fields in which to conduct research, and although they were competitive with each other and with their colleagues in other countries, their

shared European heritage, similar training, and common commitment to a global, scientific "civilizing mission" helped them develop strong personal and professional bonds with like-minded scientists both within their home scientific communities and across national and colonial borders.[48]

Such personal bonds were developed, among others, at international scientific congresses where experts established networks and generated specific knowledge repertoires. Referring to the example of the 'Congrès des sciences géographiques, cosmographiques et commerciales' in Antwerp in 1871, Claude Blanckaert has underlined the simultaneity of the institutionalization of scientific congresses and the intensification of European colonial conquest.[49] From the mid-nineteenth century onwards, universal exhibitions, mostly held in the capitals of European empires, provided favourable occasions to establish and invigorate scientific networks. The number of congresses taking place within these exhibitions steadily rose, and imperial topics proved to be of particular importance, as can be illustrated by the example of the 'Congrès colonial international' that was organized within the 'Exposition universelle' in Paris in 1889.[50] The participants of this and other congresses contributed significantly in defining colonial values, virtues and techniques, and thus helped to 'consolidate a formal, pan-European imperial moral and legal order'.[51] Florian Wagner's contribution to this volume shows how this led not only to ongoing exchanges between different national colonial associations but also to the establishment of transnational colonial endeavours.

Another strong link between empires was comparable concepts of race. Between 1870 and 1930 all imperial movements relied to a considerable degree on the assumption of racial superiority. The category of race was used to legitimize imperial conquest, to put conquered territories in hierarchical order and to set transformation goals for colonized societies. Moreover, in all empires 'boundaries of imperial citizenship coincided closely with those of race'.[52] Thus, the notion of race was not only a powerful tool to structure an empire within, but also provided common grounds for exchanges and collaborations with other empires. This was most obviously the case for concepts of whiteness playing a crucial role for European imperialisms.

Racist ideologies certainly did bind European empires together, but they were by no means exclusive to them.[53] Building its own empire from the end of the nineteenth century onwards, the United States justified the conquest of overseas territories by referring specifically to British assumptions of a largely racially defined international order.[54] The Ottoman Empire also developed concepts of a superior civilization, in which race played a significant role. In particular the Young Turk movement pursued a policy of Turkification after the revolution in 1908 and saw itself as a defender of Turkism (*Türkçülük*) in the multinational Ottoman state, so that Turkishness was to replace Islam as the basis of governing legitimacy. Even though this crude ethnic nationalism showed its sinister side as it was part of the Armenian genocide perpetrated by the Young Turks in 1915, as in Russia applying racial conceptions was considered a proof of modernity.[55] But such conceptions were also supposed to justify imperial conquests. Especially at the turn of the century, Ottoman officials discussed Western European ideas of race intensively, and Ottoman elites joined in the arabophobic discourse that characterized French colonial policies in Algeria. Paradoxically enough, the Ottoman Empire legitimized its imperial policies by referring to Western concepts of race and civilization, explicitly designed to exclude, degrade and diminish Ottoman rule.[56]

Thus, comparable concepts of science, race and civilization provided ample reasons why imperial officials and administrators closely observed the policies of other empires. For decision makers in imperial centres as well as for local officials in the colonies it made sense to look at how similar problems were addressed by their imperial neighbours.[57] Knowledge acquired on the spot was rapidly passed on to imperial experts in the metropoles and included in manuals of colonial administration. Before publishing *Die Ausbildung der Kolonialbeamten* in 1894, Max Beneke had travelled to Britain, France, the Netherlands, Spain and French territories in Africa in order to scrutinize the policies and administration techniques of these empires. He was particularly impressed by the Dutch imperial administration, which subsequently influenced the training of German colonial administrators.[58] Notwithstanding their rather critical attitude towards British policy, German colonial officials also referred frequently to the British example.[59] Similarly, American administrators were extremely interested in manuals and personal accounts of well-known British imperial officials. As a result, inspection trips to British India were organized in order to observe British administration practice on the spot.[60]

As an example, congruencies in imperial administration techniques were likely to occur when different empires were dealing with certain national groups. This was the case in Eastern and South Eastern Europe where Russian, Habsburg and Ottoman administration policies towards Bulgarians, Croats, Ukrainians and others had immediate reciprocal effects. After all, decisions on civil rights, citizenship or language policies regarding national communities in one empire were quickly communicated to their compatriots residing in other empires. Consequently, they could trigger migration or resistance processes as well as specific demands referring to more favourable policies elsewhere. The administering of certain religious communities, Jewish and Muslim among others, or certain cross-national movements as, for instance, pan-Slavism or pan-Turkism, whose founder Yusuf Akçura actually originated from Simbirsk in the Volga region, were likely to provoke similar reactions.[61] In these cases empires hardly ever had the possibility to pursue their policies without regard to those of other empires. Yet the copying and adaptation of administration techniques was not limited to empires that shared common borders, as could be seen from the legal and administrative system of the Russian Empire, which shared common ideals and was largely inspired by French, British and German examples.[62]

Even though imperial policies on the African continent proved to be manifold and sometimes antagonistic, here, too, common objectives led to similar imperial logics. As Crawford Young indicated, 'basic infrastructure and taxable activity, became the very core of colonial state construction, the hinge on which its logic turned'.[63] Thus, exploiting colonial resources and setting the ground for investments proved to be a common denominator of European imperialism in Africa. Again, this had direct repercussions on imperial policies in other regions of the world. The 1884 Berlin conference not only served European powers to divide African territories among them, but also induced the Ottoman Empire to refer from now on to its territories as genuine colonies.[64] Therefore, it is not surprising that towards the end of the nineteenth century specific facilities for colonial research, education and administration were not only founded in every single empire but also served as connecting links between them, culminating in the 'Institut colonial international' which was established in Brussels in 1894, as Ulrike Lindner demonstrates in her contribution.

The wide-ranging field of colonial violence and military action also falls within the broad scope of inter-imperial encounters. The capacity to suppress resistance was a necessary condition for all imperial presence.[65] As a consequence, imperial officials were naturally interested in the military manoeuvres of competing powers. Interestingly, the violent ways in which empires dealt with local or regional crises were used as much for consolidating as for criticizing the very idea of empire.[66] The organization of a military presence offers multiple examples of inter-imperial observations, adaptations, criticisms and copying.[67] Besides the suppression of the Boxer Rebellion in China by a joint effort of several European empires, which is discussed in detail in Susanne Kuss's contribution, the Rif-war in Morocco can serve to illustrate this point. Here, only a military collaboration between French and Spanish imperial forces was able to defeat the resistance movement led by Abd el-Krim. The Rif-war provides an example where imperial armies ultimately had no choice but to join their forces in order to achieve imperial goals, i.e. the occupation and 'pacification' of conquered territory.[68]

Certain kinds of violence to control colonized societies were in many cases informed by the example of other empires. Inter-imperial military co-operation went far beyond joint military campaigns. Japanese imperial officials incorporated ideas from various European empires before formulating a law to control 'vagabonds' that played a significant role within the exercise of violence in Japanese colonies.[69] Intelligence gathering was another domain that proved to be highly relevant to contain eventual resistance and legitimize violent reactions, as is analysed in depth in Daniel Brückenhaus' contribution.[70]

Another important field of co-operation, namely international relief organizations and humanitarian aid in general, invites interrogations of the time frame that seems most promising for investigating encounters of empires. During the Russian hunger crises of 1921, for example, organizations such as the American Relief Administration led by future US-president Herbert Hoover coordinated their efforts with European organizations firmly grounded in imperial settings. The issue of humanitarianism can help to illustrate how blurred the border between the state and the private level of inter-imperial exchanges as well as between such exchanges and broader international entanglements could be. The abolition of the slave trade, a topic intensively discussed between many empires all through the nineteenth century, is probably the most prominent example. The Brussels Conference Act of 1890, or rather the *Convention Relative to the Slave Trade and Importation into Africa of Firearms, Ammunition, and Spirituous Liquors* was signed, among others, by the British, the French, the German, the Russian, the Austro-Hungarian and the Ottoman Empires as well as the United States.

Recently, a number of publications have analysed the 'relationship between "imperialism" and "humanitarian intervention"'.[71] From the perspective of encounters of empires, these studies make valuable contributions not only by providing a great number of examples for inter-imperial collaboration. More than that, they challenge traditional boundaries and value judgements regarding the apparent blessings and evils of global imperial policies in the late nineteenth and early twentieth centuries. In one of the first comprehensive histories of the topic, Michael Barnett even identifies an age of imperial humanitarianism, which he describes as a mixture of 'colonialism, commerce, and civilizing missions'.[72]

Rob Skinner and Alan Lester also plead in favour of a strong connection between the studies of humanitarianism and empires. After all, humanitarian relief work was in most cases a collaborative effort on an international scale. Networks of international experts working within transnationally institutionalized organizations mobilized relief within a genuinely imperial framework. Especially during the time frame under consideration in the present volume, humanitarianism played an important part in imperial concepts and politics that were widely accepted across empires. 'The origins and development of humanitarianism depended on a relationship with imperial networks, ideologies and anxieties, and it seems as if the history of humanitarianism is likewise dependent upon historical approaches to, and interpretations of, empire.'[73]

While this volume is concerned with the period between 1870 and 1930, it does suggest that encounters of empires remained relevant for imperialism after World War II. Similar to the foundation of the League of Nations after World War I, the foundation of the United Nations in the late 1940s, as recently shown by Mark Mazower, was made into an international effort to protect the interests of empires around the globe.[74] Simultaneously, the so-called second colonial invasion in South-East Asia witnessed many instances of co-operation between the British, the French and the Dutch to reinvigorate their grasp on their colonial possessions.

III. Alternative empires

The fields and contact zones in which empires communicated and cooperated were predominantly constituted by correspondences, conferences, diplomatic gatherings and study commissions. Here multiple imperial elites formed all kinds of trans-imperial alliances. For that reason empires can be interpreted as specific global networks, as fields of mutual influences and as complex circuits of exchange.[75]

As can be easily detected, this approach is primarily concerned with empire elites. That is with people, in their overwhelming majority white, male, well-educated and originating in metropolitan centres, who occupied privileged positions in either the metropole or the colonies. Furthermore, this comparatively small group of imperial protagonists is characterized by highly specialized skill sets and easy access to restricted information. These elitist imperial experts felt obliged to inform themselves about specific techniques of governance that were applied within other empires and collectively elaborated general instruments of imperial rule such as demographic surveys, systems of indentured labour or technologies for transforming ethnic groups into imperial subjects.[76] These often rather abstractly constructed classification categories and knowledge patterns were instrumentalized for both theorizing about the nature and necessity of imperial rule and for concrete decision making on the spot.

Thus, imperial elites formed multiple, specialized and intertwined epistemic communities. That is, according to Peter M. Haas, 'networks of knowledge-based experts' defined by 'a shared set of normative and principled beliefs', 'shared causal beliefs', 'shared notions of validity' and 'a common policy enterprise'.[77] Such epistemic communities can be identified within and across empires in fields as diverse as science, administration, labour policies, the military,[78] even in the run on and deciphering of antiquities,[79] and, as David Schorr demonstrates in his contribution to this volume, jurisprudence and jurisdiction.

To be sure, the interaction of members of such epistemic communities with their respective empires and the influence they actually had certainly was complex, diverse and changed significantly over time. However, as Patricia Clavin has pointed out, the impact of epistemic communities on actual decision making is likely to be the strongest when they can relate to coherent political units and institutionalized intergovernmental co-operation.[80] Whenever that was the case, epistemic communities concerned with topics that promised imperial decision makers extension of power, increase of benefits or solutions for local crises could not only intensify imperialism but genuinely generate it: imperialism 'could also be the result of transnational interest groups with shared values and beliefs who pushed their governments into new kinds of interventions and supported each other in a bid to raise their credibility, gain more power, and pursue common goals'.[81]

Because of their complex interconnectedness, epistemic communities shaped and acted in imperial spaces that have little to do with traditional, red- and blue-painted maps of imperialism in Africa or Asia. With their interrelated activities they undercut 'clearly bounded geopolities, as if the color-coded school maps of a clearly marked British empire were renderings of real distinctions and firmly fixed boundaries'.[82] Recent studies have revealed the extent to which empires struggled with installing equally efficient power structures in every part of their colonial possessions. The knots in the networks of epistemic communities can serve as markers to indicate spaces where the exercise of imperial power was likely to be stronger than elsewhere. Thus, imperial territories can be described as scattered, overlapping and contested by diverging groups with often contradictory interests. Lauren Benton has convincingly demonstrated the degree of fragmentation of imperial territories and how multiple contact zones between empires existed because of that very fragmentation. 'Precisely because effective imperial control was defined by sets of narrow corridors and clusters of enclaves, multiple imperial powers could operate in the same region without producing abutting or conflicting spheres of control.'[83]

Contact zones opened different spaces for imperial action. Simultaneously, they could generate new visions of empire, new imaginary spaces of the purposes and the conditions of imperial endeavours. After all, empire was much more than a certain reality on the ground. It also included an impressive ideological framework and an evolving set of principles that in many instances existed quite independently of actual imperial situations. The immense influence, for example, that various art forms exercised on the imaginary power of the imperial idea must not be underestimated. Recently, it has even been argued that the empire not only 'came to England via the stage, but that it was in the theatre and related venues of popular spectacle that Britons came to see themselves as masters in an imperial domain'.[84] Imperialism was also a mind-set, a worldview and a fantasy and these need to be included in studies of empire.[85] This applies to imperial elites in the metropoles which often developed quite abstract blueprints of their imperial visions as well as for on the spot colonizers trying to shape – often violently – their environment according to their idealized images of society.[86] As Ashis Nandy has put it: 'Colonialism is first of all a matter of consciousness and needs to be defined ultimately in the minds of men.'[87] This statement, largely informed from a psychoanalytical point of view, has received a good deal of attention in recent historical attempts to conceptualize the notion of empire. Accordingly, 'rumour, gossip, and fantasy' should not be interpreted as phenomena exterior to actual decision making but rather as powerful and lasting discourses affecting imperial policies.[88] The transimperial epistemic communities in which large parts of these discourses were produced are therefore relevant for the historical analysis of empires.

Thus, focusing on inter-imperial collaboration rather than imperial competition not only brings new topics to the forefront but also enables alternative narratives of empire. As official imperial discourses emphasized efficiency, success and superiority to imperial rivals, inter-imperial collaboration was seldom openly advertised. Transimperial networks thus developed, as Ann Laura Stoler and Carole McGranahan phrase it, 'lateral, oblique, and global visions' that can inform diverging historical accounts. In doing so, they challenge both 'developmental and linear models' of empire as they centre, on the one hand, on multiple and conflicting visions within and across empires.[89] On the other hand, they draw attention towards ruptures, changes of guidelines, and diverging concepts within the history of single empires instead of describing them in a model of rise, decline and fall.

However, addressing inter-imperial relations runs the risk of homogenizing histories of empire. It surely makes little sense to inscribe – consciously or not – all empires into a single analytical framework. Inter-imperial relations describe affinities instead of consistencies, let alone sameness.[90] Instead, they throw the channels as well as modes of adaptation or even assimilation into sharp relief. In contrast to established research, Nadin Heé shows that German examples played a lesser role in imperial Japan whereas British models, such as floggings and other forms of punishment, were carefully adapted to local requirements.[91] Similarly, Jonas Kreienbaum analyses in his contribution the scope and limits of inter-imperial exchanges with regard to the establishment of concentration camps around 1900.

World War I brought many projects of inter-imperial collaboration to a temporary halt. The 'cooperative imperialism' that had been typical for the pre-war era vanished rather abruptly in 1914.[92] However, the belligerent alliances were formed by military co-operation between the world's leading empires. Also, the post-1918 international order was centred around a League of Nations whose main spheres of influence outside of Europe were largely identical with the territories of the entente empires and especially of Britain and France. Meanwhile, based on earlier experiences and observations, all empires put a lot of effort into professionalizing their colonial administration systems.[93] In terms of inter-imperial collaboration, the post-war era proved to be remarkably stable. Imperial powers could largely be sure that imperial rivals would not intervene in their colonial possessions and the imperial repartitioning of the world noticed few substantial changes until the outbreak of World War II.[94]

IV. Limits and delimitations

Delineating a research programme for the analysis of encounters of empires and interimperial transfers necessarily raises new questions which we do not want to ignore offhandedly. So the following paragraphs should not be misunderstood as an all-encompassing instruction sheet for handling imperial history. Rather we offer an attempt to implement practically the assumptions of imperial co-operation, and suggest how this might change our way of thinking about empires. These considerations pertain both to limits as regards content and to methodological delimitations concerning our approach. In other words: what can we learn from encounters of empires and what distinguishes this concept from other ways of writing transnational history?

Geoffrey Hosking's observation to discriminate between entities that *had* an empire and those that *were* one is critical for the understanding of imperial history. From this point of view Britain, for example, had an empire, since, as Hosking noted, it was distant, which meant that the British people could detach themselves from it 'without undue distress'. Russia, by contrast, was one because the Russian Empire 'was part of the homeland, and the "natives" mixed inextricably with the Russians in their own markets, streets, and schools'.[95] This distinction insists on a categorical difference between maritime and continental empires, in particular with regard to the treatment of colonial peripheries, resulting in supposedly different forms of organization and exercise of power.[96] States that are empires like the Russian or the Ottoman usually ruled their territory by establishing an authoritarian regime covering all subjects, whereas states having an empire, for instance Britain or France, habitually used such authoritarian methods only to control their overseas possessions; within the homeland, however, they frequently relied rather on representative systems.

From a methodological point of view, 'new imperial history' has already weakened this previously strong opposition.[97] Empirically, one can find a surprising amount of convergence and even similarity in the treatment of colonial or quasi-colonial peripheries across the maritime/territorial divide. Russia's empire-building, for example, took several directions in the course of time and in the process the different forms of its conquests were the result of specific historical situations. Reaching for territories on the eastern and western fringes started as early as the sixteenth and eighteenth centuries, respectively, and was fuelled, broadly speaking, by myths partly linked to a Byzantine, partly to a medieval Kievan understanding of Russia as a superior Christian power in the region. In the nineteenth century, however, Russia's advance in the south, i.e. the Caucasus and Central Asia, ran along the lines of clear-cut colonial conquests,[98] as Russian elites now referred to European-imperial blueprints and looked at their East 'with European spectacles if not eyes'.[99] The same was true for the Ottoman Empire.[100] This does not mean, of course, that there was only one approach, albeit diffuse, to colonial peripheries at the turn of the century. But these examples do illustrate that inter-imperial interferences already structured the administrative practices of several empires virtually in advance of conquest, even though implementation in the conquered regions could turn out differently. Instead of concentrating on the problem of comparing continental with overseas empires, the present volume is interested in general tools of governance which were thought of by imperial protagonists as being applicable to colonies in general, how these standards developed against the backdrop of inter-imperial co-operation, and what actors were involved in such border-crossing processes. Our argument is largely due to a general understanding of empire as a specific organization of power by which imperial elites seek to establish a certain set of rules to govern a heterogeneous polity.

Similarly, this also holds true for another aspect concerning the concept of the state in its relation to the self-perception of elites as being part of an empire. As state- and empire-building went hand in hand, maritime and continental empires were characterized by different attitudes towards the state. Again, Russia – and to a lesser extent the Ottoman Empire due to its late secularization of its state structures as well as polity starting with the so-called *Tanzimat* reforms in 1839 – can serve as an example. The Russian conceptualization of statehood was strongly connected with its imperial self-image; even though its concept of empire underwent a 'nationalization' during the nineteenth century, it was state institutions such as courts, ministries, committees, deputies etc. as well as state-approved societal institutions of imperial differentiation, such as estates, ethnic groups, nationalities, ideologies etc., which not only guaranteed the functioning of the polity, but strengthened the ties between the conception of Russia as a strong and expanding state as well as a heterogeneous empire insisting on the loyalty of all its subjects to the tsar.[101] By comparison maritime empires developed less consistent ideas of an amalgamation between empire and state, even though they equally relied on state institutions to exercise power in the colonies. In these cases the specific distance of the state probably correlated with the spatial separateness of the colonial peripheries and, additionally, the paternalistic-like authority of the governors could also carry on an understanding of power characterized rather by personal or face-to-face relations, as was common practice in the early modern age.[102] Here again, the volume's focus is not primarily to fathom the interplay of statehood, statecraft and imperial self-conception, but to identify an inter-imperial arena of the emergence and design of tools for control.[103] Since such tools all refer to the goal of monitoring a society either in the homeland or in the borderlands by making it 'legible',[104] i.e. by applying instruments of taxation, conscription, of preventing rebellions just as implementing means of demographic as well as social engineering, it is clear that from this point of view one cannot unambiguously distinguish between the goals of a state and those of an empire. Without claiming that these categories coincide, we contend that the instruments of hegemony and governance – whether conveyed by formal or informal channels – were of similar importance for the establishment of a state and for the formation of an empire. It is in this sense that we do not primarily differentiate but are aware that the two concepts principally designate two different spheres – one pertaining to the rational bureaucratic, the other rather to the imaginary. Yet both were in need of the function of overall control to prove each concept's cogency as well as vigour.

These considerations, however, must not obscure the distinct political and cultural characteristics of colonies in terms of resistance and opposition to their colonizers. As the contributions converge to inter-imperial encounters and therefore concentrate on high-level experts and state intervention, it could seem that focusing on inter-imperial exchanges obviously ignores the colonized subjects in the study of empires. But of course, we do acknowledge the impact, both methodologically and empirically, of the peripheral counter-movements aspiring to political participation and insisting on cultural autonomy. Recent studies, mostly with regard to the British Empire, have provided powerful arguments for the scope of exchange processes and subsequent formations of hybrid structures between the metropoles and the colonies as well as between the peripheries themselves.[105] The present volume seeks to contribute to these discussions inasmuch as in investigating the conditions and modalities of inter-imperial exchanges it raises rather more general questions about imperialism as a supposedly coherent, universal system of ideas and concepts. In order to grasp the global impact of imperialism it is important to investigate to what extent imperial power was conceptualized by authorized protagonists regardless of specific regions and circumstances. Why was imperialism constantly, though not exclusively, conceptualized as an abstract idea of rule over immense territories and heterogeneous populations? What cross-border settings and situations reveal specific mind-sets of imperial protagonists with regard to both manifestations of power and imaginations of those subjugated to power? It is the actors, venues and occasions where supposedly universal instruments for policing the colonized were invented, discussed and eventually applied that our approach is primarily interested in.

V. Imperial encounters and global connectedness

In the period between 1870 and 1930, encounters of empires represent a specific aspect within the increasing global interconnectedness of economic, financial, technical, cultural, social and political developments.[106] Our attempt at positioning empires into explicitly transnational contexts dovetails with numerous other approaches to historicize multi-layered entanglements on a global scale. Obviously, it would make little sense to bind all these significantly disparate imperial genealogies into one single master narrative. However, it is remarkable that this second globalization – as it is often referred to – occurred in a genuinely imperial setting. Therefore, actual encounters of empires must be carefully distinguished from other historically observable forms of exchange. They need to be analytically separated from concepts like globalization, modernization, cultural transfers and economic entanglements among others.[107]

Hence, a certain number of methodical delimitations are necessary, even if we are aware of the risk of overemphasizing differences with other approaches to imperial, transnational and global history. First of all, encounters of empires must avoid artificially isolating highly interrelated fields. The question is which mechanisms of collaboration and adaptation are specific for empires in the period under consideration, and what distinguishes them from co-operation between other actors such as nation-states, private businesses or international organizations. Thus, focusing on encounters does not reduce imperial history to a mere component of well-known catch-all interpretations of state-centred history. Rather, it is a specific, problem-oriented and time-bound mode of analysing techniques of power and how they were applied under imperial conditions. Historicizing these techniques contributes to understanding what empires were actually made of and what kept them together while remaining attentive to the fact that different imperial elites could conceptualize the term *empire* in different ways. Which epistemic communities imagined what kind of tools to lift colonies to the political, economic and cultural level of the metropoles? To what extent were these tools conceptualized as universal or rather as bound to concrete imperial sites?

From this perspective imperialism can be grasped as a historically specific ideological concept and as a sample of techniques to exercise power, inflict rules and generate violence not only for the purposes of actual conquest but also with regard to conducting civilizing missions.[108] Consequently, the study of encounters of empires is necessarily interested in disclosing the core of the imperialistic idea, and with regard to its specific implementations in certain locations under certain circumstances it will allow us to generate different narratives rather than straightforward and one-dimensional accounts of domination. Our approach equally incorporates general topics of imagination, legitimacy and conceptualization of empires, pointing to imperialism's broader implications beyond structural characteristics and hierarchical power relations in single colonial settings.[109] Encounters of empires also go beyond single examples within a continuous circulation of knowledge;[110] instead, they help in discussing how specific forms of knowledge were designed to serve explicitly imperial purposes and were meant to be implemented in imperial realms.

In many instances colonies were testing grounds for new concepts and techniques. But the history of imperialism also provides many examples that imperial rule could be conceptualized largely independently from concrete local requirements, because from an imperial perspective the exercise of power was confronted with quite similar threats and challenges in any given colony. The question is how and to what extent certain aspects of imperial rule were seen as specifically related to identifiable sites and when they were rather thought of as being of a more general nature. Sometimes it made sense for imperial protagonists to elaborate broader concepts to face the challenges of imperial government before applying them to a certain colonial territory. Therefore, colonies appear less as laboratories of modernity than as explicit parts of expanding structures resulting from historically evolving concepts and techniques of exercising power. The question of their global constitution and their modern potential thus transforms from a tool of analysis into an object of study.

As a result, investigating the specificities of inter-imperial encounters does not describe European imperialism as a historic exception. Imperialism is not a story of 'the West' progressively conquering 'the rest'. Rather, it is a particular aspect of expansionist state power observable in all parts of the globe. The geographical scope of the contributions reflects this approach. They include most of the European and the Asian colonial empires as well as the United States. While its conquest of territories formerly belonging to Native Americans or Mexico can arguably be considered as imperial expansion, the United States clearly took part in the global colonial venture by acquiring the Philippines, Cuba and Puerto Rico by the end of the nineteenth century. From now on the United States faced comparable dilemmas in its colonies to those its European counterparts struggled with.[111] From 1898 onward America's self-image was transformed from a continental empire into a powerful overseas actor and it began emulating especially the British model in terms of applying imperial policies and practices.[112] So encounters of empires shift away from a Eurocentric perspective on international history, even though between 1870 and 1930 European imperialism particularly seemed to dominate world history.[113] As Frederick Cooper has put it: 'To take the story of European colonization out of the metanarratives of globalization, the triumph of the nation-state, colonial modernity, or post-Enlightenment reason is, in fact, to provincialize Europe.'[114]

Thus, our approach partly intersects with and partly distinguishes itself from three influential fields of current imperial historiography. First, it broadens comparative analysis that has considerably enriched imperial studies in recent times.[115] Here, authors lament the unreflecting and inflationary use of the term *empire* and instead appeal to thorough empirical studies of similar imperial phenomena in different imperial contexts. These should be related to a kind of Weberian ideal type of empire comprising 'huge size, ethnic diversity, a multitude of composite territories as a result of historic cession or conquest, by specific forms of supranational rule, by shifting boundaries and fluid border-lands, and finally by a complex and interactive relationship between imperial centres and peripheries'.[116] This then would facilitate comparative studies concerning mechanisms of inclusion and exclusion, particularly in order to clearly distinguish empires from nation-states and furthermore to explain the very principles by which empires persisted, notwithstanding the competition with emerging nation-states. Comparing infrastructures, administrations, warfare, increasing exchange of imperial elites and the diversity of imperial agencies elucidates structural mechanisms and highlights their complex relationships to nationally constructed entities all over the world.

In emphasizing inter-imperial contact zones and exchanges, a specific transnational dimension to the understanding of single empires and common definitions of imperialism is added. In this way 'tracing trans-imperial networks [...] goes beyond comparison and looks for actual historical connections and disconnections between different sites of empire'.[117] Accordingly, the significant number of structural similarities that recent comparative studies of empires have revealed can partly be attributed to inter-imperial co-operation in various imperial sites.[118] In addition to the connection between 'larger issues of interpretation and concrete analysis of local government practices' convincingly claimed by Ulrike von Hirschhausen and Jörn Leonhard, encounters of empires include the manifold settings in which protagonists from various empires jointly reflected upon solutions for common imperial problems.[119]

Secondly, the study of inter-imperial encounters probes the very paradigm of transnationality within an imperial setting. It is not primarily concerned with the consequences certain imperial policies had in other empires. In late nineteenth-century Central Asia, for example, Russian bureaucrats kept themselves informed about British colonial experiences in India in order to better cope with their colonial issues.[120] Given the conflicted relationship between these two empires in that region this was obviously not motivated by mutual willingness to systematically cooperate. Rather, observing the British was supposed to pragmatically facilitate Russian governance on a local level by punctually putting foreign techniques to the test. There was neither the intention to define imperial rule in general nor any precedent arrangement between high-ranking imperial protagonists. Nevertheless, here, too, moments and places of transition of imperial techniques partly help elucidate concrete techniques on the spot and inform about the broader concept of imperialism.

Encounters of empires are certainly part of but not congruent with transnational transfers. It is reasonable to assume that the 'seeds of transnationalism are imperial, rather than post-colonial', because empires in general 'were the critical sites where transnational social and cultural movements took place'.[121] Migration, one of the most striking examples of manifesting transnationalism, was crucial for complex and multiple identity formations that were typical for empires.[122] But while migration processes did undoubtedly have a considerable impact on the ways an empire was experienced by its subjects, they do not inform us about the way imperialism and imperial politics were designed. While processes of diffusion, adaptation and exchanges are certainly relevant, encounters of empires concentrate on imperial settings in which elites from several empires discussed, informed and theorized such processes in order to put them into the service of well-defined and very specific imperial objectives. Consequently, the focus on exchanges between imperial experts from various fields reveals facets of the exercise of state power. These experts are concerned with 'trans-imperial networks of contact and debate' as opposed to imperial politics resulting from interaction with non-imperial actors or anti-imperial opponents.[123]

The third and most delicate delimitation, however, concerns the distinction between encounters of empires on the one hand and the broader movement of globalization on the other. To be sure, the former was often part of the latter. However, this was not always the case, and not all inter-imperial exchanges had global aims or global consequences. More importantly, it is methodically problematic to intermingle both terms. Much more than *empire*, *globalization* has meant very different things over the last decades. While it referred to international politics in the 1950s and 1960s, it was associated with economic perceptions, cultural diffusions and technological innovations in the 1970s. Triggered by increasingly worldwide financial networks and powered by the media, the idea of globalization experienced its take-off only in the 1980s.[124] Therefore, it makes little sense to conceptualize globalization as a somehow continuous, essentialized force, of which empire would have been one specific historical stage. Rather, it should be viewed as a whole range of uneven transformation processes which continuously generated a more intensified interconnectedness of states, societies, economies and cultures.[125] These transformation processes, then, also took place in imperial settings.

Additionally, while from a Western perspective globalization currently appears somehow neutrally as intensifying relationships between multiple actors, non-Westerners mostly perceive it as a form of re-colonization.[126] This fact suggests we should draw on both terms in the sense of shared/divided histories to describe the relation between different global actors embedded in imperial formations on the one hand, and the historical categories of empire and globalization on the other.

In this perspective the heterogeneous as well as asymmetrical processes of interconnecting different parts of the world have their roots partly in the history of imperial and colonial expansion. Recent studies have described the relation between imperial expansion and the idea of globalization as distinct yet not mutually exclusive. They speak of the 'growing connectedness [of empires] during a period of worldwide globalization' or of 'globalization in an imperial setting'.[127] In such diverse fields as those of political ideas, science or labour politics, examples of encounters of empires can illustrate to what extent globalization and imperialism interacted and overlapped.[128]

For our purposes, the involvement of the state and exchanges of experts regarding topics of imperial rule over foreign possessions can serve as indicators. For example, the production and distribution of quinine as a vaccine against malaria played a significant role within the imperial conquest of tropical regions in Africa. This broader story is not only an important example of globalization at the turn of the century, but, as Daniel Headrick has pointed out, was also a major tool for the establishment of imperial governance.[129] Within our approach, however, only those instances are of relevance where imperial state formations induced, altered or stopped their quinine policies due to institutional and personal exchanges of experts from different empires about explicitly imperial purposes.

Once again: inter-imperial encounters deliberately concentrate on imperial elites and therefore on a very limited group of actors. Consequently, it is necessary to determine the competence of groups entitled to discuss imperial issues, to trace the development of their ideas of empire and to investigate eventual applications. In which environments did trans-imperial networks of experts formulate such concepts? Who actually belonged to authorized groups that claimed imperial authority? What role did the interaction with colleagues from other empires play in generating concepts of imperialism? Which visions and fantasies of imperial rule informed these concepts? These questions can help explain possible ties between imperial protagonists from various origins that point to biographical as well as intellectual trajectories across different imperial settings.[130]

Finally, one might object that our approach is mostly concerned with universalistic blueprints eclipsing the specificities of single imperial entities. We do not argue, however, that local circumstances were less important or even negligible. Rather, within inter-imperial collaborations on-the-spot observations were almost automatically transposed into geographically less determined environments and more abstract ideas of imperial rule. In return, imperial officials based in specific colonial locations and learning about these ideas were to different degrees affected by the way encounters of empires led to discussions of locatable issues within a tendentially universalistic framework. By investigating the ways new tools of imperial power were implemented in concrete sites, not only the colonized but the entire range of imperial actors reappear on the scene. In many instances their actions and reactions demonstrated how futile and unrealistic some of the ideas developed within encounters of empires actually were.

Notes

1. Dominic Lieven, *Empire: The Russian Empire and its Rivals from the Sixteenth Century to the Present* (London: Pimlico, 2002); Wolfgang Reinhard, *Geschichte der europäischen Expansion*, 4 vols (Stuttgart: Kohlhammer, 1983–90). Recently, it has been convincingly argued that the Ottoman Empire should also be included in the early age of European exploration; see Giancarlo Casale, *The Ottoman Age of Exploration* (Oxford: Oxford UP, 2010).
2. Quite instructive on this issue is Craig Calhoun, Frederick Cooper and Kevin W. Moore (eds), *Lessons of Empire: Imperial Histories and American Power* (New York: The New Press, 2006). Concerning the global power of the United States more generally and referring rather to economic expansionism, see Andrew J. Bacevich, *American Empire: The Realities and Consequences of U.S. Diplomacy* (Cambridge, Mass.: Harvard UP 2002); G. John Ikenberry (ed.), *America Unrivaled: The Future of the Balance of Power* (Ithaca: Cornell UP, 2002). For further aspects of 'cultural imperialism' consult Victoria de Grazia, *Irresistible Empire: America's Advance through Twentieth-Century Europe* (Cambridge, Mass.: Belknap Press of Harvard UP, 2005). See also Leo Panitch and Colin Leys (eds), *The Empire Reloaded* [Socialist Register 2005] (London: The Merlin Press, 2004), as well as Leo Panitch and Colin Leys (eds), *The New Imperial Challenge* [Socialist Register 2004] (London: The Merlin Press, 2003).
3. Jürgen Osterhammel, *Die Verwandlung der Welt* (Munich: Beck, 2009), p. 606. If not indicated otherwise, all translations are by Volker Barth and Roland Cvetkovski.
4. Ibid., p. 615.
5. See Charles S. Maier, *Among Empires: American Ascendancy and Its Predecessors* (Cambridge, Mass.: Harvard UP, 2006), pp. 7, 20. Therefore, enlightened thinkers like Diderot, Herder and Kant had already been airing their anti-imperial attitude by passionately attacking the principal injustice of empires, see Sankar Muthu, *Enlightenment against Empire* (Princeton: Princeton UP, 2003).
6. Frederick Cooper, *Colonialism in Question: Theory, Knowledge, History* (Berkeley: University of California Press, 2005), p. 27.
7. Ann Laura Stoler, Imperial formations and opacities of rule, in: Calhoun, Cooper, Moore, *Lessons of Empire*, p. 54.
8. For an overview of the historiography of imperialism see chapter Colonial studies in Cooper, *Colonialism in Question*. See also Alain Chatritot and Dieter Gosewinkel (eds), *Koloniale Politik und Praktiken Deutschlands und Frankreichs 1880–1962* (Stuttgart: Steiner, 2010).
9. John Darwin, *The Empire Project: The Rise and Fall of the British World System 1830–1970* (Cambridge: Cambridge UP, 2009), p. 87. Italics in the text.
10. David Lambert and Alan Lester, Introduction: imperial spaces, imperial subjects, in: David Lambert and Alan Lester (eds), *Colonial Lives Across the British Empire: Imperial Careering in the Long Nineteenth Century* (Cambridge: Cambrige UP, 2006), p. 4.
11. Peter J. Cain and Anthony G. Hopkins, *British Imperialism: Innovation and Expansion, 1688–1914*, 2 vols (London, New York: Longman, 1993/94). More generally, briefly summing up the debates of approximately the last 200 years, see Anthony Webster, *The Debate on the Rise of the British Empire* (Manchester: Manchester UP, 2006). For the institutionalization of an international world market on the backdrop of increasing global interdependencies around 1900 see Niels P. Petersson, *Anarchie und Weltrecht. Das Deutsche Reich und die Institutionen der Weltwirtschaft 1890–1930* (Göttingen: Vandenhoeck & Ruprecht, 2009).

12 Jürgen Osterhammel, Europamodelle und imperiale Kontexte, *Journal of Modern European History*, 2, 2 (2004), pp. 157–82, especially p. 172; Jürgen Osterhammel, *Kolonialismus. Geschichte – Formen – Folgen* (Munich: Beck, 2003), p. 21.
13 Gayatri Chakravorty Spivak, *An Aesthetic Education in the Era of Globalization* (Cambridge, Mass.: Harvard UP, 2012); Rosalind C. Morris (ed.), *Can the Subaltern Speak? Reflections on the History of an Idea* (New York: Columbia UP, 2010); Dipesh Chakrabarty, *Habitations of Modernity: Essays in the Wake of Subaltern Studies* (Chicago: University of Chicago Press, 2002); David Ludden, *Reading Subaltern Studies: Critical History, Contested Meaning and the Globalization of South Asia* (London: Anthem Press, 2002); Vinayak Chaturvedi, *Mapping Subaltern Studies and the Postcolonial* (London: Verso, 2000).
14 For an overview see Ilya Gerasimov et al., New imperial history and the challenges of empire, in: Ilya Gerasimov, Jan Kusber and Alexander Semyonov (eds), *Empire Speaks out: Languages of Rationalization and Self-Description in the Russian Empire* (Leiden, Boston: Brill, 2009), pp. 3–32.
15 Aleksei Miller, The values and the limits of a comparative approach to the history of contiguous empires on the European periphery, in: Kimitaka Matsuzato (ed.), *Imperiology: From Empirical Knowledge to Discussing the Russian Empire* (Hokkaido: SRC, 2007), p. 30.
16 Lambert, Lester, Introduction, p. 6.
17 Sebastian Conrad and Shalini Randeria, Geteilte Geschichten: Europa in einer postkolonialen Welt, in: Sebastian Conrad and Shalini Randeria (eds), *Jenseits des Eurozentrismus: Postkoloniale Perspektiven in den Geschichts- und Kulturwissenschaften* (Frankfurt, M.: Campus, 2002), p.10; Osterhammel, *Verwandlung*, p. 620.
18 Paul Kennedy, *The Rise of the Anglo-German Antagonism 1860–1914* (London: Allen & Unwin, 1980), p. 415.
19 Frederik Cooper and Ann Laura Stoler, Between metropole and colony: rethinking a research agenda, in: Frederik Cooper and Ann Laura Stoler (eds), *Tensions of Empire: Colonial Cultures in a Bourgeois World* (Berkeley: University of California Press, 2001), p. 4.
20 Ulrike Lindner, Imperialism and globalization: entanglements and interactions between the British and German colonial empires in Africa before the First World War, *Bulletin of the German Historical Institute London*, 32 (2010), p. 4; Léonard Laborie, *L'Europe mise en réseaux: La France et la coopération internationale dans les postes et les télécommunications (Années 1850 – années 1950)* (Brussels: Lang, 2010), p. 24; Jörn Leonhard and Ulrike von Hirschhausen (eds), *Comparing Empires: Encounters and Transfers in the Long Nineteenth Century* (Göttingen: Vandenhoeck & Ruprecht, 2011), p. 15; Benedikt Stuchtey, *Die europäische Expansion und ihre Feinde: Kolonialismuskritik vom 18. bis in das 20. Jahrhundert* (Munich: Oldenburg, 2010); Martin Aust (ed.), *Vom Gegner lernen. Feindschaften und Kulturtransfers im Europa des 19. und 20. Jahrhunderts* (Frankfurt, M.: Campus, 2007).
21 'Authors writing in the *Oxford History of the British Empire* repeatedly refer to the experiences of other European and non-European empires over the past five centuries in fields as diverse as the military, administration, trade, and religion.' Benedikt Stuchtey, Introduction: towards a comparative history of science and tropical medicine in imperial cultures since 1800, in: Benedikt Stuchtey (ed.), *Science across European Empires, 1800–1915* (Oxford: Oxford UP, 2005), p. 20.
22 Kevin Grant, Philippa Levine and Frank Trentmann, Introduction, in: Kevin Grant, Philippa Levine and Frank Trentmann (eds), *Beyond Sovereignty: Britain, Empire and*

Transnationalism, c. 1880–1950 (Basingstoke: Palgrave Macmillan, 2007), p. 5. See also Tony Ballantyne and Antoinette Burton (eds), *Empires and the Reach of the Global, 1870–1945* (Cambridge, Mass: Belknap Press of Harvard UP, 2012); Martin Aust (ed.), *Globalisierung imperial und sozialistisch. Russland und die Sowjetunion in der Globalgeschichte 1851–1991* (Frankfurt, M.: Campus, 2013).

23 Richard Price, *Making Empire: Colonial Encounters and the Creation of Imperial Rule in Nineteenth-Century Africa* (Cambridge: Cambridge UP, 2008), p. XIV.
24 Crawford Young, *The African Colonial State in Comparative Perspective* (New Haven, Conn.: Yale UP, 1994), p. 95.
25 John Springhall, *Decolonization since 1945: The Collapse of European Overseas Empires* (Basingstoke: Palgrave Macmillan, 2001), p. 186.
26 As has been done in Lloyd C. Gardner, Walter F. LaFeber and Thomas J. McCormick, *Creation of the American Empire: U.S. Diplomatic History* (Chicago: Rand Mc Nally & Company, 1973).
27 Lutz Raphael, *Imperiale Gewalt und mobilisierte Nation: Europa 1914–1945* (Munich: Beck, 2011), pp. 38–81.
28 Grant, Levine, Trentmann, Introduction, p. 5.
29 Jörn Leonhard and Ulrike von Hirschhausen, Beyond rise, decline and fall: comparing multi-ethnic empires in the long nineteenth century, in: Leonhard, von Hirschhausen, *Comparing Empires*, p. 15.
30 Alexei Miller and Alfred J. Rieber, Introduction, in: Alexei Miller and Alfred J. Rieber (eds), *Imperial Rule* (Budapest: Central European UP, 2004), p. 2.
31 Lindner, *Imperialism and Globalization*, p. 5; Frank Schumacher: Kulturtransfer und Empire: Britisches Vorbild und US-amerikanische Kolonialherrschaft auf den Philippinen im frühen 20. Jahrhundert, in: Kraft, Claudia et al. (eds), *Kolonialgeschichten: Regionale Perspektiven auf ein globales Phänomen* (Frankfurt, M.: Campus, 2010), p. 311.
32 Miller, Rieber, Introduction, p. 2.
33 Jonathan Hart, *Empires and Colonies* (Cambridge: Polity, 2008), p. 16; See also Timothy H. Parsons, *The Rule of Empires: Those Who Built Them, Those Who Endured Them, and Why They Always Fail* (Oxford: Oxford UP, 2010), p. 5.
34 Duncan Kelly (ed.), *Lineages of Empire: The Historical Roots of British Imperial Thought* (Oxford: Oxford UP, 2009); David Armitage, *The Ideological Roots of the British Empire* (Cambridge: Cambridge UP, 2000); David Schimmelpenninck van der Oye, *Toward the Rising Sun: Russian Ideologies of Empire and the Path to War with Japan* (DeKalb: Northern Illinois UP 2001); Jeff Sahadeo, Empire of memories: conquest and civilization in imperial Russian Tashkent, *Canadian Slavonic Papers/ Revue Canadienne des Slavistes*, 46, 1/2 (2004), pp. 141–63; Selim Deringil, *The Well Protected Domains: Ideology and the Legitimation of Power in the Ottoman Empire 1876–1909* (London: I.B. Tauris, 1998). The point of reference was mostly the Roman Empire; a recent publication even attempts to offer an ideal-type in comparing the Roman and the American empires. Cf. Ulrich Leitner, *Imperium: Geschichte und Theorie eines politischen Systems* (Frankfurt, M.: Campus, 2011).
35 H.V. Bowen, British conceptions of global empire, 1756–83, *Journal of Imperial and Commonwealth History*, 26, 3 (1998), pp. 1–27; Peter J. Marshall, *The Making and Unmaking of Empires: Britain, India, and America c. 1750–1783* (Oxford: Oxford UP, 2005); H.V. Bowen, *The Business of Empire: The East India Company and Imperial Britain, 1756–1833* (Cambridge: Cambridge UP, 2006).
36 Bernard S. Cohn, *Colonialism and its Forms of Knowledge: The British in India* (Princeton: Princeton UP, 1996); Kapil Raj, *Relocating Modern Science: Circulation and*

the Construction of Knowledge in South Asia and Europe, 1650–1900 (Basingstoke: Palgrave Macmillan, 2007). In a recent textbook Tony Ballantyne describes 'knowledge' as the central topic of early twenty-first-century studies of empires: 'Thus "colonial knowledge" – the form and content of the knowledge that was produced out of and enabled resource exploitation, commerce, conquest, and colonization – now stands at the center of work on the history of the British Empire.' Tony Ballantyne, Colonial knowledge, in: Sarah E. Stockwell (ed.), *The British Empire: Themes and Perspectives* (Malden, Mass.: Blackwell, 2008), p. 178.

37 Keziban Acar, An examination of Russian imperialism: Russian military and intellectual descriptions of the Caucasus during the Russo-Turkish War of 1877–1878, *Nationalities Papers*, 32, 1 (2004), pp. 7–21. The adoption of the European classificatory patterns of producing colonial knowledge can be observed, for example, with the representatives of the Ottoman Empire, even though they were taking up a clearly critical position toward the colonial question, see Mustafa Serdar Palabiyik, Ottoman travelers' perceptions of Africa in the late Ottoman Empire (1860–1922): a discussion of civilization, colonialism and race, *New Perspectives on Turkey*, 46 (Spring 2012), pp. 187–212.

38 Saul Dubow, *A Commonwealth of Knowledge: Science, Sensibility, and White South Africa 1820–2000* (Oxford: Oxford UP, 2006), p. 4. Italics in the text.

39 Ulrike Lindner, Colonialism as a European project in Africa before 1914? British and German concepts of colonial rule in sub-Saharan Africa, *Comparativ*, 19 (2009), p. 106.

40 Frances Gouda, *Dutch Culture Overseas: Colonial Practice in the Netherlands Indies, 1900–1942* (Amsterdam: Amsterdam UP, 1995).

41 Ulrike Kirchberger, Deutsche Naturwissenschaftler im britischen Empire: Die Erforschung der außereuropäischen Welt im Spannungsfeld zwischen deutschem und britischem Imperialismus, *Historische Zeitschrift*, 271 (2000), pp. 623, 630.

42 Ibid., pp. 627–33, 636, 659.

43 Dubow, *Commonwealth of Knowledge*, p. 6.

44 Ballantyne, *Colonial Knowledge*, p. 185. See also Stuchtey, *Science across European Empires*; Lucile H. Brockway, *Science and Colonial Expansion: The Role of the British Royal Botanic Gardens* (New Haven, Conn.: Yale UP, 2002); Daniel Headrick: *The Tools of Empire: Technology and European Imperialism in the Nineteenth Century* (Oxford: Oxford UP, 1981).

45 These are the Historiographic Modality, Observational/Travel Modality, Survey Modality, Enumerative Modality, Museological Modality and Surveillance Modality. Cf. Cohn, *Colonialism*, pp. 3–15.

46 Michael A. Osborne, A collaborative dimension of the European empires: Australian and French acclimatization societies and intercolonial scientific co-operation, in: Roderick W. Home (ed.), *International Science and National Scientific Identity: Australia between Britain and America* (Dordrecht: Kluwer, 1991), pp. 99, 109. '[S]cientists in the colonies collaborating across the political boundaries imposed by their confederations to assist in the development of colonies under the control of other European nations.' Ibid., p. 97.

47 Claude Blanckaert, 'Eux et nous': L'Empire des sciences, in: Pierre Singaravélou (ed.), *L'empire des géographes: Géographie, exploration et colonisation (XIXe–XXe siècle)* (Paris: Belin, 2008), p. 36.

48 Deborah J. Neill, *Networks in Tropical Medicine: Internationalism, Colonialism, and the Rise of a Medical Specialty, 1890–1930* (Stanford: Stanford UP, 2012), p. 2.

49 Blanckaert, Eux et nous, p. 35.

50 Stoler, Cooper, *Zwischen Metropole und Kolonie*, p. 45; Neill, *Networks*, p. 9; Stuchtey, Introduction, p. 37; Young, *African Colonial State*, p. 147.
51 Stoler, Cooper, *Zwischen Metropole und Kolonie*, p. 28. By that it equally becomes obvious to what extent empires have to be considered decisive parts of nineteenth-century Europe's entangled history. Cf. Leonhard, von Hirschhausen, *Beyond Rise*, pp. 21, 32–3.
52 Alexander Morrison, Metropole, colony, and imperial citizenship in the Russian Empire, *Kritika*: Explorations in Russian and Eurasian History 13 (2012), p. 333.
53 Andrew Zimmermann, *Alabama in Africa: Booker T. Washington, the German Empire, and the Globalization of the New South* (Princeton: Princeton UP, 2010), p. 12.
54 Schumacher, *Kulturtransfer und Empire*, p. 310.
55 Hugh Poulton, *Top Hat, Grey Wolf and Crescent: Turkish Nationalism and the Turkish Republic* (London: Hurst & Company, 1997), pp. 50–86; Masami Arai, *Turkish Nationalism in the Young Turk Era* (Leiden: Brill, 1992); Taner Akçam, *The Young Turks' Crime against Humanity: The Armenian Genocide and Ethnic Cleansing in the Ottoman Empire* (Princeton: Princeton UP, 2012); Aviel Roshwald, *Ethnic Nationalism and the Fall of Empires: Central Europe, Russia, and the Middle East* (London, New York: Routledge, 2001). For Russia and the question of race see exemplarily Marina Mogilner, *Homo Imperii: A History of Physical Anthropology in Russia* (Lincoln: University of Nebraska Press, 2013).
56 'They hence appropriated a position that European discourse unanimously denied to them.' Zeynep Çelik, *Empire, Architecture, and the City: French-Ottoman Encounters 1830–1914* (Seattle: University of Washington Press, 2008), p. 252; Yuval Ben-Nassat and Eyal Ginio (eds), *Late Ottoman Palestine: The Period of Young Turk Rule* (London: I.B. Tauris, 2011).
57 Osborne, *Collaborative Dimension*, p. 113.
58 Jens Ruppenthal, *Kolonialismus als 'Wissenschaft und Technik': Das Hamburgische Kolonialinstitut 1908–1919* (Stuttgart: Steiner, 2007), p. 32. A similar case is A. Lawrence Lowell's *Colonial Civil Service* published in 1900, a manual for US-American colonial officials that included a chapter on the British East India's College at Haileybury. Cf. Thomas R. Metcalf, From one empire to another: the influence of the British Raj on American colonialism in the Philippines, *Ab Imperio*, 3 (2012), pp. 31–2.
59 Lindner, *Colonialism as European Project*, pp. 89, 103.
60 Schumacher, *Kulturtransfer und Empire*, p. 313.
61 Miller, Rieber, Introduction, p. 2; François Georgeon, *Aux origines du nationalisme turc: Yusuf Akçura (1876–1935)* (Paris: Éditions ADPF, 1980); Jacob M. Landau, *Pan-Turkism: From Irredentism to Cooperation* (Bloomington: Indiana UP, 1995); Andrzej Walicki, *The Slavophile Controversy: History of a Conservative Utopia in Nineteenth-Century Russian Thought* (Notre Dame, Ind.: University of Notre Dame Press, 1989), pp. 495–508.
62 Morrison, *Metropole, Colony, and Imperial Citizenship*, pp. 330–1.
63 Young, *African Colonial State*, p. 79.
64 M. Hakan Yavuz (ed.), *War and Diplomacy: The Russo-Turkish War of 1877–1878 and the Treaty of Berlin* (Salt Lake City: University of Utah Press, 2011). See also Çelik, *Empire, Architecture, and the City*, p. 247.
65 Osterhammel, *Verwandlung*, p. 610.
66 Cooper, Stoler, *Between Metropole and Colony*, pp. 28–9.
67 Morrison, *Metropole, Colony, and Imperial Citizenship*, p. 351.

68 Xavier Huetz de Lemps, La collaboration franco-espagnole pendant la guerre du Rif (1925-27): Un mariage d'amour ou de raison?, *Hesperis Tamuda*, 39 (1991), pp. 85-111, especially pp. 91-7.
69 Nadin Heé, *Imperiales Wissen und koloniale Gewalt: Japans Herrschaft in Taiwan 1895-1945* (Frankfurt, M.: Campus 2012), p. 248.
70 See for example the founding of the FBI after World War I: 'Collectively, this work showed the degree to which the members of the Bureau had learned from their collaboration with the British.' Robert Gregg, Valleys of fear: policing terror in an imperial age, 1865-1925, in: Grant, Levine, Trentmann, *Beyond Sovereignty*, p. 185.
71 Bronwen Everill, *Abolition and Empire in Sierra Leone and Liberia* (Basingstoke: Palgrave Macmillan, 2013), p. 9.
72 Michael Barnett, *Empire of Humanity: A History of Humanitarianism* (Ithaca, N.Y.: Cornell UP, 2011), p. 9.
73 Rob Skinner and Alan Lester, Humanitarianism and empire: new research agendas, *The Journal of Imperial and Commonwealth History*, 40, 5 (2012), p. 740.
74 Mark Mazower, *No Enchanted Palace: The End of Empire and the Ideological Origins of the United Nations* (Princeton: Princeton UP, 2009).
75 Andrew Thompson, The power and privileges of association: co-ethnic networks and the economic life of the British imperial world, *South African Historical Journal*, 56 (2006), 43-59. 'empire as a phenomenon of overlapping networks through which knowledge and ideas were exchanged, goods were traded, and people travelled'. Ibid., p. 44.
76 Karl Ittmann, Dennis D. Cordell and Gregory H. Maddox (eds), *The Demographics of Empire: The Colonial Order and the Creation of Knowledge* (Athens: Ohio UP, 2010); Daniel R. Headrick, *Tentacles of Progress: Technology Transfer in the Age of Imperialism, 1850-1940* (Oxford: Oxford UP, 1988); Daniel R. Headrick, *Power over Peoples: Technology, Environments, and Western Imperialism, 1400 to the Present* (Princeton: Princeton UP, 2010); Matthew H. Edney, *Mapping an Empire: The Geographical Construction of British India, 1765-1842* (Chicago: University of Chicago Press, 1990); Sebastian Conrad, *Globalisierung und Nation im Deutschen Kaiserreich* (Munich: Beck, 2006).
77 Peter M. Haas, Introduction: epistemic communities and international policy coordination, *International Organizations*, 46, 1 (1992), pp. 2-3.
78 Neill, *Networks*, p. 6.
79 Astrid Swenson and Peter Mandler (eds), *From Plunder to Preservation: Britain and the Heritage of Empire, c. 1800-1940* (Oxford: Oxford UP, 2013), p. 21. We are grateful to John MacKenzie for drawing our attention to this publication.
80 'The relationship between a transnational community of experts and the history of intergovernmental relations is complex. [...] transnational networks and epistemic communities need coherent nations and intergovernmental cooperation to have its biggest impact.' Patricia Clavin, Introduction: conceptualising internationalism between the world wars, in: Daniel Laqua (ed.), *Internationalism Reconfigured: Transnational Ideas and Movements Between the World Wars* (London: I.B. Tauris, 2011), p. 5.
81 Neill, *Networks*, p. 11.
82 Ann Stoler and Carole McGranahan: Introduction: refiguring imperial terrains, in: Ann Stoler, Carole McGranahan and Peter C. Perdue (eds), *Imperial Formations* (Santa Fe, N.M.: School for Advanced Research Press, 2007), p. 9; 'political geographies that were uneven, disaggregated, and oddly shaped – and not at all consistent with the

image produced by monochrome shading of imperial maps'. Lauren Benton, *A Search for Sovereignty: Law and Geography in European Empires, 1400–1900* (Cambridge: Cambridge UP, 2010), p. 2.
83 Benton, *Search for Sovereignty*, p. 37.
84 Marty Gould, *Nineteenth-Century Theatre and the Imperial Encounter* (London, New York: Routledge, 2011), p. 2.
85 Susan Zantop, *Colonial Fantasies: Conquest, Family and Nation in Precolonial Germany, 1770–1870* (Durham: Duke UP, 1997). 'Most important of all, discerning the impact "meanings", "representations" or "colonial knowledge" requires something more than a sampling of texts: the careful reconstruction of economic and political contexts must be the starting point of enquiry.' Darwin, *Empire Project*, p. 7. Cf. Thomas Richards, *The Imperial Archive: Knowledge and the Fantasy of Empire* (London: Verso, 1993); John M. MacKenzie, *European Empires and the People. Popular responses to Imperialism in France, Britain, the Netherlands, Belgium, Germany and Italy* (Manchester: Manchester UP, 2011).
86 'Colonizers live in what has elsewhere been called "imagined communities".' Laura Ann Stoler, Rethinking colonial categories: European communities and the boundaries of rule, *Comparative Studies in Society and History*, 31 (1989), p. 137.
87 Ashis Nandy, *The Intimate Enemy: Loss and Recover of Self under Colonialism* (Delhi: Oxford UP, 1983), p. 63.
88 'It is only when we focus on the production of the colonial archives and on the sorts of narratives contained within it that we find how much rumor, gossip, and fantasy pervaded the official field.' Cooper, Stoler, *Between Metropole and Colony*, p. 21. Zantop, *Colonial Fantasies*.
89 Stoler, McGranahan, Introduction, p. 14. 'Dutch authorities who sought comparison with Australia's colonization of its hinterlands or with Spanish authorities in the Americas rarely did so across the board.' Ibid., p. 15.
90 Çelik, *Empire, Architecture, and the City*, p. 247.
91 Heé, *Imperiales Wissen*, pp. 247ff.
92 Darwin, *Der imperiale Traum*, p. 346.
93 Young, *African Colonial State*, p. 101. Concerning the beginning of colonization in Africa: 'During this stage the dominant objective was to construct an apparatus of domination that would transform military (sometimes political) subordination into permanent rule. [...] The superstructure of colonial domination was institutionalized, rationalized, and routinized.' Ibid., p. 10.
94 Darwin, *Der imperiale Traum*, pp. 388–9. 'Following the interplay between transnationalism and empire suggests many lines of continuity that cut across the markers of the two world wars.' Grant, Levine, Trentmann, Introduction, p. 13.
95 Geoffrey Hosking, The Freudian frontier, in: *Times Literary Supplement*, 10 March 1995, p. 27, quoted after Roman Szporluk, *Russia, Ukraine, and the Breakup of the Soviet Union* (Stanford: Hoover Institution Press, 2000), p. 401.
96 Probably most explicit and, due to historical circumstance, also furnished with a civilizing gradient in Carl Schmitt, *Land und Meer: Eine weltgeschichtliche Betrachtung* (Leipzig: Reclam, 1942).
97 Jürgen Osterhammel, Russland und der Vergleich zwischen Imperien: Einige Anknüpfungspunkte, in: *Comparativ*, 18, 2 (2008), pp. 11–26; Guido Hausmann, Maritimes Reich – Landreich: Zur Anwendung einer geografischen Deutungsfigur auf Russland, in: Guido Hausmann and Angela Rustemeyer (eds), *Imperienvergleich: Beispiele und Ansätze aus osteuropäischer Perspektive* (Wiesbaden: Harrassowitz, 2009), pp. 489–509.

98 See exemplarily Michael Khodarkovsky, *Russia's Steppe Frontier: The Making of a Colonial Empire, 1500–1800* (Bloomington: Indiana UP, 2002); Daniel R. Brower, *Turkestan and the Fate of Russian Empire* (London: Routledge 2003); Robert D. Crews, *For Prophet and Tsar: Islam and Empire in Russia and Central Asia* (Cambridge, Mass.: Harvard UP, 2006); Jeff Sahadeo, *Russian Colonial Society in Tashkent, 1865–1923* (Bloomington: Indiana UP, 2007); Alexander S. Morrison, *Russian Rule in Samarkand 1868–1910: A Comparison with British India* (Oxford: Oxford UP, 2008); Michael Khodarkovsky, Of Christianity, enlightenment, and colonialism: Russia in the North Caucasus, 1550–1800, *The Journal of Modern History*, 71, 2 (1999), pp. 394–430; Marie Bennigsen-Broxup (ed.), *The North Caucasus Barrier: The Russian Advance Towards the Muslim World* (London: Hurst, 1992); Austin Jersild, *Orientalism and Empire: North Caucasus Mountain Peoples and the Georgian Frontier, 1845–1917* (Montreal: McGill-Queen's UP, 2002); Michael Khodarkovsky, *Bitter Choices: Loyalty and Betrayal in the Russian Conquest of the North Caucasus* (Ithaca: Cornell UP, 2011).

99 Szporluk, *Russia*, p. 403.

100 Selim Deringil, 'They live in a state of nomadism and savagery': the Late Ottoman Empire and the post-colonial debate, *Comparative Studies in Society and History*, 45, 2 (2003), pp. 311–42.

101 The literature on this topic is abundant. See, for instance, the excellent article by Jane Burbank, who investigates the example of township courts. Jane Burbank, Thinking like an empire: estate, law, and rights in the early twentieth century, in: Jane Burbank, Mark von Hagen and Anatolyi Remnev (eds), *Russian Empire: Space, People, Power, 1700–1930* (Bloomington: Indiana UP, 2007), pp. 196–217. For the Russian conception of the state in comparison especially to the British case consult Oleg Kharkhordin, What Is the state? The Russian concept of Gosudarstvo in the European context, *History and Theory*, 40, 2 (2001), pp. 206–40. For the Ottoman Empire see the impressive synthesis of Kemal H. Karpat, *The Politicization of Islam: Reconstructing Identity, State, Faith, and Community in the Late Ottoman State* (Oxford: Oxford UP, 2001).

102 For the British case see Matthew Lange, *Lineages of Despotism and Development: British Colonialism and State Power* (Chicago: University of Chicago Press, 2009). Distance as well as personalization of power was also an issue in continental empires. David Feest, In Amt und Würden? Die Beleidigung dörflicher Amtsleute und die Repräsentation des Staates im ausgehenden Zarenreich, in: Jörg Baberowski, David Feest and Christoph Gumb (eds), *Imperiale Herrschaft in der Provinz: Repräsentationen politischer Macht im Zarenreich* (Frankfurt, M.: Campus 2008), pp. 102–20; Susanne Schattenberg, *Die korrupte Provinz? Russische Beamte im 19. Jahrhundert* (Frankfurt, M.: Campus, 2008); Deringil, *The Well Protected Domains*; Lisa Anderson, *The State and Social Transformation in Tunisia and Libya 1830–1980* (Princeton: Princeton UP, 1986).

103 Perhaps the best known and most common empirical implement since the eighteenth century to make territory as well as its inhabitants visible for rule was statistics. Heinrich Hartmann, *Der Volkskörper bei der Musterung: Militärstatistik und Demographie in Europa vor dem Ersten Weltkrieg* (Göttingen: Wallstein, 2011); Lars Berisch (ed.), *Vermessen, Zählen, Berechnen: Die politische Ordnung des Raums im 18. Jahrhundert* (Frankfurt, M.: Campus, 2006); Alain Blum, *L'anarchie bureaucratique: Pouvoir et statistique sous Staline* (Paris: Édition la Découverte, 2003); Andrea Alice Rusnock, *Vital Accounts: Quantifying Health and Population in Eighteenth-Century*

England and France (Cambridge: Cambridge UP, 2002); Alain Desrosières, *La politique des grands nombres: Histoire de la raison statistique* (Paris: Édition la Découverte, 1993); Brian R. Mitchell, *European Historical Statistics, 1750–1970* (London: Macmillan, 1975).

104 James C. Scott, *Seeing like a State: How Certain Schemes to Improve the Human Condition Have Failed* (New Haven, Conn.: Yale UP, 1998), p. 2. The legibility of society is tantamount to mapping both its territory and its people, usually ascribed to the typical tasks of the state, see for the French case the classic of Pierre Rosanvallon, *L'état en France de 1789 à nos jours* (Paris: Seuil, 1990).

105 Esme Cleall, *Missionary Discourses of Difference: Negotiating Otherness in the British Empire, 1840–1900* (Basingstoke: Palgrave Macmillan, 2012); Richard Gott, *Britain's Empire: Resistance, Repression and Revolt* (London: Verso Books, 2011); Richard Price, *Making Empire: Colonial Encounters and the Creation of Imperial Rule in Nineteenth-Century Africa* (Cambidge: Cambridge UP, 2008); Ashwini Tambe and Harald Fischer-Tiné (eds), *The Limits of British Colonial Control in South Asia: Spaces of Disorder in the Indian Ocean Region* (London, New York: Routledge, 2009); Simon J. Potter, *News and the British World: The Emergence of an Imperial Press System, 1876–1922* (Oxford: Clarendon Press 2003); Lambert, Lester, Introduction, p. 11.

106 Christopher A. Bayly, *The Birth of the Modern World. Global Connections and Comparisons* (Oxford: Blackwell, 2004).

107 Gary B. Magee and Andrew S. Thompson, *Empire and Globalisation: Networks of People, Goods and Capital in the British World, c. 1850–1914* (Cambridge: Cambridge UP, 2010); Walter Goebel and Saskia Schabio (eds), *Locating Transnational Ideals*, (New York: Routledge, 2010); John M. Headley, *The Europeanization of the World: On the Origins of Human Rights and Democracy* (Princeton: Princeton UP, 2008); James Livesey, *Civil Society and Empire: Ireland and Scotland in the Eighteenth-Century Atlantic World* (New Haven, Conn.: Yale UP, 2009); Kevin H. O'Rourke and Jeffrey G. Williamson, *Globalization and History: The Evolution of a Nineteenth-Century Atlantic Economy* (Cambridge, Mass.: MIT Press, 1999).

108 All, in doing so, encounters of empires still stay aware of the risk of analytically inscribing imperialism into the narrative of modernization and thus perpetuating hierarchical and misbalanced explanations of historical processes. 'Modern empire was not an aberrant supplement to the history of modernity but rather its constituent part.' Partha Chatterjee, *The Black Hole of Empire. History of a Global Practice of Power* (Princeton: Princeton UP, 2012), p. XI.

109 See the discussion of the term in Bernard Porter, *The Absent-Minded Imperialists. Empire, Society, and Culture in Britain* (Oxford: Oxford UP, 2004), pp. 312–14.

110 Blanckaert, Eux et nous; Stuchtey, Introduction, p. 2.

111 Lanny Thompson, *Imperial Archipelago: Representation and Rule in the Insular Territories under U.S. Dominion after 1898* (Honolulu: University of Hawaii Press, 2010); Julian Go, Imperial power and its limits: America's colonial empire in the early twentieth century, in: Calhoun, Cooper, Moore, Lessons of Empire, pp. 201–14.

112 Julian Go, *Patterns of Empire: The British and the American Empires, 1688 to the Present* (Cambridge: Cambridge UP, 2011).

113 This was contended at least in a recent German textbook. See Reinhard Wendt, *Vom Kolonialismus zur Globalisierung: Europa und die Welt seit 1500* (Paderborn: Schöningh, 2007), pp. 221–52.

114 Cooper, *Colonialism in Question*, p. 30.
115 Leonhard von Hirschhausen, *Comparing Empires*; Dominic Lieven, *Empire: The Russian Empire and Its Rivals* (London: Murray, 2000); Guide Hausmann and Angela Rustemeyer, *Imperienvergleich: Beispiele und Ansätze aus osteuropäischer Perspektive* (Wiesbaden: Harrasowitz, 2009).
116 Leonhard von Hirschhausen, *Comparing Empires*, p. 12.
117 Lambert, Lester, Introduction, p. 30.
118 Go, *Patterns of Empire*, p. 13; Morrison, *Russian Rule*, p. 3; Benno Gammerl, *Untertanen, Staatsbürger und Andere: Der Umgang mit ethnischer Heterogenität im britischen Weltreich und im Habsburgerreich, 1867–1918* (Göttingen: Vandenhoeck & Ruprecht, 2008), p. 335.
119 Ulrike von Hirschhausen and Jörn Leonhard, Zwischen Historisierung und Globalisierung: Titel, Themen und Trends der neuen Empire-Forschung, *Neue Politische Literatur*, 56 (2011), p. 403.
120 Morrison, *Russian Rule*.
121 Grant, Levine, Trentmann, *Beyond Sovereignty*, p. 2.
122 Mojúbàolú Olúfúnké Okome and Olufemi Vaughan (eds), *Transnational Africa and Globalization* (Basingstoke: Palgrave Macmillan, 2012), pp. 2–3; Caroline Elkins and Susan Pedersen (eds), *Settler Colonialism in the Twentieth Century: Projects, Practices, Legacies* (New York: Routledge, 2005).
123 Ronin A. Butlin, *Geographies of Empire: European Empires and Colonies c. 1880–1960* (Cambridge: Cambridge UP, 2009), p. 17. Zimmermann, *Alabama in Africa*, p. 10; Clavin, Introduction, p. 3; Stuchtey, *Die europäische Expansion*, p. 20.
124 Olaf Bach, *Die Erfindung der Globalisierung: Untersuchungen zu Entstehung und Wandel eines zeitgeschichtlichen Grundbegriffs* (Bamberg: Difo-Druck GmbH, 2007).
125 Magee, Thompson, *Empire and Globalisation*, p. 2; Jürgen Osterhammel and Niels P. Petersson, *Geschichte der Globalisierung: Dimensionen, Prozesse, Epochen* (Munich: Beck, 2003), pp. 7–15; Sebastian Conrad and Andreas Eckert, Globalgeschichte, Globalisierung, multiple Modernen. Zur Geschichtsschreibung der modernen Welt, in: Sebastian Conrad, Andreas Eckert and Ulrike Freitag (eds), *Globalgeschichte. Theorien, Ansätze, Themen* (Frankfurt, M.: Campus, 2007), pp. 7–49.
126 Andreas Eckert and Shalini Randeria, Geteilte Globalisierung, in: Andreas Eckert and Shalini Randeria (eds), *Vom Imperialismus zum Empire: Nicht-westliche Perspektiven auf Globalisierung* (Frankfurt, M.: Suhrkamp, 2009), pp. 9–33, especially pp. 9–13. Goebel, Schabio, *Locating Transnational Ideals*.
127 Ulrike Lindner, Transnational movements between colonial empires: migrant workers from the British Cape Colony in the German diamond town of Lüderitzbucht, *European Review of History*, 16 (2009), p. 689; Darwin, *The Empire Project*, p. 102.
128 See for example Grant, Levine, Trentmann, Introduction, p. 6; Stuchtey, Introduction, p. 22; Alan Lester, *Imperial Networks. Creating Identities in Nineteenth-Century South Africa and Britain* (London, New York: Routledge, 2001), p. 6.
129 Headrick, *Tools of Empire*, p. 234.
130 Desley Deacon, Penny Russell and Angela Woollacott (eds), *Transnational Lives: Biographies of Global Modernity, 1700–Present* (Basingstoke: Palgrave Macmillan, 2010); Rosamund Dalziell (ed.), *Selves Crossing Cultures: Autobiography and Globalisation* (Melbourne: Australian Scholarly Publishing, 2002).

1

European Imperialism: A Zone of Co-operation Rather than Competition?[1]

John M. MacKenzie

Historians have an inevitable tendency to look backwards: it is in the nature of the practice of their profession. The search for origins and causes is hard-wired into the very systems of their methodologies. Thus they take great epoch-making turning points, such as World War I of the twentieth century, and seek to establish the roots of such transformatory events. The decades preceding the outbreak of that war are invariably constructed as a prelude, as a time of developing conflict which ultimately breaks out into the major conflagration. But when some form of counterfactual approach is adopted and historians look at those years through an alternative lens from that of 1914–18, perhaps they would come up with rather different perspectives. If the very words 'empire' and 'imperialism' seem to carry within them the notion of competition and conflict, perhaps the new focus creates a different spin. Yet it is hard to escape the idea that empires are by their nature expansionist and expansionism leads to violence at a number of levels, violence against the people over whom dominance is established, frontier tensions with other expanding states, and struggles for supreme power (in the case of this period) within Europe itself. Perhaps we may add, more unconventionally, the violence done to the domestic, metropolitan populations of empires, not least as a result of their implication in the culture of violence which they seem to engender.

Such a belief in the essential violence of empires is clearly something of a truism. Violence and empire are indeed conjoined in a baleful historical twinning. It also seems to be a revealed truth of the era of European imperialism from the sixteenth century to the twentieth that the rivalries of the ambitious states of Europe led to a succession of wars that almost inevitably culminated in the global conflicts of the twentieth century. Of course such a statement subsumes all sorts of historical debates, but the concept of a 400-year period of conflict, ultimately sparked by forms of global expansion, seems to hold sway in a European historical orthodoxy.[2] From the point of view of the worldwide victims of empire it seems to offer a useful vision of European iniquity in seizing indigenous destinies and identities, often in a violently destructive or even genocidal embrace. Thus for them it may be that modern globalization was conceived in rape and born in the midst of much violence. Some historians, notably Niall Ferguson, have attempted to give this a much more positive ring, the notion that modern (alleged) capitalist freedoms and global liberalism suggest that some aspects at least of the imperial period had beneficial outcomes.[3] Whatever we may think of this revision, perhaps we should inject another into the mix, the possibility that the image of continuous conflict has been overdrawn, that it needs to be reconsidered in certain crucial ways. This does not, by any means, have the effect of reducing the scale of the violence of imperialism, but it may revise the potentially violent relationships of the imperial powers themselves.

I. Two eras of European imperialism?

It is perhaps useful to reflect on the background to the late nineteenth- and early twentieth-century period, for historical context is surely important. A central dilemma that arises from this is one of continuity and change. Should we see the period of European expansion as essentially continuous from the voyages of exploration of the fifteenth and sixteenth centuries to the wars of the twentieth? Many major historians of imperialism seem to do so, even if they recognize key economic developments or transformations during that era. Or should we distinguish a considerable rupture in the late eighteenth century? We are accustomed to think of the so-called New Imperialism as being a characteristic of the second half or final quarter of the nineteenth century,[4] but should we perhaps see a new imperialism actually arising in the later eighteenth, one that is as much inspired by intellectual, religious and cultural changes as by economic and technological ones? And perhaps it is the case that while the earlier period was essentially nationalist, the second tended towards the internationalist. Were there perhaps two very distinct forms and periods of imperialism, the one highly competitive and riddled with conflict, the other often marked by some aspects of co-operation? Does this distinction help to create the essential background to the material of this book? Thus I am suggesting that while most historians have concentrated on economic transformations in the later eighteenth century, notably the shift towards industrial capitalism and new forms of trade, should we instead be concentrating on the intellectual, religious and cultural characteristics of the new forms of imperialism of the nineteenth and twentieth centuries?[5]

There are indeed major contrasts between the empires of the age of mercantilism and those of the age of industrialism, between early modern and modern empires. It has generally been accepted that European mercantile empires were inevitably about conflict. The central mercantilist notion of a finite global resource, a limited world trade underpinned by protectionism and bullionism (limited precious metal supply to underpin currencies), implied this.[6] This apparent inevitability of conflict was heightened by two factors, first the great sense of a religious struggle between the Catholic and Protestant empires, between on the one hand the centralized Crown-led empires of Spain and Portugal, united from 1580 to 1640, then later France, and on the other, the assertive new Protestant empires, those of the Netherlands and England. And the second was the tendency of these latter countries to create chartered companies, notably the Dutch and English East India Companies, aggressive capitalism incarnate, empire at arm's length, contrasting with the Catholic empires held very close to the royal chest. This highly conflictual era of European empires was to last from the sixteenth to the eighteenth centuries with the field gradually simplifying itself, as Spain, Portugal and the Netherlands declined, into a straight battle between Britain (after 1707) and France. Nowhere better reflects this sense of violent competition than the Caribbean. There, some islands, like St Lucia in the Antilles, repeatedly changed hands. Others, like Antigua, were ringed by forts, garrisoned by troops, and became settings of major naval bases and engagements.[7] While Caribbean islands were often small and at that time exceptionally rich from the imperialists' point of view, similar examples of the expectation of continual conflict, and the measures taken to cope with it, can be found around the world.

Obviously we think of the Napoleonic Wars as the powerful and enduring struggle that brought this first phase of European imperial conflict to an end. But this era had already overlapped with a supremely influential intellectual flowering. The Enlightenment has been a source of much controversy in respect of its relationship with imperialism. Did it set the mental groundwork for modern empires? Or was it essentially opposed to imperialism? Evidence for the first can be found in stadial theory – a form of historical evolution of human societies from hunting and gathering, through the pastoral, the agricultural and finally the commercial, with industrial to be added on later. This was formulated in Edinburgh by William Robertson and others.[8] The second notable intellectual and cultural development was the hugely influential notion of the heightened contrast between civilization, so often associated with classical empires, and barbarism, that vision of the Huns, Goths and Vandals at the gates.[9] This central concept led in two directions, firming up a sense of imperial superiority, but also tending towards a dominant idea that empires were doomed to fail, that the prime characteristic of historic empires, as reflected in the experience of the classical world, was to overreach themselves. The British were influenced – and perhaps this influence spread to the rest of Europe through translations – by two titanic eighteenth-century figures, Edward Gibbon and Edmund Burke.[10] Both were obsessed with the fateful and violent decline of empires and their visions, together with the later rather more optimistic one of Thomas Lord Macaulay, infused the education and world-views of British imperialists in the late nineteenth and twentieth centuries.[11] For them and for many others, empires implied decay, human moralities that failed to live up to heroic visions of grandeur. Burke spoke of the 'dilapidation into which a great empire must fall';[12] Gibbon wrote of the 'vicissitudes of fortune [...] which buries empires and cities in a common grave' (and incidentally, note that assumed synergy between empires and cities).[13] The romantic poet William Wordsworth, who had warmly welcomed the French Revolution, proclaimed 'Another year [...] Another mighty empire overthrown'.[14] This view of empires as always doomed to fail through ruinous and violent collapse seems to me to be a distinctive characteristic of the Age of the Enlightenment. This became a great lesson for imperialists, a fateful and much-feared bogey to be avoided in the modern age.

Moreover, there were other supposedly anti-imperial aspects of the Enlightenment, notably in the development of the science of economics. Adam Smith's powerful critique of mercantilism and his elevation of the concepts of free trade as a new orthodoxy was to be phenomenally influential.[15] On the question of colonies, his work was however ambiguous. It is interesting that in book four of *The Wealth of Nations*, he wrote of 'the general advantage which Europe, considered as one great country, has derived from the discovery and colonization of America' which he saw as leading to an 'increase of its enjoyments' and an 'augmentation of its industry', producing a variety of commodities for pleasure and for ornament. Thus he implies a consideration of Europe acting together rather than in fierce mercantilist confrontation. But he also wrote positively of the free trade area which was constructed in the region of North America and the Caribbean within the British Empire.[16] In the nineteenth century, the free trade school, which owed its intellectual origins to Smith, certainly believed that trade had the power to overwhelm conflict, that freedom of trade and empires, formerly so protectionist, were essentially incompatible. But this also cut two ways: the reality was that free trade, rather than rendering mercantile or any other form of imperialism redundant, came to underpin and perhaps facilitate British imperialism.[17] And the phobia which that imperialism developed was the notion that other empires might indulge in neo-protectionism, might cut into the free trading ideal.

We can also identify a significant cultural relativism in some Enlightenment figures, not least Jean-Jacques Rousseau's concept of the 'noble savage', duly reflected in many of the paintings of the time. This cultural relativism had its British Indian expressions in the scholarly interests of Sir William Jones, Warren Hastings and many other figures associated with them.[18] But such scholarly approaches were, perhaps, to be less influential than Smith's free trade and cultural relativism had a somewhat chequered career. It came to lose its influence as those oppositional dualities set up by Gibbon and others moved centre stage. Thus, as the nineteenth century progressed, it seemed to be apparent that one of the common and uniting effects of European imperialism was precisely those sets of binaries which seemed to be born out of the Enlightenment, but which were in a sense raised and educated through social Darwinism and the development of pseudo-scientific racism. These became the essential imperial dualities of civilized/savage; superior/inferior; advanced/primitive. All of these had their origins, however inaccurately, in the Rome/German tribes conflict, now massively re-emphasized by racial ideas.

Commerce and free trade were seen as one of the markers of the civilized/superior/advanced paradigm. But the great irony was that while free trade was seen as a supposed dissolver of conflict, its application, or lack of it, became a source of tension. On the other hand, there can be little doubt that whereas mercantile conflict was based on genuinely different world-views, religious and political, modern European imperialism had common intellectual origins. To a certain extent, the progress of forms of secularism facilitated this shift towards supposedly rational approaches to the outer world, even in an era when evangelicalism became central to the religious impulse. Through these triple developments, intellectual, commercial and religious, the gulf represented by the binaries was widened and deepened. And with the almost tectonic opening up of these fissures, the conceits of empire grew accordingly.

So what are these conceits of empire? The common feature of all historic empires is that they are both inspired by and in turn develop visions that are essentially illusory and fantastical. But they are of course no less real in the minds of imperialists, no less instrumental and inspirational for that. These visions involve concepts not only of racial, but also of intensely national superiority, notions of unique capacities. They involve fantasies of global rule and world government or monarchy. For the citizens – not the subjects – of empires they also involve fantasies of world taxonomies, of engrossing the globe into intellectual and scientific systems that will create forms of archival and scientific order.[19] And along with those go fantasies of universal medical, scientific and educational systems, of world-encompassing religion, freedom of travel, and globalized orders facilitating trade and communications. All of these constitute the manifestations and confirmations of those binaries or dualities that underpin all nineteenth-century empires. Clearly, in the modern era, these fantasies of empire are held in common, but also potentially lead to conflict. Just as there is a tendency for each institutionalized religious system to see itself as uniquely inspired, uniquely plugged into the ur-source of the respective spiritual authority, so too does each empire consider itself to hold the particular set of unique justifications for its fantasies of superiority and authority. Anyone who has read through the school textbooks, the juvenile literature, the heroic biographies, the foundational works of history of the British in the nineteenth century, would know how far this is true.[20] But of course equivalent bases can readily be found for the Dutch, French, German, Italian, Russian and indeed Japanese Empires. Thus while the intellectual foundations and the fantastical visionary structures built upon them are in a sense common, the national styles are qualitatively different.

II. Conflict or co-operation?

So we appear to be back in an era of conflict. Not the least of this conflict lay in another great contrast between the shared ideas and the clashes to which they seemed to lead. If intellectual ideas were held in common, but leading to competing national visions, so too were new forms of economic and demographic transformations shared by all imperial states. Thus modern empires developed equivalent economic foundations, industrialism and its spread around Europe, the United States, and later Japan, in the concentration of populations in rapidly, even explosively, growing urban settings, and in the development of increasingly sophisticated technologies – of war, transport, communications, visual displays and publications. The 'tools of empire' were generally shared tools.[21] Even the organization of time itself was an imperial innovation which was held in common across empires.[22] Yet just as intellectual systems broke down into competing conceits, so too did these common economic bases for empires and the technologies to facilitate them become sources of tension. The principal source of such friction is easy to find. The fact of the matter was that industrial techniques were reliant on raw materials that were not always available in Europe – and were largely absent in the case of Japan. Industrial imperialism with so much in common competed for the raw materials necessary to feed it. Another source of conflict lay in geography. If commerce was the vital adjunct of power, then access to commerce was key – access to the North Sea for the Germans, access to the Mediterranean for the Russians, access to India and the Indian Ocean for the British, access to South America and the Far East for the Americans. The language of the new nineteenth-century imperialism seems to confirm this: the 'hands off' policy of the Monroe Doctrine, the 'Scramble for Africa', the 'Open Door' in China (violently kept open that is), the forcing open of Japan, the efforts to prop up the 'Sick Man of Europe' against the forcing open of the Bosphorus and so on. Political, diplomatic and military historians have sometimes (though not always) emphasized such conflicts and some, at least, have seen World War I as the climactic war of empires, the war which would at the very least result in the victors' redistribution of the spoils of empire (which was indeed what happened).

On the other hand, some have emphasized the manifest yearnings for international approaches. These arose out of the conference at Vienna and the diplomatic settlements of the Napoleonic wars and had their particular expression in the later nineteenth century. As is well known, the imperial powers tried to settle potential conflicts by treaty-making. The most significant of these was perhaps the General Act of the Conference of Berlin of 1885.[23] This enshrined the British passion for free trade, freedom of navigation of waterways, freedom of missionary societies to operate in the territories of rival empires, methods of notification of land grabs and the like, as well as pledges on the abolition of the slave trade, along with ground rules for dealing with African chiefs. How effective all this was is of course another matter, but other treaties followed with regard to Africa, multilateral ones involving firearms and slavery as well as bilateral examples dealing with negotiated settlements of boundary disputes and expansionary moves.[24] And indeed on the eve of World War I, the British and the Germans were busily making plans for what they envisaged as the break-up of the Portuguese Empire in Africa in the wake of the collapse of the Portuguese monarchy in 1910. This more or less secret agreement cheerfully re-carved up the Portuguese African colonies between them.[25] It was partly this diplomatic activity and potential conflict resolution which led some historians to suggest that World War I had nothing whatsoever to do with empire.

III. Co-operation: the environment, science, medicine and Christian missions

If the post-1815 period seemed to be a time of attempted diplomatic rapprochement, we need to explore the significant areas of cross-imperial co-operation in such fields as the environment, scientific and medical endeavour, and Christian missionary activity. In the case of the environment, it is of course an obvious truth that the environment is no respecter of political boundaries and it is indeed the development of environmental history which helped to promote notions of a co-operative imperialism. Richard Grove dated this back to the eighteenth century, and even earlier, linking it to the environmental and scientific interests of the Enlightenment.[26] Theories about progressive desiccation, notably on oceanic islands, but also in continental contexts, were particularly developed in an international setting, spreading from French and German environmental savants to Britain primarily through the Scottish Enlightenment and a scientific community in the northern part of the United Kingdom which was much more highly developed than in England. Such desiccation – and sometimes even desertification – was allegedly connected with tree cover. The rapacious clearance of trees in Caribbean islands (for example, almost all the indigenous tree cover of Barbados was cleared within a few decades of the arrival of the English there in 1627) as well as the great sugar-producing French islands of the Indian Ocean, Ile de France and Ile de Bourbon, later Mauritius and Réunion, was key here. Whether desiccation theory was influential or not in transforming attitudes to environmental exploitation and change, it is certainly the case that scientific research generally has long been an international endeavour. Sir Joseph Banks, botanist on Captain Cook's first voyage and later the powerful polymath and president of the Royal Society in London, had considerable international networks.[27] Moreover, forestry as a discipline was well developed in France and Germany ahead of the emergence of such skills in Scotland or England.[28] Thus the British set out to learn from their continental neighbours, often sending their own personnel across the English Channel for training. It took some time for education in England, notably in the universities, to catch up in the provision of such technical expertise.

All of this led to the emergence of an international group of practitioners. It is now well known that the leading foresters in British India had very non-English sounding names such as J.G. Koenig, Wilhelm Schlich, Dietrich Brandis and Berthold Ribbentrop. The appearance of non-British names in key technical areas of imperial endeavour is now a familiar phenomenon. Anyone interested in the development of the botanical gardens and scientific enterprises will find German and French names abounding in the record.[29] This is certainly true in the founding of museums in the British Empire.[30] Tamson Pietsch has also unveiled the same effect in her work on the origins of the universities of the Anglophone world.[31] James Braund has recently edited a collection of essays examining the influence of German-speaking scientists upon the development of science and natural history in New Zealand, notably the geologist Ferdinand Hochstetter.[32] Braund has also researched the wider incidence of this phenomenon in the Pacific and elsewhere. To all of this we could add the influence of continental Europeans in the history of art across the British Empire. Many of the images we have of the imperial environment, both through constructions of landscape (and its potential bounty) and of indigenous peoples were executed by travelling artists from European countries, again partly because in some respects art education was so much better developed there.[33]

One popular subject of art was animals and hunting. This became a key area of co-operation within European imperialism from the 1890s, as the exploitation of the animal resource of Africa in particular was reaching its climax.[34] There had developed here an elite fellowship of the hunting fraternity. The British considered the Germans not only to be admirable and fervent hunters, but also as people from whom lessons could be learned. When the British came to consider the framing of game law for their East African and other colonial territories, as well as the gazetting of game reserves, they turned to the examples of such law already put in place in German East Africa, Tanganyika, by the commissioner, later governor, Hermann von Wissmann. (Wissmann's life, ironically or appropriately enough, was brought to an end prematurely in a hunting accident.) The British Foreign Office (which at that time was still administering the East African colonies before handing them over to the Colonial Office) asked for copies of German game law to be sent to it so that they could be used as a template for their own legislation. Lord Salisbury obtained these from Berlin and then sent them out to the commissioners of the East African protectorates – and indeed to other colonies in Central and Southern Africa. Extensive correspondence was subsequently gathered together into a parliamentary command paper.

In 1900 the first international conference on African wildlife was held in the Foreign Office in London. Representatives of all European countries with African possessions attended, although it was apparent that the event was dominated by the British and the Germans. The Germans were indeed represented by Baron von Lindelfels as well as the said Hermann von Wissmann, who was still considered as the great expert on the subject. The resulting convention (which not all the participating countries ratified) proposed a whole range of regulations that were to be more or less influential in the control of hunting, particularly African access to it, in the twentieth century. The convention also invoked the regulations on guns and ammunition (notably keeping them out of African hands) that had been agreed at the Brussels conference of 1889–90. Moreover, the movement towards the founding of game reserves and the later national parks was essentially an international one, starting in the western United States, that archetypal region of American imperialism, and spreading throughout the world, initially within the imperial territories of the European powers. These areas of co-operation have now been studied much more extensively by Bernhard Gissibl and others.[35] But one of the key points that must be made is that one of the objectives of all these regulations was to exert control over Africans, over their access to firearms and also to hunting, as well as to deny them the extensive lands set aside for reserves and parks. The age of internationalist imperialism always had an eye to self-preservation, particularly in respect of indigenous peoples.

By the 1890s we can carry this study of personnel co-operating across empires into the realms of tropical medicine and the new science of microbiology. Once again Scots tended to operate in tandem, or sometimes in competition, with European scientists. In the study of the pathology of malaria, Italians were prominent, not least because malaria was a problem in Italy, even close to Rome, and rival claims were established for the discovery of transmission by mosquitos between Robert Ross in India and Italian experts, though medical researchers also co-operated.[36] In the study of cattle diseases such as East Coast fever in Africa, not to mention trypanosomiasis and the tsetse fly, Scots worked together with Robert Koch, although occasionally the British Colonial Office expressed some anxiety about the prominence of Germans in such studies.[37] Other tropical diseases experienced in the imperial context also invariably involved international co-operation.[38] The international character of imperial science in the late nineteenth century was developed in an important collection of essays edited by Benedikt Stuchtey, though with the exception of Stuchtey's introduction and the chapter with the title 'Fraternity in the age of jingoism' the contributions to this volume often operated in parallel rather than in a truly comparative way.[39] Public health was yet another area in which imperial powers co-operated, once again very often, but not exclusively, in the interests of protecting imperial administrators and white settlers from what were perceived to be the dangers of the proximity of indigenous populations.[40] Other significant studies have unveiled scientific research in various national contexts, but nonetheless the striking characteristic of an age in which institutions proliferated together with their publications was the way in which such research journals and bulletins were exchanged across the world.[41] Environmental anxieties in this period were also shared among the empires, particularly concerning aspects of forestry and agricultural development.[42] Thus these trans-European networks operated not only in the exchange of personnel, but also of scientific and technical information. Scientists, museums and other scientific institutions transferred specimens in respect of natural history, other scientific disciplines and also ethnography, right across Europe.

Ulrike Lindner has pointed out various areas of imperial co-operation between Britain and Germany in the supposed era of imperial rivalry.[43] It is of course true that the German, as well as the French, Belgian and Portuguese, Empires were dependent upon the extraordinary network of submarine and overland telegraph cables that the British had established across the globe. This was inevitably to present a major problem to the Germans on the outbreak of World War I and it was fortunate for Germany that radio communications had been invented by then. Transport systems were also invariably shared. For example, Germany established a very effective shipping line to East Africa and, for a period, the British – including imperial officials – found it the most convenient means of reaching British imperial territories in the region, although they did often deprecate the fact. British railway companies and engineers often built the railway lines in colonies of other empires.[44] To shift the focus towards the Far East, it is also true that the Japanese navy and expertise in transport technology, including shipbuilding, marine engineering, lighthouse building and railway building, were all developed in league with Scottish models, as well as with the shipyards of Aberdeen or of Barrow-in-Furness in North-West England.[45] Japanese students were prominent at Scottish universities in the final decades of the nineteenth century. In different ways, we can also see areas of co-operation with the Russian and Ottoman Empires as well as in the realm of informal imperialism in China. Returning to Britain and Germany, Lindner has also pointed to the ways in which those imperial powers were tied up, even if often reluctantly, in colonial campaigns, such as those against the Herero and Nama in what is now Namibia, while the Germans were also keen to tap into the convenient sources of Indian and Chinese labour which British capitalist enterprises in railway building, plantations and mines had utilized not only in South Africa, but also in East Africa as well as in Caribbean and Indian Ocean islands.

We can, however, go further. The vast growth of capitalist enterprise in the nineteenth century often took on international tendencies. Although, as Magee and Thompson have pointed out, the ties between settler colonies in the British Empire and London or other metropolitan centres were fairly intense,[46] still there is a good deal of evidence of international cross-investment during the period, for example in the gold mines of South Africa.[47] Banks and stock exchanges were also seldom respecters of political frontiers, at least until war broke out. Money generally headed for the places where profits could be made regardless of national sentiment – and of course cross-border risk capital could produce higher returns. This was particularly true of areas of informal imperialism. While we now know a fair amount about the characteristics of such 'soft power' imperialism in South America and China, it would be helpful to have more detailed studies of investment flows and international company activity in regions like these where direct imperial sentiment was absent. It is certainly the case that German shipping and trading companies as well as German banks and insurance operators were highly active in South American countries where there was also a considerable amount of German settlement, not least in Argentina.[48]

We should also note that the flow of settlers across the world additionally failed to adhere to imperial boundaries, a fact sometimes adduced by French, German and later Italian propagandists in their efforts to establish more effective territories of settlement across the globe. The French seemed to be well supplied with settlement areas in North Africa, but the others struggled to find equivalents. The massive power of the United States of course sucked in settlers not just from Britain and Ireland, but from throughout Scandinavia (notably Norway), Western, Southern and Eastern Europe. This ensured that all the empires, well-established like the British, French and Portuguese, or nascent such as the German and Italian, were united in viewing such migrants as lost to their own national ambitions. But in the nineteenth and early twentieth centuries, Germans in particular headed in quite large numbers for Canada, South Africa, Australia and New Zealand, obviously taking their expertise and labour with them. In South Africa, 2,000 members of the German Legion who had fought on the side of the British in the Crimean War were settled by the Governor Sir George Grey as armed farmers on the frontier of the Cape Colony in order to create a buffer zone against what were seen as the threatening African people beyond that frontier.[49] In the colonies of settlement, towns with German names can be found to illustrate this movement. In Ontario there was a Berlin until, in a supremely unsympathetic move, the Canadians renamed it Kitchener during World War I. There are still a lot of people with German names living there. Further west, Germans and people from Eastern Europe settled on the prairies and in British Columbia. In the Transvaal, now Gauteng, there is a Heidelberg while in South Australia there is the celebrated Hahnsdorf, where the visitor is disorientated not only by the ubiquitous presence of German-ness everywhere, in its band, its shops, its fairs, but also by all the German names on its war memorial until the realization dawns that in fact they all fought on the British side. James Belich has suggested that, putting aside the enormous migration to the USA, 400,000 Germans migrated to Canada by 1950, most before 1914. There are said to be several hundred thousand New Zealanders of German descent and 27 per cent of the supposedly Dutch population of the Cape in South Africa in 1807 (that is after the British had taken it over) was actually German and there were notable fresh injections in the 1850s and during the diamond and gold booms later in the century. Some 6.2 per cent of settlers in Queensland and 7.7 per cent in South Australia were Germans.[50] Belich refers to the Germans as 'important allies of Anglo-Settlement' and suggest that this may be explained by a sense of shared Anglo-Saxon-ness on the part of the British, the racial myth of German origins flourishing alongside other forms of racialism. Germans indeed may have been more highly valued in the propaganda of the times than the Catholic and supposedly Celtic Irish. While such migration does suggest a co-operative settlerdom in the 'replenishing of the earth' (to use Belich's title) it also implies a source of tension, a sense of loss of fellow citizenry and a competitive desire for territories of chauvinistic settlement in Africa or the Pacific.

Germans were also prominent as explorers and missionaries. One leading British imperialist who was complimentary about the German contribution in this field was the artist, naturalist, explorer and administrator Sir Harry Johnston. In his autobiography, he was particularly complimentary about Württembergers whose characteristics as Protestants, scholars and African travellers he was keen to extol. The objects of his praise included Reverend Sigismund Koelle who established himself in Sierra Leone on behalf of the Church of England, conducting linguistic research in the course of his missionary work; Johan Ludwig Krapf and Johannes Rebmann, discoverers of Mounts Kenya and Kilimanjaro in East Africa; Carl Mauch whom Johnston credited with revealing the Zimbabwe Ruins; and Theodor Wanner, the founder of the Württemberg Geographical Society. Johnston addressed the German Colonial Society offering suggestions for German colonization and, in 1910 and 1911 delivered lectures in Stuttgart as a guest of the King of Württemberg. He argued that the Germans should settle the Alsace–Lorraine problem with France, presumably by giving those former French territories back, and that France would then look kindly on German ambitions through the Balkans, into Asia Minor and Mesopotamia.[51]

German settlers inevitably took their churches, as well as their language and culture, with them. In the eighteenth century, German Lutherans and French Protestants had been welcomed in North America as allies in the fight against what was seen as the dangers of 'Popery'.[52] And this inevitably leads me to a consideration of Christian missions. The emergence of evangelicalism and the phenomenally energetic dispersal of missions across the globe surely represents a considerable area of co-operative imperialism in the late nineteenth century, though one that has been little recognized. German Moravians were among the pioneer missionaries, not only in North America and notably in southern Africa from as early as the eighteenth century, but also in other colonial empires.[53] Various British evangelical societies fanned out across the globe from the 1790s onwards, but most notably in the second half of the nineteenth century. Catholic missions soon followed. As we have seen with regard to the 1885 Treaty of Berlin, missions of a variety of European nationalities were founded in the African territories of the imperial powers. British territories not only contained several English and Scottish denominations, but also Catholic White Fathers and others, while the Paris Evangelical Mission (which was Protestant) operated in Northern Rhodesia (Zambia) and Basutoland (Lesotho).[54] It is true that there was occasionally a scramble among the denominations for particular influence in specific areas, but nonetheless almost every colony contained missions from other states. It is also true that during the international campaign against Leopold's Congo, some Belgian Catholic interests imagined this to be an essentially Protestant and anti-Catholic movement, particularly as several Protestant missions operated in the Congo and supplied E.D. Morel and others with information and photographs relating to the atrocities.[55] Nonetheless, a general policy of religious laissez faire existed across Africa and often, to protect themselves, missionaries were respectful of the civil power. This was also true of India and other parts of the British Empire. Just as examples, there were British missions in German African territories and German missions in Australia. Such a situation continued into the postcolonial era. Missionaries vied with each other in ethnographic studies, in the collection of artefacts, in the translation of the Bible into African and other languages, as well as in the provision of educational and medical facilities, but nonetheless most seemed to recognize that they were working towards the same ends and even regularly co-operated with each other on the ground. Moreover, the international missionary movement commenced a series of conferences, the first in Edinburgh in 1910, not so very long before the outbreak of World War I.[56]

All these missionary societies used similar techniques to drum up support from the populations of their home countries, both in the sense of raising funds and in recruiting both clerical and lay missionaries. They invariably mounted exhibitions, published magazines and illustrations, sent missionaries on leave on lecture tours. This was all part of the imperial culture of European states, cultural forms which were strikingly similar, albeit with some differences (for example, related to levels of literacy) across Europe. Shared technologies and cultural phenomena, in print and publishing capitalism, in photography and later moving film, in theatrical displays, in exhibitions, in museums, zoos and botanic gardens, also in pressure groups and religious associations, led to similar effects – the dissemination of imperial ideas to the home population, even if some of the effects might be different.[57] Some of these missionaries were granted heroic status, particularly those who were seen to have been 'martyred' in the field. Sometimes, such martyrdom occurred as a result of the killing of missionaries by indigenous forces who saw them, sometimes rightly, as the forerunners of the extension of imperial rule.[58] Sometimes the martyrdom took place as a result of the rigours of the environment, which may be seen to have been the case with David Livingstone, the most celebrated missionary explorer of his day who unquestionably acquired fame across international borders – though the Portuguese may have been less sympathetic to him than some other European peoples. More commonly, imperial heroes were military figures, as has been demonstrated by Berny Sèbe in a book which considers the parallel creation of heroes and the projection of their exploits to the populace in Britain and France.[59] Kitchener and Marchand may be seen as figures who symbolized imperial rivalries on the ground, yet their construction as heroic figures and, in a sense, as courts of appeal for domestic politicians, pressure groups and others took place in strikingly similar ways.

After World War I, co-operation continued although obviously the Germans were removed from the field. One of the most influential of colonial theorists of the twentieth century, Frederick Lugard, wrote of the ways in which the decline of jealousy and friction between the British and the French led to greater co-operation. This extended from the extradition of criminals across colonial boundaries to support in the suppression of a Muslim rising just north of the Nigerian border in 1917. Nigerian railways were also vital to the trade of the French colonies in the interior.[60] Lord Hailey, in his monumental *African Survey* also stressed co-operation between the British and the French, not least in forestry and including a joint commission on desiccation which was set up in the 1930s. He surveyed French, Belgian, Italian and Portuguese methods in Africa as well as British, and pointed out that botanists, botanic gardens and agricultural officers all co-operated. Moreover, the mines of both Southern Rhodesia (Zimbabwe) and South Africa were significant users of African labour from Portuguese Mozambique.[61]

Thus, official commentators were themselves well aware of significant patterns of co-operation right down to World War II. With notable exceptions, modern scholars have been less inclined to follow them. Thus studies of modern imperial co-operation still have a long way to go. The most fruitful way forward, in this and in wider fields, lies in an escape from European national perspectives into much more comparative approaches. It may well be true that too many British imperial historians – perhaps because of the sheer scale of that empire, the range of studies required, as well as the limitations of language – have remained far too introspective. As a result they have often failed to recognize the necessity of such cross-national studies for a full understanding of the British experience itself. It remains the case that comparative work is still relatively in its infancy.[62] This book represents one important advance.

IV. Co-operation: benign or malign?

The approach opened up by Ulrike Lindner requires further work. She implicitly suggests that the problem is that past studies of co-operation, concentrating as they did on scientific, medical, animal and forest conservation, and perhaps even religious and humanitarian phenomena, divert attention into benign outcomes. This approach was perfectly encapsulated in Richard Grove's original book with its defiant title *Green Imperialism*.[63] Lindner has directed our attention into more malign aspects of co-operation, in colonial wars verging on genocide, or indeed tipping over the edge, as well as on the 'new systems of slavery', to quote the title of the late Hugh Tinker's book, that constituted the indentured labour movements of the nineteenth century.[64] But it may be that such an attempt to divide co-operation into benign and malign is itself simplistic. It is surely the case that conservation activity could, in effect, be designed to the detriment of indigenous peoples. Moreover, it may be that shared intelligence systems, as well as pseudo-scientific racial studies based on anthropometric activities in which museums and other institutions indulged would demonstrate that some of the scientific activity would decidedly fall into the malign category. In any case all of this broke down in 1914, when intelligence systems, scientific activities, the so-called 'tools of empire' and much else were dedicated to the most violently destructive of wars, a true *weltkrieg* that sucked peoples across the world into its horrendously violent maw.

It may be suggested that although the war led to the development of the diplomatic internationalism of the League of Nations (at least on the part of the victors), this ran counter to a new wave of nationalism in scientific and educational institutions. The period of apparent internationalism which unquestionably developed to something of a climax at the end of the nineteenth and the beginning of the twentieth centuries gave way to rather more chauvinistic approaches. We need further research here, but it can be said that British imperial museums, as well as forestry departments, were drawing almost exclusively on personnel either from the colonial territories themselves or from the United Kingdom during that period.[65] Pietsch has demonstrated that this was also true of universities, although here the significance of the United States grows considerably, particularly, as might be expected, in Canada.[66] Perhaps the key point is that the connection between Britain and Germany, which had been most highly developed in these international contacts, was disrupted and the Anglophone world (as an example) became more introspective. As it happened, the war had perhaps further stimulated scientific and technical areas in which, to a certain extent, England had lagged behind.

V. Conclusion

A preliminary summing up may therefore lead us to suggest that we do have a period of intensely nationalist imperialism in the mercantile era contrasted with a much more internationalist one in the period of modern industrial imperialism. It is of course true that there were cross-national mercenaries operating in the armies of the early modern period (the Dutch Scots brigade is a good example), that various promiscuous nationalities can be found turning up in trading contexts. But nonetheless, the rivalry between the Catholic and Protestant states was intense, while that between the Dutch and the English led to the notorious so-called massacre of Ambon or Amboina in 1623 when twenty English traders were tortured and executed by the Dutch. In the later period it was much more likely that such violence would be perpetrated against indigenous people. Perhaps this highlights another contrast between the two imperial periods. Imperialism in the modern era seems to have a very different feel to it with, as we have seen, a great deal more co-operation across national boundaries. The really rich paradox about the modern period is that the most active time of such co-operation occurred in the decades before World War I, supposedly the time of intense imperial rivalries, while the retreat to a more nationalist approach occurred during the interwar years when we have allegedly moved into a time of experimental internationalism symbolized by the League of Nations. Meanwhile, it is in the years after World War II that what remained of the European empires became increasingly porous. Migration to the territories of settlement of the former British Empire then became truly international, with many more people from Southern and Eastern Europe heading for Canada and Australasia. Within a few years, large numbers of Asian people, for example Vietnamese in Australia, Hong Kong Chinese in Canada, were also migrating, ensuring that the so-called replenishing of the earth had become a genuinely global movement.[67] Other co-operative phenomena can be identified. Recent books, drawing on newly-opened secret archives, have demonstrated the ways in which the British and the Americans were alarmed at the possibility of communist successor states to empire in the era of the Cold War.[68] They pooled their intelligence resources to avoid such eventualities. Two distinguished historians have even written of the imperialism of decolonization – when American policy makers rapidly forgot their anti-colonial stance in the 1950s when they supported and indeed urged on the British in attempting to ensure that successor politicians after independence would be pro-West in their outlook.[69] Other oddities have continued to emerge. More recently, ex-Portuguese territories aspired to join the Anglophone Commonwealth, while English began to replace French and Portuguese as languages of former colonies as people reached out for forms of international communication. Empires were never watertight, but as they sank, they began to leak like sieves, losing a great deal of their original national character as they did so. But it is a fact that whatever else may be said about imperialism, it has always been replete with paradoxes. These perhaps become more apparent as we develop these studies of imperial co-operation.

Notes

1. This chapter was originally constructed as a keynote for the Cologne conference on which this book is based. It therefore takes a synoptic form before focusing on some key areas of co-operation among European empires.
2. D.K. Fieldhouse's *The Colonial Empires: a Comparative Survey from the Eighteenth Century* (London: Weidenfeld & Nicolson, 1966 – first published in Germany in 1965) was epoch-making as a comparative survey and it did date the second period of imperial expansion from 1815. But there is little or nothing on intellectual underpinnings – and the Enlightenment does not even merit an index entry.
3. Niall Ferguson, *Empire: How Britain Made the Modern World* (London: Allen Lane, 2003).
4. For example, E.J. Hobsbawm's celebrated work *The Age of Empire 1875–1914* (London: Weidenfeld & Nicolson, 1987). This was the third of his trilogy, starting with *The Age of Revolution 1789–1848* and *The Age of Capital 1848–1875*.
5. Richard Drayton, Knowledge and empire, in: P.J. Marshall (ed.), *The Oxford History of the British Empire (OHBE): the Eighteenth Century* (Oxford: Oxford UP, 1998), pp. 231–52. But there is no specific chapter on the Enlightenment or on science.
6. The classic work on mercantilism is Charles Wilson, *Mercantilism* (London: Routledge, 1958), although there has been a vast literature since then.
7. Hilary McD. Beckles, The 'Hub of Empire': the Caribbean and Britain in the Seventeenth Century, in: Nicholas Canny (ed.), *OHBE: The Origins of Empire* (Oxford: Oxford UP, 1998), pp. 218–40; Richard B. Sheridan, The formation of Caribbean plantation society, 1689–1748, and J.B. Ward, The British West Indies in the age of abolition, 1748–1815, in: Marshall, *OHBE*, pp. 394–414 and 415–39.
8. William Robertson elaborated his stadial theory in his *History of America*, the first three volumes of which were published in 1777 and the final volume in 1796. See S.J. Brown (ed.), *William Robertson and the Expansion of Empire* (Cambridge: Cambridge UP, 1997).
9. For concepts of barbarism, savagery and civilization, see the five volumes of J.G. Pocock, particularly *Barbarism and Religion Vol. 4: Barbarians, Savages and Empires* (Cambridge: Cambridge UP, 2005).
10. Pocock, *Barbarism*, contains useful discussions of Burke and Gibbon. See also J.G. Pocock, *Barbarism and Religion, vol. 1: The Enlightenment of Edward Gibbon, 1737–1764* (Cambridge: Cambridge UP, 1999) and Pocock, *Barbarism and Religion vol. 3: The First Decline and Fall* (Cambridge: Cambridge UP, 2003); and additionally, Adam Rogers and Richard Hingley, Edward Gibbon and Francis Haverfield: the Tradition of Imperial Decline, in: Mark Bradley (ed.), *Classics and Imperialism in the British Empire* (Oxford: Oxford UP, 2010), pp. 189–209. For the influence of the classics on British imperial practice, see C.A. Hagerman, *Britain's Imperial Muse: The Classics, Imperialism, and the Indian Empire, 1784–1914* (Basingstoke: Palgrave Macmillan, 2013).
11. Catherine Hall, *Macaulay and Son: Architects of Imperial Britain* (New Haven, Conn.: Yale UP, 2012)

12 This comes from Burke's Speech on the Nabob of Arcot's Debts, *Oxford Dictionary of Quotations* (London: Oxford UP, 1959), p. 101, no. 30.
13 This quotation is taken from Gibbon's *Decline and Fall of the Roman Empire*, Chapter 71. It can be found in the *Oxford Dictionary of Quotations*, p. 217, no. 13.
14 William Wordsworth, National Independence and Liberty, part 1, quoted in *Oxford Dictionary of Quotations*, p. 578, no. 4.
15 Adam Smith, *An Enquiry into The Nature and Causes of the Wealth of Nations* (London, 1776).
16 R.H. Campbell and A.S. Skinner, *Adam Smith* (New York: St Martin's Press, 1985), pp. 160–1.
17 This notion was proposed in a seminal article by John Gallagher and Ronald Robinson, The imperialism of free trade, *Economic History Review*, Second Series, 6, 1 (1953), pp. 1–15.
18 Garland Cannon, *The Life and Mind of Oriental Jones: Sir William Jones, the Father of Modern Linguistics* (Cambridge: Cambridge UP, 1990). Philology became an international discipline, particularly in respect of Germany. For later examples, see Avril A. Powell, *Scottish Orientalists and India: the Muir Brothers, Religion, Education and Empire* (Woodbridge: Boydell, 2010).
19 Thomas Richards, *The Imperial Archive: Knowledge and the Fantasy of Empire* (London: Verso, 1993).
20 These were surveyed in John M. MacKenzie, *Propaganda and Empire: the Manipulation of British Public Opinion, 1880–1960* (Manchester: Manchester UP, 1984).
21 Daniel R. Headrick, *The Tools of Empire: Technology and European Imperialism in the Nineteenth Century* (Oxford: Oxford UP; 1981); Daniel R. Headrick, *The Invisible Weapon: Telecommunications and International Politics 1851–1945* (Oxford: Oxford UP; 1991). With increasing sophistication, it may perhaps be said that such tools were less likely to be shared in time of war. See also Michael Adas, *Machines as the Measure of Men: Science, Technology, and Ideologies of Western Dominance* (Ithaca, NY: Cornell UP, 1989).
22 Clark Blaise, *Time Lord: Sir Sandford Fleming and the Creation of Standard Time* (London: Weidenfeld & Nicolson, 2000); Giordano Nanni, *The Colonisation of Time: Ritual, Routine and Resistance in the British Empire* (Manchester: Manchester UP, 2012).
23 General Act of the Conference of Berlin, 1885. See the centennial volume of the German Historical Institute London: Stig Forster, Wolfgang J. Mommsen and Ronald Robinson (eds), *Bismarck, Europe and Africa: the Berlin Africa Conference 1884–1885 and the Onset of Partition* (Oxford: Oxford UP, 1988).
24 See for example the Brussels slave trade conference of 1889–90 and the resulting treaty.
25 P.H.S. Hatton, Harcourt and Solf: the Search for an Anglo-German Understanding through Africa, 1912–1914, *European History Quarterly*, 1, 2 (1971), pp. 123–45.
26 Richard Grove, *Green Imperialism: Colonial Expansion, Tropical Island Edens and the Origins of Environmentalism, 1600–1860* (Cambridge: Cambridge UP 1995).
27 John Gascoigne, *Science in the Service of Empire: Joseph Banks, the British State and the Uses of Science in the Age of Revolution* (Cambridge: Cambridge UP, 1998); Richard Drayton, *Nature's Government: Science, Imperial Britain and the 'Improvement' of the World* (New Haven, Conn.: Yale UP, 2000).
28 Gregory A. Barton, *Empire Forestry and the Origins of Environmentalism* (Cambridge: Cambridge UP, 2002). See also John M. MacKenzie, *Empires of Nature and the Nature*

of Empires: Imperialism, Scotland and the Environment (East Linton: Tuckwell, 1997), pp. 67-71.
29 Donal P. McCracken, *Gardens of Empire: Botanical Institutions of the Victorian British Empire* (Leicester: Leicester UP, 1997); Donal P. McCracken, Fraternity in the age of jingoism: the British Imperial botanic and forestry network, in: Benedikt Stuchtey (ed.), *Science Across the European Empires 1800-1950* (Oxford: Oxford UP, 2005), pp. 49-62. To a certain extent this was also true of zoological gardens. See Natalie Lloyd, Australian zoological gardens 1860-1939: empire, nation, nature and the city, PhD University of Western Australia, 2005.
30 John M. MacKenzie, *Museums and Empire: Natural History, Human Cultures and Colonial Identities* (Manchester: Manchester UP, 2009).
31 Tamson Pietsch, *Empire of Scholars: Universities, Networks and the British Academic World, 1850-1939* (Manchester: Manchester UP, 2013).
32 James Braund (ed.), *Ferdinand Hochstetter and the Contribution of German Scientists to New Zealand National History in the Nineteenth Century* (Frankfurt, M.: Lang, 2012). See also Braund, German-speaking scientists in New Zealand, 1773-1951: research past, present and future, in: Bernadette Luciano and David G. Mayes (eds), *New Zealand and Europe: Connections and Comparisons* (Amsterdam: Rodopi, 2005), pp. 173-87 and Braund, Enlightenment Austria and the South Seas: the Pacific voyages of Thaddeus Haenke 1761-1816, *Europe-New Zealand Research Series*, 6, 3 (2011), pp. 1-22.
33 John M. MacKenzie, Art and the empire, in: P.J. Marshall, *The Cambridge Illustrated History of the British Empire* (Cambridge: Cambridge UP, 1996), pp. 296-315; Timothy Barringer, Geoff Quilley and Douglas Fordham (eds), *Art and the British Empire* (Manchester: Manchester UP, 2007).
34 MacKenzie, *Empire of Nature*. For the material that follows, see particularly Chapter 8. See also Bernhard Gissibl, The nature of colonialism: hunting, conservation and the politics of wildlife in the German colonial empire, PhD Universität Mannheim, 2009, particularly Chapters 8 and 9.
35 Bernhard Gissibl, German colonialism and the beginnings of international wildlife preservation in Africa, *German Historical Institute Bulletin Supplement*, 3 (1996), pp. 121-43; Bernhard Gissibl, Sabine Hohler and Patrick Kupper (eds), *Civilising Nature: National Parks in Global Historical Perspective* (New York: Berghahn, 2012); Bernhard Gissibl, *The Nature of German Imperialism: Conservation and the Politics of Wildlife in Colonial East Africa* (Oxford, forthcoming).
36 Gordon Harrison, *Mosquitoes, Malaria and Man: A History of the Hostilities since 1880* (New York: Dutton, 1978); Edwin R. Nye and Mary E. Gibson, *Ronald Ross Malariologist and Polymath: a Biography* (Basingstoke: Palgrave Macmillan, 1997).
37 Paul E. Cranefield, *Science and Empire: East Coast Fever in Rhodesia and the Transvaal* (Cambridge: Cambridge UP, 1991).
38 Maryinez Lyons, *The Colonial Disease: A Social History of Sleeping Sickness in Northern Zaire, 1900-1940* (Cambridge: Cambridge UP, 1992); John Farley, *Bilharzia: A History of Imperial Tropical Medicine* (Cambridge: Cambridge UP, 1991).
39 Stuchtey, *Science*, Introduction, pp. 1-45 and McCracken, Fraternity in the age of jingoism, pp. 49-62.
40 Alison Bashford, *Imperial Hygiene: A Critical History of Colonialism, Nationalism and Public Health* (Basingstoke: Palgrave Macmillan, 2004).
41 One example of a growing literature is Michael A. Osborne, *Nature, the Exotic and the Science of French Colonialism* (Bloomington, Ind.: Indiana UP, 1994); for connections

across the British Empire and beyond, see also Saul Dubow, *A Commonwealth of Knowledge: Science, Sensibility and White South Africa 1820–2000* (Oxford: Oxford UP, 2006).
42 James Beattie, *Empire and Environmental Anxiety: Health, Science, Art and Conservation in South Asia and Australasia, 1800–1920* (Basingstoke: Palgrave Macmillan, 2011).
43 Ulrike Lindner, Imperialism and globalization: entanglements and interactions between the British and German colonial empires in Africa before the First World War, *Bulletin of the German Historical Institute London*, 32, 1 (2010), pp. 4–28. See also Lindner, Encounters over the border: the shaping of colonial identities in British and German colonies in Southern Africa, in: Ulrike Lindner et al. (eds), *Hybrid Cultures – Nervous States: Germany and Britain in a (Post) colonial World* (Amsterdam: Rodopi, 2010), pp. 3–22; and Ulrike Lindner, German colonialism and the British neighbour in Africa before 1914: self-definitions, lines of demarcation and co-operation, in: Volker Langbehn and Mahamad Salamaa (eds), *Colonial (Dis)continuities: Race, Holocaust and Post-War Germany* (New York: Columbia UP, 2011), pp. 254–72.
44 Simon E. Katzenellenbogen, *South Africa and Southern Mozambique: Labour, Railways and Trade in the Making of a Relationship* (Manchester: Manchester UP, 1982). This offers but one of many examples. The British also built railways in areas of informal empire such as South America and China.
45 Alexander McKay, *Scottish Samurai: Thomas Blake Glover 1838–1911* (Edinburgh: Canongate, 1993); Michael Gardiner, *At the Edge of Empire: The Life of Thomas Blake Glover* (Edinburgh: Birlin, 2007). Barrow-in-Furness supplied the *Mikasa*, the flagship of Admiral Togo Heihachiro at the Battle of Tsushima in 1905. This ship is still preserved at Yokosuko naval base in Japan.
46 Gary B. Magee and Andrew S. Thompson, *Empire and Globalisation: Networks of People, Goods and Capital in the British World, c. 1850–1914* (Cambridge: Cambridge UP, 2010), particularly Chapter 2.
47 Robert V. Kubicek, *Economic Imperialism in Theory and Practice: The Case of South African Gold Mining Finance 1886–1914* (Durham, N.C.: Duke UP, 1979).
48 For German communities and enterprises in South America, see Robert Bickers (ed.), *Settlers and Expatriates* (Oxford: Oxford UP, 2010).
49 Richard Price, *Making Empire: Colonial Encounters and the Creation of Imperial Rule in Nineteenth-Century Africa* (Cambridge: Cambridge UP, 2008), p. 339.
50 James Belich, *Replenishing the Earth: the Settler Revolution and the Rise of the Anglo-World, 1783–1939* (Oxford: Oxford UP, 2009), pp. 62–5 and *passim*.
51 Sir Harry Johnston, *The Story of My Life* (London: Chatto & Windus, 1923), pp. 445–51.
52 Eliga H. Gould, The Christianizing of British America, in: Norman Etherington (ed.), *Missions and Empire* (Oxford: Oxford UP, 2005), p. 46. For Germans in missions in British India in the nineteenth century, see Eric Frykenberg, Christian missions and the Raj, in Etherington, *Missions*, 118–19.
53 J.E. Hutton. *A History of the Moravian Missions* (London: Moravian, 1922).
54 C.W. Mackintosh, *Coillard of the Zambezi: The Lives of François and Christina Coillard, of the Paris Missionary Society, in South and Central Africa* (New York: American Tract Society, 1907).
55 T. Jack Thompson, *Light on Darkness? Missionary Photography of Africa in the Nineteenth and Early Twentieth Centuries* (Grand Rapids, MI: Eerdmans, 2012), pp. 190–1 and 197.

56 Brian Stanley, *The World Missionary Conference, Edinburgh 1910* (Grand Rapids, MI: Eerdmans, 2009).
57 John M. MacKenzie, Giuseppe Finaldi, Bernhard Gissibl, Vincent Kuitenbrouwer, Berny Sèbe and Matthew Stanard, *European Empires and the People: Popular Responses to Imperialism in France, Britain, the Netherlands, Belgium, Germany and Italy* (Manchester: Manchester UP, 2011).
58 *A.M. MacKay: Pioneer Missionary of the Church Missionary Society in Uganda* by his sister (London: Hodder & Stoughton, 1893).
59 Berny Sèbe, *Heroic Imperialists in Africa: The Promotion of British and French Colonial Heroes, 1870–1939* (Manchester: Manchester UP, 2013).
60 Frederick Lugard, *The Dual Mandate in British Tropical Africa* (London: Blackwood, 1922), pp. 30, 181, 222, 279.
61 Lord Hailey, *An African Survey: a Study of the Problems Arising in Africa South of the Sahara* (Oxford: Oxford UP, 1938), pp. 653–4, 952, 1104.
62 *The Journal of Imperial and Commonwealth History* recently had a special issue (47, 4, (2013)) devoted entirely to German colonialism. The articles in this mainly concentrate on German colonialism itself, though one consists of a discussion of Nazi expansionism in the light of Mussolini's imperialism. But it may be that all this may encourage British historians into more comparative approaches.
63 See footnote 26 above.
64 Hugh Tinker, *A New System of Slavery: the Export of Indian Labour Overseas 1830–1920* (London: Oxford UP, 1974).
65 MacKenzie, *Museums and Empire*.
66 Pietsch, *Empire of Scholars*.
67 Eric Richards, *Destination Australia: Migration to Australia since 1901* (Manchester: Manchester UP, 2008), Chapters 9–12; Marjory Harper and Stephen Constantine, *Migration and Empire* (Oxford: Oxford UP, 2010), Chapters 6 and 12; Patricia E. Roy, *A White Man's Province: British Columbia Politicians and Chinese and Japanese Immigrants, 1858–1914* (Vancouver: University of British Columbia Press, 1989); Marilyn Lake and Henry Reynolds, *Drawing the Global Colour Line: White Men's Countries and the International Challenge of Racial Equality* (Cambridge: Cambridge UP, 2008), Chapter 14.
68 Calder Walton, *Empire of Secrets: British Intelligence, the Cold War and the Twilight of Empire* (London: Harper, 2013).
69 William Roger Louis and Ronald Robinson, The imperialism of decolonisation, *Journal of Imperial and Commonwealth History*, 22 (1994), pp. 462–511.

Part Two

Connecting Colonialisms

2

New Forms of Knowledge Exchange Between Imperial Powers: The Development of the Institut Colonial International (ICI) Since the End of the Nineteenth Century

Ulrike Lindner

I. Introduction

In 1912, forty delegates from different imperial powers met in Brussels for three days to discuss a wide variety of colonial topics such as the regulation of labour, the acclimatization of the white race in tropical countries as well as colonial monetary policy. They came together as members of the Institut Colonial International (ICI) that was founded in 1894 and has held regular international meetings since then. At the session in 1912, there were French, German, British, Belgian, Dutch, Italian and Portuguese delegates present, but the institute also had members from Russia, the USA and Latin American countries.[1] Among other topics the delegates discussed problems of tropical hygiene, debated how forms of colonial administration could be decentralized and how indigenous leaders could be included. They also deliberated about how imports from the colonies could be increased. Solutions from different colonies of different empires were discussed in detail.[2] One would assume these discussions to have taken place within the administration of a *single* imperial power and not in an international meeting attended by high-profile members of the administrations of several empires. After all, many of the participating states saw themselves as major rivals in Europe and overseas in 1912, two years before the outbreak of World War I. This self-perception is shared by the established historiography on the pre-war period. Still, the amicable exchange on colonial matters seemed to be a matter of course in 1912. Recent research on colonial empires during the period of high imperialism has confirmed that forms of co-operation between imperial powers in the colonial world were rather frequent and common.[3] However, the discussions in the ICI seem to have reached a surprising level of institutionalized exchange.

Certainly, the ICI and its meetings have to be considered in the context of growing internationalization since the 1870s. Numerous international institutions had emerged since then, often residing in cities of small European states, as in Geneva, Gent or Brussels. The Institut de Droit International (IDI) founded in Belgium in 1873 or the International Institute of Statistics established in Brussels in 1885, for example, brought together new experts in newly created or newly reorganized fields.[4] In the world of colonies and empires, strategies of internationalization became important features, with the ICI being the most prominent organization.[5] Strangely, the ICI, with its secretariat in Brussels, its annual or biannual meetings and its huge reservoir of publications is not well researched in the history of empire and colonialism. During the last twenty years only a few articles have addressed some aspects of the history of the institute.[6]

This chapter will first address how actual forms of co-operation and knowledge transfer evolved between imperial powers at the end of the nineteenth century and by what factors these developments were shaped. It will also engage with the question of how new groups of colonial experts were involved in transimperial knowledge transfer. In the next section, the chapter will focus on the institutionalization of imperial knowledge exchange between colonial powers within the ICI and examine the foundation and the main principles of the institute. It will survey some of the topics and themes discussed until the end of the 1920s and examine whether forms of collective imperial knowledge existed in the sphere of the ICI.[7] The ICI was an institutionalized space that allowed a rather free exchange of expert knowledge. However, there were quite obvious boundaries and limits that formed those exchange processes and these have to be addressed as well. The chapter will shed some light on these developments and ask whether and how the institute served as a nodal point in colonial knowledge networks. I will use the term 'colonial knowledge' to identify certain reservoirs of knowledge being connected with colonial expansion and colonial rule. I thus follow the research of Helen Tilley who has argued convincingly against the term 'colonial science', as it would suggest that Western science and colonial science existed as distinct phenomena, a highly problematic concept overlooking the intertwining of colonial and metropolitan contexts.

II. Evolving forms of knowledge exchange between imperial powers

Convergence of imperial knowledge

During the long nineteenth century the development and advancement of sciences was strongly linked with the expansion of empires, as many scholars have argued for the British Empire.[8] The exploration of new territories was made possible by colonial expansion or by imperial strategies and became likewise one of the instruments of colonial growth. Colonial and imperial knowledge could be developed by groups of experts working in the colonies of one imperial power or travelling between colonial territories of several European powers. Local knowledge influenced the collection of colonial knowledge significantly, as research during the last decades has convincingly shown, even if this was ignored in the history of science for a long time.[9] Unsurprisingly, old colonial powers such as Great Britain had developed quite elaborate and practiced ways of generating knowledge on colonial topics. National institutions such as the Royal Geographical Society became important motors of imperial exploration.[10] France, having lost most of its colonies during the Napoleonic era, had built up a huge empire once again since the 1830s. France reinvented itself as a 'modern' colonial power, particularly with its colonial expansion in West Africa from the 1880s onwards.[11] At the end of the nineteenth century, countries such as Germany and Italy as well as the Belgian King Leopold II entered the colonial realm and took over new territories, mainly in sub-Saharan Africa.[12] Experts from the new colonial powers took experienced empires like Britain and France as an example when they started their colonial endeavours.[13] However, inter-imperial observation and learning became a more general trend at the turn of the century. Colonial knowledge started to wander and to be exchanged on a much broader scale.

Several aspects stimulated these changes. First, one has to look at general developments in the sciences and at the application of science and scientific methods to colonial government, environment and society. During the last decades of the nineteenth century, scientific institutions not only became dominant around the world but were strongly connected with the growing worldwide expansion of Europe.[14] In most European empires, methods such as statistical surveys, cartographical surveys or legal codification processes gained enormous influence, being always connected with international debates.[15] Explorers and scientists who added their part to colonial knowledge reservoirs often worked internationally and were supported by different European or Western states.[16] They substantially contributed to the exchange between colonial empires. The exchange of knowledge was also strongly advanced by the development of certain fields in science. From the mid-nineteenth century a growing body of experts in all European countries dealt with different aspects of colonialism. They came from newly-developed disciplines such as anthropology and ethnology or from fields like tropical agriculture, tropical medicine, forestry, language studies, geography and colonial economics. International science congresses flourished at the end of the nineteenth century, also addressing colonial topics.[17] These experts exchanged their knowledge over national borders quite freely and scientists certainly furthered the interest in a more intense exchange in the semi-political fields of colonial economy and colonial administration.[18]

A second development which furthered knowledge exchange between empires was the structural change through economic and technical globalization at the end of the nineteenth century. The acceleration of information exchange and its growing density made distant territories more accessible.[19] The years between the 1880s and the beginning of World War I resulted in a world which was interconnected in many ways. In particular, the speed at which information travelled changed. Globalization reached the colonies as well. European powers co-operated on technical matters such as laying telegraph lines and establishing steamer connections.[20] Connections between the motherland and the colony as well as between colonies of different European empires became closer.[21] The various aspects of technical and economic globalization made it possible for the European powers and their colonies to take a close interest in each other. On the other hand, the perceived risks of a globalized and more comparable world mad the institutionalization of comparison, knowledge transfer and co-operation highly necessary.

As a third factor, new colonial acquisitions by colonial empires at the end of the nineteenth century posed similar problems to different colonizers. Italy, Germany and King Leopold II of Belgium occupied their first colonial territories, mostly in Africa. There was a general imperial expansion, also by the older colonial powers. The main sub-Saharan French African possessions were occupied from the 1870s onwards. Great Britain added Botswana, Egypt, Kenya, Nyasaland, the Gold Coast and other regions to its colonial territories.[22] For all the European powers, the process of establishing colonial rule in the new African territories was full of tensions. The colonizers faced similar logistic, administrative and economic problems. The self-definition as colonial ruler in the new colonial environment was first and foremost connected with a concept of white, European superiority over the indigenous population. This again created and reinforced commonalities between the European colonizers.[23]

Fourth, racist and social Darwinist theories became highly influential in all European nations during the second half of the nineteenth century and had a huge impact on colonial policies as well as on the relations between Europeans and non-Europeans.[24] In such a setting, the inferiority of the indigenous populations and the right to rule over them was taken as a given fact and was backed up ideologically no longer mainly by a civilizing mission, but also by justifications from various racist theories, mixing in varying forms of cultural racism.[25] Even in the French Empire, where administrators and theorists upheld a strong notion of a *mission civilisatrice*, universalistic concepts had their narrow limits. As in other empires, French colonial policy was dominated by racialized notions of society.[26] Against this ideological background and despite ongoing rivalries in Europe it was quite self-evident for administrators, experts and politicians from different European empires and colonies that they should develop forms of co-operation and exchange, as one can observe in the meetings of the ICI. Until World War I, their central aim remained to uphold white superiority over the colonized population. In the contemporary perception this goal could only be reached by the exchange of knowledge and skills.[27]

As a fifth point, one should mention that economic colonial policies of various European powers began to aim more strongly at making the colonies effective through employing a so-called modern, scientific form of colonialism. Not only the exploitation of natural resources but also the exploitation of indigenous labour and more generally the utilization of colonial people was now at the centre of colonial discussions. During the last decade of the nineteenth century and the first decade of the twentieth these concepts gained prominence.[28] Indigenous labour was no longer debated only in connection with cheap labour for plantations but also in terms of the local production of cash crops that would yield a stronger surplus for the metropole. Generally, the colonies were supposed to bring more profit by using indigenous labour more systematically, as the publications of the ICI during the 1890s show convincingly.[29] In France the term *mise en valeur* became prominent in colonial discussions around 1900.[30] In Germany, a similar concept of *Inwertsetzung der Kolonien* was developed after 1900, particularly under colonial secretary Bernhard Dernburg and the governor of German East Africa, Albert von Rechenberg.[31] In turn, Dernburg referred to British forms of colonial economy as role model for his plans. In British African tropical colonies the concept of indirect rule became prominent, often connected with a system of peasant crop production for export.[32]

Taking these different factors and aspects together, one can observe a substantial convergence of colonial knowledge reservoirs in various fields, making the foundation of an international institute quite likely.

Colonial experts and exchange between expert groups

At the end of the nineteenth century, colonial experts might be colonial politicians or administrators who often tried to apply scientific methods to their administrative and political tasks. They might be scientists who were interested in colonial medicine, agriculture, economy and law, or in the new fields of anthropology and ethnology. Sometimes the political and scientific fields overlapped significantly. Colonial politicians became part of the scientific exploration of the colonies. They often qualified themselves as experts through scientific expeditions and publications. In these fields of so-called 'scientific colonialism' an understanding between colonial experts of different empires could be more successful than in the political sphere.[33] Furthermore, new groups of experts emerged from the new technical occupations, particularly from the field of engineering. Engineers might be considered to be the most important international expert group of the twentieth century.[34] People tried to follow careers in the new fields. They created new groups, edited new publications and founded institutions that were interested in knowledge exchange between colonial empires. Many of these experts were members of national colonial associations of their own countries, as Florian Wagner shows in his chapter in this volume, but they also started to work transnationally.

When looking at the group of colonial administrators and politicians we can observe a growing tendency towards exchange between people from different motherlands at the end of the nineteenth century, particularly on the side of the new colonizing nations. This is quite obvious when we look at German colonies and their personnel. In Germany we find endless articles in colonial journals and countless publications on British colonialism as a role model. Paul Rohrbach was a typical colonial expert, being a successful publicist on colonial matters and a colonial administrator in German South-West Africa for some years (1903–6). He addressed the British Empire as the exemplary concept for German colonization in most of his publications.[35] The German officials in the colonial administration in Berlin translated and studied many official British government publications on colonial questions, particularly the organization of indigenous and local labour.[36] British positions were regularly analysed before Germany developed its own concepts, for example in the case of the management of indigenous labour.[37]

It is less known that the exchange with other colonizers became an important factor for experienced colonizers as well. In France, being itself an old colonial power, Dutch and English colonies became a role model during the last decades of the nineteenth century. The French colonial expert Joseph Chailly-Bert, lawyer and lecturer at the Ecole Libre des Sciences Politiques and one of the founders of the ICI saw British and

Dutch forms of colonialism in South-East Asia as important role models for French colonialism. He published on Dutch Java and British Indochina and always stressed the importance of comparative approaches in his own articles and books.[38]

On the British side, one would find colonial experts and publicists such as Louis Hamilton, who wrote programmatically in an article for the journal *United Empire* in 1912 that British colonizers should not only focus on their own empire but also learn from other colonial experiences, particularly from the German side.[39] Co-operation and knowledge transfer also became recurring themes for the experienced British colonizers.[40] The British *Journal of the African Society* started to translate articles from non-British colonial journals and offered knowledge on these colonies to a British expert audience.[41] As a further example, *The Times* widely covered the German colonial congresses in 1902, 1905 and 1910 with their expert talks on many features of colonialism, from agriculture to linguistics to colonial law.[42]

In the Netherlands, a long-established colonial power with economically very successful colonies in South-East Asia there was also a growing tendency towards transnational exchange. Pieter van der Lith (1844–1901), professor of colonial law at the University of Leiden, founded the *Revue coloniale internationale* in 1884 that, despite its relatively brief life would publish in different languages and address colonial problems in a comparative perspective.[43] He became one of the co-founders of the ICI and published quite substantially on the British colonial empire in India.[44]

Not only experts in the metropole, but also administrators in the colonies became more interested in neighbouring colonies of other imperial powers. As an example one can look at the lawyer Robert Asmis, who worked as colonial administrator in the German colonies Cameroon and Togo between 1906 and 1902 and was also a scholar and publicist. He tried to join the British Colonial Service in his younger years, however, he failed. After his doctoral degree he made a career in the German Colonial Service and later in the Consular Service of the German Foreign Office. He became an expert in colonial law and travelled in the British colonies of the Gold Coast and Nigeria.[45] He published articles on his research on British and German colonies in the journal *Koloniale Rundschau* and translated versions of these articles were soon published in British colonial journals.[46]

For scientists in the colonial realm, tropical medicine was certainly the most important transnational and transcolonial project around 1900, particularly after the turn to experimental medicine and bacteriology at the end of the nineteenth century.[47] Robert Koch is remembered in the colonial context for exploring sleeping sickness in East Africa with redoubtable human experiments. His expedition was itself a transnational undertaking. He worked with German scientists but his main experiments took place in British Uganda on the Ssese Islands of Lake Victoria. In 1900, there was a large epidemic in British Uganda, killing more than 100,000 people. All colonizers of the region feared for their working populations. Therefore, in April 1906, the German government sent a team under Robert Koch to East Africa to combat the disease. They studied all aspects of the disease from symptomatology to laboratory diagnosis and prevention. Therapeutic trials of atoxyl indicated that large doses were effective against sleeping sickness, but of 1,633 patients treated, twenty-three became permanently blind from optic atrophy. Atoxyl was by no means as successful as the scientists had hoped for.⁴⁸ Earlier, Koch had worked with various teams in other British colonies. He undertook studies of cholera in Alexandria and Calcutta in 1883/4 and also worked in the Indian veterinary institute between 1897 and 1898.⁴⁹ Such co-operations and expeditions show the impact of international science on knowledge exchange and on transnational expert careers in the colonial realm. These topics were also taken up in institutions such as the ICI. Many sessions dealt with the problems of tropical medicine, often addressed as the precondition of European rule in tropical countries.⁵⁰

There were also new groups of technical experts. The railway projects in most of the European colonies in Africa and South Asia became meeting points for engineers from many different empires and nations. Dirk van Laak has pointed at the growing significance of engineers as a worldwide expert group for the twentieth century.⁵¹ However, this was already a phenomenon around 1900 when many colonies supported huge infrastructural railway projects. As an example, the British engineer and geographer Clement Gillman came from a German-British background. As a British citizen, he was educated in Freiburg by his grandfather and studied engineering in Zürich. In between Britain and Germany he decided on a colonial career. In 1905 he started to work for the company Philipp Holzmann in German East Africa, developing the new rail connection in the hinterland of the colony.⁵² He wrote a diary of his experiences. His fluent English became an important factor, as he had to work with Indian workers on the German railway project. During World War I he was interned by the Germans as a British citizen.⁵³ After the war he could follow his career again and started to work for the British administration of the now British Tanganyika as a railway engineer, his British citizenship now being an asset. He worked until 1936 in British Tanganyika as chief engineer of the railway.⁵⁴ These new colonial experts were technical experts who could work in many different settings and could be hired as international specialists.⁵⁵ The new forms of technical experience also added to the notion that colonial knowledge should be transferred and exchanged. The ICI took up such technical questions as irrigation, railway construction and mining techniques in its conferences and publications.⁵⁶

Thus, the founding of the ICI has also to be seen in the context of those emerging or newly established colonial expert groups.

III. ICI – institutionalizing knowledge transfer and expert meetings

All these developments furthered forms of exchange between different colonial empires. Colonial knowledge was amassed in new dimensions. It is not surprising that it went along with new forms of institutionalization. The 1912 session of the ICI in Brussels that this chapter opened with seems to be less astonishing within the context of growing colonial and imperial exchange.

The ICI was founded in Brussels in 1894, mainly by French, Belgian and Dutch colonial administrators and experts as an institution to promote the exchange of colonial knowledge between imperial powers.⁵⁷ The foundation of the institute was strongly linked with the development of French colonialism and the new French concept of *colonisation comparée*. The notion of 'comparative colonialism' was first represented by the French expert Paul Leroy-Beaulieu in the new colonial department of the Ecole Libre des Sciences Politiques in Paris, founded in 1886. Joseph Chailly, one of the most important French experts on colonial affairs at the end of the nineteenth and the beginning of the twentieth century, strongly promoted the concept of comparative colonialism in the following years. It became a new and important subject in colonial discussions and was supposed to bring together French colonial experiences with the experiences of other imperial powers. In 1892, Chailly described it as a modern method to avoid serious mistakes in the colonial realm that would help French colonialism to prosper and make it economically successful.[58]

Another forerunner of the ICI was the already mentioned *Revue coloniale internationale*, published in Amsterdam from 1885 and edited by the Dutch professor of colonial law Pieter van der Lith. The journal was able to attract many colonial experts from different nations and empires and published articles in several languages on a wide variety of themes.[59] Chailly met Lith during the 1880s. The meeting of the two colonial experts certainly fostered the idea of promoting international exchange.

Chailly was also highly active in French national colonial affairs, being one of the co-founders of the Union Colonial Française (UCF) (the French Colonial Association) in 1893, and being its secretary-general for over twenty years.[60] In the same year, he also played a significant role in the process of inaugurating the ICI. He organized a meeting of international colonial experts in Paris on 6 October 1893. The founding members of the ICI comprised Chailly Léon Say, an economist and former French minister of finance, along with Professor Pieter van der Lith and Isaac Fransen van der Putte from the Netherlands, van der Putte being a former Dutch colonial minister. From Belgium came Albert Thys, who was engaged in the administration of the Congo Free State, and Camille Janssen, honorary governor general of the Congo Free State and former minister of finance. Lord Reay, one of the British founding members along with Sir Alfred Lyall, had been the governor of Bombay and was a member of the Royal Asiatic Society.[61] He had strong ties to the Netherlands, having been born in The Hague and becoming a British citizen only later in life. His connections to the Dutch sphere remained tight.[62] He hardly figures as a typical expert of the British Empire as he was very much inclined towards exchange with continental Europe. Thus, from the beginning, the ICI was clearly a French-Dutch-Belgian-centred enterprise, a fact that is also mirrored in the leading figures of the institute. The offices of president and vice-president that changed after each session were taken over by French, Belgian and Dutch active members on a regular basis. The post of secretary-general of the ICI remained in the hands of the founding Belgian member Camille Janssen for thirty-two years. He was followed by another Belgian colonial expert, Octave Louwers.[63]

The small office of the ICI was in Brussels, and the yearly or biannual sessions of the institute took place either in Belgium (Brussels and The Hague) or in cities of other members. The institute laid down its statutes at its first conference in 1894 in Brussels and organized fourteen more sessions up to the outbreak of World War I.[64]

The discussions of the meetings were published in the proceedings of the ICI, the so-called *compte rendu* of each session. The proceedings were themselves a reservoir of colonial knowledge, as they included substantial debates on various colonial topics.[65]

Additionally, the ICI edited a book series called *La bibliotheque coloniale internationale*. The series, comprising over forty volumes, was published between 1895 and the 1930s and covered more than ten different topics in sub-series: colonial labour, the training of colonial administrators, land management in the colonies, the organization of protectorates, colonial education, railways, mining, forestry, hunting, colonial law etc.[66] Each sub-series consisted of several, mostly massive, volumes, mainly assembling regulations and methods of colonial organization in European and Western colonies around the world, from India over the South Seas to Africa and the Caribbean. It is obvious that the ICI publication series concentrated on the gathering of regulations and on the compiling of administrative principles in various areas of common interest to the institute's members. The publications of the *Bibliotheque Coloniale Internationale* rarely developed theories or future concepts of colonialism. Rather, it is characteristic of the ICI that the sub-series on colonial law was the most extensive of all and was published over the longest period of time, from 1906 to 1927; a similar focus was laid on the problems of the legal system of colonial protectorates.[67] Legal regulations were clearly at the centre of interest for many members of the ICI, also owing to the fact that most founders of the institute were lawyers by training. Some years later, many of the now over forty members of the ICI also came from the legal profession. For example, at the meeting in 1900, the active delegate of the United States was a professor of international law at Columbia University, New York and three of the six active French members worked as professors of law at French universities.[68] Furthermore, from 1911, the ICI also published the *Recueil International de Législation Coloniale*, a collection of colonial laws, underlining the focus on colonial legal problems.[69]

More than being the publications of an international learned society on colonialism bringing together national colonial societies, the periodicals and series of the ICI generally served as a place for collecting information on various areas of colonial knowledge. They provided material for the new expert groups mentioned earlier in this chapter. Colonial engineers and economists would profit from the information on colonial railway construction and irrigation, scientifically-oriented colonial administrators would benefit from the compilations on colonial labour and colonial administration. Doctors engaged in colonial and tropical medicine would employ the expert discussions of the ICI on these issues.

The tasks of knowledge production and storage were executed with modern techniques, following the common use of modern governmental reports and statistics in European empires.[70] For example, the scientific commission of the ICI developed questionnaires on certain colonial topics and sent them to the active members of different colonial empires to collect their diverse assessments of certain questions.[71] The answers were collected by the ICI and were used during the next meeting. Such an approach was also employed in most of the book series, as for example in the publications on mining in the colonies. The first volume presented a number of questions the ICI had sent to various colonies, for example:

1. What is the nature of the lodes bearing precious metals and precious stones? Which are the chief mining centres?
2. Is the mining carried on by small or by large undertakings? [...]

4. What were the areas of workings in operation in 1890, 1895 and 1905 [...]
8. Give the yearly production.[72]

The secretariat of the ICI followed up the answers from the colonies and would often give short-term contracts to experts who would elaborate on critical issues identified by the questionnaires.[73]

Publications of the institute were certainly read in the colonial administrations of the members. They can for example be found in German and in British colonial files.[74] In what way they had an actual impact on colonial decisions of the participating nations is hard to evaluate. However, topics from the journals and publications were taken up in ongoing national discussions. As an example, at the meeting of the ICI in London in 1913, a medical expert reported on the training of indigenous nurses and midwives in the French colony of Madagascar and the British colony of Nigeria.[75] This was quoted in a petition of the Society of Protection of Natives in Germany in 1914, when it asked the German Parliament to establish training for native nurses, health personnel and midwives to combat infant mortality in German colonies.[76] Obviously, expert circles of the participating nations were aware of the ICI discussions, particularly of the proceedings of the ICI conferences.

Taking these different examples together, one of the main aims of the institute was thus to order, organize and store knowledge on colonial issues by using an inter-imperial approach. The ICI certainly created forms of collective imperial knowledge that were shared between colonial powers and developed processes of information-gathering and knowledge production.[77] The ICI could also be regarded as a form of continental European 'imperial archive' following the argument of Thomas Richards, who identified the existence of a British Imperial Archive, calling it a 'fantasy' of knowledge collected and united in the service of state and empire. Even if Richards's analysis is mainly based on literary fiction, his interpretation might also be used to describe the undertakings of the ICI.[78]

The other important aim of the ICI was to bring together international experts on colonialism in its meetings and to offer them a forum for discussions. They should work comparatively, as stated in the first session in 1894. Besides the collection of colonial knowledge this exchange should help to develop new concepts of colonialism and to initialize reforms that would make the colonies more profitable.[79] Clearly, the idea of developing a modern, scientific form of colonialism prevailed. The members defined the institute as a scientific organization, not a political one.[80] Researchers dealing with the ICI have characterized it as a 'learned association'.[81] Still, the members of the ICI saw colonial knowledge as expert knowledge on colonial politics, colonial administration, colonial law and economy. Thus, the main issues the institute dealt with were actually those of colonial policy. The rich body of expert literature that was generated by the institute during the next decades was intended to be received and read by the governments and colonial administrations of member states. In this, the institute aimed at scientific exchange but also at forms of international political consulting.

The ICI constituted itself as an international but non-governmental institution and was not financed by the member states. However, most of the states having active members in the ICI subsidized the organization quite substantially.[82] Further funds came from membership fees, donations and the publications of the institute.

Subjects that could cause political controversy between the participating nations were formally excluded in the statutes of the ICI.[83] Debates over the frequent border disputes between colonial powers or discussions about the many colonial wars the participating nations fought in their colonial territories would not be found in the proceedings or publications of the institute, but in the files of the colonial administrations.[84] The transfer of military knowledge on colonial wars – being quite common between imperial powers around 1900 – was also excluded from the topics of the institute.[85] The ICI tried to aim at a better understanding of the participating nations, as Lord Reay said in 1895: the institute should try to combat prejudices between the nations and to establish an entente cordial between the nations that were represented in the institute.[86]

Soon after its foundation, the institute attracted members of many different imperial nations who joined it in its endeavour to develop a systematized knowledge reservoir on colonial administration, colonial law and generally on colonial knowledge. There was a distribution key allocating a certain number of active member places to certain nations, in order to guarantee the internationality of the institute. In 1894, sixty active members were allowed. According to the perceived prominence of each empire, the distribution key allowed eleven active members from the UK, seven from France, six from the Netherlands, five each from Germany and Russia, three each from Italy, Belgium, Portugal, Spain, the USA and Latin America as well as two from Denmark. Six members could attend the sessions coming from other destinations.[87] However, the actual number of active members varied between thirty in 1894 to forty-three in 1900 to fifty-seven in 1913. Furthermore, not all of the active members joined every conference. The French, German, Belgian and Dutch delegates figured most prominently in the debates of the institute until 1914, whereas British delegates were often absent. The institute also allowed associated and corresponding members (respectively from motherlands and colonies of the participating nations). The active members could choose these additional members on the basis of their possessing a useful expertise for the ICI.[88]

The ICI was able to attract some high-profile experts among its active members. In 1907, Bernhard Dernburg, German colonial secretary, and the president of the German Colonial Society, Count Mecklenburg, were members. From the British side came Sir Alfred Lyall, former governor of India, and Sir Alfred Moloney, former governor of Honduras. From Belgium, Baron Descamps, one of the ministers in the Belgium government dealing with the Congo, and from France Prince August d'Arenberg, president of the Committee of French Africa, and president of the Sues-Canal Compagnie.[89]

Interestingly, not only nations with overseas colonies became members. There were also delegates from territorial empires and independent nations in Latin America. The following nations had permanent active delegates at the institute before World War I: Germany, Latin America (with two members from Chile), Britain, Austria-Hungary, Belgium, Denmark, the USA, France, Italy, the Netherlands, Portugal and Russia. It is striking that the ICI integrated different forms of empires as a matter of course in 1900.

Territorial empires such as Austria-Hungary and Russia were members as well as empires with overseas colonies, and non-European empires such as the USA, then administrating a colony in the Philippines.[90] Obviously, Latin America, with its forms of internal colonization, was also part of the concept of a colonization *comparée* in the ICI.[91] Whereas historical research started only very recently to compare territorial, overseas and non-European empires, as recent works on empires by Burbank and Cooper, Stoler and McGranahan, and Leonhard and von Hirschhausen show,[92] the ICI worked more than 100 years ago on such a comparative basis.

However, the ICI excluded certain empires in its comparative approach. Neither Japan, being a successful imperial power in the East after the Russo-Japanese War of 1904–5, nor the Ottoman Empire, had delegates at the institute before World War I.[93] In the debates within the institute it was obvious that only European or Western states could be members of even if the statutes did not explicitly adhere to such exclusion mechanisms. The notion of being a white superior European colonizer played a significant role in the self-understanding of the ICI. Already in the first session of the institute in 1894 questions were discussed about how European colonizers could survive in tropical climates, how Europeans could prepare themselves for their task and how European and indigenous bodies would function differently. Similar debates on colonialism and tropical hygiene emerged in the session of 1895 in The Hague.[94] As in other discussions at the end of the nineteenth and beginning of the twentieth century, 'European' was used synonymously with 'white' in these debates. Against such a background of racial assumptions, it was clear that the membership of the institute could only be taken up by 'white Europeans'. In the session of 1895, it was stated that the aim of the institute remained to consolidate European rule over other races.[95] The concept of European rule obviously included the USA and Latin American countries and their delegates as being of European ancestry, but not deputies from Japan and 'oriental countries' such as the Ottoman Empire.

As to the limitations of the ICI there are several points to be mentioned. Besides serving as a place for colonial knowledge collection and beyond providing a discussion forum for comparative colonization, the ICI did not figure as a paramount and highly influential institution for colonial policy in the two decades before World War I. If one looks at decision-making in colonial administrations, the British example was still in many ways the benchmark for any successful colonization at the end of the nineteenth century. For example, even if German colonial secretary Bernhard Dernburg (1906–10) and the governor of German South West Africa and subsequent colonial secretary Friedrich von Lindequist (1910–11) were highly active in the ICI in the period between 1907 and 1914,[96] the German colonial administration under colonial secretaries Dernburg and Wilhelm Solf (1911–18) was still inclined to follow British colonial approaches. A strong influence of the ICI in actual colonial decisions cannot be traced in German files. The German administration remained, as my research has shown, fixed on British colonization as a role model throughout the whole period of active German colonization.[97]

The ICIs sphere of influence was also constrained by the fact that it rarely launched new initiatives and rather mirrored the discussions in the main colonial metropoles. As Benoit Daviron has shown in his research, one of the initiatives the institute tried to launch between 1895 and 1905, an international regulation of Asian indentured labour in the colonies, failed completely. The ICI drafted a regulation that should have led to an international treaty. However, the discussions made it quickly clear that an international treaty of labour migration would never succeed. Furthermore, Great Britain, as the main supplier of indentured work, was not interested in the ICI's arrangements. The whole discussion was quickly dropped.[98]

Furthermore, many of the active delegates of the ICI were retired ministers or former governors. The British delegation within the ICI consisted almost completely of former colonial governors.[99] Other countries sent retired politicians as well.[100] As an additional prominent example, Lord Frederick Lugard, who has to be seen as one of the architects of colonial rule in British Africa during the first two decades of the twentieth century, was an associated member of the institute in the 1930s, long after his active and most influential period.[101] Thus, the ICI was not always at the forefront of colonial debates and colonial politics.

Generally, the ICI was most strongly hampered by the indifference of its British members. They hardly engaged themselves in the debates of the institute. Great Britain had a high number of active representatives in the official rota of the institute, however they were not present at most of the meetings and remained uninterested.[102] Therefore, the largest worldwide empire with the most elaborate knowledge reservoir on colonization, as well as a huge publication record on colonial issues, was rather absent in the ICI. This substantially weakened the claim of the institute to present an international forum on colonization.

The main reason for British indifference was certainly the founding of the ICI as a French-Belgian-Dutch expert group.[103] The ICI understood itself in some ways as a continental alternative to British imperial dominance. Furthermore, the British Empire was economically most successful in its trade with the settlement empire, i.e. with Canada, Australia, New Zealand and South Africa.[104] Therefore, British colonial administrators and economists were not greatly interested in the French project of 'mise en valeur' for the new tropical colonies in Africa that dominated the discussions within the ICI. Besides an economic focus on the white settlement colonies, India had always been at the centre of British colonial interest. The British Raj was not seen as comparable to other European colonies and their administrative and economic problems.[105] The British view on forms of comparative colonization as they were represented by the ICI remained reserved. As a consequence, the institute could only execute a limited influence on international developments in the colonial world that was being dominated by the British Empire.

World War I meant a long break in the history of the institute. After a meeting in 1913, the institute next reassembled two years after the end of the war in Brussels in 1920.[106] Germany, having lost its colonies, was excluded. Italy became much more engaged and sent a growing number of active and associated members to ICI meetings.[107] The conferences of the 1920s were held in Paris in 1921, in Rome in 1924, in The Hague in 1927, and again in Brussels in 1929. The number of active delegates increased to seventy in 1920, now with a new quota regulation.[108] The racial scheme of the ICI also changed during the 1920s. At the meeting in Paris in 1931, three Japanese delegates appeared. Masaji Inouye, president of an international development company from Tokyo, Shunji Miyao, vice-president of the Japanese Colonial Bureau, former director for the government in Korea and Kunio Yanagida, professor of the history of colonialism at the University of Waseda represented the Japanese Empire.[109] This clearly meant a shift in the understanding of imperial networks within the ICI. Formerly only including 'European' colonizers or rulers of 'European descent' (the US and Latin American States), the presence of Japanese experts meant a rather pragmatic opening up of concepts of imperial internationalism.

In the international context, the arguments of colonizers started to change generally after World War I – a transformation that had a strong impact on the ICI. A first impetus of change was provided by the Versailles Treaty, with the mandates of the League of Nations that emphasized the trusteeship of the colonial powers for indigenous populations. 'Colonial development' became the new key term. The new trusteeship ideology put a great deal of pressure not only on the mandate powers to invest in development and social programmes in their territories, but on all colonizing powers.[110] The concept of *mise en valeur* the ICI had committed itself to before World War I now seemed outdated, as it concentrated mainly on plantation management in the colonies. The ICI developed some new concepts dealing with an expansion of indigenous agriculture in the colonies in the 1920s.[111] However, new organizations such as the International Labour Organization (ILO) that was founded in 1919 in connection with the peace conference at Versailles quickly developed a strong expertise and could exert a dominant influence in these fields, pushing back the ICI.[112] Also, population decline was now seen as an immense threat to productivity in the colonies. From the mid-1920s onwards, health problems in the colonies were connected with issues of subsistence. As Michael Worboys has shown, the 'discovery' of malnutrition in Africa happened in 1925 in association with research on cattle diseases and on the diets of different African peoples. The consequences of this research were now debated in British expert groups and in international forums. New attention was directed to social welfare and development in the colonies.[113] However, these topics were hardly taken up by the ICI in the 1920s.

Generally, other new organizations such as the League of Nations and the League of Nations Health Organization started to take a great interest in the situation of colonial populations and societies after World War I. Their wish to develop international programmes influenced the colonizing powers in their outlook on colonies.[114] Clearly, the ICI found itself now in the second row of institutions furthering international transfer on colonial issues.

The ICI continued to be a place for exchanging colonial knowledge on legal and economic matters. For example, after the economic crisis in 1929, the session of 1931 was partly devoted to the effects of the crisis in the colonies. The institute also published detailed reports on different consequences of the crisis in various types of colonial economies.[115]

What should remain important is the fact that the ICI institutionalized colonial knowledge transfer and created new forms of regular discussion and meetings between political and scientific experts. The institute certainly excelled in systematically ordering knowledge on colonialism. However, local knowledge that was always integrated in the process of collecting material on colonial issues was hardly mentioned and was not addressed as valuable. The ICI has to be seen in the strong tradition of stabilizing Western hegemony in the fields of science and knowledge.[116]

III. Conclusion

Exchange of colonial knowledge was an expanding field at the end of the nineteenth century. Explorers, scientists and colonial merchants had always had mobile careers between colonial empires and had added to a growing body of colonial knowledge. Now, with the increasing scientific interest in colonization, with the emerging of new fields of science, with a further differentiation of colonial knowledge and with more expert groups engaged in colonial matters, the exchange of imperial knowledge reached new dimensions. Information and knowledge on colonial matters were read, translated and commented upon by a growing number of people. Furthermore, the administrations of different colonial empires became more interested in their neighbours and tried to learn from each other's experiences; political and scientific experts mingled. New careers emerged, connected with the systematic exploitation of the colonies and with the building up of infrastructural systems.

The ICI as an international, non-governmental institution can be seen as a typical outcome of all these developments.[117] Exchange of colonial knowledge between empires is something quite unknown in historical research, still, constant mutual observation and a desire to learn from each other was a rather common phenomenon in the interactions between empires at the end of the nineteenth and the beginning of the twentieth century.[118] The ICI is an exemplary case showing the extent of these developments. Until 1914 it certainly served as a nodal point in the networks of European and Western colonial experts. Even if the disinterest of British experts curtailed the influence of institute, the ICI was an important exchange forum for colonial knowledge, at least for the colonial empires of continental Europe. After 1918, the role of the ICI became less prominent. New concepts emerged. Other international organizations such as the ILO and the League of Nations now addressed colonial politics and provided more important international networks and more influential forums for knowledge exchange. However, the ICI continued to offer a growing reservoir of colonial knowledge that accommodated the demands of its members.

As a last point it should be mentioned that the development of an international exchange forum of colonial knowledge involved first and foremost the aim of stabilizing European rule over dependent colonies. The ICI was keen to reform colonialism in a form that helped to preserve European or Western rule over colonized people. Seeing it from the perspective of postcolonial studies it served to institutionalize forms of constructing knowledge about colonized people and helped to stabilize European hegemony over certain reservoirs of knowledge.[119] Even if it created knowledge exchange and international connections, the ICI always displayed various layers of exclusion and considerable differences in levels of power.

Notes

1 Institute Colonial International, *Compte-Rendue de la Session tenue à Bruxelles les 29, 30 et 31 Juillet 1912* (Brussels et al.: Augustin Challamel, 1912) (in the following: *Compte Rendu*, 1912), p. 43.

2 *Compte Rendu*, 1912, pp. 311–14.
3 For the tensions between co-operation and rivalry that shaped the relations of European empires and for strong proofs of co-operation see Ulrike Lindner, *Koloniale Begegnungen: Deutschland und Großbritannien als Imperialmächte in Afrika 1880–1914* (Frankfurt, M., New York: Campus 2011); Ann Laura Stoler, Carole McGranahan and Peter C. Perdue (eds), *Imperial Formations* (Santa Fe, N.M., Oxford: School for Advanced Research, 2007).
4 Madeleine Herren, *Internationale Organisationen seit 1865: Eine Globalgeschichte der internationalen Ordnung* (Darmstadt: Wiss. Buchgesellschaft, 2009), pp. 15–17.
5 See e.g. John Boli and George M. Thomas (eds), *Constructing World Culture: International Nongovernmental Organizations since 1875* (Stanford: Stanford UP, 1999).
6 Janny de Jong, Kolonialism op een Koopje: Het International Koloniale Instituut, 1994–1914, *Tjidschrift voor Geschiedenis*, 109 (1996), pp. 45–72; Jan Henning Böttger, Internationalismus und Kolonialismus: Ein Werkstattbericht zur Geschichte des Brüsseler 'Institut Colonial International' (1894–1948), *Jahrbuch für europäische Überseegeschichte*, 6 (2006), pp. 165–73; Jan Henning Böttger, Bienvue dans la capital de l'Empire! Die Tagung des Institut Colonial International in Berlin (1897), in: Ulrich van der Heyden and Joachim Zeller (eds), *Macht und Anteil an der Weltherrschaft: Berlin und der deutsche Kolonialismus* (Unrast: Münster, 2005), pp. 109–15; Benoit Daviron, Mobilizing labour in African agriculture: the role of the International Colonial Institute in the elaboration of a standard of colonial administration 1895–1930, *Journal of Global History*, 5 (2010), pp. 479–501; Pierre Singaravélou, Les strategies d'internationalisation de la question colonial et la construction transnational d'une science de la colonization à la fin du XIXe siècle, *Monde(s)*, 1 (2012), pp. 135–57. See also the chapter by Florian Wagner in this book and his forthcoming PhD thesis that will deal with the ICI more thoroughly.
7 Frederick Cooper and Ann Laura Stoler, Between metropole and colony: rethinking a research agenda, in: Frederick Cooper and Ann Laura Stoler (eds), *Tensions of Empire: Colonial Cultures in a Bourgeois World* (Berkeley: University of California Press, 1997), p. 13.
8 Robert A. Stafford, Scientific exploration and empire, in: Andrew Porter (ed.), *The Oxford History of the British Empire: The Nineteenth Century* (Oxford: Oxford UP, 1999), pp. 294–319; Benedikt Stuchtey, Introduction: towards a comparative history of science and tropical medicine in imperial cultures since 1800, in: Benedikt Stuchtey (ed.), *Science Across the European Empires, 1800–1950* (Oxford: Oxford UP, 2005), pp.1–2; see also Christopher Bayly and Roy MacLeod (eds), *Nature and Empire: Science and the Colonial Enterprise* (Chicago: University of Chicago Press, 2000); or more generally: Daniel R. Headrick, *The Tools of Empire: Technology and European Imperialism in the Nineteenth Century* (Oxford: Oxford UP, 1981).
9 Helen Tilley, Global histories, vernacular science, and African genealogies; or, is the history of science ready for the world?, *Isis*, 101 (2010), pp. 113–14; see more generally Kapil Raj, *Relocating Modern Science: Circulation and the Construction of Scientific Knowledge in South Asia and Europe 1650–1900* (Basingstoke, New York: Palgrave Macmillan, 2007).
10 For the history of the Royal Geographical Society see Ian Cameron, *To the Farthest Ends of the Earth: The History of the Royal Geographical Society 1830–1980* (London: Macdonald, 1980).
11 Lewis Pyenson, *Civilizing Mission: Exact Sciences and French Overseas Expansion 1830–1940* (Baltimore: Johns Hopkins UP, 1993).

12 Tony Ballantyne and Antoinette Burton, Empires and the reach of the global, in: Emily S. Rosenberg (ed.), *A World Connecting 1870-1945*, (Cambridge, Mass.: Harvard UP, 2012), pp. 288-90.
13 For the British Empire as role model for German colonialism see Lindner, *Koloniale Begegnungen*, p. 43.
14 Tilley, Global histories.
15 Ulrike von Hirschhausen, People that count – the imperial census in nineteenth- and early twentieth-century Europe and India, in: Jörn Leonhard Leonhard and Ulrike von Hirschhausen (eds), *Comparing Empires. Encounters and Transfers in the Long Nineteenth Century* (Göttingen: Vandenhoeck & Ruprecht, 2011), pp. 145-70.
16 An infamous example is the explorer and publicist Henry Morton Stanley, who was supported by the British Empire, by the Belgian King Leopold II and by several other financiers. See Frank McLynn, *Stanley. The Making of an African Explorer* (Oxford: Oxford UP, 1991).
17 Stuchtey, Introduction, pp. 20-1.
18 Lindner, *Koloniale Begegnungen*, pp. 95-7.
19 Christopher A. Bayly, *The Birth of the Modern World: Global Connections and Comparisons* (Oxford: Wiley-Blackwell, 2004), p. 461; John Darwin, *After Tamerlane: The Global History of Empire Since 1405* (London: Bloomsbury, 2008), pp. 300-4.
20 Roland Wenzlhuemer, *Connecting the Nineteenth-Century World: The Telegraph and Globalization* (Cambridge: Cambridge UP, 2012).
21 Lindner, *Koloniale Begegnungen*, p. 459.
22 Bouda Etemad, *Possessing the World: Taking the Measurements of Colonisation from the Eighteenth to the Twentieth Century* (New York: Berghahn, 2007), pp. 212-18.
23 Lindner, *Koloniale Begegnungen*, pp. 309-10.
24 H.L. Wesseling, *The European Colonial Empires: 1815-1919* (London: Routledge, 2004), pp. 125-30.
25 Christian Geulen, *Geschichte des Rassismus* (Munich: Beck 2007), p. 85.
26 Alice Conklin, *A Mission to Civilize. The Republican Idea of Empire in France and West Africa, 1895-1930* (Stanford: Stanford UP, 1997), pp. 239-41.
27 Lindner, *Koloniale Begegnungen*, p. 90.
28 Sebastian Conrad, *Deutsche Kolonialgeschichte* (München: Beck, 2008), p. 37.
29 See the massive publications of the ICI on colonial labour and labour management during the 1890s: ICI (ed.), *La Main-d'oeuvre aux colonies. Tome I : Documents officiels sur le contrat de travail et le louage d'ouvrage aux Colonies (Colonies allemandes, Etat indépendant du Congo, Colonies françaises, Indes orientales néerlandaises)* (Paris: A. Colin, 1895); ICI (ed.), *La Main-d'oeuvre aux colonies, Tome II: Documents officiels sur le contrat de travail et le louage d'ouvrage aux colonies (Indes anglaises, Colonies anglaises)* (Paris: A. Colin, 1897); ICI (ed.), *Main-d'oeuvre aux colonies, Tome III: Documents officiels sur le contrat de travail et le louage d'ouvrage aux Colonies (Colonies françaises, Surinam)* (Paris: A. Colin, 1898) .
30 Stuart Michael Persell, *French Colonial Lobby 1889-1938* (Stanford, Ca.: Hoover Press Publications), pp. 97-9.
31 Bernhard Dernburg, *Zielpunkte des deutschen Kolonialwesens* (Berlin: Ernst Friedrich Kittler 1907). See for Rechenberg, Detlef Bald, Die Reformpolitik von Gouverneur Rechenberg. Koloniale Handelsexpansion und indische Minderheit in Deutsch-Ostafrika, in: D. Oberndörfer (ed.), *Africana Collecta II* (Düsseldorf 1971), pp. 242-61.
32 Crawford Young, *The African Colonial State in Comparative Perspective* (New Haven: Yale UP, 1994), p. 82; B.R.Tomlinson, Economics and empire: the periphery and the

imperial economy, in: Andrew Porter (ed.), *The Oxford History of the British Empire. The Nineteenth Century* (Oxford: Oxford UP, 1999), pp. 53-74. There was quite a successful programme of local cash crop production (cocoa) in the British African colony of the Gold Coast.

33 Lindner, *Koloniale Begegnungen*, p. 83; for the growing significance of scientific colonialism see also Nadin Hée, *Imperiales Wissen und koloniale Gewalt. Japans Herrschaft in Taiwan 1895-1945* (Frankfurt, M.: Campus, 2012), pp. 14-17. See e.g. the German colonial secretary Wilhelm Solf who published as a colonial expert and translator before and while working for the colonial service. For Solf see Eberhard von Vietsch *Wilhelm Solf: Botschafter zwischen den Zeiten* (Tübingen: Wunderlich, 1961).

34 Dirk van Laak, *Imperiale Infrastruktur: Deutsche Planungen für eine Erschließung Afrikas* (Paderborn: Ferdinand Schöningh, 2004), pp. 35-40, 91-3.

35 Paul Rohrbach, *Deutsche Kolonialwirtschaft. Kulturpolitische Grundsätze für die Rassen- und Missionsfragen* (Berlin: Hilfe 1909); Paul Rohrbach, *Der deutsche Gedanke in der Welt*, (Königstein i.T.: Langewiesche, 1912); Paul Rohrbach, *Zum Weltvolk hindurch* (Stuttgart: Engelhorn, 1914).

36 Bundesarchiv Berlin-Lichterfelde (in the following BAB), R 1001/8739, Cape of Good Hope, Blue Book of Native Affairs, 1891; as a summary of a British colonial report: R 1001/8729, Swaziland, after the colonial report No. 559, Cd. 3729/23, 1908.

37 BAB, R 1001/8741, German General Consulate South Africa to Chancellor von Bülow, 2.5.1905, BAB, R 1001/8748, report of the Chief Native Commissioner Matabeleland, Southern Rhodesia, 1908, f. 52-6. This report that was specifically requested by colonial secretary Bernhard Dernburg.

38 Joseph Chailly-Bert, *Java et ses habitants* (Paris: Armand Colin, 1900); Joseph Chailly-Bert, *La colonisation de l'Indo-Chine: L'expérience anglaise* (Paris: Armand Colin, 1892); Joseph Chailly-Bert, *L'impôt sur le revenue: Législation comparée et économie politique* (Paris: Guillaumin, 1884). For Chailly and his admiration of the Dutch role model see also Frances Gouda, *Dutch Culture Overseas: Colonial Practice in the Netherland Indies, 1900-1942* (Amsterdam: Amsterdam UP 1996), pp. 45-6.

39 Louis Hamilton, The German colonies 1910-1911, *United Empire*, 3 (1912), p. 970; see also articles by Wyatt Tilby, Germany as a colonising factor, *United Empire* 3 (1912), pp. 57-9 and The German record in colonising, *United Empire* 5 (1914), pp. 711-15.

40 Anon., Interkoloniales Verständnis: Eine Wertschätzung deutscher Leistungen von englischer Seite, *Deutsche Kolonialzeitung*, 7 May 1910.

41 Extracts from the *Deutsche Kolonialzeitung* being translated into English celebrating the thirtieth anniversary of the German Colonial Society: Anon., German view on colonisation: extracts from German sources, *Journal of the African Society*, 14 (1914), pp. 40-52.

42 Anon., The German colonies, *The Times*, 11 October 1902, p. 7.

43 See *Revue Coloniale Internationale* 1 (1885) for the international character of the journal. For Pieter van der Lith see Lith, *Nieuw Nederlandsch Biografisch Woordenboek vol. 8* (Leiden 1911-37), p. 1063.

44 Pieter van der Lith and Arnold Pistorius, *De grondslagen voor het British-Indisch beheer* (The Hague: Martinus Nijhoff, 1876); Pieter van der Lith, Bombay onder het bestuur van Lord Reay, *De Gids* 56 (1892).

45 On Asmis see Bettina Brockmeyer, Der Kolonialbeamte Rudolf Asmis, in: Rebekka Habermas and Alexandra Przyrembel (eds), *Von Käfern, Märkten und Menschen:*

Kolonialismus und Wissen in der Moderne (Göttingen: Vandenhoek & Ruprecht, 2013), pp. 84–94.
46 The German article, W. Asmis, Eingeborenenrecht und Eingeborenenpolitik in der Goldküste und in Nigerien, *Koloniale Rundschau* (1912), pp. 678–706, was translated and published as W. Asmis, Law and policy: relating to the Natives of the Gold Coast and Nigeria, *Journal of the African Society*, 12 (1912/13), pp. 17–51.
47 Ulrike Lindner, The transfer of European social policy concepts to tropical Africa, 1900–50: the example of maternal and child welfare, *Journal of Global History*, 9 (2014), p. 211.
48 Wolfgang U. Eckart, *Medizin und Kolonialimperialismus: Deutschland 1884–1945* (Paderborn: Ferdinand Schöningh, 1997), pp. 340–1.
49 Christoph Gradmann, *Krankheit im Labor: Robert Koch und die medizinische Bakteriologie* (Göttingen: Wallstein, 2005), pp. 278–82.
50 See the discussion on tropical medicine and hygiene during the first session of the institute: ICI (ed.), *Compte-Rendu des Séances Tenues à Bruxelles les 28 et 29 Mai 1894* (Brussels: Typographie-Lithographie Populaire 1894), pp. 43–69.
51 Van Laak, *Imperiale Infrastruktur*, p. 243.
52 B.S. Hoyle, *Gillmann of Tanganyika 1882–1946: The Life and Work of a Pioneer Geographer* (Aldershot: Avebury, 1987), pp. 47–53, 56.
53 Hoyle, *Gillmann*, pp. 85–6.
54 Rhodes House, Oxford, MSS Afr.s.900 (1), Clement Gillman, History of Tanganyika Railway, 1921; also Hoyle, *Gillmann*, pp. 198–332.
55 Singaravélou, Les stratégies, pp. 149–150. See also Pierre Singaravélou, *Professer L'Empire. Les Science coloniales en France sous la IIIe République* (Paris: Publications de la Sorbonne, 2011).
56 ICI (ed.), *Bibliothèque Coloniale Internationale, no. 5: Les Chemins de fer aux colonies et dans les pays neufs* (Brussels et al.: Établissements généraux d'Imprimerie et al., 3 vols, 1900–1); ICI (ed.), *Bibliothèque coloniale internationale, no. 6: Le régime minier aux colonies* (Brussels et al.: Établissements généraux d'Imprimerie et al., 3 vols, 1902–3); ICI (ed.), *Bibliothèque coloniale international, no. 7: Les différents systèmes d'Irrigation* (Brussels et al.: Établissements généraux d'Imprimerie et al., 4 vols, 1906–9).
57 ICI (ed.), *Compte-Rendu des Séances tenues a Bruxelles les 28 et 29 Mai 1894* (Brussels: Établissements généraux d'Imprimerie, 1894) (in the following *Compte Rendu*, 1894). See p. 4: 'De créer des relations internationales entre les personnes qui s'occupent d'une façon suivie de l'étude du droit et de l'administration des colonies, hommes politiques, administrateurs, savants, – et de faciliter l'échange des idées et des connaissances spéciales entre hommes compétents.'
58 Singaravelou, Les strategies, p. 150.
59 See *Revue coloniale internationale*, 1 (1885). The first volume featured German, French and English articles by authors from many different colonial empires covering a wide variety of subjects.
60 Daviron, Mobilizing labour, p. 480; see for the development of the national colonial unions in continental Europe the chapter by Florian Wagner in this volume.
61 Singaravélou, Les stratégies, p. 151; for the professions of the founding members see *Compte Rendu* 1894, pp. 21–5.
62 Thomas Baty, Lord Reay, *Journal of the Society of Comparative Legislation*, 13 (1912), pp. 9–10.
63 *Compte Rendu*, 1894, p. 21; *Compte Rendu*, 1912, p. 11; ICI (ed.), *Compte Rendu de la session tenue à Paris, les 17, 18 et 19 mai 1921* (Brussels et al.: Établissements Généraux

d'Imprimerie et al., 1921), (in the following *Compte Rendu* 1921), p. 13; ICI (ed.), *Compte Rendu de la XXIe session tenue à Paris, les 5-6-7 mai 1931* (Brussels et al.: Établissements généraux d'Imprimerie et al., 1931), pp. 18–19.

64 1895 in The Hague, 1897 in Berlin, 1899 in Brussels, 1900 in Paris, 1901 again in The Hague, 1903 in London, 1904 in Wiesbaden, 1905 in Rome, 1907 in Brussels, 1908 in Paris, 1909 in The Hague, 1911 in Brunswick, 1912 in Brussels and 1913 in London. See for the locations of the conferences *Compte Rendu*, 1894–1913.

65 *Compte Rendu*, 1894–1937.

66 For the publications of the ICI see ICI (ed.), *Bibliothèque Coloniale Internationale, no. 1: La main-d'oeuvre aux colonies* (Paris: Armand Clon et Cie., 3 vols, 1895–7); ICI (ed.), *Bibliothèque Coloniale Internationale, no. 2: Les fonctionnaires coloniaux* (Brussels et al.: Adolph Mertens et al., 3 vols, 1897–1910); ICI (ed.), *Bibliothèque coloniale international, no. 3: Le régime foncier aux colonies* (Brussels et al.: Adolph Mertens et al., 6 vols, 1898–1905); ICI (ed.), *Bibliothèque Coloniale Internationale, no. 4: Le régime de protectorats* (Brussels et al.: Établissements généraux d'Imprimerie et al., 2 vols, 1899); ICI (ed.), *Bibliothèque Coloniale Internationale, no. 5: Les Chemins de fer aux colonies et dans les pays neufs* (Brussels et al.: Établissements généraux d'Imprimerie et al., 3 vols, 1900–1); ICI (ed.), *Bibliothèque coloniale internationale, no. 6: Le régime minier aux colonies* (Brussels et al.: Établissements généraux d'Imprimerie et al., 3 vols, 1902–3); ICI (ed.), *Bibliothèque Coloniale International, no. 7: Les différents systèmes d'Irrigation* (Brussels et al.: Établissements généraux d'Imprimerie et al., 4 vols, 1906–9); ICI (ed.), *Bibliothèque coloniale international, no. 8: Les lois organiques des colonies* (Brussels et al.: Établissements généraux d'Imprimerie et.al., 3 vols, 1906–27); ICI (ed.), *Bibliothèque Coloniale Internationale, no. 9: L'enseignement aux indigènes* (Brussels et al.: Établissements généraux d'Imprimerie et al., 2 vols, 1909–10); ICI (ed.), *Bibliothèque Coloniale International, no. 10: Les droits de chasse dans les colonies et la conservation de la faune indigène* (Brussels et al.: Établissements généraux d'Imprimerie et al., 2 vols, 1911); ICI (ed.), *Bibliothèque coloniale international, no. 11: Le régime forestier aux colonies* (Brussels et al.: Établissements généraux d'Imprimerie et al., 3 vols, 1914).

67 ICI (ed.), *Bibliothèque Coloniale International, no. 8: Les lois organiques des colonies* (Brussels et al.: Établissements généraux d'Imprimerie et al., 3 vols, 1906–27).

68 *Compte Rendu*, 1900, p. 10: Bassett-Moore, professor of International Law at Columbia University, New York; Despagnet, professor of law at Bordeaux; Girault, professor of law at Poitiers; Leseur, professor of colonial law at Paris.

69 Karl Rathgen, ICI, in: Heinrich Schnee (ed.), *Deutsches Koloniallexikon*, vol. 2 (Leipzig 1920), p. 99.

70 See e.g. Ann Laura Stoler, *Along the Archival Grain. Epistemic Anxieties and Colonial Common Sense* (Princeton: Princeton UP, 2009), pp. 158–60; see also von Hirschhausen, *People that Count*.

71 *Compte Rendu*, 1894, pp. 35–7.

72 See e.g. ICI (ed.), *Bibliothèque Coloniale Internationale, no. 6: Le régime minier aux colonies* (Brussels et al.: Établissements généraux d'Imprimerie et al., 3 vols, 1902–3), vol. 1, pp. 9–10.

73 *Compte Rendu*, 1894, p. 37.

74 Boettger, *Internationalismus*, p. 171.

75 *Compte Rendu*, 1913, pp. 86–8.

76 Eingabe der Deutschen Gesellschaft für Eingeborenenschutz an den Reichstag und das Reichs-Kolonialamt, *Koloniale Rundschau*, 1914, pp. 129–32.

77 Cooper, Stoler, *Between Metropole and Colony*, p. 13.

78 Thomas Richards, *The Imperial Archive. Knowledge and the Fantasy of Empire* (London: Verso, 1993), p. 6.
79 *Compte Rendu*, 1894, p. 3: De faciliter et de répandre l'étude comparée de l'administration et du droit des colonies, mainly: 'différents systèmes de gouvernement des colonies, la législation coloniale and des ressources des diverses colonies, de leur régime économique et commercial'.
80 *Compte Rendu*, 1894, p. 3.
81 Daviron, *Mobilizing labour*, p. 499.
82 Böttger, Internationalismus und Kolonialismus, p.168.
83 Article 13 of the Regulations of the Institute, see *Compte Rendu*, 1894, p. 9.
84 See e.g. the longstanding negotiations between Britain and Germany on the drawing up of a definite frontier between Kenya and Tanzania. BAB, R 1001/6931, Vermerk über weiter bestehende Differenzen mit England wegen Grenzstreitigkeiten auf kolonialem Gebiet, 19 April 1904; BAB, R 1001/6936, Deutsch-englisches Abkommen vom 19.5.1909 über die endgültige Festlegung der Grenze zwischen Deutsch-Ostafrika und Uganda, 19 May1909.
85 On the exchange of military knowledge between colonial powers see Ludwig von Estorff, *Wanderungen und Kämpfe in Südwestafrika, Ostafrika und Südafrika, 1894–1910* (Windhoek: John Meinert, 1968), pp. 91–6; Eckard Michels, Das Ostasiatische Expeditionskorps des Deutschen Reiches in China 1900/01, in: Tanja Bührer, Christian Stachelbeck and Dierk Walter (eds), *Imperialkriege von 1500 bis heute. Strukturen, Akteure, Lernprozesse* (Paderborn: Ferdinand Schöningh, 2011), pp. 401–18.
86 ICI (ed.), *Compte-Rendu de la Session tenue à la Haye, les 9, 10, 11 et 12 septembre 1895* (Paris: Armand Clon et Cie., 1895), (in the following *Compte Rendu*, 1895), p. 41. 'Nos discussions ont pour but de faire une trêve à bien des malentendus, de commbattre les préjugés. D'établir une entente cordiale entre les nations que nous représentons, d'améliorer le sort des populations de nos colonies.'
87 *Compte Rendu*, 1894, p. 6.
88 Articles 7 and 8 of the regulations, *Compte Rendu*, 1894, p. 7.
89 ICI (ed.), *Compte Rendu de la Session tenue à Bruxelles les 17, 18 et 19 juin 1907*, (Brussels et al.: Établissements généraux d'Imprimerie et al., 1907) (in the following *Compte Rendu*, 1907), pp. 13–17.
90 *Compte Rendu*, 1907, p. 14; *Compte Rendu*, 1912, p. 21; *Compte Rendu*, 1921, pp. 15, 21.
91 The discussions on internal colonization in Latin America and the colonial situation in European empires in the nineteenth century are still separate issues in contemporary research; on the lack of connections between these research areas see Enrique Dussel, C. Jáuregui and Mabel Moraña (eds), *Coloniality at Large: Latin America and the Postcolonial Debate* (Durham: Duke UP, 2008).
92 Jane Burbank and Frederick Cooper, *Empires in World History* (Princeton: Princeton UP, 2010) or Stoler, McGranahan and Perdue, *Imperial Formations*; Jörn Leonhard and Ulrike von Hirschhausen (eds), *Comparing Empires: Encounters and Transfers in the Long Nineteenth Century* (Göttingen: Vandenhoeck & Ruprecht, 2011).
93 See *Compte Rendu*, 1894, pp. 23–5; *Compte Rendu*, 1895, p. 17; *Compte Rendu*, 1900, pp. 8–12; *Compte Rendu*, 1907; *Compte Rendu* 1912.
94 *Compte Rendu*, 1894, pp. 52–7; *Compte Rendu*, 1895, pp. 45–74.
95 *Compte Rendu*, 1895, p. 21, '[…] à cause de la diversité des systèmes de colonisation adoptés et pratiqués par les différentes nations européennes, à cause des différences de race et de caractère des populations auxquelles ces systèmes étaient appliqués; que ses divergences de race, de climat […] de tirer des conclusions générales.'

96　*Compte Rendu*, 1907, p. 12; *Compte Rendu*, 1912, p. 43.
97　Lindner, *Koloniale Begegnungen*, pp. 43–9.
98　Daviron, Mobilizing labour, pp. 481–3.
99　*Compte Rendu*, 1907, p. 13.
100　See the member lists in the *Compte Rendu* of 1894, 1895, 1900, 1903, 1907, 1912.
101　ICI (ed.), *Status et Réglement, Liste de Membres, Listes de Publication*, (Brussels, 1931), p. 22.
102　Jong, Kolonialisme, pp. 50–1; Daviron, *Mobilizing labour*, p. 485.
103　Jong, Kolonialisme, pp. 45–6.
104　P.J. Cain, Economics and empire: the metropolitan context, in: Porter, *Oxford History*, pp. 42–5.
105　Robin J. Moore, Imperial India 1858–1914, in: Porter, *Oxford History*, pp. 441–2.
106　See ICI (ed.), *Compte Rendu de la session tenue à Bruxelles les 24, 25 et 26 mai 1920* (Bruxelles: Établissements Généraux d'Imprimerie, 1920) (in the following: *Compte Rendu*, 1920).
107　See ICI (ed.), *Compte Rendu de la session tenue à Rome les 22, 23 et 24 avril 1924* (Bruxelles: Établissements Généraux d'Imprimerie, 1924).
108　*Compte Rendu*, 1920, p. 29. The number of active delegates was limited to seventy with the following regulations: England: fourteen, Belgium: eight, Spain: two, USA: three, France: twelve, Italy: six, Netherlands: nine, Portugal: three, further countries: thirteen.
109　ICI (ed.), *Status et Réglement, Liste de Membres, Listes de Publication*, (Brussels: Établissements Généraux d'Imprimerie, 1931), p. 33.
110　Joanna Lewis, *Empire State-Building. War & Welfare in Kenya 1925–52* (Oxford: James Currey, 2000), pp. 25–6; Vernon Marston Hewitt, Empire, international development & the concept of good government, in: Mark R. Duffield and Vernon Marston Hewitt (eds) *Empire, Development & Colonialism: The Past in the Present* (Woodbridge: Currey, 2009), pp. 30–44.
111　Daviron, Mobilizing labour, p. 497.
112　See for the history of the ILO Daniel Maul, *Menschenrechte, Entwicklung und Dekolonisation – Die Internationale Arbeitsorganisation (IAO) 1940–1970*, (Essen: Klartext, 2007).
113　Michael Worboys, The discovery of malnutrition between the wars, in: David Arnold (ed.), *Imperial Medicine and Indigenous Societies*; (Manchester: Manchester UP, 1988), pp. 210–11.
114　Tilley, *Africa*, pp. 177–81.
115　ICI (ed.), *Compte Rendu de la XXIe session tenue à Paris les 5-6-7 et 8 mai 1931* (Bruxelles: Établissements Généraux d'Imprimerie, 1931).
116　Veronika Lipphardt and David Ludwig, Wissens- und Wissenschaftstransfer, in: Institute for European History (IEG) Mainz (ed.), *Europäische Geschichte Online (EGO)*, 2011-09-28. URL: http://www.ieg.-ego.eu/lipphardtv-ludwigd-2011-de.
117　Herren, *Internationale Organisationen*.
118　Ann Laura Stoler and Carole McGranahan, Introduction: refiguring imperial terrains, in: Stoler, McGranahan, Perdue, *Imperial Formations*, p. 12.
119　Edward Said, *Orientalism*. Reprint with a new Preface (London: Penguin 2003), pp. 44–5.

3

Private Colonialism and International Co-operation in Europe, 1870–1914

Florian Wagner

We, the friends of colonial expansion in Germany and in France, shall cherish one ideal that we found on the journeys we have made, at the remote places we have seen and during the strenuous and adventurous life we have led. We should cherish that ideal among all people and in all the different climes. This ideal is certainly not more beautiful than the nationalist thought, but it complements it in the most useful and human way: it is the European ideal.

Albert Comte de Pouvourville, French colonial activist[1]

Albert Comte de Pouvourville, a veteran of the French Colonial Service who had turned to expansionist journalism when released from his duties, wrote these lines in a heated atmosphere of imperial rivalry in Europe in 1907.[2] Provided that Pouvourville's fraternization with German colonialists was not due to the mollifying effect of opium consumption – a taste that Pouvourville had acquired while serving in French Indochina – his behaviour seems to be at odds with his time.[3] Instead of closing ranks, Pouvourville's Europe threatened to go to war over colonial conflicts.

At the turn of the century, the colonizing powers had identified the sultanate of Morocco as one of the few remaining territories to lack European domination. France, Germany, Great Britain and Spain had asserted their rights to the sultan's lands and media carried the conflict down to the tables of European pubs and inns.[4] A conflict so pertinent arose, that historians of the twentieth century had seen no other choice but to interpret it as the curtain-raiser of World War I.[5] Colonial rivalry, the chroniclers argued, culminated in a 'cold war' on the Morocco question, which was about to dump into a real war when Germany sent the gunboat *Panther* to the North African coast. According to this narrative of historical continuity, the preliminary settlement of the conflict in 1911 only deferred the outbreak of a European war and was far from preventing it. Pouvourville's contribution to the *Deutsche Kolonialzeitung* in 1907 does not seem to fit that story. Or, to put it more dramatically, his plea for a Franco-German colonial entente as a cornerstone of a 'European ideal' seems to be anachronistic.

In this chapter I will show that Pouvourville's collaboration with German colonial activists does not make him a maverick to his own time. He was not the only one to raise his voice in favour of an international colonial co-operation, but was on the contrary accompanied by an internationalist choir of colonial activists. German colonial experts had asked him to contribute the above cited article to the *Deutsche Kolonialzeitung* (*German Colonial Revue*), which regularly gave a forum to expansionists from other nations. Pouvourville had even written regularly for the *Kolonialzeitung*, in a column on Franco-German 'intercolonial' co-operation, since 1905. In that year he had established contacts with representatives of the German colonial movement at a session of the Institut Colonial International, founded in 1894 with its headquarters in Brussels.[6] During the biennial meetings of the Institut Colonial International, Pouvourville had made friends with the Dutch Pieter Antoine van der Lith, who had issued the *Revue Coloniale Internationale* in the 1880s.[7] He had also encountered Édouard Descamps, a Belgian internationalist and promoter of the État Indépendant du Congo (Congo Free State), which had been created with the help of the International African Association at the Brussels International Geographical Conference (1876).[8] Several international colonial congresses were to follow until World War I and gave colonial activists like Pouvourville, Van der Lith or Descamps the chance to meet and discuss colonial issues. This chapter analyses these different manifestations of colonial internationalism and seeks to retrace their origins as well as their long-term effects.

Doing justice to the fact that private initiatives were the origin of colonial internationalism since the 1870s, the first part of the chapter analyses the emergence of an unprecedented non-governmental colonial movement in Europe from the 1870s onwards. With Great Britain setting the benchmark for other colonizing powers, the chapter will mainly focus on continental Europe and the co-operation between private colonial associations in France, Germany, Belgium and Spain. Each of these countries had a colonial tradition of its own. But during the late nineteenth century, dynamics of convergence both in colonial theory and practice unfolded. Contemporaries sought to describe these developments of unprecedented scope by using a new terminology: by the end of the nineteenth century, the expressions 'colonialism' and 'internationalism' found their way into European vocabularies and made explicit what had appeared urgently obvious for a long time.[9]

The second part of the chapter challenges Pouvourville's assumption that internationalism and colonialism were 'natural' phenomena, or 'movements' autonomous of human agency. Both ideologies served personal interests, even though their promoters portrayed them as being 'uninterested' ideals. Rather, they served to codify and legitimize nationalist and exploitative practices and were used by individuals and groups to shape reality according to their interests.

Colonial interest groups were known to introduce colonial concepts to European societies and to exaggerate their importance for these societies. Some contemporaries had already noted that colonial interest groups assumed the character of a 'political party' that tried to promote colonialism against a plurality of other interests.[10] In order to impose themselves, they made extensive use of media and 'propaganda' to promote colonialism. By analysing social composition and the propagandistic activity of lobby groups, the traditional historiography concluded that only small groups backed colonial expansion and 'sold' it to their compatriots as a necessity for the survival of their own society.[11] Whether Europeans bought this story or not, remains a matter of debate.[12]

The numeric marginalization of colonial lobby groups within their own countries is only one reason why they turned to like-minded expansionists in other European countries to demonstrate a transnational solidarity among colonial experts. Since the 1870s, some colonial activists had called themselves 'internationalists'. Definitions of the term 'international' varied and contemporaries used the term interchangeably with 'European'. It is not the purpose of this chapter to define 'internationalism' or 'colonialism', but to show how colonial activists used these terms and to what extent they hoped to gain agency by calling themselves 'internationalists' or 'Europeans'. There is no doubt that colonial activists hoisted nationalist or Europeanist colours depending on the respective circumstances and situations. Nobody was surprised when German nationalist and racist Carl Peters – who headed the Gesellschaft für Deutsche Kolonisation (Society for German Colonisation, 1884) – joined the Institut Colonial International in Brussels.[13] Likewise, while many colonial activists claimed to act on the authority of humanity, civilization or an imagined international community, they did not necessarily abandon their aggressive nationalism.[14] When colonial activists make use of these abstract concepts to substantiate their claims for colonial projects, the historian needs to be cautious of the hypocrisy inherent to the colonialists' affirmation of 'Europeanness' and 'internationalism'. This hypocrisy will be discussed in the second part of this chapter.

The third part will focus on the alleged contradiction between nationalist and internationalist positions. Much has been written about the nationalist origins of colonial expansion. Max Weber was one of the first to describe colonial expansion as the logical and supposedly inevitable outcome of nineteenth-century nation-building.[15] In this part I will argue that nationalism and transnational co-operation did not necessarily enter into conflict. Pouvourville's perspective, in which 'the national thought' and the 'European ideal' were not contradictory, but complemented each other to merge into a 'humane' symbiosis, is consistent with the contemporary self-portrait of this period.[16] For nineteenth-century Europeans, their continent was not a homogenous spatial entity, but a competitive community.[17] Europe's apparent success, called 'progress' by its inhabitants, seemed to originate in an internal commercial and political rivalry. Colonial theorists not only adopted this view, but helped to promulgate it by declaring that the ability to colonize delivered the proof of being a progressive and indeed 'European' country. I will argue in the last part of the chapter that the notion of Europe as a competitive society, which saw its progress based in national and commercial rivalry, prevailed among the colonial internationalists. However, for all rivalry, they wanted creative competition, not a destructive war. And above all, they did not want to risk a war that threatened to put an end to the colonial project.

I. Private colonial societies in Europe between nationalism and internationalism

The significance of private colonial initiatives in Europe

The 1870s witnessed the emergence of colonial lobby groups all over Europe. Especially in France, Germany, Belgium and Spain, but also in the Netherlands and Italy, colonial activists pooled, organized and institutionalized a phenomenon that contemporaries referred to as the 'colonial movement'. Acting as a private citizen and not as the head of state, Belgian King Leopold II had created the Association Internationale pour l'Exploration et la Civilisation de l'Afrique Centrale (shortened as Association Internationale Africaine) in 1876.[18] In the same year, the French Société des etudes coloniales et maritimes made its first appearance, before the more professional associations, the Comité de l'Afrique Française (1890) and the Union Coloniale Française (1894) came to the fore.[19] The Spanish Sociedad Geográfica de Madrid (1876) had been created to encourage colonial expansion, before the Sociedad Española de Africanistas y Colonistas (1883) and the Sociedad Española de Geografía Comercial (1885) helped to popularize colonization in Africa.[20] The Deutsche Afrikanische Gesellschaft (1876) pioneered in advocating German colonial commitment, but only the Deutscher Kolonialverein (1882) and the Deutsche Kolonialgesellschaft (1887) eventually succeeded in winning the Germans' support for colonial projects.[21]

These associations were not initiated by official top-down politics, but arose from an allegedly 'democratic' necessity to organize and institutionalize colonial interests. By creating pressure groups, pro-colonial activists appeared as interest groups that took the form of 'colonial parties', the most famous among them being the '*parti colonial*' in France.[22] The German Kolonialgesellschaft was the biggest colonial interest group in Europe, with its membership amounting to 40,000 in 1914.[23] In France, the '*coloniaux*' were less numerous and their number did not surpass a total of 10,000 registered members before World War I. Only 200 of them played an active role between 1890 and 1914.[24] In Spain and Belgium, the membership lists rarely contained more than 1,000 entries.[25] Most of the colonial associations' members remained inactive, with some of them not even paying the subscription fees – a problem the steering committee of the German Colonial Society frequently complained about.[26] Nevertheless, the German Colonial Society remained the biggest, yet not the most effective, colonial interest group in Europe. In France, colonial activism seemed to go back to a few but particularly active colonialists like the French Algerian Eugene Etienne, who appeared on the membership lists of no fewer than nineteen colonial lobby groups and had created many of them himself.[27] Joaquin Costa played a similar role for Spain and set up the four most important groups there.[28]

These colonial associations were multifunctional: being primarily private interest groups, they also functioned as learned societies that tried to accumulate and popularize colonial knowledge. Some members used them to increase political prestige, others just enjoyed the sociability or banquets the groups' leaders hosted.[29] But their main purpose was to win support for their interests by competing with other interest groups, which were thematically different but equally concerned with asserting themselves. They were devoted to winning the favour of what they called 'public opinion'. In order to succeed in the task to portray colonial expansion as a contribution to national wealth and strength, they set up a programme of – to use their own expression – 'colonial education' of their compatriots.[30]

The close link between colonization and education programmes is illustrated by French educational reformer and colonial propagandist Jules Ferry or by the Spanish Joaquin Costa who, besides his colonial activities, contributed to the creation of a laicist university, the Institución Libre de Enseñaza. The Deutsche Kolonialgesellschaft initiated the Hamburg-based Kolonialinstitut, while the French Union Coloniale set up a school for colonial medicine.[31] All colonial associations were eager to establish colonial sciences at European universities and played an important part in creating training schools for colonial administrators.[32]

Colonial education was accompanied by colonial propaganda and both took on the scale of an internal civilizing mission: lobby groups issued periodicals and monographs and set up colonial libraries and colonial museums. By organizing travelling exhibitions, slide lectures and trade shows with colonial products, they tried to excite all Europeans with colonial expansion, regardless of class or residence.[33] Moreover, they arranged huge national congresses that brought together all the different groups interested in colonial topics.[34]

Inducing linguists, anthropologists, physicians, geographers or cartographers to participate in these congresses gave colonial activism a new quality: while colonial activists had formerly made advances to other scientific disciplines in order to be accepted as a new science, they intended to subordinate the other disciplines by the end of the nineteenth century. By bowing to the new colonial master science, anthropology or geography were reduced to mere auxiliary sciences of colonialism. Once colonial 'methods' became autonomous 'sciences', and developed into the collective singular of 'colonial science', they also inherited the attributes assigned to 'science'. Colonial science was described as being rational, verifiable and contributing to the progress of mankind. But above all, colonial science was said to emancipate itself from nationalist ideology. Representing colonialism as a science provided the basis for its internationalization.

Finally, colonial interest groups were well informed about colonial realities on the spot. Colonial lobby groups financed scientific expeditions and sent them to overseas territories, only to publish comprehensive reports about the success of these missions. Most of them opened branches in the colonies and invited administrators or colonists to contribute to their colonial propaganda machine. Colonial journals appeared periodically (the *Dépêche Coloniale* in France was a daily newspaper) and recorded meticulously all colonial news as well as reviewing recent expansionist publications. Their editors even sent pre-formulated articles to the daily press and thus functioned as colonial press agencies that addressed a wider public.[35]

From this point of view, it is hard to deny that colonial associations – for all their numeric weakness – played an important role in producing a colonial discourse in the colonizing societies. The pro-colonial discourses they produced may have been far from gaining cultural hegemony. But their omnipresent propaganda certainly made a mark on European societies.[36]

While the colonial propaganda failed to raise the necessary capital for extensive colonial projects,[37] it nevertheless played an important role in acquiring territories in Africa and in pushing national governments to officially acknowledge them as colonial possessions. The contracts completed by Carl Peter's Gesellschaft für deutsche Kolonisation (Society for German Colonisation), Costa's Sociedad Española de Africanistas y Colonistas (Spanish Society of Colonists and Africanists) or Stanley's Association Internationale Africaine with 'indigenous' chiefs, led to the establishment of official colonies in East Africa (1885), Equatorial Guinea (Spanish, 1885) and the Congo Free State (private state owned by Leopold II, 1885).

After colonial societies had contributed significantly to trigger the scramble for Africa and had been busy acquiring overseas territory for decades, they finally turned to the exploration and exploitation of the colonies and their inhabitants. To achieve this goal, interest groups had evolved into more professional colonial expert groups and formed specialized subdivisions like the Kolonialwirtschaftliches Komitee, the Sociedad Española de Geografía Comercial or the Société belge d'Études Coloniales by the end of the nineteenth century.[38] These organizations wanted to 'manage' colonies more effectively and render them more profitable. The alleged need to economically develop the colonies boosted interest in foreign, economically more successful colonies as well as the imperial strategies of other colonizing powers. The exchange of colonial knowledge had developed into a vital instrument to improve colonial rule and economic exploitation. In order to achieve this goal, the colonial associations had to intensify the exchange of colonial knowledge.

However, traditional historiography has analysed these colonial interest groups merely within a national framework and laid emphasis on their importance for national societies. While colonial interest groups had been a cornerstone of nationalism studies, only a few historians understood them as learned societies, which cultivated their image as expert groups and portrayed strategies of colonial management as a 'science'.[39] Their self-conception as scientific expert groups made explicit international co-operation and exchange thinkable.

By cultivating their own image of experts, they contributed to establishing the myth of colonial expertise, which helped them to justify aggressive expansion and conquest in the name of scientific progress. Colonial experts claimed to spread high-tech civilization by colonial interventions. These self-proclaimed experts soon turned Africa into a 'living laboratory', as Hellen Tilley described their production of colonial knowledge.[40] The 'triumph of the expert' finally led to the development doctrine, which boosted the career of many European scholars and gave colonial expansion a humanitarian touch.[41] The idea of the colonial expert has its origins in the colonial associations. Their transnational co-operation derived from the idea that colonial expertise could be universally applied and was part of an 'uninterested' and 'utilitarian' habitus that obscured underlying interests.[42]

Their turn to colonial internationalism does not necessarily prove the nationalists' views wrong, but complete them by painting a fuller picture that brings both narratives together. The analysis of colonial associations, with their dual character as colonial interest groups and learned societies, allows us to understand the dialectic modus operandi between national interests and transnational expertise. The Institut Colonial International – an institution created by European colonial associations in order to stimulate exchange between colonizing countries – stands for the dialectics of colonial associations that were situated between national interests and an international epistemic community of colonial experts.

So far, only a few collective works have assembled case studies from different European countries and have tried to expose similarities in the colonial theory and practice of these countries. Nevertheless, they fail to provide a synthesis in comparative and transnational perspectives.⁴³ A current trend in imperial historiography, instead, highlights transnational interactions and global contexts. Ulrike Linder's book on colonial encounters between Britain and Germany, Sebastian Conrad's analysis of the German Empire in a global perspective and Andrew Zimmerman's entangled history of cotton production in Togo are excellent examples of this historiographical trend.⁴⁴

All of these authors make reference to colonial interest groups as one of the prime movers behind inter-imperial exchange, caught between national interest and international co-operation. Given this critical part of private colonial initiatives for the colonial project, I will show in the following section how the colonial interest groups emerged within an explicitly European context. They situated themselves between nationalist purposes and different forms of international co-operation.

Private colonialism and international co-operation

The idea of transnational co-operation in colonial matters originated in the debates at international geographical congresses held in Europe from the 1870s. Participants of these congresses deliberated on the interconnectedness of geographical exploration, economic expansion, mass emigration and colonization.⁴⁵ These phenomena were manifestations of a gradual process of globalization that seemed to require international interventions. At the 1875 *Congrès international des sciences géographiques* in Paris, the Argentine Carlos Calvo – a recruitment agent for European emigrants and founding member of the famous Institut de Droit International (Institute for International Law) – presented an exhaustive report on the past and present of colonial expansion. According to the migration expert Calvo, colonial expansion originated in global flows of emigration and resettlement. This human mobility was anything but organized and required international coordination.

The congresses' participants were deeply impressed by Calvo's presentation and called for international co-operation in colonial matters.⁴⁶ International co-operation should help to control mass emigration, settlement and colonization, it was thought. Following the 1875 geographical congress, colonially-minded Europeans tried to make use of international networks provided by geographical societies and advocated transnational co-operation. Geographical societies all over Europe were infiltrated by colonial activists and partly converted into colonial lobby groups.⁴⁷

Inspired by the debates at the Paris geographical congress in 1875, the Belgian King Leopold II seized the opportunity to organize his own geographical conference in 1876. For several decades, Leopold had been searching for colonial territory worldwide, sending his agents to Africa, America and Asia. Unlike Calvo and the members of the 1875 international geographical congress, Leopold desisted from promoting mass emigration and colonial settlement. Instead, he drew on traditional examples of personal enrichment by colonial exploitation. He identified the profitable Spanish colonial empire and the Dutch exploitative cultivation system in Java as a model for personal enrichment.

Leopold had studied foreign colonial literature and even visited the Spanish colonial archives in Seville, where he informed himself about the empire's economic return. Besides seeking inspiration from the Spanish archives, he studied the infamous 'cultivation system' in Dutch Java, a system of forced agricultural labour that had made Java one of the most profitable colonies of the nineteenth century. Both the Spanish possessions in the West Indies and the Dutch colonies in the East Indies were notorious for ruthless economic exploitation of local resources and populations.[48]

But Leopold had understood that he had to disguise his private economic interests in order to win the support of the European powers for his colonial ambitions. In 1876, just one year after the geographical congress had been held in Paris, he invited members of geographical societies, abolitionist associations and philanthropic groups to Brussels. Obscuring his real intentions, he characterized his colonial project as a humanitarian intervention against the slave trade. In his inaugural speech, Leopold spoke on the authority of humanity and civilization and proclaimed to 'open the last unpenetrated part of the globe to civilization'. He had identified the Congo Basin to be that territory, which, by 'a crusade that glorifies the age of progress' should be civilized and opened to economic penetration by the European powers. He called for international co-operation under the leadership of Belgium, a small nation with no interests, which guaranteed the neutrality of the territory: 'I would be happy if Brussels became a sort of headquarters of the civilising movement.'[49]

The creation of the Association Internationale Africaine was the outcome of the 1876 International Geographical Conference, which was organized by Leopold to win support for his attempt to colonize the Congo Basin. Its alleged aim was to open up the Congo region for European trade. Leopold, who organized the Brussels conference as a civilian and not as the king of Belgium, portrayed this project of colonization as a necessary intervention to abolish the slave trade, explore the territory scientifically and develop the country in a rational way to the benefit of humanity. He succeeded in depicting his personal project of colonial exploitation as a European duty and a contribution to the progress of humanity.[50]

As soon as the international participants of the conference returned to their home countries, they set up colonial associations – modelled upon similar societies in other countries – and founded national branches of the Association Internationale Africaine. The German delegates were particularly active in that regard: the renowned explorers Gustav Nachtigal, Gerhard Rohlfs and Georg Schweinfurth, along with the rising star of German geography, Ferdinand von Richthofen, set up a national committee. Baptized the Deutsche Afrikanische Gesellschaft (German African Society), the society was to inspire several colonial start-ups and was finally merged into the German colonial umbrella organization, the Deutsche Kolonialgesellschaft (German Colonial Society).[51] The French committee was in no way inferior to the Germans, and Austrian or Dutch branches were eager to follow. Even in Spain, which was about to be stripped of its morbid empire, geographers were carried away by the international colonial enthusiasm and arranged a revival of colonial optimism. In the wake of the Brussels conference, military geographer and colonial activist Francisco Coello established a Spanish branch of the International African Association called the Asociación Española para la Exploración del África.[52] He also created the Real Sociedad Geográfica de Madrid (Spanish Geographical Society), which dedicated itself immediately to the promotion of colonial projects. Similar associations mushroomed all over Europe and directed their attentions to Africa, which became the main target of potential colonial expansion.

For the ambitious Belgian king, Europe was not enough. He was particularly concerned with winning the favour of the Anglo-Saxon world, knowing that without the consent of Great Britain and the United States of America his energetic Association Internationale Africaine would be reduced to inaction.[53] With the help of the adventurer and boasting journalist Henry Morton Stanley, he succeeded in winning them over. Stanley explored the Congo Basin, acquired land by doubtful contracts and violent coercion and, by doing so, made himself a hero of civilization in US-American, English and European newspapers.[54] Leopold re-baptized his enterprise Association Internationale du Congo and sent several multinational expeditions to the region. He made his way into the Congo and the world seemed to go into raptures over his speeches about civilizing duties, human progress and philanthropic abolitionism.

The Brussels conference was the opening ceremony for a new age of colonial movements in Europe and the world. Likewise, it provided new strategies of legitimizing colonial domination. But first and foremost, it claimed that colonizing and civilizing central Africa was an international duty.

Less than a decade later, Leopold saw himself accorded the right to turn the African possessions of his international association into a proper state, the État Indépendant du Congo (Congo Free State). By force of habit he crowned himself head of state. An international conference held in Berlin in 1884/5 had given him the right to do so. Fourteen nations had accepted Bismarck's invitation to the German capital to solve urgent problems concerning the colonization of Africa. In exchange for the promise of absolute neutrality and the warrant for the freedom of commerce, Leopold had obtained permission to turn his possessions into a state. That is why the Belgian king was quick at getting over the fact that Bismarck had taken the initiative to organize such an international diplomatic conference, even though Leopold had always planned to do that himself.

While the conference converted the private Association Internationale du Congo into an independent state, it was far from being professional. Diplomats were not experienced in matters concerning Central Africa. Colonial experts for this region were rare. As a consequence, the diplomats, ignorant of the African continent, were backed by 'technical' experts who had been leading figures of the private colonial movement. Most of them were familiar faces. Among them was Leopold's one-man think-tank, Emile Banning, who had organized the Brussels conference in 1876. Spain had sent the geographer Francisco Coello, the founding father of the Spanish colonial movement, and Germany the owner of the Hamburg-Africa shipping line, Adolf Woermann, who was a member of the Deutsche Kolonialgesellschaft. Also, Henry Morton Stanley featured prominently in the negotiations. And the Berlin conference was only one episode in a series of international congresses to settle disagreements that derived from colonial expansion and rivalry.[55]

In the meantime, the newly founded État Indépendant du Congo turned into a training ground for European colonialists. Leopold's Association Internationale Africaine had not only employed the British-born Stanley to explore the Congo and acquire territory, but employed also other Europeans, like the German officers Hermann von Wissmann and Curt von François, who led the by-then biggest European expedition to Central Africa and 'explored' the Kasai region. After leaving the service of the Association Internationale Africaine, Wissmann became governor of German East Africa, while von Curtois held positions in German Togo and Cameroon, before pulling together the *Schutztruppe* in German West Africa.[56]

Leopold recruited his administrators from among all Europeans and also built the famous Congo railway from Matadí to Léopoldville with the help of an international group of engineers and workers, comprising Italian, Danish, German, Swiss, Dutch, Greek and Luxembourger citizens. Moreover, the railway-builders recruited an African labour force from all over the black continent. Recruitment agents enrolled workers in Zanzibar, British Nigeria, French Senegal, German Togo or Portuguese Angola, mostly under suspicious circumstances. This seemed to have happened with the consent of the foreign authorities. The multitude of languages spoken during the construction of the Congo railway from Matadí to Leopoldville in the Belgian Congo brought to mind the 'legendary construction site of the Babel tower', as a keen observer put it.[57]

While most of Europe had turned its attention to the practical exploitation of the Congo, representatives of the Dutch Colonial Association made a rather intellectual attempt to bring together European colonial theorists. Since 1885, Dutch colonial activists under the guidance of Leiden law professor P.A. van der Lith had issued the *Revue Coloniale Internationale*. By inviting colonial experts from Europe and the Americas, they hoped to accumulate knowledge about economic resources, ethnographical research and administrative strategies in the colonies. Being rather an accumulative than a synthezising expert journal, the different articles stood side by side in a seemingly disorganized way. This might have been one of the reasons why the *Revue Coloniale Internationale* disappeared after some years. What remained was a pioneer project to familiarize European colonial activists with each other's work.[58]

It took colonial activists another decade to provide their scattered attempts at internationalist co-operation with a permanent institution. Once again, delegates of colonial associations from France, Belgium and the Netherlands took the initiative and set up the Institut Colonial International in 1894. Brussels became the seat of its general secretary, which worked the whole year through. The secretary organized biennial meetings for the members, who were delegates sent by private colonial organizations and not by official authorities. P.A. van der Lith was one of the founding fathers, together with the head of the Union Coloniale Française, Joseph Chailley. Representatives of the Deutsche Kolonialgesellschaft numbered high in the membership lists, while the only British delegate who participated regularly in the initial sessions was the Scottish Lord Reay, president of the Royal Asiatic Society in London.

In the first year of its existence, the Institute established a quota system and invited delegates of colonizing countries in direct proportion to their assumed colonial importance. There were delegates from France (seven members), the Netherlands (six), Belgium (three), Britain (eleven), Germany (five), Austria-Hungary (one), Denmark (two), Italy (three), Portugal (three), Spain (three) and Russia (five). Colonial experts from the USA and South America were also appointed to the Institute. The idea behind this selection was to nominate delegates from European or neo-European nations, which had given proof of their national sovereignty, and had therefore become part of an imagined international community.[59]

The Institut Colonial International aimed at institutionalizing and substantiating the exchange of colonial experiences and styled itself as a scientific organization. Its founding fathers made the comparison of the different nations' colonial administration and laws their favourite topic. Both international lawyers and jurists – specializing in comparative colonial legislation – joined the Institute. In close co-operation with the Institut de Droit International, they tried to design international regulations for trans-colonial labour recruitment and general laws facilitating labour migration.[60] They found support among colonial entrepreneurs like Albert Thys, the Belgian builder of the Congo railway, who figured prominently in the Institute's meetings. Thys's railway building company even financed the Institute's comprehensive publications on comparative railway construction in the colonies.[61]

Another field which induced the colonial internationalists to set up global rules was the trade in opium and alcohol. The Institute's members were keen on finding solutions to illegal trafficking or harmonizing the various regulations in force in different colonies. The institute published several volumes, comparing the existing regimes.[62] Moreover, the strong presence of colonial lawyers mirrored the Institute's interest in the legitimization of colonial dispossessions that had occurred during the period of conquest in the 1880s. It recommended the establishment of land registers in order to codify the possessions that white invaders had acquired by making legally doubtful treaties with the indigenous populations.[63]

Apart from those legal debates, the Institute discussed the technical details of how to organize economic development and exploitation, such as the construction of railways, irrigation systems or sanitation systems.[64] These discussions were supposedly free of any hidden political agendas and seemed to be purely technical. These expert debates represented the Institute's vow to science and neutrality, outlawing all kinds of imperial rivalry.

To back this image, and in order to avoid friction among the participating members, the Institute's regulations banned 'political' discussions from the its regular meetings that might lead to 'irritating debates among nations'.[65] For the Institute's members, colonial science should be free of interest and transnational, while nationalism belonged to the realm of politics. Before the Institute's members discussed colonial legislation, international arrangments, or technical co-operation, they designated specialists, who prepared reports on the different topics under discussion. Once submitted to the Institute, the expert reports were at the centre of the debates during the biennial meetings.

Both the reports and the conference proceedings were published in the *International Colonial Library*. The library's comprehensive volumes constituted a veritable archive of colonial knowledge, and the publications were widely read in colonial ministries as well as among colonial administrators on the spot. In addition, colonial ministries provided the Institute with insider information, which helped in conducting their comparative surveys about colonization.

By the turn of the century, the Institute had developed into an institution of colonial expertise. Meetings were held almost annually now and leading authorities in the colonial field, like Bernhard Dernburg or Hubert Lyautey, participated frequently. Due to the membership of those famous colonial administrators and due to their busy comparison of official colonial documents, the Institute gained its reputation as a truly international institution of colonialism.

The International Colonial Institute has a legacy that penetrates well into the twentieth century.[66] Pouvourville, who – as I mentioned in my introduction – called for a colonial 'European ideal' in 1907, was one of its most active members. And here we see that Leopold's dream of Brussels as an international hub of colonialism had come true – yet he had already stopped dreaming about it. Shortly after he created the Congo Free State, Leopold abandoned his internationalist strategy, which gave way to a policy of personal enrichment. His exploitation of the Congo caused the deaths of thousands of Congolese. When the Belgian cruelties committed by Leopold's representatives in the Congo Free State were uncovered the monarch had to resign as head of the colony. The Belgian state inherited the territory and thereby took on a heavy load of moral debt. Had Leopold's reputation not already faded a long time ago, he ended up certainly becoming a persona non grata for internationalist colonialism after 1908.[67]

While Leopoldian internationalism ended, Pouvourville continued to celebrate a continental German-French Europe in the German *Kolonialzeitung*. Like Pouvourville, French colonial activists had turned to Germany, seeking for an ally against the British colonial predominance. At the centre of the Franco-German rapprochement was the deputy of the Algerian Département of Oran, Eugène Etienne. He headed the so-called 'colonial party' in the French chamber from 1892 to 1913 and founded several colonial associations and periodicals in France. As the *spiritus rector* of French colonial propaganda and a member of the Institut Colonial International, he was fascinated by the German Colonial Society whose members numbered around 30,000 in 1900. Nevertheless, his attempt to establish an equally numerous umbrella organization in France failed.

Etienne was more successful in finding a peaceful solution for the German-French conflict over Morocco. This conflict had dominated colonial debates since the turn of the century. After the British side had received carte blanche in Egypt as a compensation in the entente cordiale in 1904, France, Germany and Spain continued to show interest in the Sultanate.[68] The German government staked out its claim in an aggressive way, while the French government tried to outdo German influence in Morocco. In this heated atmosphere, Etienne travelled to Germany and urged the Emperor Wilhelm to propose an agreement to settle the conflict over Morocco. While he gained Wilhelm's goodwill, the predominantly Anglophile French government rebuked him for his impertinence.[69] Ignoring the official position of their government, French political activists continued to co-operate with like-minded Germans. French colonial activists, like Lucien Hubert, delivered speeches in front of the Deutsche Kolonialgesellschaft in Berlin and members of the Hamburg-based Kolonialinstitut visited the French Union Coloniale. Although Lucien Hubert's proposal to hold a European Colonial Congress did not materialize due to the outbreak of World War I, the pre-war era abounded with declarations of mutual friendship.[70] As a consequence, Pouvourville's 1907 call for colonial co-operation fell on a fertile ground in continental Europe and beyond.

II. The nationalist paradigm and the use of European and internationalist concepts

However, transnational exchanges and international co-operation were confined to clear limits. All of the colonial activists were aware of the fact that the 'European ideal' was confronted with a nationalist reality.

When Leopold II convoked the Brussels' Geographical Conference in 1876, all of the participants knew that he did so for his own glory. He organized the conference on his own account and set up the private Association Internationale Africaine to win moral and financial support among Europeans. Leopold was well aware of the fact that Belgians and the Belgian government were not able nor willing to support his cause. But more importantly, he and his entourage knew that they needed the support of the great powers to secure freedom of action for the Congo project. Thus, they portrayed Belgium as being weak enough to not threaten the world's superpowers, but as being strong enough to open the Congo Basin for European and American free trade. It was his collaborator, Emile Banning, who framed this policy in Europe and in Africa in terms of Belgian neutrality.[71] This was a more subtle nationalist strategy born out of the world's power relations. Leopold could appeal to Europe or to an 'international community' and used this community in order to win support for his Congo enterprise, but also to strengthen Belgium's national position within the world community.[72] When the participants of the Brussels conference left Belgium, they were well aware of this.[73] Shortly after the conference, a process of re-nationalization alienated the branches in other countries from the International African Association. And once the Congo Free State was established in 1885 – with Leopold at the head of the state – the promise of establishing free trade soon fell into oblivion.

Spanish attitudes towards internationalism were equally ambiguous. While the French Pouvourville wrote for the German *Kolonialzeitung*, Spanish-German attempts at co-operation had failed, due to nationalist confrontations. Already in 1885, a member of the Spanish Geographical Society, Saturnino Jiménez, had used the *Kolonialzeitung* to press for a German-Spanish agreement on Morocco in order to provide the basis for a broader European co-operation without confrontation. Unfortunately, his article appeared while Germany made a first and aggressive attempt to acquire the Spanish Caroline Islands in the Pacific Ocean. His initiative was thus deemed unpatriotic and he was forced to leave Madrid's Geographical Society.[74] Internationalist rhetoric was omnipresent, but too close a fraternization with other colonizing countries was still considered as being treason to the national cause.

Despite their participation in internationalist projects, the attitude of Spanish colonialists towards Europe had been ambiguous. This derived from the fact that nineteenth-century Europe had come to interpret the Iberian power as a decadent and failed empire. Being frequently cited as the main example of imperial immorality, the Spanish Empire came off worst in accounts of European expansion. Comparative studies on empires, as published by the Institut Colonial International, led to the establishment of a veritable hierarchy of nations according to their colonial abilities. Colonial theorists never failed to mention that Spain was at the very bottom of this hierarchy.

Moreover, Spain's long-lasting orientation towards the extra-European 'New World' was said to alienate the country from Europe. This idea was taken further and merged with the black legend into a myth of Spanish otherness. While 'modern Europe' sailed to overseas territories under the flag of civilization and progress, the Spanish expansion was portrayed as being the exact opposite of a specifically European modernity.[75]

The so-called 'black legend', a term coined at the end of the nineteenth century in the context of colonial comparisons and competition,[76] popularized the idea that Spain's management of its vast empire had been an economic and moral failure. Its proponents identified exploitation and slavery as the main markers of Spanish colonial policy, which inescapably led to the moral and physical breakdown of its empire. The decolonization of Latin American territories seemed to prove Spain guilty of all these allegations. Spanish intellectuals partly shared the view of Spanish decadence and backwardness included in the black legend. Already before the loss of Cuba, Puerto Rico and the Philippines in the 1898 war with the USA, intellectuals called for a 'regeneration' of the country.[77]

One of the regenerationists was Joaquín Costa, a self-taught scholar and reform thinker. Costa joined Francisco Coello's Sociedad Geográfica in 1883 and helped to transform it into a veritable colonial lobby group. That same year, he organized the first *Congreso Español de Geografía Comercial y Mercantil* and created the Sociedad Española de Africanistas y Colonistas. Several associations were to follow and Costa became the most eminent promoter of Spanish colonialism. Stating that Spain could only recover when it colonized parts of Africa,[78] Costa wanted Spain to prove its ability to colonize in a modern way and, as a consequence, find its way back to Europe. Colonizing in a 'European' and modern way could thus strip Spain off its discredited 'anachronistic' empire and rehabilitate it as a progressive nation. He laid out his ideas in a book called *Reconstitution and Europeanisation of Spain. Program for a national party*, published in 1900.[79]

After 1898, when Spain lost the last remains of its former empire, Spanish representatives had disappeared from the membership lists of the Institut Colonial International.[80] But in portraying themselves as a progressive European nation that had put its inglorious colonial past behind it, the Spanish could return to the international stage. Acting as a colonial power on the authority of 'Europe' allowed Spain finally to participate in the partition of Morocco in 1912. Shortly after, Spanish delegates made their comeback at the Institut Colonial International. Like in the Belgian case, the small Spanish nation tried to assert itself by portraying itself as a modern nation that was part of the European concert while improving its national scope of action.

Using 'Europe' to improve personal or national scopes of action was also the strategy France employed. It was quite obvious that French expansionists tried to assume colonial leadership over continental Europe. Although several attempts were made to co-operate with British colonialists, French colonialists preferred to co-operate with the less powerful Germans, Belgians or Dutch. Colonial activists in these countries rarely challenged French supremacy overseas. The journal *L'Europe Coloniale – organe hebdomadaire des interests coloniaux de l'Europe Continentale*, which was edited in

Paris and explicitly directed to colonialists in 'continental' Europe represented the French leadership in colonial matters.

French was the language of internationalism in general and of the colonial internationalists in particular. The Institute Colonial International's official language was French. Even if the regulations stipulated that the conference proceedings and publications should be published both in French and English, the latter was not in use before World War I.[81] The Institute's meetings were also held in French, which prevented some Anglophone members from participating actively in the debates. Thus, a British member, Alfred Lyall, complained in the 1890s: 'We meet in a large official room, where speeches are made and papers discussed on colonial questions; the official language being French, I have not yet made any oratorical display.'[82]

In Germany, the situation was more complex. While the steering committee of the Deutsche Kolonialgesellschaft tended to be internationally minded, the various local branches assumed explicitly nationalist positions.[83] Moreover, colonialists drew a strict line of demarcation between the more cosmopolitan Deutsche Kolonialgesellschaft and a pan-German breakaway faction that called itself Alldeutscher Verband (Pangerman League), whose membership outnumbered the Kolonialgesellschaft by far. The pan-German ideological blend of nationalism, anti-Semitism and militaristic imperialism guaranteed a permanent influx of new members, while the colonialists had the reputation of being more moderate, technical and therefore less attractive.[84] Time and again, the Deutsche Kolonialgesellschaft embraced pan-German ideologies, knowing that these fell on fertile ground among the German petite bourgeoisie. But generally speaking, its internationalist attitude also derived from a need to distinguish itself from the Alldeutscher Verband.

As a consequence, competitive emulation remained a main reason for the interest in co-operation. In France for instance, colonial societies employed experts on German, English or Italian colonialism. One of them, Camille Fidel, delivered detailed reports about the colonial activity in Germany and Italy.[85] The Belgian journalist Victor Gautier spied into the secret of German colonial policy and recorded variation of German public opinion towards the Congo. Based in Berlin, he regularly sent the latest news to Leopold.[86] Most of the expansionist and colonial publications were read and reviewed all over Europe. The colonial press organs, like the *Deutsche Kolonialzeitung*, the *Dépêche Coloniale* or the *Bulletin de la société d'études colonials belges* collected foreign expansionist literature and reviewed it or screened it for useful expert knowledge.

While national colonial interest groups showed a natural interest in 'improving' their own colonial policy, the Institute Colonial International also struggled with its own role and responsibility to represent internationalist colonialism in a context of growing European nationalism. Its members refused to formulate 'doctrines', or to make recommendations to men on the spot, let alone official authorities. Styled after a scientific institution, its members emphasized its independence and neutrality. When it came to the implementation of common international rules or concrete co-operation among colonizing powers, the Institute kept a low profile. Internationalism was certainly a cherished ideal, as Pouvourville claimed, but the Institut Colonial International did not issue compulsory guidelines for colonial policies.

As has been shown above, internationalist ideas were confronted with nationalist realities. But, following Pouvourville in his argument, internationalism was not necessarily opposed to nationalist attitudes. According to his interpretation, internationalism – or a notion of Europeanness – ran parallel to nationalist confrontation and 'complemented it in the most human way', but also in the 'most useful' way as he put it in the initially cited article of the *Deutsche Kolonialzeitung*. Colonial activists could use spatial categories like 'international community' or 'Europe' as arguments or as strategies to win support for their national cause.

III. Making use of the international space

The interest in European or transnational co-operation derived from private colonial associations and notably from their dual character: as learned societies, they showed great interest in the international exchange of technical knowledge; as national colonial pressure groups, they observed imperial rivals enviously to avoid missing a novel move to expand their own nation's colonial domination. Both characteristics stem from a desire to imitate and apply successful strategies of ruling the colonized. Colonial experts tried to learn from each other and imitate successful strategies of colonization. As the ability to colonize was a proof of modernity, it was necessary to be at the cutting edge. Thus, competitive emulation was the driving force behind an intense exchange between European colonial administrators and theorists.

Nevertheless, this transnational exchange created a unified colonial discourse in Europe and beyond. The transfer of knowledge occasioned the technical enhancement of colonial exploitation and provided a pool of universally applicable arguments in favour of colonization. Colonizing powers all over Europe thought of 'civilizing mission', 'pacification' or 'development' as useful concepts to justify violent expansion and exploitation of overseas territories. These legitimizing ideologies emanated especially from Belgium and France, whose theorists produced 'internationalist' and 'Europeanist' ideologies. Both countries propagated an overarching universalism, be it the French civilizing mission or the Belgian humanitarianism, which made the combat of slavery the main argument for intervention in Central Africa. Both French and Belgian colonial activists were particularly active in developing strategies to legitimize their colonial oeuvre, including the Belgian anti-slavery rhetoric or the French concept of '*mise en valeur*' (economic development to the benefit of humanity).[87] In Germany, Spain and the Netherlands, colonial activists copied these concepts and used them to enrich their own colonial language and to substantiate their pro-colonial arguments. By making reference to these universal concepts, colonial activists legitimized colonial expansion. And by pretending to act on the authority of 'a superior Europe' or an 'international community of civilized nations', they enhanced their prestige.

Institutions like the Institut Colonial International were at the heart of the exchange of expert knowledge. In fields as different as irrigation, engineering, colonial legislation or the construction of railway lines in undeveloped territories, the transfer of technical knowledge should help to improve colonial exploitation to the benefit of the white colonizers and the colonized alike. Realizing infrastructure programmes and the '*mise en valeur*' of colonial resources helped to give moral legitimacy to colonial projects. The self-proclaimed colonial experts were still situated between individual materialism, nationalist ideology and racist 'othering', and were therefore far from being the 'neutral scientists' they pretended to be. Learning from others how to colonize more efficiently was the most important reason for the exchange of knowledge and the improvement of individual or national positions in a 'competitive community'.

For most of the colonial activists the 'European' or 'international' society stood for a competitive community of colonizing powers. The colonies thus divided nations because of imperial rivalry *and* united them on the common grounds of colonial projects. Contemporaries did not consider this dialectic concept contradictory. Moreover, despite all imperial rivalry, the competition between colonizing powers was rarely considered to be a *casus belli* for the members of colonial associations. Colonial activists like Pouvourville understood the dialectic relation between nationalism and internationalism. His proclamation of transnational co-operation stated that the European ideal complemented nationalist attitudes, instead of replacing them. In the view of most Europeans, competition among nations, regions and economies was the engine of the progress and superiority of colonizing societies. Thus, competition and rivalry were necessary to progress and helped to maintain the superiority of such societies. The most important marker of their superiority was political sovereignty, which distinguished them from the dependent and 'immature' territories. Political sovereignty and independence established a feeling of solidarity among European and neo-European states alike. Because these states were considered sovereign nation states, they were invited to send delegates to the International Colonial Institute. According to the regulations, only members of sovereign nations were admitted to the Institute.[88]

But competition – if it remained peaceful and guaranteed economic and technological progress – required rules. Internationalist projects in the colonial field, like the diplomatic congresses in Brussels or Paris, aimed at establishing international rules to avoid imperial conflicts.[89] Private institutions, like the Institut Colonial International, were equally inclined to formulate international regulations on more practical issues like intercolonial labour recruitment or the fight against alcohol contraband, and formed the basis for international colonial thought. Prominent international lawyers like Édouard Descamps had joined the Institute and contributed significantly to set its agenda. Although drafting international regulations and advocating for their enforcement, the Institute refrained from issuing official statements or recommendations and carefully watched over its reputation as a 'scientific' and 'neutral' institution. In doing so, it pioneered the portrayal of colonialism as a rational way of 'improving' the world to the benefit of humanity. This idea became the most important argument for maintaining colonial empires beyond World Wars I and II, and colonial co-operation continued to play an important role in the legitimization of colonial empires.

IV. Conclusion

In this chapter I have shown that private colonial interest groups emerged all over Europe from the 1870s. They were organized in a similar way and tried to win the support of their compatriots for colonial ventures. However, they originated not only within a national framework, but were embedded in an international context inspired by international conferences in general and by Leopold's 1876 conference in particular. After contributing significantly to the scramble for Africa in the 1880s, they evolved into expert institutions and accumulated colonial knowledge by transnational exchange. International co-operation was then institutionalized in the International Colonial Institue (1894). Colonial experts from all the 'colonizing' European and American countries participated in the Institute's biennial meetings and exchanged colonial knowledge via publications and deliberations. But this international co-operation did not dilute nationalist attitudes. Most of the colonialists were also nationalists. They used the international exchange of knowledge to strengthen their national position or to make their own country's colonial rule more efficient. Moreover, the use of spatial categories transcending the national sphere, such as the 'European civilization' helped to legitimize national expansion in specific situations. Colonising on the authority of the international community, civilization or even humanity helped to substantiate national colonial claims. As a consequence, the imagined international community of colonizing states was often referred to in colonial discourses. Colonial theorists used notions of international law to guarantee colonial possessions or to distribute colonial territory, as in the Berlin West Africa Conference in 1884/5 or in the partition of Morocco between 1904 and 1912. Pouvourville, the French colonial expert who wrote for the *Deutsche Kolonialzeitung*, got to the heart of this attitude: 'This ideal is certainly not more beautiful than the nationalist thought, but it complements it in the most useful and human way: it is the European ideal.'

Notes

1 Albert Comte de Pouvourville, Deutschlands Beteiligung am Französischen Kolonialkongreß 1907, *Deutsche Kolonialzeitung*, 33, 17 February 1907, p. 329.
2 Albert Comte de Pouvourville was general secretary of the French *Congrès Coloniaux* and wrote for the most prominent colonial journal in France, the *Dépêche Coloniale*; see: Deutsch-Französische Beziehungen, *Deutsche Kolonialzeitung*, 29, 22 June 1905, pp. 301ff.
3 Pouvourville, a disciple of Taoist philosophy, wrote under his *nom de plume* 'Matgioi' in favour of a moderate consumption of opium, which he believed to stimulate brainpower and to be an adequate remedy for all kinds of maladies: Matgioi (Albert de Pouvourville), *L'Esprit des Races Jaunes. Les Sept Élements de l'Homme et de la Pathogénie Chinoise* (Paris: Chamuel, 1895), p. 50.
4 Willibald Gutsche, Zu Hintergründen und Zielen des 'Panthersprungs' nach Marokko von 1911, *Zeitschrift für Geschichtswissenschaft*, 28, 2 (1980), pp. 133–51.
5 Most vivid: Geoffrey Barraclough, *From Agadir to Armageddon: Anatomy of a Crisis* (London: Weidenfeld & Nicolson, 1982), with reference to colonial lobby groups: James Joll and Gordon Martel (eds), *The Origins of the First World War* (Harlow: Pearson Longman, 2007), p. 63. Generally: Margaret MacMillan, *The War that Ended Peace, the Road to 1914* (New York: Random House, 2013) pp. 378–9; Hugh Strachan, *The First World War*, Vol. 1: *To Arms* (Oxford: Oxford University Press, 2001); see also the articles by Jean-Jacques Becker and Gerd Krumeich, in J.J. Becker and S. Audoin-

Rouzeau (eds), *Encyclopédie de la Grande Guerre 1914-1918* (Paris: Bayrd, 2004), pp. 151-69. A different view of the origins of World War I: Christopher Clark, *Sleepwalkers: How Europe Went to War in 1914* (London: Penguin Books, 2013).

6 Deutsch-Französische Beziehungen, *Deutsche Kolonialzeitung*, 29, 22 June 1905, pp. 301-2. So far, the Institut Colonial International has been studied by: Janny de Jong, Kolonialisme op een koopje. Het Internationale Koloniale Instituut, 1894-1914, *Tijdschrift voor geschiedenis*, 109 (1996), pp. 45-72; Benoit Daviron, Mobilizing labour in African agriculture: the role of the International Colonial Institute in the elaboration of a standard of colonial administration, 1895-1930, *Journal of Global History*, 5 (2010), pp. 479-501. See also Ulrike Lindner's contribution to this volume.

7 P.A. van der Lith created the *Revue Coloniale Internationale* as a representative of the Dutch Colonial Association, which intended to exchange and enhance colonial knowledge. See: Introduction, *Revue Coloniale Internationale* 1 (1885), pp. I-XVI.

8 See for example: Édouard Descamps, *L'Afrique nouvelle : Essai sur l'état civilisateur dans les pays neufs et sur la fondation, l'organisation et le gouvernement de l'État indépendant du Congo* (Paris: Hachette & Cie., 1903).

9 The term 'colonialism' became part of European vocabulary after it was introduced by socialist Paul Louis, *Le Colonialisme* (Paris: Soc. nouv. de libr. & d'éd., 1905). Regarding internationalism see Martin Geyer and Johannes Paulmann (eds), *The Mechanics of Internationalism: Culture, Society and Politics from the 1840s to the First World War* (Oxford: Oxford UP, 2001); Glenda Sluga, *Internationalism in the Age of Nationalism* (Philadelphia: University of Pennsylvania Press, 2013); Daniel Laqua, *The Age of Internationalism and Belgium, 1880-1930: Peace, Progress and Prestige* (Manchester: Manchester UP, 2013); Madeleine Herren, *Internationale Organisationen seit 1865: Eine Globalgeschichte der internationalen Ordnung* (Darmstadt: Wissenschaftliche Buchgesellschaft, 2009).

10 Charles-Robert Ageron, *France Coloniale ou Parti Colonial?* (Paris: Presses Universitaires de France, 1978); Peter Grupp, *Deutschland, Frankreich und die Kolonien: Der französische Parti Colonial und Deutschland von 1890-1914* (Tübingen: Mohr, 1980); Christopher M. Andrew and Alexander S. Kanya-Forstner, The French Colonial Party: its composition, aims and influence 1885-1914, *The Historical Journal*, 14, 1 (1971), pp. 99-128; Vincent Viaene, King Leopold's imperialism and the origins of the Belgian Colonial Party, 1860-1905, *The Journal of Modern History*, 80, 4 (2008), pp.741-90.

11 See on this topic: Tony Chafer (ed.), *Promoting the Colonial Idea: Propaganda and Visions of Empire in France* (Basingstoke: Palgrave Macmillan, 2002); Matthew G. Stanard, *Selling the Congo: A History of European Pro-Empire Propaganda and the Making of Belgian Imperialism* (Lincoln: University of Nebraska Press, 2012); John Mackenzie, *Propaganda and Empire: The Manipulation of British Public Opinion, 1880-1960* (Manchester: Manchester University Press, 2003).

12 The most prominent scholarly debate involves Bernard Porter and John MacKenzie, who take opposite positions regarding the question of whether British society was 'imperial' or not: John M. MacKenzie, 'Comfort' and conviction: a response to Bernard Porter, *The Journal of Imperial and Commonwealth History*, 36, 4 (2008), pp. 659-68.

13 Institut Colonial International, *Compte Rendu de la Session tenue à la Haye, le 9, 10, 11 et 12 septembre 1895* (Paris: Colin, 1895), p. 3; see also Arne Perras, *Carl Peters and German Imperialism, 1856-1918: A Political Biography* (Oxford: Clarendon Press, 2004).

14 Alice Conklin, *A Mission to Civilize: The Republican Idea of Empire in France and West Africa, 1895-1930* (Stanford: Stanford University Press, 1997).

15 Birthe Kundrus, *Moderne Imperialisten: Das Kaiserreich im Spiegel seiner Kolonien* (Köln: Böhlau, 2003), p. 37.
16 The most active propagators of colonial, international and humanitarian arguments were the propagandists employed by Leopold II of Belgium to justify his colonial project in the Congo. Emile de Laveleye, for example, claimed that Leopold's International African Association was an 'international and humanitarian work in the most significant sense', cit. in: Jan Vandersmissen, The king's most eloquent campaigner ... Emile de Laveleye, Leopold II and the creation of the Congo Free State, *Belgisch Tijdschrift voor Nieuwste Geschiedenis* (2011), p. 22.
17 Eric Hobsbawm, *The Age of Capital, 1848–1875* (London: Weidenfeld & Nicolson, 2003), pp. 354–6.
18 The best first-hand descriptions of the International African Association's foundation: Émile Banning, *L'Afrique et la Conférénce de Géographie de Bruxelles* (Brussels: Muquardt, 1877) ; Émile Banning, *L'Association Internationale Africaine et le Comité des Hautes Études du Haut-Congo 1877–1882 travaux et résultats de décembre 1877 à octobre 1882* (Brussels, 1882). About the Belgian colonial movement in general: Lewis H. Gann and Peter Duignan, *The Rulers of Belgian Africa 1884–1914* (Princeton: Princeton University Press, 1979); Stanard, *Selling the Congo*; Viaene, King Leopold's Imperialism; Jean Stengers, *Congo: Mythes et Réalités* (Brussels: Éditions Racine, 2005).
19 See Origines de la Société, *Bulletin de la Société des études coloniales et maritimes* 5 (1876). There are extensive studies of the French colonial movement: Andrew and Kanya-Forstner, The French 'Colonial Party'; Christopher M. Andrew and Alexander S. Kanya-Forstner, French business and the French colonialists, *The Historical Journal* 19, 4 (1976), pp. 981–1000; Ageron, *France Coloniale*; Grupp, *Deutschland, Frankreich und die Kolonien*; Stuart M. Persell, *The French Colonial Lobby, 1889–1938* (Stanford: Hoover Institution Press, 1983); See also: Chafer, *Promoting the Colonial Idea*; Pascal Blanchard et al. (eds), *Culture Coloniale en France : De la Révolution Française à nos jours* (Paris: CNRS Éditions, 2008).
20 Elena Hernandez Sandoica, *Pensamiento burgués y problemas coloniales en la España de la Restauración (1875–1886)*, (Diss. Univ. Complutense de Madrid, 1982); J.A. Rodriguez Esteban, *Geografía y Colonialismo: La Sociedad Geográfica de Madrid 1876–1936*, (Madrid: UAM Ed., 1996); J. Nogué and J.L. Villanova, Spanish colonialism in Morocco and the Sociedad Geografica de Madrid 1876–1956, *Journal of Historical Geography* 28, 1 (2002), pp. 1-10; Víctor Morales Lezcano, *El Colonialismo hispano-francés en Marruecos (1896–1927)*, (Granada, 2002); see also Christopher Schmidt-Nowara and John M. Nieto-Phillips (eds), *Interpreting Spanish Colonialism: Empires, Nations, Legends* (Albuquerque: University of New Mexico Press, 2005).
21 Klaus J. Bade, *Friedrich Fabri und der Imperialismus in der Bismarckzeit* (Freiburg: Atlantis Verlag, 1975); Victor Pierard, *The German Colonial Society 1882–1914* (PhD Diss., State University of Iowa, 1964); Klaus Klauß, *Die Deutsche Kolonialgesellschaft und die deutsche Kolonialpolitik von den Anfängen bis 1895* (Diss., Berlin [East], 1966); Edgar Hartwig, Deutsche Kolonialgesellschaft (DKG) 1887–1936, in: D. Fricke (ed.), *Lexikon zur Parteiengeschichte 1789–1936*, vol. 1, (Leipzig: Bibliographisches Institut, 1983–6), pp. 724–48; Hartmut Pogge von Strandmann, *Imperialismus vom Grünen Tisch: Deutsche Kolonialpolitik zwischen wirtschaftlicher Ausbeutung und 'zivilisatorischen' Bemühungen* (Berlin: Links, 2009); see also Ulrich van der Heyden and Joachim Zeller (eds), *Kolonialismus hierzulande: Eine Spurensuche in Deutschland* (Erfurt: Sutton, 2007); Kundrus, *Moderne Imperialisten*; forum: The German Colonial

Imagination with Lora Wildenthal, Jürgen Zimmerer, Russell A. Berman, Jan Rüger, Bradley Naranch and Birthe Kundrus, *German History*, 26, 2 (2008), pp. 251–71; Horst Gründer, *Geschichte der deutschen Kolonien*, (Paderborn: Schöningh, 2012).

22 Ageron, *France Coloniale*; Grupp, *Deutschland, Frankreich und die Kolonien*; Viaene, 'King Leopold's imperialism'.

23 Hans-Ulrich Wehler, Transnationale Geschichte. Der neue Königsweg historischer Forschung?, in: Gunilla F. Budde et al. (eds), *Transnationale Geschichte: Themen, Tendenzen und Theorien* (Göttingen: Vandenhoeck & Ruprecht, 2006), pp. 161–74, here p. 162.

24 Andrew and Kanya-Forstner, French business and the French colonialists, p. 988.

25 Concerning the Spanish case: Elena Hernandez-Sandoica, La ciencia geográfica y el colonialismo español en torno a 1880, in: Santiago Garma Pons (ed.), *El científico español ante su historia: la ciencia en España entre 1750–1850* (Madrid: Diputación Provincial de Madrid, 1980), pp. 527–44, esp. p. 531.

26 Die deutsche Kolonialgesellschaft im Reichstag, *Deutsche Kolonialzeitung*, 12, 20 March 1902, p. 110; Die Hauptversammlung der Deutschen Kolonialgesellschaft in Königsberg und ihre Kritik in der Tagespresse, *Deutsche Kolonialzeitung*, 25, 23 June 1906, p. 242.

27 Peter Grupp, Parti Colonial Français und deutsche Kolonialbewegung, in: C. Metzger et al. (eds), *Machtstrukturen im Staat in Deutschland und Frankreich* (Stuttgart: Steiner, 2007), pp. 148–63, here p. 157.

28 Hernandez-Sandoica, *La ciencia geográfica y el colonialismo español*, p. 531.

29 See, for the political function of the German Colonial Society, Geoff Eley, *Reshaping the German Right: Radical Nationalism and. Political Change after Bismarck* (New Haven: Yale UP, 1980).

30 Alte Aufgaben, *Deutsche Kolonialzeitung*, 36, 5 September 1901, p. 350; La vraie situation, *Bulletin du Comité de l'Afrique Française*, June 1909, p. 217; Nogué and Villanova, Spanish colonialism in Morocco, p. 6.

31 See Hans Kai Möller, *Universität oder Kolonialinstitut: Ein Wort zur Kritik der Senatsvorlage über die Hamburger Universität* (Hamburg: Seippel, 1913) and Jens Ruppenthal, *Kolonialismus als Wissenschaft und Technik: Das Hamburgische Kolonialinstitut 1908 bis 1919* (Stuttgart: Steiner, 2007); Raphael Blanchard, *L'Institut de médicine coloniale. Histoire de sa fondation. Extrait des Archives de Parasitologie* (Paris: F.-R. de Rudeval, 1902).

32 The German Colonial Society initiated the establishment of the Hamburger Kolonialinstitut, but the goverment in Berlin did not provide it with money, see Ruppenthal, *Kolonialismus als Wissenschaft*. Also in France colonial lobby groups helped to establish the École Coloniale: Sophie Dulucq, *Écrire l'histoire de l'Afrique à l'époque coloniale* (Paris: Éditions Karthala, 2009), p. 46. In Spain many colonial activists were linked to the Institución Libre de Enseñanza: Martin Eloy Corrales (ed.), *Marruecos y el Colonialismo Español (1859–1912): De la guerra de África a la 'penetracion pacifica'* (Barcelona: Ed. Bellaterra, 2002), pp. 140–1; Leopold II wanted to create an 'École Mondiale' open to all individuals from civilized countries and closely tied to the Congo Free State: Madeleine Herren, *Hintertüren zur Macht: Internationalismus und modernisierungsorientierte Außenpolitik in Belgien, der Schweiz und den USA 1865–1914* (Munich: Oldenbourg, 2000), pp. 87–8.

33 Concerning colonial exhibitions see Arbeitsausschuss der Deutschen Kolonial-Ausstellung (ed.), *Deutschland und seine Kolonien im Jahre 1896: Amtlicher Bericht über die erste deutsche Kolonial-Ausstellung* (Berlin: Reimer, 1897); Catherie Hodeir

and Michel Pierre, *L'exposition coloniale 1931* (Bruxelles: Éditions Complexe, 1991); Alexander C.T. Geppert, *Fleeting Cities: Imperial Expositions in Fin-de-Siècle Europe*, (Basingstoke: Palgrave Macmillan, 2010); Nicolas Bancel, Pascal Blanchard, Gilles Boëtsch, Éric Deroo and Sandrine Lemaire, *Zoos humains* (Paris: Éditions La Découverte, 2002); Marieke Bloembergen, *Colonial Spectacles: The Netherlands and the Dutch East Indies at the World Exhibitions, 1880–1931* (Singapore: Singapore University Press, 2006).

34 See for example Deutscher Kolonialkongress, *Verhandlungen des Deutschen Kolonialkongresses*, (Berlin: Verlag Kolonialkriegerdank, 1902); René Worms et al., *Congrès colonial français de 1905, séance d'ouverture, compte rendu des conférences et des séances de section, analyse des travaux, rapport général* (Paris: Au secrétariat général des Congrès coloniaux français, 1905); *La politique financière du Congo belge: rapport au Comité permanent du Congrès colonial [compte rendu de la séance plénière du 11 déc. 1925]* (Brussels: Goemaere, 1925); Sociedad Geográfica de Madrid (ed.), *Congreso Español de Geografía Colonial y Mercantil Circular* (Madrid : Fortanet, 1883).

35 Leopold's propaganda office, the Comité pour la représentation des intérêts coloniaux en Afrique paid foreign journalists for placing articles in favour of Leopold's Congo Free State in European newspapers. For Spain and France see José Maria Sanz Garcia, Un geopolítico ante el Conflicto de las Carolinas (1885), *Anales de la Fundación Joaquín Costa*, 4 (1987), pp. 139–58, here pp. 145–6; *Bulletin du Comité de l'Afrique Française*, March 1904, p. 77.

36 See for example Blanchard et al., *Culture coloniale*.

37 Despite sporadic support from banks and enterprises, the colonial interest groups were at pains to raise funds to finance their colonizing projects: Gilbert Ziebura, Interne Faktoren des französischen Hochimperialismus 1871–1914. Versuch einer gesamtgesellschaftlichen Analyse, in: Wolfgang J. Mommsen (ed.), *Der moderne Imperialismus* (Stuttgart: Kohlhammer, 1971), pp. 85–139; Jacques Marseille, *Empire Colonial et Capitalisme Français: Histoire d'un Divorce* (Paris: Seuil, 1984); Boris Barth, *Die deutsche Hochfinanz und die Imperialismen : Banken und Außenpolitik vor 1914* (Stuttgart: Steiner, 1995).

38 Moreover, they created regional groups or female branches, like the Frauenbund der Deutschen Kolonialgesellschaft: Lora Wildenthal, *German Women for Empire 1884–1945* (Durham: Duke UP, 2001); see also J.L. Vellut (ed.), *Femmes coloniales au Congo belge. Essais et documents* (Louvain la Neuve: Centre d'histoire de l'Afrique, 1987); Marie-Paule Ha, The making of the 'Coloniale' under the Third Republic, in: Robert Aldrich and Kirsten McKenzie (eds), *The Routledge History of Western Empires* (London: Routledge, 2014), pp. 222–35.

39 Marxist, Social and Cultural historians mostly interpreted private colonial movements within a national framework. The literature cited in the preceding footnotes gives proof of the nationalist paradigm.

40 Hellen Tilley, *Africa as a Living Laboratory: Empire, Development and the Problem of Scientific Knowledge, 1870–1950* (Chicago: University of Chicago Press, 2011).

41 Joseph Hodge, *Triumph of the Expert: Agrarian Doctrines of Development and the Legacies of British Colonialism* (Athens, OH: Ohio University Press, 2007); see also Monica van Beusekom, *Negotiating Development: African Farmers and Colonial Experts at the Office du Niger, 1920–1960* (Portsmouth, N.H.: Heinemann, 2002).

42 Emmanuelle Sibeud, *Une science impériale pour l'Afrique? La construction des savoirs africanistes en France, 1878–1930* (Paris: Éditions de EHESS, 2002).

43 John MacKenzie (ed.), *European Empires and the People: Popular Responses to Imperialism in France, Britain, the Netherlands, Belgium, Germany and Italy* (Manchester: Manchester UP, 2011); Lorin Amaury and Christelle Traud (eds), *Nouvelle Histoire des Colonisations Européennes, XIXe–XXe siècles* (Paris: Presses Universitaires de France, 2013); older contributions are still valuable: Grupp, Deutschland, *Frankreich und die Kolonien*; Winfried Baumgart, *Imperialism: The Idea and Reality of British and French Colonial Cxpansion, 1880–1914* (Oxford: Oxford UP, 1982).

44 Ulrike Lindner, *Koloniale Begegnungen: Deutschland und Großbritannien als Imperialmächte in Afrika 1880–1914* (Frankfurt a.M.: Campus, 2011); Sebastian Conrad, *Globalisation and the Nation in Imperial Germany* (Cambridge: Cambridge UP, 2010); Andrew Zimmerman, *Alabama in Africa: Booker T. Washington, the German Empire, and the Globalization of the New South* (Princeton: Princeton UP, 2010).

45 See for example Carlos Calvo, *Etude sur l'Emigration et la Colonisation réponse à la première des question du Groupe V soumises au Congrès International des Sciences Géographiques de 1875* (Paris: not specified, 1875).

46 Programme, *Bulletin de la Société des etudes coloniales et maritimes*, 1 (1876–7), p. 6.

47 The literature on colonial activities of geographical lobby groups is vast: Rodriguez Esteban, *Geografía y Colonialismo*; Nogué and Villanova, *Spanish Colonialism in Morocco*; Iris Schröder, *Das Wissen von der ganzen Welt: Globale Geographien und räumliche Ordnungen Afrikas und Europas 1790–1870* (Paderborn: Schöningh, 2011); Hélène Blais, Florence Deprest and Pierre Singaravelou (eds), *Territoires impériaux: Une histoire spatiale du fait colonial* (Paris: Publications de la Sorbonne, 2011); Pierre Singaravelou, *L'Empire des géographes. Géographie, exploration et colonisation (19e–20e s.)* (Paris: Belin, 2008); Marc Poncelet, *L'invention des sciences coloniales belges* (Paris: Éditions Karthala, 2008).

48 Jan Vandersmissen, *Koningen van de wereld: Leopold II en de aardrijkskundige beweging* (Leuven: Acco 2009).

49 Ferdinand von Richthofen, Bericht über die unter dem Vorsitz Sr. Majestät des Königs der Belgier vom 12. bis 14. September in Brüssel abgehaltene internationale Conferenz zur Berathung der Mittel für die Erforschung und Erschliessung von Central-Afrika, *Verhandlungen der Gesellschaft für Erdkunde zu Berlin*, 7 and 8 (1876), pp. 168–82, here pp. 178–9.

50 Emile Banning, *L'Afrique et la Conférence*; Émile Banning, *L'Association Internationale Africaine*; see also Association Internationale Africaine, in: *Deutsches Koloniallexikon*, Vol. 1 (Leipzig: Quelle und Meyer, 1920), p. 90; Viaene, King Leopold's imperialism.

51 Richthofen, Bericht.

52 Francisco Coello, Discurso en la fundación de la Sociedad Geográfica de Madrid, *Boletín de la Sociedad Geográfica de Madrid*, 1 (1876), pp. 113–69 and Francisco Coello, Asciación Internacional para la Exploración y Civilisación del África Central, *Boletín de la Sociedad Geográfica de Madrid*, 1 (1876), pp. 501–22.

53 See Leopold's correspondence in Archives du Palais Royal à Bruxelles, Archives du Cabinet du Roi Leopold II. Documents relatifs au developpement exterieur de la Belgique.

54 Dorothy Stanley (ed.), *The Autobiography of Sir Henry Morton Stanley: The Making of a 19th-Century Explorer* (Santa Barbara: Narrative Press, 2001 [1909]).

55 Stig Förster, Wolfgang J. Mommsen and Ronald Robinson (eds), *Bismarck, Europe, and Africa: The Berlin Africa Conference 1884–1885 and the Onset of Partition* (Oxford:

Oxford UP, 1988); Antony Anghie, *Imperialism, Sovereignty and the Making of International Law* (Cambridge: Cambridge UP, 2007).
56 Conradin von Perbandt, Die Erforschung des Kassai-Gebietes, in: A. Becker, C. von Perbandt et al. (eds), *Hermann von Wissmann, Deutschlands größter Afrikaner: Sein Leben und Wirken unter Benutzung des Nachlasses* (Berlin: Schall, 1906), pp. 69–70.
57 See Chemin de fer du Congo. Personnel Ouvrier, *Le Congo Illustré: voyages et travaux des belges dans l'État indépendant du Congo*, 1 (1892), p. 52.
58 'Introduction', *Revue Coloniale Internationale*, 1 (1885), pp. I–XVI.
59 Institut Colonial International (ed.), Brussels, *Compte-rendu de la Session de 1894* (Brussels: Institut Colonial International, 1894).
60 Institut Colonial International, *Compte Rendu de la Session tenue à Bruxelles les 5,6,7 avril 1899* (Brussels: Institut Colonial International, 1899), pp. 53–4 ; Institut Colonial International (ed.), *La Main d'Oeuvre aux Colonies. Documents officiels sur le contrat de travail et le louage d'ouvrage aux colonies*, 3 vols (Brussels: Institut Colonial International, 1895–8), see also Benoit Daviron, Mobilizing labour in African agriculture: the role of the International Colonial Institute in the elaboration of a standard of colonial administration, 1895–1930, *Journal of Global History*, 5 (2010), pp. 479–501.
61 Institut Colonial International (ed.), *Les Chemins de fer aux colonies et dans les pays neufs*, 3 vols (Brussels: Institut Colonial International, 1900).
62 See for example Albert de Pouvourville, *L'Opium et l'Alcool en Indochine* (Paris: Établissements Généraux d'Imprimerie, 1909).
63 Institut Colonial International (ed.), *Le Régime Foncier aux Colonies: Documents officiels* (Brussels: Institut Colonial International, 1902).
64 Institut Colonial International (ed.), *Les différents systèmes d'irrigation: Documents officiels précédés de notices historiques* (Brussels: Institut Colonial International, 1909).
65 Article 12 of the Statutes, in: Institut Colonial International (ed.), Compte Rendu de la Session tenue à la Haye (Brussels: Institut Colonial International, 1909), p. 30.
66 It continued to work even after World War I under the name of 'Institute of Differing Civilizations'.
67 Felicien Cattier, a specialist in colonial law and member of the Institut Colonial International, was one of the first to criticize Leopold's policy in the Congo: Martti Koskenniemi, *The Gentle Civilizer of Nations: The Rise and Fall of International Law 1870–1960* (Cambridge: Cambridge UP, 2004), pp. 155–66.
68 The British and French governments divided their zones of influence in Africa. Great Britain received Egypt, while France was given carte blanche in Morocco; See MacMillan, *War*, pp. 142–71.
69 Peter Grupp, Eugène Etienne et la tentative de rapprochement franco-allemand en 1907, *Cahiers d'Études Africaines*, 15, 58 (1975), pp. 303–11.
70 Koloniale Vorlesung des französischen Deputierten L. Hubert, *Deutsche Kolonialzeitung*, 10, 9 March 1907, pp. 93–4.
71 Émile Banning, *Les origines et les phases de la neutralité belge* (Brussels: Dewitt, 1927).
72 See particularly the correspondence with Victor Gautier, a Belgian journalist who tried to win the favour of the German public and government for Leopold's cause: *Archives du Palais Royal à Bruxelles*, Archives du Cabinet du Roi Leopold II. Documents relatifs au développement exterieur de la Belgique, Correspondance 56, Victor Gautier.
73 For example: Richthofen, Bericht, Coello, Asciación Internacional.
74 Nogué and Villanova, *Spanish Colonialism in Morocco*, p. 15.

75 Luis Español Bouché, *Leyendas Negras: Vida y Obra de Julian Juderías* (Salamanca: Junta de Castilla y León, 2007); María DeGuzmán, *Spain's Long Shadow: The Black Legend, Off-Whiteness, and Anglo-American Empire* (Minneapolis: University of Minnesota Press, 2005).
76 Julián Juderías, *La leyenda negra: estudios acerca del concepto de España en el extranjero* (Salamanca: Junta de Castilla y León, 2003 [1914]) popularized the term, which had been in use since 1899.
77 E. De Jongh-Rossel, *El Krausismo y la Generación de 1898* (Valencia: Albatros, 1985).
78 Azucena Pedraz Marcos, El Pensamiento Africanista hasta 1883. Cánovas, Donoso y Costa, *Anales de la fundación Joaquín Costa*, 11 (1994), pp. 31–48.
79 Joaquín Costa, *Reconstitución y europeización de España. Programa para un partido nacional* (Madrid: Impreta de San Francisco de Sales, 1900); O.I. Mateos y de Cabo, *El pensamiento político de Joaquín Costa. Entre nacionalismo español y europeísmo* (Diss. Universidad Complutense de Madrid, 1996); Eloy Fernandez Clemente, *Estudios sobre Joaquín Costa* (Zaragoza: Universidad de Zaragoza, 1989); George J.G. Cheyne, *A Bibliographical Study of the Writings of Joaquín Costa (1846–1911)* (London: Tamesis Books, 1972).
80 It is not certain whether they were excluded from the Institute, or if they retired by their own choice. As there was one Spanish associate member remaining in the Institute after 1898, it is more likely that they backed out voluntarily.
81 Article 2 of the Regulations, in : Institut Colonial International (ed.), *Compte Rendu de la Session tenue à la Haye* (Brussels: Institut Colonial International, 1909), p. 26.
82 Sir Mortimer Durand, *The Life of the Right Hon. Sir Alfred Comyn Lyall* (Edinburgh and London: Blackwood, 1913), p. 364.
83 See for example Eley, *Reshaping the German Right*.
84 Peter Grupp, Die Deutsche Kolonialgesellschaft in der Agadirkrise 1911, *Francia* 7 (1979), pp. 285–307.
85 Camille Fidel, *L'opinion allemande et la question du Maroc* (Paris: Comité du Maroc, 1905); Camille Fidel, *Les intérêts italiens en Tunesie* (Paris: Publication du Comité de l'Afrique Française, 1911).
86 *Archives du Palais Royal à Bruxelles*. Archives du Cabinet du Roi Leopold II. Documents relatifs au développement exterieur de la Belgique, Correspondance 56, Victor Gautier.
87 For the '*mise en valeur*' see Albert Sarraut, *La mise en valeur des colonies françaises* (Paris: Payot, 1923); Bernhard Dernburg, *Zielpunkte des deutschen Kolonialwesens. Zwei Vorträge* (Berlin: E.S. Mittler & Son, 1907); see also Sebastian Conrad, *Globalisierung und Nation im Deutschen Kaiserreich* (München: Beck, 2006), p. 212.
88 Article 4 of the regulations, in: Institut Colonial International (ed.), *Compte Rendu de la Session tenue à la Haye* (Brussels: Institut Colonial International, 1909), p. 27.
89 Much has been written on the connection between colonialism and the rebirth of international law in the nineteenth and twentieth centuries: Koskenniemi, *Civilizer*; Anghie, *Imperialism*; Andrew Fitzmaurice, The justification of King Leopold II's Congo enterprise by Sir Travers Twiss, in: Shaunnag Dorsett and Ian Hunter (eds), *Law and Politics in British Colonial Thought: Transpositions of Empire* (New York: Palgrave Macmillan, 2010), pp. 109–28.

Part Three

Law Transfers

4

Riparian Rights in Lower Canada and Canada East: Inter-imperial Legal Influences[1]

David Schorr

I. Introduction: inter-imperial law in an inter-imperial court

One of the most dynamic areas of law in the nineteenth-century Anglo-American world was that of water rights, or, as it was typically denoted then, 'riparian rights'. This body of law dealt with the relative rights of owners of land adjacent to water – riparian land – to use the flowing waters, whether for power, irrigation, transportation, fishing or waste disposal. The historical development of the law in this field in the nineteenth century has been analysed from several points of view, including economic property theory and Marxian legal history.[2] Transnational aspects of the subject have not been neglected, as some have highlighted the transatlantic – that is, Anglo-American – framework in which this body of doctrine developed, and others have examined the use of Continental, civil law sources by some of the American jurists responsible for that development.[3] Yet the inter-imperial aspect of this story, in particular the meeting of the laws of the British and French Empires, has gone unremarked.

The court case of *Miner* v. *Gilmour* can be seen as the epicentre of this inter-imperial encounter. The case began as a conflict in the 1850s between two prominent citizens of the Eastern Townships village of Granby, in the part of Canada then known as Canada East (in the half-century preceding 1841 called Lower Canada, the southern part of today's Quebec). Harlow Miner's tannery on the south bank of the Yamaska River, the town's major industrial enterprise, was powered by water directed from a dam in the river, but Francis Gilmour, the town's store-keeper, had been opening a sluice on the north side of the dam in order to allow the water to flow through and power his gristmill downstream (Figure 4.1). In order to put a stop to Gilmour's interference with his business, Miner brought a lawsuit in the Superior Court of the District of Montreal.[4] When the court ruled in Miner's favour, ordering Gilmour to cease and desist diverting water away from Miner's mill, Gilmour brought an appeal to the Court of Queen's Bench of Canada. Here the decision went in his favour, and the court dismissed the plaintiff's suit. Unsatisfied with this result, it was Miner who appealed this time, making use of the only remaining judicial recourse available to him, an appeal to the Judicial Committee of the Privy Council in London.

Figure 4.1 View of the Miner's Dam, Granby, QC, about 1910. Image MP-0000.1049.9, McCord Museum

The Privy Council, an organ of the British monarchy, was for years the executive body through which British overseas possessions were governed, also hearing appeals from the courts of these colonies.[5] In 1833, in an effort to give these appeals a more judicial character, Parliament created the Judicial Committee of the Privy Council (Figure 4.2) (hereinafter the 'Judicial Committee' or 'Privy Council'), composed primarily of judges from other British high courts (but also with some non-judicial politicians to ensure political influence when such was felt to be necessary). Though formally not a court of law – the members of the committee did not wear judicial garb, they sat around a table with the parties' counsel and their decisions were, strictly speaking, merely recommendations to the monarch, who would then issue an order giving force to the recommendation – in practice it functioned like a court, and was treated as such by all. This new judicial body was tasked with hearing appeals from overseas possessions (as well as from the British court of Admiralty and ecclesiastical courts).[6]

The Judicial Committee, hearing cases from far-flung possessions around the globe, was an imperial institution par excellence. The nature of litigation in the common law, adversarial, system – in which the parties, not the state, generally determined if and when court proceedings would be conducted, and on what legal grounds – meant that the court's agenda was largely shaped by the decisions of litigants in the courts below. Nonetheless the Judicial Committee's worldwide jurisdiction, along with its judges' parallel tenures on other British high courts, gave it a potentially harmonizing and homogenizing role; 'The assumption was that there could be cohesion

Figure 4.2 Sitting of a Judicial Committee of the Privy Council. *Illustrated London News*, vol. 8, no. 206, 11 April 1846, p. 1. Image courtesy of Nandini Chatterjee

and certainty in the legal system of the empire only if appeals could be referred up to a judicial body in London.'[7]

At the same time the Judicial Committee was in effect an *inter*-imperial institution. British law distinguished between territories acquired through 'settlement' of supposedly unoccupied lands, as in the case of Australia and many American colonies, and those acquired by 'conquest' or cession from other 'civilized' states, such as the various Indian possessions and lands taken from other European powers. In the former case, in which the British viewed the legal situation prior to their arrival as a vacuum, English law was held to follow the settlers into the new possession as far as was practical; but in the latter – the colonies acquired by conquest – the existing laws remained in force until modified by new legislation by the conquering British.[8] With the acquisition of a host of new colonies during and in the wake of the wars with France and its allies, the British Empire came to include a large number of jurisdictions in which the law of other empires became part of the law of the British Empire, as well. The judges of the Privy Council were thus expected to rule on numerous appeals in which the applicable law was not English law but the law of another empire, whether French, Dutch, Spanish or Mughal.

These foreign imperial laws, even the European ones, were different from the English law not only in content, but in overall structure and culture. The legal systems of the countries of Continental Europe, along with most of their colonies, applied what is known as the civil law, based on Roman law and local custom, with great weight given to the opinions of learned jurists who had developed the Roman principles over the medieval and modern periods. In the period under consideration, many civil law countries were engaged in a process of codification, in which the principles of the civil law were reorganized and enacted into law on a national basis. In England, on the other hand, though pockets of the civil law existed (primarily in ecclesiastical courts, Admiralty courts and in the Court of Chancery), most legal issues were governed by the common law, the body of judicial precedent built up over hundreds of year of English court decisions, supplemented by statutes passed by Parliament. Colonies of 'settlement' continued to apply the common law rules (as do their successor states today, from Australia to the United States to most of the Canadian provinces). With different sources of law and legal traditions, the common law and civil law were likely to give divergent answers to any given legal question. Yet the Privy Council, hearing appeals not only from common law jurisdictions such as New South Wales and Upper Canada (today's Ontario), but from civil law ones formerly held by other imperial powers, such as Mauritius (French law) and Cape Colony (Dutch law), was a potential site for the fertilization of the common law by doctrines and principles of the civil law.

As we will see, the case of *Miner v. Gilmour*, arising in a formerly French province, seems to have been a prominent inter-imperial legal encounter, with a British imperial court being tasked with applying French imperial law, the intertwining of French, British and American legal discourses, and the product of this case affecting the development of the law throughout the British Empire. Yet this legal encounter raises a series of questions about the paradigm of inter-imperial encounters.

First is the problem of differentiating the inter-imperial from the transnational. The characterization of empires as 'the critical sites where transnational social and cultural movements took place'[9] seems, at first glance, to fit quite nicely the history of water law as it developed in and around the case of *Miner v. Gilmour*. Yet, on further examination, as we will see, it becomes difficult to distinguish the encounter of legal norms and ideas in the French and British Empires from the diffusion of laws between metropolitan France, Britain and the USA.

Second is the question of intentionality. In many of the examples mentioned in this volume's Introduction, along with some of the case studies examined in the chapters, the paradigmatic inter-imperial encounter is one in which agents of empire actively and consciously seek out interaction with agents of other empires, then act, to some extent, in concert. Yet while legal developments may have proceeded in this manner in some cases, the inter-imperial encounter of water law norms examined in this chapter departed somewhat from this model. The legal history presented in this chapter may thus fulfil a dual function in terms of the subject of this volume; while illustrating the inter-imperial development of one area of law, it also calls into question the boundaries of the 'encounters of empires' model.

II. The law in *Miner v. Gilmour*

As the judges of the Privy Council recognized, the law governing the conflict between Miner and Gilmour over the waters of the Yamaska was not English law. Quebec, before being conquered by the British in 1760, had been part of the French Empire. A royal edict of 1663 had declared the law of New France to be the law as applied in the *Parlement* of Paris.[10] This law included royal ordinances, Roman law as expounded by jurists, and the sixteenth-century official collection of the customary law of Paris known as the *Coutume de Paris*.[11] The Quebec Act of 1774, passed by the British Parliament a few years after the British conquest of Canada from France, declared that the laws of property existing in the province of Quebec pre-conquest would remain in force under British rule.[12] The water law applicable to the case at hand was thus the law of the old French Empire, that is to say the law of *ancien régime* Paris, ironically no longer in force in France itself after the adoption of the Napoleonic Code in 1804, but preserved in British colonies that had been conquered from the French. Indeed, the lawyers arguing the case before the British court in Westminster cited the civilian *Digest* of Justinian, the great French scholar Pothier and said Custom of Paris.[13]

The encounter between French and English law did not end with this infusion of French imperial law into a British imperial courtroom, nor with its application by British judges at the seat of imperial power. Despite the lack of formal authority for English common law in the civil law jurisdiction of Canada East, the lawyers for Miner and Gilmour before the Privy Council cited not only the civilian sources mentioned above, but also recent English case law on the subject of riparian rights. The judges of the Judicial Committee were impressed with the 'great learning and ingenuity' displayed by counsel, and scheduled an unusual second round of oral arguments.[14] Yet after all this learning and argument, they arrived at a surprising conclusion: 'It did not appear that, for the purposes of this case, any material distinction exists between the French and the English law'. According to both legal systems, the court opined, Miner could not demand that Gilmour keep the dam gate closed all the time, since a riparian proprietor had 'no right to interrupt the regular flow of the stream, if he thereby interferes with the lawful use of the water by other proprietors, and inflicts upon them a sensible injury'.

The decision's exposition of this and other principles of what Lord Kingsdown, writing for the court, termed the 'general law applicable to running streams' – that is to say the law of riparian rights, according to him common to French and English law – went on to be cited extensively throughout the British Empire and beyond as the definitive statement of the rules of riparian rights in the common-law world, as will be discussed in Part VI below.[15]

One might frame this episode as one in which the expanding British Empire encountered legal norms of the old French Empire through conquest, assimilated them into the common law, and then spread them throughout its possessions around the world. Alternatively, one might frame it as one in which British lawyers, despite their professed recognition of the legal distinctiveness of the civil-law province, essentially ignored French law and imposed, in an expression of imperial power, their own law on the conquered land. Yet deeper reading in the law of Canada East reveals that the crossed legal history of the British and French Empires was more complex than either of these two stories suggests.

So do two hints in the *Miner* opinion itself. The first is the Privy Council's reference to 'the general law of running streams'. This way of presenting the legal environment went beyond a simple statement that the water law of pre-revolutionary French law in force in Canada East was essentially the same as the common law in force in most of the rest of the British Empire; it seems to rather have reflected a view that there was a 'general law', not specific to particular legal systems, that applied in the case at hand.[16]

The second hint that something more than simple merging of two imperial legal traditions was at work involves the sources cited before the court. In addition to the civil-law sources discussed above, the parties relied upon two sources neither French nor English, but American: James Kent's *Commentaries on American Law*, a highly influential work by one of the premier American jurists of the age, and the leading American water case of *Tyler* v. *Wilkinson*.[17] To understand why American sources were cited in a British court adjudicating an issue meant to be determined by seventeenth-century French law, we need to go back across the Atlantic to Canada East and Lower Canada.

III. American sources of French-Canadian water law

Canada's broad St Lawrence River and its tributaries were the sites of intensive water use in the mid-nineteenth century. They served as fishing grounds, highways for water craft, conduits for floating logs and sources of power for both traditional grist mills and new industrial facilities. Uses and users often came into conflict, and these conflicts often landed up in court.

The earliest fully reported case of this type was the 1832 case of *Oliva* v. *Boissonnault*. James Oliva sued Nicolas Boissonnault in the court of King's Bench, District of Quebec, for placing obstructions in the Rivière du Sud, blocking the floating of logs downstream to the St Lawrence.[18] Chief Justice Jonathan Sewell ruled for Oliva, explaining that under French law the public had a right of passage on every stream capable of floating logs or rafts. Alongside his discussion of French law, he noted that the public's right was the same in England and America, citing Kent's *Commentaries* with regard to the latter.[19] Two years later *St Louis* v. *St Louis*, another water law dispute, reached the courts. This time the case involved a riparian landholder diverting water through a canal to his sawmill so that it bypassed the gristmill and carding and fulling mill of his downstream neighbours. Sewell, sitting this time in the Provincial Court of Appeals, again cited Kent, here in support of the proposition that a riparian landowner might 'conduct such portion of the stream as he requires for the amelioration of his property by canals or otherwise through the extent of the land which he occupies, but he must return it to the stream before it reaches the confines of his neighbour's estate'.[20]

Sewell was not alone in his affection for Kent and other American authority. Probably the most salient example was the dissenting opinion filed by Judge Thomas Aylwin in the appeal of *Brown* v. *Gugy* to the Queen's Bench of Lower Canada. This judicial opinion was really a brief intended to set before the Privy Council Aylwin's view of the law, as it was written especially to include with the appeal to the London court, well after judgement had been delivered by the Queen's Bench and leave granted for further appeal to the Privy Council.[21] Aylwin's 1861 opinion included a verbatim quote of ten pages from Kent's discussion of riparian rights, footnotes and all, and went on to say that the reasons given by the lower court 'are in my opinion bad & I prefer the ruling of the Supreme Court of Louisiana in the case of Allard & al vs Lebau [sic] cited at the bar'.[22]

One might conclude that this familiarity with and reliance on American law was a result of American connections. Aylwin had studied briefly at Harvard, where he must have been exposed to some American law (though not to Kent's *Commentaries*, which had yet to be published).[23] Sewell was born in Massachusetts (to a Loyalist family) and spent his childhood there, and he had been elected to the American Philosophical Society in 1830 and received an honorary doctorate from Harvard in 1832, the year of his *Oliva* decision.[24]

Yet reliance on American sources was not a simple matter even for Anglophone judges with American connections. It was Aylwin, formerly a *Patriote* politician, who had written, in a criminal case, a year before this opinion in *Brown* v. *Gugy*:

> I will shew the danger of referring to American authorities in criminal cases [...]. I hope we will hear [...] no more of them. The practice of late has been to create great confusion, by the habit has prevailed to too great an extent of citing American, English and French authorities in all cases indiscriminately, and it is time to put an end to such confusion.[25]

Moreover, Francophone lawyers, too, relied on American water law sources. Advocates Simon Lelièvre and François-Réal Angers cited the American Joseph Angell's *Treatise on the Law of Watercourses* in support of their position on property in water in a case before the Superior Court of Quebec City.[26] This source, as well as Louis Houck's *Treatise on the Law of Navigable Rivers*, was cited by C.B. Langlois in an appeal before the Queen's Bench decided in 1877.[27] B.C.A. Gugy, a lawyer who had campaigned against annexation of Canada to the United States, cited the American Angell's treatise on the law of tidewaters in arguing his own case in a dispute with a landowner on the opposite bank of the Beauport River.[28] Charles-Chamilly de Lorimier, a clerical-nationalist conservative and stalwart proponent of the civil law as a 'bulwark of French Canadian and Catholic values', nonetheless cited in a judicial decision a Wisconsin case among a string of Quebec cases on the question of whether a seasonally navigable stream was public or not.[29] Most extreme was Lorimier's Montreal law office partner Désiré Girouard, whose long and learned brief in a case in which he was a party cited and quoted (in French translation) a host of American sources on riparian law, from Thomas Jefferson to Angell to the latest American case law.[30]

IV. The attraction of American law

Why did lawyers and judges from the French-law province of Lower Canada/Canada East look south of the border for legal principles and rules in water law cases, to a jurisdiction that had never belonged to the old empire from which the local law derived, and no longer belonged to the new empire of which Canada was now a part?[31]

In his dissent in the 1859 case of *Boswell* v. *Denis* Judge Aylwin indicated one reason why Canadians may have preferred American law over French in some cases. According to French law, a 'navigable and floatable' river was a public one, in which the public enjoyed rights that could not be impaired by the riparian owners. As the river in question in *Boswell*, the Jacques-Cartier, contained rapids and was therefore not 'navigable' by boat traffic, the majority of the court straightforwardly applied the French test and ruled that it could not be considered a public river. Aylwin objected to this analysis: 'Our rivers cannot be compared with those of France or Europe; the *Jacques Cartier* is a good sized river and has plenty of water, – it has rapids it is true, but [...] I believe the river to be both *navigable* and *flottable*.'[32] Following a tradition going back to Montesquieu and further, Aylwin argued that French law could not apply unmodified in North America, as it was developed for a different set of environmental circumstances. Similarly, in a 1905 case Justice Trenholme of the Quebec King's Bench noted that American authorities on the question of navigability 'possess more than ordinary interest for Canadian Courts, as the conditions there were and are precisely like those in our country'.[33]

Yet it seems this was not the only reason for Canadians' turn to American water law. Returning to *Brown* v. *Gugy*, it is significant that the American case which Judge Aylwin preferred over the lower court's ruling was from Louisiana, the only American state which based its legal system on (French) civil law. Moreover, Kent's discussion of water law (like his discussions of many other subjects) was replete with references to civilian sources. In the pages quoted in Aylwin's opinion (sections 6 and 7 of Kent's Lecture 52), the American jurist cited a large number of American and English cases, as was appropriate for a work purporting to be a commentary on American law, but his very first citations were to civilian sources: Justinian's *Digest*, Pothier's *Traité du Contrat de Société* and Toullier's *Droit Civil Français*.[34] Later in the section, he cited again to Pothier, quoted with approval a maxim of Roman law and stated that the *Code Napoléon* established the same rule as said maxim.[35]

Later commentators have divided as to what extent Kent's use of civilian sources was substantial or rather mere window dressing, with Alan Watson arguing that Kent's use of the Roman and French sources in the section cited above was riddled with errors and that it provided little support to his exposition of riparian rights.[36] Nonetheless it seems that Judge Aylwin saw Kent as a good civilian source, prefacing his long quote from the *Commentaries* thus: 'I think it proper to avail myself of the valuable observations of Chancellor Kent, upon the subject of possessory rights in running streams acquired by prior occupancy. They are so apposite and so conformable to the principles of Civil Law, that I cite them with as much confidence, as if I were citing from Civilians or French writers.'[37] Aylwin, it seems, while wary of using American legal sources indiscriminately (as indicated by his quote in Part III above), was more than willing to use American sources as statements of the civil law, applicable in his Canadian jurisdiction.

Aylwin was not the first to think this way. Returning to *St Louis* v. *St Louis*, we find Chief Justice Sewell citing Kent as the last in a string of French authorities supporting the proposition that a riparian proprietor had to return the water he used to the stream before it reached his neighbour's land.[38] Kent himself in the relevant passage cites the

Digest and Pothier.³⁹ It seems that Aylwin, here, too, was citing Kent as an authority on the French law applicable in Canada East, not on American law.

But perhaps the clearest instance of reliance on Kent as a civilian writer was in *Oliva v. Boissonnault*. Here Sewell cited Kent not only in support of his discussion of American law, as discussed above, but also in support of another proposition: 'In the law of France, navigable rivers have always been regarded as public highways and as such dependencies of the public domain; and floatable rivers (rivieres flottables, as they are there termed) have been viewed in the same light.'⁴⁰ The referral to Kent in support of a description of French law was no mistake, as Kent writes on the cited page: 'In the French law, navigable or floatable rivers, as they are termed, have always been regarded as dependencies of the public domain.'⁴¹ So here, too, an American source was explicitly cited by a Canadian judge as authority on French law.

It seems, then, that Canadian lawyers and judges were attracted to American water law not just because of similar geographic conditions, but because they saw the law expounded in the American sources, particularly Kent's *Commentaries*, not as American law per se, but as reflecting the French law of waters applicable in their jurisdiction, as well.

As remarkable as this reliance on American sources as authorities on *ancien régime* French law might seem, it should be pointed out that some of the French sources cited by Canadian courts were themselves authorities on the relevant French law only at a remove. Toullier's exposition of water law quoted by Chief Justice Sewell in *Oliva v. Boissonnault*, for instance, was actually a commentary on the *Code Napoléon*, law which had no legal force in Canada, having been legislated decades after the Quebec Act confirmed the force of French law in Quebec as it existed at the date of British conquest.⁴² While courts were often correct in presuming that the rules enshrined in the Napoleonic Code reflected pre-Revolutionary French law, this reliance on contemporary French legal sources to explicate norms of old French law was only a step removed from using American sources to do the same.⁴³

V. Encounters of legal empires in *Miner*?

Returning now to London and the Privy Council in *Miner* v. *Gilmour*, the reliance by counsel on American sources for a question of French law, along with the court's conflation of the French law and the common law (discussed in Part III of this chapter), would seem to be a faithful expression of the water law of Canada East, with its own heavy reliance on American sources and blending of the French law and common law, often by way of citing those same American sources.

Moreover, the incorporation of the civil law into the common law of waters and the export of this *mélange* throughout the common-law world might be seen as the product not only of a one-time encounter with the law of Canada East in *Miner* v. *Gilmour*, but of an ongoing engagement with this odd jurisdiction, at once an integral part of the ascendant British Empire and the offspring of the old French Empire. Thus we find the Lower Canada case of *St Louis* v. *St Louis*, discussed in Part III above for Chief Justice Sewell's use of Kent as authority for a point of French law, making its way to the Privy

Council in 1841.⁴⁴ The judge who delivered the judgement of the Judicial Committee, Stephen Lushington, a prominent and knowledgeable English civilian lawyer (he was a judge on ecclesiastical and Admiralty courts, enclaves of civil law in the English legal system), was also a member of the panel that decided *Miner* v. *Gilmour*.⁴⁵ Might the bold statement of the court in *Miner*, according to which riparian rights in the common law were essentially the same as in the civil law, have been influenced by Lushington's exposure to precisely this attitude by the American-Canadian judge Sewell in *St Louis*?

Sewell's view in *St Louis* may have influenced the common law of waters through yet another route, as well. Sitting alongside Lushington on the Judicial Committee to hear the appeal of Sewell's judgment in *St Louis* v. *St Louis* was James Parke, the dominant judge on the English Court of Exchequer.⁴⁶ Within the decade, his court decided two cases – *Wood* v. *Waud* and *Embrey* v. *Owen* – which were the first English cases to adopt the American law of riparian rights, relying heavily on Kent, *Tyler* v. *Wilkinson* and French sources.⁴⁷ Could the Lower Canada case of *St Louis* v. *St Louis* have made an impression on Baron Parke, leading his court to base modern English riparian law on French and American sources?

Here we encounter a methodological difficulty – distinguishing between inter-imperial influences on the one hand, and transnational influences of the 'ordinary' kind, between two national jurisdictions, whether imperial metropolises or not, on the other. Put more concretely, was the intermixture of the laws of the old French Empire and the new American one in the courts of the British Empire a true inter-imperial encounter?⁴⁸ Or might it be better conceived of as a case of British judges being influenced by the laws of France and the United States, two national jurisdictions the laws of which they were inclined to consider by factors such as geographic proximity, cultural affinity, common legal origins and the availability of law books, independently of their crossed imperial histories?

Some support for the latter framing might be found in the fact that significant Roman-law influence on English water-law cases had a long pedigree dating to medieval and early modern times; in the period under discussion it was evident already in the important King's Bench case of *Mason* v. *Hill*.⁴⁹ Chief Justice Denman's decision in that case, quoting extensively from Justinian and the Dutch civilian commentator Vinnius, was handed down in 1833, eight years before the Privy Council ruled in the Lower Canada case of *St Louis* v. *St Louis*.

As for American and French water law, English judges were exposed to these independently of cases coming up from Canada. One important channel was Gale's *Treatise on the Law of Easements*, the first edition of which was published in London in 1839, a couple of years before the appeals of Sewell's decision in *St Louis* was heard by Lushington, Parke and the other judges sitting on the Privy Council appeal.⁵⁰ In the preface to the work, Gale explained that a majority of English cases on easements made recourse to the Romanist civil law, and so his treatise would rely on civilian authorities on servitudes. Moreover, he wrote:

> With the same view the authority of decisions in the American Courts has been called in aid upon the subject of water-courses – questions which the value of water as a moving power, and the frequent absence of ancient appropriation have

often given rise to in the United States. In those judgments the law is considered with much care and research, and the rights of the parties settled with precision. The result of the authorities is stated by Chancellor Kent, in his well-known Commentaries, with his usual ability.[51]

Like the Canadian judges discussed above, Gale, too, thus viewed American sources, especially Kent, as authorities on the civil law. When it came to water law, Gale did not cite Kent, but he quoted extensively from the leading American case *Tyler* v. *Wilkinson*.

There is no doubt that English courts were influenced by Gale on easements. The Court of Exchequer in *Wood* v. *Waud* and *Embrey* v. *Owen,* and counsel arguing before Privy Council in *Miner* v. *Gilmour*, all cited Gale's discussion of water rights under American law, along with *Tyler* v. *Wilkinson*. They all cited, too, to Kent's exposition of riparian rights, particularly the pages (discussed above in Part IV) in which he summarized the law, relying on civilian sources.[52] Given that Gale did not cite these pages, it can be assumed that while they may have read *Tyler* only as quoted by Gale, they read Kent in the original.

What brought the English lawyers and judges to turn to Kent's discussion of water law? It is possible that Kent's coverage of the topic was simply the best that was available at the time, and it is possible that Gale's recommendation pointed them in that direction, but it is also possible that their exposure to the opinions of Canadian judges and their reliance on Kent in *St Louis* v. *St Louis* and later in *Miner* v. *Gilmour* were decisive, or at least primed them for the easy acceptance of American and French authority on water law. In any case, the conflation of the civil and common law of waters continued in the reception of *Miner* v. *Gilmour* into the law of the British Empire, as we will now see.

VI. *Miner* as an inter-imperial legal authority

Lord Kingsdown's summary of the relative rights of riparian owners, regarded as definitive for the rest of the nineteenth century and beyond, was cited widely throughout the British Empire and beyond.[53] Though arising in a case in which the applicable law was the old French law of Canada East, on the imperial periphery, it was taken as a faithful exposition of the common law of England, the imperial metropolis. In the 1876 case of *Lyon* v. *Fishmongers' Company*, for instance, dealing with the right of access of riparian owners to the River Thames, the House of Lords (at the time the highest court for cases arising in Britain itself) referred to it as one of 'the best authorities' on riparian doctrine.[54]

Perhaps the most interesting reliance on *Miner* (for our purposes) in the water jurisprudence of the British Empire came in two decisions authored by the British judge Colin Blackburn.[55] In the House of Lords case of *Orr Ewing* v. *Colquhoun* (1877), Blackburn rejected the rule of Scottish law applied by the Scottish court below, arguing (*inter alia*), 'If such be the law of *Scotland* it is different from what Lord *Kingsdown*, in [*Miner* v. *Gilmour*], states to be the law of *England* and *France*.'[56] Lord Blackburn, it seems, was ready to modify the law of the metropolis (albeit of Scotland, a jurisdiction of secondary importance, and one in which the civil law, not the common law, applied), bending it to conform to the law as laid down in *Miner*, a case governed by the law of a foreign empire.

A few years later came *Commissioners of French Hoek* v. *Hugo*, an appeal to the Privy Council of a judgement of the supreme court of the Cape Colony, in today's South Africa.[57] Governing the dispute over the waters of two small watercourses was what is known as Roman-Dutch law. This was the law in force in the Cape Colony when it was ceded by the Dutch to the British at the end of the Napoleonic Wars (the metropolitan Netherlands had by this point adopted the Napoleonic Code for use in the home country), and, as the colony had been conquered from another state, not 'settled', this was the law that remained in force under British rule. Like the pre-Revolutionary French law in force in Quebec, Roman-Dutch law was based largely on the writings of learned 'civilian' jurists writing in the Roman law tradition. Indeed, in addition to Cape Colony cases and Roman-Dutch sources, lawyers for the appellants cited French treatises in support of their argument.

Writing for the Privy Council in *French Hoek*, Lord Blackburn referred approvingly to the summary of the law of riparian rights in *Miner* v. *Gilmour*, seeming to attach some importance to the similar positions of the Roman-influenced civil law in Canada East and the Cape Colony:

> In *Miner* v. *Gilmour* this Board had to decide as to the Canadian law, which is founded on the old French law, not on that law as altered by the Code Napoléon, and Lord Kingsdown, in delivering the judgment, used [...] expressions which have often been cited, and always with approval. He said: 'It did not appear that, for the purposes of this case, any material distinction exists between the French and the English law.'[58]

Finding, however, that an important difference was said to exist between Roman-Dutch law – in which a landowner might do as he pleased with a stream arising within his land, without regard to effects on downstream riparians – and the English common law as laid down in *Miner* – according to which a riparian owner could in general not interfere with the uses made by downstream owners – Lord Blackburn made an odd argument, explaining that his court had 'a very grave doubt, whether that which was alleged to be the Dutch-Roman law could be so, the English law as laid down by Lord Kingsdown being so much more convenient'.[59]

Blackburn's attitude to the plural legal world of the British Empire is thus revealed as ambiguous. On the one hand, he recognized that the governing law in *Miner* v. *Gilmour* was the law of the old French Empire, a fact that seemed to imbue it with particular relevance for the case at hand, also governed by pre-Revolutionary, Romanist civil law. On the other hand, the Privy Council's rejection in *French Hoek* of the accepted understanding of the Roman-Dutch law (as expounded by the Roman-Dutch authority Voet, the lower court sitting in the Cape and appellants' counsel) in favour of what it termed the 'English law' as laid down in *Miner* seems to reflect a sort of legal patriotism or at least homogenizing tendency, with the British judge not bothering to determine the applicable law imported from another imperial system, since the English rule was 'so much more convenient'. In this encounter with the law of a foreign empire, far from making the British law conform to the foreign imperial law, as in *Orr Ewing*, Blackburn made the foreign law (in force in the British Cape) conform to the English common law.

It should be noted that Blackburn was no foe of the civil law of the Continent, no common law chauvinist; one of his most noted judgements, on English contract law, made heavy use of civilian sources.[60] So his rejection of the Roman-Dutch rule in *French Hoek* in favour of the 'more convenient' English law seems not to have been the product of a general predilection in favour of English law, but of a preference for the specific rule of the common law of water rights relevant to the case over the Roman-Dutch one. Nonetheless, his varying characterizations of the rules of riparian rights explained in *Miner* v. *Gilmour*, first as based on 'the old French law', then as 'the English law as laid down by Lord Kingsdown', raise the question of whether the Canadian case's wide influence on the law of the British Empire should be properly viewed as reflecting the impact of French imperial law on the British, or simply as the result of particularly persuasive British authority.

VII. Conclusion

It is clear, then, that Quebec/Lower Canada/Canada East was a fertile ground for the transfer of legal norms from the French Empire to the British one. It is also clear that it was the site for the intermixing of laws from the civil and common law systems, catalysed with the aid of legal sources from a growing, third, empire – the American one.

What is less clear is whether this inter-imperial mixing was primarily a local phenomenon, limited to the law of this one province of the British Empire, or whether its influence radiated back to the imperial metropolis, Britain, and from there outwards again throughout the Empire. British courts in Westminster made use (like their subordinate counterparts in Quebec City and Montreal) of French and American sources to work out the relative rights of private citizens and the public in watercourses, and were certainly cognizant to some extent of water-law developments in Canada. The appellate review by the Judicial Committee of the Privy Council of a Canadian dispute, *Miner* v. *Gilmour*, was the occasion for the authoritative judicial pronouncement on the unity of French and English water law, and for the export of this homogenized conception of the law to lands as far afield as India, Australia and South Africa. Yet we cannot say for certain that it was the particularly imperial combination of the French and English law in Canada that led to this transplantation of American and French law into the common law; factors inherent in the development of English law itself, on its home turf, may have been responsible for the reception.

Beyond the legal history of water, the doubts raised by this analysis may have implications for imperial histories in general. Inter-imperial influences may be hard to distinguish from transnational influences of the more prosaic kind, especially when centralized institutions of empire – in the case examined here, British courts at the imperial centre hearing cases from the imperial periphery – are involved. Their cognizance of foreign imperial practices and norms may have come through the imperial network, but it may also have come from straight country-to-country influence, without the medium of empire. Put another way, while the circumstances of this inter-imperial encounter certainly had inter-imperial elements in fact, it is not entirely clear if the imperial dimension was fundamental or rather coincidental, whether the encounter was actually one of empires or rather one between nation-states. Nonetheless, the story of *Miner v. Gilmour* shows that, at the very least, the mechanics of particular transnational phenomena may owe much to the imperial frameworks of the nations in question. It is possible that the import of civil law norms into English water law would have come about without inter-imperial contact; yet the fact is that it was the existence of imperial institutions like the Privy Council and inter-imperial encounters like the conquest of Quebec and the Cape Colony that forced British courts to engage in a sustained way with French law and facilitated its export to jurisdictions around the world.

Yet even if the imperial aspects of this episode are viewed as significant or even dominant, we remain with the question of whether the influence of French imperial law on that of the British Empire was a paradigmatic 'encounter of empires'. While the legal system of the Empire, with its preservation of foreign imperial laws in 'ceded' territories and the Privy Council at the apex of the judicial pyramid, had the inherent potential to facilitate the mixing of foreign legal norms into the laws of England and the empire at large, the inter-imperial diffusion of ideas thus produced seems to have departed in some important aspects from other cases of encounters between empires. There was no inter-imperial discussion of this process; little, if any, theorizing about it; and it is unclear that any imperial objectives were served by it. The inter-imperial development of water came about not as a result of any co-operation between French and British imperial officials, nor even as a result of a conscious decision of any British official to look to another empire for inspiration in the development of British imperial water law, but in response to lawsuits and appeals instigated by private parties and prosecuted by their lawyers, each seeking advantage for themselves or their clients, with little regard to larger questions of imperial legal policy. Imperial judges enthusiastically embraced the civil law of the French Empire, but seemingly more for its prestige and utility than for any imperial objectives. Moreover, theirs was a very one-sided embrace; their interaction was not with living French legal officials, nor even with the living law of the French Empire, but mainly with the law of the pre-revolutionary French Empire, which ironically had largely passed from the world outside of the British Empire.

Notes

1 Funding for this research was provided by the Israel Science Foundation (grant no. 1108/11); the US National Endowment for the Humanities; the Judging Empire project at the University of Plymouth; the Osgoode Society for Canadian Legal History; and the Berg Institute for Law and History and Cegla Center for the Interdisciplinary Study of the Law at Tel Aviv University. Any views, findings,

conclusions or recommendations expressed in this chapter do not necessarily reflect those of the National Endowment for the Humanities or any other funder. Thanks to the volume editors and to the Internationales Kolleg Morphomata, Universität zu Köln, for organizing the conference which sparked my thinking on the topic.
2 See Morton J. Horwitz, *The Transformation of American Law, 1780–1860* (Cambridge, Mass., London: Harvard University Press, 1979); Carol M. Rose, Energy and efficiency in the realignment of common-law water rights, *Journal of Legal Studies*, 19 (1990), pp. 261–96.
3 For the dialogue between American and English law on this subject, see Joshua Getzler, *A History of Water Rights at Common Law* (Oxford: Oxford UP, 2004). For the use of civil law sources by American jurists, see the rather different appreciations of Samuel C. Wiel, Waters: American law and French authority, *Harvard Law Review*, 33 (1919), pp. 133–67 and Alan Watson, Chancellor Kent's use of foreign law, in: Mathias Reimann (ed.), *The Reception of Continental Ideas in the Common Law World: 1820–1920* (Berlin: Duncker & Humblot, 1993), pp. 45–62; Alan Watson, *The Evolution of Western Private Law: Expanded Edition* (Baltimore: Johns Hopkins UP, 2001), pp. 138–92; Arthur Maass and Hiller B. Zobel, Anglo-American water law: who appropriated the riparian doctrine, *Public Policy*, 10 (1960), pp. 109–56.
4 For background on Miner and Gilmour see *Historical Sketch of Granby, The Granby Directory for 1912–1913* (Sherbrooke: L.A. Belanger, 1912), p. 9; Cecilia Capocchi, History of the Miner family, *Miner Heritage Farm* www.fermeheritageminer.ca/en/about-us/miner-family (accessed 16 January 2014). The judgement of the Superior Court is reproduced in the file of the Queen's Bench case *Gilmour v. Minor*, Case No. 154 of 1855, Bibliothèque et Archives nationales de Québec (BAnQ), Montreal. Miner's name is spelled 'Minor' in some of the case reports and documents, including most documents in the case file held by BAnQ and the case as printed in *Lower Canada Reports*, 9, p. 115. Unless referring to a source in which the spelling is otherwise, this chapter will in general use 'Miner', following the spelling in the non-legal historical materials cited above and in *Miner v. Gilmour, Moore's Privy Council Cases* 12, p. 131, *English Reports*, 14, p. 861.
5 See William Cornish, Michael Lobban and Keith Smith, Empire's law, in: *The Oxford History of the Laws of England: Volume XI: 1820–1914 English Legal System* (Oxford: Oxford UP, 2010), pp. 234–54.
6 For the history of the Judicial Committee of the Privy Council, see Thomas Mohr, A British empire court – a brief appraisal of the history of the Judicial Committee of the Privy Council, in: Anthony McElligott et al. (eds), *Power in History: From Medieval to the Post-Modern World* (Dublin: Irish Academic Press, 2011), pp. 125–42; Patrick Polden, The judicial roles of the House of Lords and Privy Council, 1820–1914, in: *Oxford History of the Laws of England: Volume XI*, pp. 528–68; Charlotte Smith, The Judicial Committee: an introduction to the Judicial Committee of the Privy Council, *Privy Council Papers Online* www.privycouncilpapers.org/judicial-committee-privy-council (accessed 18 February 2014).
7 Cornish, Lobban, Smith, Empire's Law, p. 245.
8 See J.E. Cote, The reception of English law, *Alberta Law Review*, 15 (1911), pp. 29–92.
9 Kevin Grant, Philippa Levine and Frank Trentmann (eds), *Beyond Sovereignty: Britain, Empire and Transnationalism, c. 1850–1950* (Basingstoke: Palgrave Macmillan, 2007), p. 2. See also the Introduction to this volume by Volker Barth and Roland Cvetkovski.

10 See Edit de création du conseil supérieur de Quebec, in *Edits, Ordonnances Royaux, Declarations et Arrêts du Conseil d'Etat du Roi Concernant le Canada* (Quebec: Fréchette, 1854), I, p. 37.

11 See F.P. Walton, The legal system of Quebec, *Columbia Law Review*, 13 (1913), pp. 213–31. Certain French legislative enactments of the seventeenth century treating water may have also applied, but as these were never registered in New France their legal force in Canada was uncertain, and the case law mostly ignored them; see Henri Brun, Le droit québécois et l'eau (1663–1969), *Cahiers de Droit*, 11 (1970), pp. 7–45.

12 An Act for making more effectual Provision for the Government of the Province of Quebec in North America, 14 Geo. III, c. 83 (1774).

13 *Miner v. Gilmour, English Reports*, 14, p. 865. The citation to the *Coutume de Paris* is inferred: Edmund Moore's standard report of the case states (*Moore's Privy Council Cases*, 12, p. 141; *English Reports*, 14, p. 865) that the parties cited at argument before the Privy Council, Douet's [sic] Princ. of the Law of Lower Canada, Art. 186, pp. 189, 265. The work in question is presumably N.B. Doucet's *Fundamental Principles of the Laws of Canada* (Montreal, 1841–3), and 'Art. 186' presumably refers to article 186 of the *Coutume de Paris* (ibid., pp. 254–5), stating that a servitude may be extinguished by thirty years of contrary use, a point probably raised by Gilmour in response to a claim that he had abandoned his claim to river water (*English Reports*, 14, pp. 862, 867, 870). As pages 189 and 265 of Doucet have nothing to do with the issues litigated in the case, 'pp. 189, 265' may be corrupted citations to articles 89 and 266 of Doucet's summary of the civil law of Canada (2, pp. 62, 108), the former stating that a usufructuary may give away his right, the latter setting the term of prescription for immoveable and incorporeal things at ten years.

14 The re-hearing may have been due to a 2–2 split among the judges on the original panel; see Polden, *Judicial Roles*, p. 565.

15 The quotes are from *Miner v. Gilmour, English Reports*, 14, p. 870.

16 Michel Morin, La perception de l'ancien droit et du nouveau droit français au Bas-Canada, 1774–1866, in: H. Patrick Glenn (ed.), *Droit québécois et droit français: communauté, autonomie, concordance* (Cowansville: Éditions Yvon Blais, 1993), p. 16 (citing, *inter alia, Miner v. Gilmour*) notes a number of decisions from Quebec and Lower Canada stating that French and English law led to the same result. The claim of the Privy Council in *Miner*, however, that the French and English laws of water were materially the same, went further than a claim with regard to results alone. The reference to a transnational 'general law of running streams' went further still.

17 The citation in *Miner v. Gilmour* is to Volume 3, page 544 of Kent's *Commentaries*, probably referring to the 8th edition (New York: Kent, 1854), in which page 544 opens the section on running waters, but possibly the 7th edition (New York: Kent, 1851), in which the page treats prescription in water rights. *Tyler* is reported at *Federal Cases*, 24, p. 472 (Circuit Ct Dist Rhode Island 1827).

18 *Oliva v. Boissonnault, Stuart's Lower Canada Reports*, p. 524 (KB 1832). The St Thomas River mentioned in the report is identified as the Rivière du Sud in the report of the appeal, *Boissonnault v. Oliva, Stuart's Lower Canada Reports*, p. 564 (Ct App 1833). In the earlier cases of *Harrower v. Babin* (*Revue de Legislation* 2, p. 469 (KB 1817)) and *Stein v. Seath* (*Rapports Judiciaires Revisés*, 24, p. 134 (KB Montreal 1828)) the reported holdings were simply that 'an action [...] can be maintained against a neighbouring proprietor for impeding a water course to the plaintiffs prejudice' and that 'no person may obstruct a navigable river with impunity', without further explanation or supporting authority.

19 *Oliva* v. *Boissonnault*, p. 526, citing Kent's *Commentaries*, 3, p. 344 (New York: Halsted, 1828).
20 *St Louis* v. *St Louis, Stuart's Lower Canada Reports*, p. 579 (Ct App 1834), citing Kent's *Commentaries*, 3, p. 353.
21 The judgement of the Queen's Bench, from which Aylwin dissented without filing an opinion, was delivered on 7 May 1861 (not 1860, as printed in *Brown* v. *Gugy, Lower Canada Reports*, 11, p. 401). Record of Proceedings, *Brown* v. *Gugy* Printed Papers, shelfmark P.P. 1316, vol. 177G, British Library, pp. 315–16 (also at BAnQ Québec, cote TL999, contenant 1960-01-343/56). Leave to appeal to the Privy Council was granted the next day, ibid., while Aylwin's dissenting arguments were filed only on 13 November 1861, Judge Aylwin's Opinion, *Brown* v. *Gugy* Printed Papers. The Privy Council criticized this practice, stating that the dissenting judges' 'reasons for dissenting from their colleagues should have been stated publicly at the hearing below, and should not have been reserved to influence the decision in the Court of appeal', *Brown* v. *Gugy, English Reports*, 15, p. 939.
22 Aylwin's opinion, 13 November 1861, pp. 11–14, quoting Kent's *Commentaries*, 3, pp. 439–48 (apparently 3rd ed., New York: Clayton, Van Norden, 1836), and citing *Allard* v. *Lobau, Martin's Reports (n.s.)*, 2, p. 317 (1824).
23 See André Garon, Aylwin, Thomas Cushing, in *Dictionary of Canadian Biography*, 10 (University of Toronto/Université Laval, 2003–), www.biographi.ca/en/bio/aylwin_thomas_cushing_10E.html.
24 See F. Murray Greenwood and James H. Lambert, Sewell, Jonathan, in *Dictionary of Canadian Biography*, 7, www.biographi.ca/en/bio/sewell_jonathan_7E.html (accessed 21 January 2014). For the dominance of Anglophone judges in nineteenth-century Quebec, and their affinity for English law at the expense of reigning French law, see Morin, *Perception*, pp. 10–11.
25 *R.* v. *Creamer, Lower Canada Reports*, 10, p. 407 (KB 1860). See Morin, *Perception*, p. 16.
26 *Larue* v. *Dubord, Lower Canada Reports*, 1, p. 35 (Sup Ct Quebec 1850), citing Angell's *Law of Watercourses* (probably 2nd ed., Boston: Hilliard, Gray, 1833).
27 *Bell* v. *Corporation of Quebec, Quebec Law Reports*, 7, p. 106 (PC 1879), citing Angell, *Law of Watercourses* (probably 5th ed., Boston: Little, Brown, 1854), and Louis Houck, *A Treatise on the Law of Navigable Rivers* (Boston: Little, Brown, 1868).
28 D.R. Barry, An eminent Quebec lawyer of the last century, *Canadian Law Times*, 32 (1912), pp. 427–38; Jacques Monet, Gugy, Bartholomew Conrad Augustus, in: *Dictionary of Canadian Biography*, 10, www.biographi.ca/en/bio/gugy_bartholomew_conrad_augustus_10E.html (accessed 21 January 2014); *Brown* v. *Gugy, English Reports*, 15, p. 936; Josheph K. Angell, *A Treatise on the Right of Property in Tide Waters* (2nd ed., Boston: Little & Brown, 1847).
29 *Pierce* v. *McConville, Revue de Jurisprudence*, 5, p. 547 (Sup Ct Joliette 1898), citing *Olson* v. *Merrill, Wisconsin Reports*, 42, p. 203 (1877). The quote is from Brian Young, Lorimier, Charles-Chamilly de, in: *Dictionary of Canadian Biography*, 14, www.biographi.ca/en/bio/lorimier_charles_chamilly_de_14E.html (accessed 24 March 2014).
30 *Dunning* v. *Girouard, La Revue Légale*, 9, pp. 187–241 (QB 1877). Michael Lawrence Smith, Girouard, Désiré, in: *Dictionary of Canadian Biography*, 14, www.biographi.ca/en/bio/girouard_desire_14E.html (accessed 24 March 2014).
31 G. Blaine Baker has noted the general openness of Canadian law to American law in this period, as part of a general 'cross-pollination in law throughout the North Atlantic

world'; The reconstitution of Upper Canadian legal thought in the late-Victorian Empire, *Law and History Review*, 3 (1985), pp. 219–92, especially at 242–5. The question of why particular areas of law, such as riparian law, were sites for this phenomenon nonetheless requires explanation.

32 *Boswell v. Denis, Lower Canada Reports*, 10, pp. 298–99 (QB 1859).
33 *Lefaivre v. Attorney General, Rapports Judiciaires (B.R.)*, 14, 125 (1905). For other Canadian justifications for borrowing from American, as opposed to English, law, see Baker, *Reconstitution*, p. 248.
34 See Kent's *Commentaries*, 3rd ed., 3, p. 439, note a.
35 See ibid., p. 441, notes a and b.
36 See Watson, *Chancellor Kent*. For the divergence between American riparian law and the civil law see also Wesley Vos, The Riparian principle in South Africa and other countries, *South African Law Journal*, 68 (1951), pp. 200–9. For the view that Kent's exposition of water law was heavily influenced by civil law, particularly French law, see Wiel, *Waters*.
37 Aylwin's opinion, *Brown v. Gugy* Printed Papers, pp. 10–11.
38 *St Louis v. St Louis*, p. 579, note (a).
39 See Kent's *Commentaries*, 1st ed., 3, p. 353, citing in note b 'Dig. 39. 3, 4 and 10' (should read 39.3.1.4 and 10, see Watson, *Chancellor Kent*) and Robert Joseph Pothier, *Traité du Contrat de Société* (1764), second app. No. 236, 237. Watson's judgement that the cited passages from Justinian and Pothier provide no support for the rules state by Kent is perhaps too harsh; while it is true that those sources deal with the issue of damage from flowing rainwater and not with diminution of flow by upper riparians, Kent may have sought to rely on the more general points that 'one ought to improve one's land in such a way that it does not make a neighbour's land worse' (*Digest*, 39.3.1.4, Pothier no. 236), and that if water 'is turned back [...] suit may be brought' (*Digest*, 39.3.1.10, Pothier no. 237).
40 *Oliva v. Boissonnault*, p. 526, citation to Kent in note (c).
41 Kent's *Commentaries*, 1st ed., 3, pp. 342–3.
42 *Oliva v. Boissonnault*, pp. 525–6. The quote, found in C.B.M. Toullier, *Le Droit Civil Français*, 3, pp. 90–1 (Paris: Jules Renouard, 5th ed., 1839), is an explanation of the law in Art. 644 of the Code.
43 For reliance on post-Revolutionary French law in Lower Canada cases see Morin, *Perception*, 24.
44 *St Louis v. St Louis, English Reports*, 13, p. 161 (PC 1841).
45 See S.M. Waddams, Lushington, Stephen (1782–1873), in: *Oxford Dictionary of National Biography* (Oxford: Oxford UP, 2004), www.oxforddnb.com/view/article/17213 (accessed 24 March 2014).
46 See Gareth H. Jones, Parke, James, Baron Wensleydale (1782–1868), in: *Oxford Dictionary of National Biography*, www.oxforddnb.com/view/article/21283 (accessed 24 March 2014).
47 *Wood v. Waud, English Reports*, 154, p. 1047 (Ex 1849); *Embrey v. Owen, English Reports*, 155, p. 579 (Ex 1851).
48 For the American Empire see, for example, Sam W. Haynes and Christopher Morris (eds) *Manifest Destiny and Empire: American Antebellum Expansionism* (College Station: Texas A&M UP, 1997).
49 *Mason v. Hill, English Reports*, 110, p. 700 (KB 1833). For Roman influence on English water law generally, see Getzler, *Water Rights*.
50 See C.J. Gale and T.D. Whatley, *Treatise on the Law of Easements* (London: S. Sweet, 1839); Getzler, *Water Rights*, pp. 268–9, 282.

51 Gale and Whatley, *Easements*, pp. v–vi.
52 *Wood v. Waud*, pp. 1055, 1056; *Embrey v. Owen*, pp. 585, 586; *Miner v. Gilmour*, p. 865.
53 For *Miner* as the definitive statement of the law in the rest of the nineteenth century and beyond, see Getzler, *Water Rights*, p. 294. For citations of *Miner* see, for example, in addition to the cases discussed in this section, cases cited in the report of the case, p. 871; *Hough v. Van der Merwe, Buchanan's Reports*, 1874, p. 154 (Cape Colony, 1874); *Lomax v. Jarvis, New South Wales Reports*, 6, p. 242 (1885); Lal Mohun Doss, *The Law of Riparian Rights, Alluvion & Fishery*, p. 278 (Calcutta: Thacker, Spink & Co., 1891); *Wiggins v. Muscupiabe Land & Water Co., California Reports*, 113, p. 190 (1897); *Debi Pershad Singh v. Joynath Singh, Indian Appeals*, 24, p. 66 (PC, 1897); *Nagle v. Miller, Victorian Law Reports*, 29, p. 785 (1904); *Nga Pi v. Nga Kyan Tha, All India Reporter (Upper Burma)*, 1914, p. 20; *Mahabir Sahu v. Ram Saran, All India Reporter (Patna)*, 1919, p. 179; *Sec'y. of State v. Damisetti Surayya, All India Reporter (Madras)*, 1929, p. 229; *Murli v. Hanuman Prasad, All India Reporter (Allahabad)*, 1936, p. 521.
54 *Lyon v. Fishmongers' Co., Appeals Cases*, 1, p. 683. See also *Nuttall v. Bracewell, Law Reports Exchequer*, 2, p. 9 (1866).
55 Blackburn was Scottish by birth but was educated in England and practised law in the English courts. Gareth H. Jones, Blackburn, Colin, Baron Blackburn of Killearn (1813–1896), *Oxford Dictionary of National Biography*, www.oxforddnb.com/view/article/2510 (accessed 20 August 2014).
56 *Orr Ewing v. Colquhoun, Appeals Cases*, 2, p. 856 (1877). Emphases in original.
57 *Commissioners of French Hoek v. Hugo, Appeals Cases*, 10, p. 335 (1885).
58 Ibid., p. 344.
59 Ibid., p. 346.
60 *Taylor v. Caldwell, English Reports*, 122, p. 309 (QB 1863); see Jones, *Blackburn*.

5

Creating a Colonial *Shari'a* for Russian Turkestan: Count Pahlen, the *Hidaya* and Anglo-Muhammadan Law*

Alexander Morrison

I had invited a group of learned mullahs with the object of studying and editing a Russian translation of rules based on the Shari'a which I had prepared [. . .] I had found supporting material for the Russian text in French codified collections from Tunis and Algiers, and in compendiums and digests by English magistrates on cases where the litigants were Mohammedan.[1]

The Russian Empire's propensity to import expertise and borrow techniques and technology from its rivals is a well-known phenomenon. As the most backward of the nineteenth century's 'Great Powers', Russia's modernization was in large part financed by foreign capital, and made extensive use of foreign machinery and ideas: French battleships, British railway engineers and Prussian uniforms all figured prominently.[2] What is less familiar, and more controversial, is the Russian 'borrowing' of specifically colonial ideas and techniques from the empires of their French and British contemporaries. Many Russian historians today prefer to argue that Russia was never a colonial power, and that the political relationship between European Russia and the empire's territories in the Caucasus, Central Asia and Siberia cannot be compared to that between metropole and colony in Western Europe.[3] The Soviet period imposed a vision of the 'friendship of peoples' on the Tsarist past, which cast the Russians as an 'elder brother' protecting the empire's more backward inhabitants from conquest and exploitation by western imperialist powers (primarily Britain).[4] This chapter will argue that in fact Russian statesmen, administrators and military officers often shared similar attitudes to their counterparts in western colonies, and drew on a shared colonial episteme for techniques of conquest, pacification and governance. This pattern of

---

* My thanks to Volker Barth, Jane Burbank, Roland Cvetkovski, Ulrike von Hirschausen, Thoralf Klein, Jonas Kreienbaum, Ulrike Lindner and Frank Schumacher for their comments, which have greatly improved this chapter.

colonial borrowing is particularly clear in the empire's Central Asian territories, which before 1917 were explicitly considered to be analogous to the colonies of other European powers. The appeal of borrowing ideas and techniques lay partly in the fact that they had already been tested and, in principle, found effective, but also – as Lauren Benton has suggested when looking at colonial legal practices – because in many cases they carried a certain prestige.[5] Their adoption could be used to demonstrate a colonial regime's maturity and legitimacy: as we shall see, this desire for recognition through emulation was important for Russian colonialism. This chapter, however, explores a case of 'failed transfer', showing that while prestige and access to European networks of knowledge helped to determine which particular pieces of colonial know-how were borrowed, they could not ensure that the transplant would be successful.

I. Russia's colony and its comparators

The governor-generalship of Turkestan was created by imperial decree in 1867, from territory in Central Asia which had been conquered by the Russians since 1853, with its capital in Tashkent. Beginning with just two provinces, Semirechie and Syr-Darya (modern-day southern Kazakhstan and northern Kyrgyzstan), further conquests expanded its territory to almost a million square miles. Samarkand was added in 1868, with the remainder of the Bukharan emirate becoming a Russian protectorate. Khiva also became a vassal state in 1873, Ferghana was annexed in 1876, Transcaspia (modern Turkmenistan) in 1885 and the Pamir region in 1895. From the very outset, Turkestan became the most 'colonial' of the Russian Empire's borderlands: it was governed by military administrators under a series of special statutes that gave considerable autonomy to its governor-general.[6] Its overwhelmingly Muslim inhabitants did not acquire even the rudimentary rights associated with Russian citizenship at this date. Legally they were placed in the category of *inorodtsy* ('aliens'), although in practice the Russians almost always described them as *tuzemtsy*, 'natives', emphasizing both their lack of mobility within the Empire, and the status of the Russians as incomers from Europe.[7] If the racial boundaries between colonizer and colonized in Turkestan were less important and less assiduously policed than those of British or French colonies, religion played much the same role as the key marker of the difference and inferiority of the local population. Turkestanis could not aspire to serve in the higher administration of their own province, as district commandants or governors: nor could they serve elsewhere in the Empire. Turkestan was governed predominantly, though not exclusively, by ethnic Russians, with Ukrainians, Baltic Germans, Poles, Georgians and the occasional Muslim Tatar or Bashkir making up the balance. It remained under military rule until 1917, and was never granted the independent civilian courts or *zemstva* (provincial elected assemblies) created by the Great Reforms in European Russia, nor, later, full representation in the State Duma. By the late nineteenth century Turkestan also became a colony of settlement, as Russian peasants occupied supposedly 'spare' land not needed by nomadic pastoralists. This was predicated on the principle that Europeans, and above all Orthodox Great Russians, had a pre-eminent right to the Empire's land that trumped that of the indigenous population.[8] By every meaningful criterion then, Turkestan was a colony, politically and culturally subordinated to the Russian metropole.⁹

The parallels between Russian Turkestan and other European colonies were obvious to contemporary observers, whether they were British, French or Russian. Most famously G. N. Curzon devoted the bulk of his 1889 account of a journey along the newly-completed railway from the Caspian to Samarkand to comparisons of Russian rule in Central Asia with British rule in India, which were surprisingly often to the favour of the former.¹⁰ On the Russian side Turkestan was often referred to as *Nasha Koloniya* ('our colony'),¹¹ and compared with both British rule in India and French Algeria. Using the language of colonialism in this way allowed Russian officials to lay claim to what at the time was a fashionable form of modernity. Unlike in the Soviet period, in late Tsarist Russia there was nothing taboo or incongruous in comparing Russian rule with that of other 'imperialist' powers, although it is only recently that historians have begun to appreciate these parallels once again.¹²

Given this awareness that they were engaged in a common enterprise, and their frequent invocation of a *mission civilizatrice* (the more usual term in Russian was *prosvetitel'noe dvizhenie* or 'enlightening movement') it would have been surprising if the Russian military authorities in Turkestan had not also observed the experience of other European powers in ruling over Muslims and sought to borrow from them. The British historian Francis Skrine suggested 'That so much of the Russian edifice is built on Anglo-Indian models is the strongest proof of their intrinsic excellence. We were pioneers, and had difficulties to encounter with which our neighbours were never perplexed; they have profited by our experience and mistakes.'¹³ While the Russians were rarely as uncritical and accepting as this quotation blithely suggests, they did study the French and British colonial experience attentively, particularly the officers of the General Staff, the intellectual elite of the Russian Army.¹⁴ The Russian conquest of the Northern Caucasus and the French conquest of Algeria took place concurrently, and were frequently compared by Russian officers seeking guidance on methods of defeating and administering 'fanatical' Muslims.¹⁵ In 1874, immediately after his participation in the campaign to conquer the Khanate of Khiva, Captain A.N. Kuropatkin (later minister of war) was sent on an official mission to Algeria to observe the *Armée d'Afrique* in action and collect information on French methods of subduing Islamic 'fanaticism' and administering Muslim populations.¹⁶ Over twenty years later in 1898, in the aftermath of an uprising led by a Sufi leader against the Russians in Andijan, publications on the conspiratorial and fanatical nature of Sufi brotherhoods drew heavily on the work of the French colonial ethnographer Louis Rinn on the Sanussiyya of North Africa.¹⁷ In 1905 A. Gubarevich-Radobyl'skii produced an in-depth economic comparison of the French protectorate in Tunisia and the Russian protectorate in Bukhara, concluding with a rousing invocation of the common European civilising mission of the two powers in 'barbarous Asiatic lands'.¹⁸

Russian views of British rule in India varied considerably from admiration for its technological achievements to (distinctly hypocritical) condemnation of its racism, but here too the Russians thought there were lessons to be learned.¹⁹ In the military sphere one of the clearest, so far as they were concerned, came from the 1857 rebellion, which demonstrated the foolishness of relying on 'native troops' for security, whatever the cost savings.[20] As M. D. Skobelev, the most notoriously brutal of all the Russian commanders in Central Asia, noted when disbanding the Kazakh militias established by his predecessor in Transcaspia: 'In my view it does not do to revive in them the spirit of military comradeship.'[21] The Russians exempted the local population of Turkestan from military service, banned them from owning firearms, and did all they could to ensure they never acquired knowledge of modern weaponry. They also studied British campaigns on the North-West frontier, partly to assess strategic and technological weaknesses that could perhaps be exploited in the event of a war between Britain and Russia on the Central Asian frontier, but also because it offered lessons for the chastisement of Russia's own *gortsy* ('mountain-dwellers') in Central Asia and the Caucasus.[22] On the civilian side they showed interest in Anglo-Indian methods of civil service recruitment and training: as Nil Lykoshin, a prominent Orientalist-administrator, noted wistfully in 1905: 'Administrative posts in the English colonies in material respects are better organized than in ours [...] the English Government only sends "choice" public servants to its colonies, and such can only be found at a good salary. They give civil servants in their colonies the kind of privileges that we cannot even dream about',[23] although his pleas for better training (particularly in languages) and higher salaries for Russian military administrators fell on deaf ears.[24] Anglo-Indian irrigation projects also attracted Russian attention when they began building new canals in Turkestan, as the engineer S.F. Ostrovskii wrote in 1906 that 'Yes, India is a land of wonders from the irrigation point of view, and before beginning work on the hungry steppe [North of Djizakh], we should have studied the Indian canals, which in their grandiosity are considered the first in the world: the Upper Ganges canal is thirty times larger than the Nicholas I canal in the Hungry Steppe.'[25] The Russians also studied Anglo-Indian systems of revenue collection, land surveying and tax distribution, all areas where they struggled throughout the first thirty years of their rule in Central Asia, ensuring that Turkestan ran a substantial deficit.[26] In 1913 A.I. Gippius, the governor of Ferghana Province, produced a report entitled *The resolution of the task of decentralising agriculture in British India*, which quoted, amongst others, John Stuart Mill, Sir John Strachey and Sir Henry Maine, as part of an attempt to both improve revenue collection and potentially allow Turkestan's provinces greater budget autonomy.[27] Perhaps the most comprehensive descriptions of British India in Russian were those of A.E. Snesarev and V.F. Novitskii, both staff officers who travelled there extensively, who while they condemned British rule as racist and lacking in civilising zeal, also admired its economic and technical accomplishments, and envied the way in which the British had managed to turn their colony in India into a source of world power.[28]

This grudging desire to emulate British colonial practice could result in full-blown colonial Anglophilia in some, more elevated, circles. In 1906 the well-known Russian jurist and Baltic German aristocrat Baron Boris Nolde published an article in *Vestnik Evropy*, the most important of Russia's opinion-forming 'Thick' journals, entitled 'England and her autonomous colonies'.[29] This was a detailed and admiring study of the systems of devolved government established in Britain's white settler colonies, concentrating primarily on Lord Durham's 1839 report recommending responsible Government for Canada and the granting of this by the Act of Westminster in 1867. As

David Mcdonald has argued, Nolde's primary purpose here was to emphasize the need for responsible government in Russia, with ministers appointed by and answerable to the legislature rather than the monarch.[30] However, his ideas seem to have struck a chord with at least one of his fellow Baltic Germans, Senator Count Konstantin Konstantinovich von der Pahlen, who in 1908 would be sent to Turkestan to conduct an official inspection ('*Senatorskaya Reviziya*') and make recommendations for the reform of its administration.[31] The enormous report which resulted from this contained many ideas borrowed from or inspired by the example of British India.[32] Pahlen considered Turkestan's administration to be hopelessly over-centralized: 'These insufficiencies present themselves especially clearly on comparison of our system for ruling the area with that of other Governments over Asiatic possessions, especially with the most prominent and extensive – the British Indian Colony.'[33]

Pahlen wrote that in India power was devolved to the viceroy and his council, and that this local autonomy continued down to the lowest levels of the Indian Civil Service. He wanted to see a more devolved system of government in Turkestan, with greater powers for the governor-general and, in turn, for military governors and district commandants.[34] Pahlen's recommendations on this and most other points were not adopted, but one episode in particular from his tour of inspection stands out as the pre-eminent case of attempted colonial 'borrowing' in pre-revolutionary Turkestan, namely the Commission's recommendations for the so-called 'People's Judges' (*Narodnye Sudy*) or *qazi*s who administered Islamic law under Russian auspices in Turkestan, and their attempt to draw up a single 'code' of *shari'a*. This occupies a prominent place both in the Commission's report and in Pahlen's later memoirs, and offers irresistible parallels with similar colonial legal codifications elsewhere.[35] It is also a perfect illustration of something Pahlen and his commission got almost comically wrong through relying on analogy with another colonial power's experiences. Moreover, the Commission's lack of understanding of Islamic law was arguably no greater than that of officials who had served in Turkestan all their lives: as we shall see, the Pahlen Commission chose this path largely because of advice from local orientalists, and ignored counter-advice from scholars working in St Petersburg.

II. *Qazi*s and Islamic law in colonial Turkestan

Unlike in British India, where they were abolished in 1864 and replaced with a code of Muslim personal law administered through British courts, state-appointed *qazi*s survived in Russian Turkestan until their suppression by the Bolsheviks after 1926.[36] The preservation of the Islamic judiciary in Turkestan, albeit in modified form, despite the rhetorical hostility towards Islam of many of the first generation of Russian colonial officials,[37] was an excellent example of the compromises and adjustments to local conditions that characterize all colonial regimes. In Russia, where legal pluralism was more or less the norm, Jane Burbank has described this as an aspect of an 'imperial rights regime', which sacrificed formal legal equality but conformed to local customs and needs, whether of Russian peasants or of Turkestan Muslims.[38] While this was sometimes a consequence of Russian legal pluralism, it is not clear that it was always deliberate. The preservation of Turkestan's Islamic courts owed as much to pragmatism and paranoia as to any positive or coherent colonial policy: the Russians had neither the knowledge nor the resources to create a new legal system from scratch in Central Asia after the conquest, and they feared provoking an Islamic revolt if they interfered too strongly with local customs; it also served as a clear indication of the separateness of the local population.[39] Unlike in the Volga region, however, the Russians did not create a state-sponsored Islamic hierarchy to administer Muslim courts, educational institutions and endowments, instead abolishing the most senior offices of *Qazi-Kalan* and *Sheikh ul-Islam*, and subjecting the courts to the (usually rather loose) supervision of Russian military officials.[40] This was owing to the first governor-general of Turkestan, K.P. von Kaufman's mistaken belief that in the absence of state support Islam in Turkestan would wither away and die.[41] Under this policy (known as *Ignorirovanie*), Christian missionaries were also banned from proselytizing in Turkestan.

Among the innovations introduced by the Russians to the pre-conquest judicial system was to make the post of *qazi* elected, the term being three years and the franchise restricted to so-called *pyatidesyatniki* (*ellikbosh* or *panjahbosh*), who represented groups of fifty households, a measure which Adeeb Khalid believes was designed specifically to undermine their authority as scholars, although it is unlikely that this was the conscious intention.[42] Another consequence was the creation of a reified and largely artificial distinction between the spheres of *shari'a*, which was supposed to be restricted to the sedentary population, and customary law or *'adat*, which was to be used by nomads.[43] The Turkestan Statute of 1886 had subsequently restricted the responsibilities of *qazi*s, renamed them *Narodnye Sudy* ('People's Judges') and stated that they were supposed to pass judgement in accordance with 'local custom', officially dropping the term *shari'a*.[44]

By the early 1900s von Kaufman's policy of *Ignorirovanie* was widely discredited among Russian officials, particularly after the Andijan Uprising of 1898 had supposedly revealed the continued vitality and dangerousness of Central Asian Islam. Governor-General Dukhovskoi's proposals for tighter and more intrusive regulation of Islamic institutions had been rejected, however, and no new policy had been put in their place.[45] As Paolo Sartori has shown, despite the formal policy of non-interference, the cumulative effect of Russian policy over forty years was to bring about some significant (if sometimes unintended) changes in Islamic legal practice in Central Asia, notably the eclipse of the *mufti* as an authority on Islamic law, the removal of many criminal offences from its jurisdiction, and the creation of an appellate system that encouraged the local population to use the authority of the colonial state to challenge *qazi*s' judgements.[46] Recent work on a collection of *qazi*s' judgements in the Samarkand Museum of local history suggests initial continuity of form and content, but ultimately quite substantial compositional and notarial changes, particularly from the 1890s.[47] However, what primarily concerns us here is how *qazi*s were perceived by local officials and by the Pahlen Commission, and the degree to which the Russian interpretation of problems with the Islamic judiciary and the solutions proposed for these drew on the experience of other colonial powers.

Pahlen devoted a whole volume of his report to the question of the *qazi*s in Turkestan, and another to the question of Islamic and customary law in the region.[48] By and large the report's criticisms of the *qazis*' courts echoed those made by administrators, the Russian press and legal reformers over the previous twenty years.⁴⁹ Almost from the outset of Russian rule in Turkestan, the military bureaucracy had been bombarded with petitions complaining of corrupt decisions, ignorance of the *shari'a* or electoral fraud by Islamic judges. In 1908 the Samarkand provincial administration alone received forty-four such petitions relating to *qazis*, and they were a common feature of the workings of the 'Native administration', something that swallowed an immense amount of official time.⁵⁰ The report strongly criticized the electoral system in this, as in other, branches of the 'native administration', stating that it had simply turned the appointment of judges into a battleground for party intrigues, the prize being the bribes that could be extorted during a three-year term of office.⁵¹

> One of the popular judges of the town of Samarkand, in a note about the popular courts which he gave to *me*, openly attests, that the *pyatidesyatniki*, pursuing profit, bring in as popular judges individuals in no way worthy of this position. The electoral expenses grow year by year; those who have acquired the position of popular judge, in order to get back the money they have spent, resort to evil practices and decide matters incorrectly; those candidates who have failed to become judges, and having no means of returning the money they borrowed before the election, submit petitions about the bad faith of the electors and foment accusations of corruption against their successful rivals.⁵²

The report noted that *qazis*' pay continued to be linked to the value of the cases they were judging, at levels fixed far too low to remove the incentive to corruption,⁵³ and often varying widely from district to district. Pahlen claimed that many levied fees three or four times as high as those they received from the state, and frequently took bribes in addition.⁵⁴ The sheer number of complaints received by the Russian authorities, the Commission's report concluded, betrayed a deep discontent amongst the population with the *qazis* and their courts. Pahlen did not pay a great deal of attention to this question in his memoirs, referring to corruption among the *qazis* only in the context of the unreformed judicial system in the protectorate of Bukhara, about which he can have known very little.⁵⁵

The reliability of the Pahlen Commission's conclusions on these points is debatable. My own research on Samarkand revealed numerous apparently proven cases of corruption amongst *qazis* in the documentary record, although these of course were also produced by and for colonial officials, and I may have given them too much credence.⁵⁶ The report's conclusions were based not only on reports from local officials, but on the petitions the Commission itself received directly from large groups of the local population during its tour of Turkestan. Three lengthy ones came 'from the inhabitants of Samarkand', and were highly conservative in character. One of them spent six pages complaining about the privileged status of Jews under Russian rule, claiming that they were selling diseased meat to Muslims, and asking that all those who had arrived in Samarkand from Bukhara, Persia or Afghanistan since the Russian conquest be expelled, and that the *qazis* be given jurisdiction over them again. The other two were largely concerned with securing the integrity of *waqf* endowments, and all were probably instigated by the Samarkand *'ulama*.[57] Two petitions from Chimbai in the Amu-Darya region (modern-day Karakalpakstan) criticized the election of *qazi*s and called for a revival of the office of *Ra'is* (an official who under the pre-conquest regime had been responsible for inflicting corporal punishment on those found guilty of crimes against religion), and for a greater role to be given once again to *mufti*s, interpreters of Islamic law who, they claimed, were increasingly being ignored by corrupt and venal *qazi*s:

> In the name of all the inhabitants of the Chimbai district, we inform your radiance that in earlier times there existed *ra'is*es and *mufti*s, to whose responsibility fell the supervision over the correct interpretation of the *shari'a* by *mufti*s, the decisions of the popular judges, marriages, and the verification of shopkeepers' and bakers' weights. Now these positions have been abolished, because of which each of the officials and tradesmen mentioned above do as they please. And because of this for the good of the people we request you to revive the abolished position of *ra'is*, if there is that possibility.[58]

> We, Muslims, on the basis of the published laws of Muhammad, from ancient times have had particular religious officials, *mufti*s, *qazi*s and *ra'is*es. From the conquest of the region by the Governor-General and his commanders it was declared to us that the order of things which existed from ancient times would be left without changes, because of which we were very glad and prayed for his health. Indeed the old way of doing things survived for a few years without changes – the *qazi*s were appointed from amongst individuals, who knew the *shari'a* well, the *mufti*s and *ra'is*es existed, thanks to which the well-being of Muslims was high. At the present time the *qazi*s are chosen for three-year terms by *pyatidesyatniki*, and the *pyatidesyatniki* in most cases are illiterate and immoral and choose for the duties of People's Judge individuals who resemble them – entirely ignorant of the *shari'a*, thanks to which there is a noticeable decline of Muslims from the religio-moral point of view.[59]

These were also presumably inspired by conservative *'ulama*, and there is, of course, no way of knowing how representative such views were, or the degree to which they had been tailored to match what the Russians wanted to hear. On the other hand, scholars working with sources in Turki and Persian have found very similar criticisms of the *qazis*' courts in reformist Muslim journals such as *Al-Islah*, and it seems patronising to suppose that these are no more than reflections of a colonial discourse.[60] What seems fairly clear is that factionalism was rife in judicial elections, and that increasingly many *qazi*s could attain office, not because of their qualifications as *ulama* and jurists, but because they were able to command the support of a powerful group in local society, although considerably more research is needed on this point.

Such appeals for the upholding of the *shari'a* and greater control of the *qazi*s appear to have struck a chord with Pahlen, although he was not prepared to contemplate returning to the pre-conquest judicial system or reviving the *ra'is*, and dismissed such suggestions as being inspired by Panislamic sentiments.[61] There was an alternative solution available to him: the judicial expert I.I. Kraft had argued strongly in 1898 that Turkestan's judiciary should no longer be regarded as a special case, but be brought into line with the rest of the Empire: *qazis* and the *shari'a* should be abolished altogether.[62] However, the Commission fell short of proposing anything so radical and potentially disruptive. Pahlen had little sympathy with advocates of purely military rule in Turkestan, still less with Islam, and had he felt that sufficient progress had been made towards *grazhdanstvennost'* (civic values) in Turkestan over the previous forty years, he would have recommended the abolition of the popular courts – in some of his unpublished notes he regretted that lack of funds and other considerations made this impossible, as they were a source of Muslim 'fanaticism' which prevented the native population from fully appreciating the benefits of Russian rule.[63] Fundamentally, Pahlen believed that Turkestan was still a region with very particular, colonial problems, which required colonial solutions,[64] and like Senator F.K. Giers, who had conducted the last inspection of Turkestan twenty-five years earlier, he decided that abolition of the *shari'a* courts would be premature.[65] Apart from anything else, the Turkestan administration simply lacked sufficient personnel with even rudimentary legal training to be able to take over and 'Russify' the *qazis*' role.[66]

Instead the report suggested increasing the staff of the Russian district courts and allowing a representative from them, trained in Muslim law, to preside over the congresses of *qazis*. While deploring the corruption of the electoral system, the Commission reluctantly concluded that Russian district commandants lacked the time and specialist knowledge to be able to appoint judges themselves, and instead advocated a more direct electoral system, with one candidate being chosen in each village by the heads of households. It also recommended that *qazis* be paid regular salaries, on a par with those of native canton administrators – that is, 500 roubles a year, plus a total of 1,400 roubles for expenses related to their duties, and suggested that it be rendered easier for those classified as *tuzemtsy*, 'aliens' under Russian law, to acquire full citizenship and thus escape the jurisdiction of the Islamic courts altogether.[67] However, the most ambitious aim of the Pahlen Commission was to create a single, written *shari'a* code for the use of all *qazis* in Turkestan, in place of the ad hoc system of precedent and local custom which had hitherto obtained. This was intended both to place greater constraints on *qazis* to deliver judgements in accordance with universal norms, and to harmonize the system of Islamic law used in Turkestan with the General Laws of the Russian Empire.[68] What is striking, however, is that rather than looking either to all-imperial legal norms or to earlier attempts to regulate Islamic law within Russia, the Pahlen Commission's attempt at codification would be borrowed from the experience of another European colonial power – British India.

III. Colonial codifications of the *shari'a*

Since the introduction of the 1886 Turkestan Statute, in theory the *qazis* of Turkestan had not been formally obliged to follow *shari'a*, as the relevant articles in the new administrative law simply referred to an ill-defined 'local custom'. It is doubtful whether this made a great deal of difference in practice (it was really no more than a change in nomenclature, mirroring that from *qazi* to 'People's Judge'). Islamic law in all parts of the world is a mixture of the textually-based (the Qu'ran and canonical compilations of Hadith) and local custom, and *qazi*s have always had an important interpretative role to play.[69] The *shari'a* is 'no codification of the law in any sense, nor can there ever be one'.[70] This is something that was rarely understood by colonial officials, however, and the Pahlen report considered the change in wording to be of great importance, and the source of much arbitrariness and corruption.[71] The report demonstrated an absolute conviction that, before the conquest, amongst the settled population the *shari'a* had constituted a strict and uniform code, while customary law was 'rudimentary'.[72] This backward but consistent system, the report went on to argue, had been progressively eroded under Russian rule by: 'A whole range of innovations, so that on the pretext of preserving the settled population's popular judges they were given new courts which were entirely different in their organisation, together with which no real measures to reduce their fanaticism were introduced, nor any to remove the barriers to a *rapprochement* with the Russians.'[73]

What was needed was a 'return' to the consistency of the pre-conquest period, to restore Islamic justice in Turkestan to its former purity and to harmonize it, so far as possible, with Russian law. As by this date *qazi*s dealt primarily with matters of property and family law, the first step was to create a recognized 'code' in these areas which could be referred to both by Russian judges and by the interested parties in any case in order to ensure that the *qazi*s' judgements were in full conformity with it.

> The creators of the 1886 statute did not decide to give for the direction of the 'People's Judge' a codex that would be accessible to general understanding, adapted to local demands and in agreement with the basic principles of Russian law, but restricted themselves to the publication of article 210, enabling the People's Judges, both of the nomadic and sedentary population, to decide matters 'on the basis of custom', entirely overlooking that the settled population do not possess judicial customs, as these are comprised entirely within the written regulations of Muslim law – the *shari'a*.
>
> Accordingly the reorganization of the 'People's Judges', in the sense of the creation of appeals and cassation authorities linked to the general courts, in view of the obvious impossibility of altering the currently existing rule of the *shari'a*, rooted unshakeably amongst the people, it is essential both for the Russian courts, and for those people who are interested, the possibility of mastering the substantive laws [*material'nyi zakon*] employed by the People's Judges, and until now only known to them. Only by this means, in the view of the Inspecting Senator, will it be possible to attain the control over them both by the administrative and judicial powers, and by the population itself, which is essential for the regular delivery of justice, and banish that disgraceful judicial arbitrariness, sheltered by the sanction of Russian power, which it has fallen to the inspection to establish.[74]

Pahlen's was not the first attempt to 'codify the *shar'ia*' in the Russian Empire: indeed, given how widespread a tendency this was amongst colonial regimes, the fact that such a measure had never been successfully implemented in Turkestan is an effective measure of the weakness of the Russian colonial state.[75] There was already a lengthy Russian tradition of *shari'a* scholarship at Kazan University, represented in particular by the figure of Mirza Alexander Kazem-Bek, a Persian from Resht who had converted to Christianity and had produced translations of a number of standard juridical works directly from the Arabic. The use of these by the muftiate in Orenburg had apparently led to a hardening of the norms of *shari'a* in the Volga region and the fringes of the Steppe.[76] However, the most important 'code' of Muslim law used by the colonial authorities in Turkestan was not based upon any of this material. Instead, it was a translation of a text called the *Hidaya* edited by N.I. Grodekov, the then governor of Syr-Darya Province, who would later go on to become governor-general of Turkestan in 1906–8. This was first published in 1893, and then reprinted in 1905.[77] The Orientalist N.P. Ostroumov, the principal advisor on matters Islamic to successive governors-general of Turkestan, was an enthusiastic advocate of its use, noting regretfully that owing to a very short print-run even the second edition had rapidly become unavailable.[78] This was partly, perhaps, because a copy of Grodekov's *Hidaya* had been placed in all provincial libraries in Turkestan for consultation by military administrators.[79]

Scholarly opinion was far from united on the merits of the work, however: in 1905 the commission overseeing the expansion of Oriental language instruction amongst Russian officers had also suggested teaching them the rudiments of Muslim law using Grodekov's edition of the *Hidaya*, a proposal which the St Petersburg University Orientalist V.V. Barthold attacked in forthright terms:

> The *Hidaya* in its translation (from English) by N. I. Grodekov, [...] presents, in the commission's opinion, 'a fundamental work and important juridical guidance'. We can set this opinion against the judgement of Professor V. R. Rosen,[80] in whose words 'speaking definitively, there was no need to waste time and money on the *Hidaya*, as the vast mass of the casuistic material in it is capable only of crushing the desire of non-specialists to study the *shari'a* [...] Unfortunately, it is entirely possible that a future administrator, having completed a course in Muslim law according to the programme recommended by the Commission, will come to judge the legal views of the natives according to the Testament of Timur, as laid down centuries ago in India, or even, armed with the four volumes of the *Hidaya*, lodge protests against every decision of the popular judges, if they are not in agreement with the conditions of that book.[81]

Barthold had two principal objections to Grodekov's *Hidaya*, which he would later summarize in his *History of Cultural Life in Turkestan*.[82] Firstly he understood, as most colonial officials did not, that within the Islamic legal tradition a single commentary, however distinguished, should not be interpreted as a binding, inflexible and unchanging code. In a pioneering critique which anticipated Saidian *Orientalism* by seventy years, Barthold ridiculed local Russian 'experts' on Islam such as A. Shishov and O. Shkapskii for their belief that *shari'a* could be pinned down in this way, and their expectation that Muslims in modern Turkestan would live their lives precisely in accordance with ancient religious texts[83]:

Past experience allows us to apprehend that those who use these texts will look on the provisions laid down in them not as theories derived from the distant lives of jurist-theologians, re-worked in the calm of their cells and, with the exception of the fields of family and inheritance law, almost nowhere applicable to real life, but as generally recognized, really existing juridical norms in everyday use. Such a misunderstanding has been disposed of among academics, but among non-specialists continues to reign. One can bring forward many examples of how these preconceptions render the correct understanding of modern life and its historic origins more difficult.[84]

Secondly, Barthold had considerable reservations about the text itself. As the Russians were aware, the *Hidaya* was in origin a twelfth-century legal digest by the famous Central Asian jurist Burhan ud-din 'Ali ibn Abu Bakr al-Marghinani, a native of Marghelan in the Ferghana valley who died in Samarkand in AD 1197, and whose descendants had monopolized the positions of *Sheikh ul-Islam* and *Qazi-Kalan* of the city under the Timurids;[85] his tomb was still an important landmark in the early nineteenth century.[86] However, the text of the *Hidaya* available to the colonial authorities in Turkestan had a rather distant relationship to the original. As Barthold had noted, Grodekov's edition was a translation not from the Arabic original, but from English. This was because the *Hidaya* had become the founding text of Anglo-Muhammadan jurisprudence in India. It had originally been translated into English in 1791 by Charles Hamilton, not from Arabic, but from a Persian version drawn up at the behest of Warren Hastings by four Calcutta *munshi*s, using an unknown Arabic original. It had various sections added to it from another text called the *Sirajiyyah*[87] to fill gaps covering property and inheritance law, and was thus turned into a strict code heavily influenced by British jurisprudential ideas.[88] The Russian edition reproduced this almost without alteration, also translating Hamilton's original preface, with Grodekov's contribution limited to a very occasional explanatory footnote.

The history of the *Hidaya*, and the manner in which it was remade into 'Anglo-Muhammadan law' is thus a classic case study in the creation of 'colonial knowledge',[89] although it should be noted that a similar legal reform had been pushed through (with rather greater success) by Amir 'Abd ur-Rahman Khan's modernizing state in Afghanistan.[90] There, however, they were using the Arabic original, whilst Grodekov's *Hidaya* was really an Anglo-Indian text, and unlikely to correspond very closely to Islamic justice as it was practised in Turkestan. It did carry, however, the imprimatur of what was widely acknowledged to be the most successful European colonial regime, that of the British in India, which seems to be what caused Pahlen to overlook or reject earlier models from within the Empire, such as the (broadly successful) codification of '*adat* in Daghestan.[91] In Turkestan, the opinion of N.P. Ostroumov counted for more than that of St Petersburg-based Orientalists such as Barthold and Rosen, and he did not see any objections either to the use of the *Hidaya* or to the project of codification. In a series of articles which appeared in *Turkestanskie Vedomosti* in 1909, just as the Pahlen Commission was drawing up its new 'code', Ostroumov outlined his understanding of what was meant by '*shari'a*', which helps to explain why Pahlen and other Russian officials assumed that what was used in India would also be appropriate for Turkestan.

> [...] the *shariat*, which is applied identically to popular life in Russia, Bukhara, Afghanistan, Egypt, Syria, India, Java, Arabia, Algeria, China – its teachings are acknowledged in every land of Islam [...] in other words: Turkestani, Bukharan, Turkish and other Muslims conduct themselves in their creed and in everyday life by a single law, not by different codes as do the Russians, French, English etc.[92]

Pahlen's memoirs reveal that he was entirely in agreement with this view of the *shari'a* as a uniform 'code' which applied throughout the Muslim world: 'the fact that the Hanafite sect [...] ruled the medresehs in both India and Turkestan, so that the same interpretation of the Muhammadan faith was practised in both places, was of very great assistance in this task'[93] and British India – specifically Anglo-Muhammadan Law – was to become the model for Pahlen's Turkestan reforms. He appears to have been unaware of the *shari'a* scholarship of Mirza Kazem-Bek, and although instead he made some use of Grodekov's *Hidaya*,[94] Pahlen decided that on its own even this text would not be sufficient:

> Having permitted the native population to regulate itself according to its own laws, Russian power, in order to avoid the reproach of sanctioning injustice and arbitrariness, not only has the right, but is obliged to oversee the application of juridical norms. Pursuing this aim, the British government, with a view to establishing supervision over native justice in India, and recognized as essential for Indian judges the *Hidaya* of Burhan-Eddin-Ali [sic] (who lived in the twelfth century) as the most authoritative of the books, constituting the *shari'a*.
>
> However, neither the *Hidaya*, nor any of the other collections that constitute the *shari'a*, can settle all or even the majority of the manifestations of legal life that are subject to standardization. The majority of these collections are monographs on separate legal questions, and in general diffusion only separate parts are used, or even sometimes only separate judgements; other Russian and foreign works on Muslim law present theoretical research, the creation of a system of law on the basis of this or that collection of a separate Muslim scholar.
>
> At the same time, the independent creation, with the aid of a congress of those knowledgeable in the law, of a complete compilation of the laws of the *shari'a* would be an unrealisable aim; only the scrutiny of a pre-existing collection, put together in a manner as close as possible to the existing judicial situation, and the introduction of corrections and additions, would seem to be the sort of work that would be feasible for a group of experts called together by the Inspecting Senator.
>
> Accordingly, a collection of Muslim Law of the Hanafi School currently used in India compiled by Professor Roland Wilson of the Department of Indian Law at Cambridge University was put forward as the basis of this work.[95]

Anglo-Muhammadan law thus became the basis for Pahlen's proposed codification of Turkestani *shari'a*, moving even further away from the Central Asian origins of the

Hidaya.⁹⁶ This was unfortunate: leaving aside the degree to which Indian Islam and *shari'a* had been affected by local conditions, Wilson's code had been produced to meet specific Anglo-Indian administrative needs, and to view it as a convenient summary of the *shari'a* that would apply to all Sunni Hanafis, as Pahlen did, was inviting confusion.

IV. Conclusion: rejecting the colonial *shari'a*

In May 1909 a congress was held in Tashkent to debate this issue – a consultative process quite characteristic of Russian statecraft, but also reflecting the 'non-European foundations' of Russian rule in Turkestan, and the colonial regime's dependence on elite collaborators and their specialized knowledge.⁹⁷ Together with fifteen representatives from the local administration, eight Russian judges and four education officials were invited, and twenty-nine *qazis* and Muslim jurists from Samarkand, Syr-Darya and Ferghana provinces were selected by the military governors and prosecutors of the regional courts to attend.⁹⁸ All 500 paragraphs of the text Pahlen had prepared were exhaustively examined over eight days, which he recalled as a great success: 'I must here place on record how immensely impressed I was by the earnest work of the mullahs [...] Never had it been my privilege to preside over a gathering so keen to accomplish the task set before it.'⁹⁹

However, Pahlen's recollections on this point were rose-tinted. The correspondent who described the congress for the liberal daily newspaper *Turkestanskii Kur'er*, one Antonovich, produced an account strongly at odds both with the conclusions of the report and with Pahlen's memoirs:

> The principal aim of the congress is to establish whether or not the translation of the *Hidaya* is accurate, and to what degree the *Hidaya* is in agreement with local customs [...] This *Hidaya* is a book of the Hanafi doctrine, written in the Arabic language in India in the nineteenth century, when the British were already ruling there. There is no doubt that the book shows clear signs of Anglicization. The *Hidaya* was translated into English from Persian, and from English into Russian, thus the Russian translation, through the particularities of language [...] inevitably suffers from gross insufficiencies and distortions.
>
> In Turkestan the *Hidaya* is largely unknown, and when at the first session they began to read out articles from this book, the 'scholars' looked blank, their faces became gloomy and they curtly uttered just the one word: 'No'.¹⁰⁰

While Antonovich was wrong to suggest that the *Hidaya* itself was little-known in Turkestan, as we have seen the text produced by Pahlen had only the most distant relationship to the original. It was to prove very difficult to persuade the jurists of Turkestan to accept a bastardized form of Islamic law codified by Englishmen in India. Antonovich noted various interpellations made in the *Hidaya* by its English editors, and the fact that British policy towards Islam in India had not been successful in defusing tensions and bringing about peace. He also argued that the proposed reform was viewed with misgivings by the wider population as well, and could perhaps provoke precisely the sort of 'fanatical' reaction that had worried the Russians since the Andijan uprising: 'The first day of the Congress passed very guardedly. Neither the Muslims, nor the Russians understood what its purpose was. A suspicion grew amongst the Muslims, that a Russian official had decided to re-create Muslim laws, and at every crossroads in the town, in the bazaars and *chaikhanas* the Sarts talked exclusively about the Congress.'[101]

Although the rumours in the bazaars had no immediate serious consequences, the congress ended on a sour note: 'There was much surprise, when the *qazis* announced that they had been insulted by Count Pahlen's opening speech, in which he had suggested that they, the *qazis*, were susceptible to the temptation of bribes, and asked him politely to take back his assertions.'[102] Pahlen had clearly aired some of the suspicions that would later appear in his report. The official account of the results of the conference was also less fulsome than Pahlen himself seems to have remembered, stating that roughly half of the articles in the translated code had proved acceptable to those assembled, while the remainder, relating to property and family law, required substantial revision or were entirely unsuitable. The conclusion was that this was still an 'unfinished work', and it was never destined to be completed.[103] The Russian text of Pahlen's code printed in the report was circulated to the Russian military courts in Turkestan, and, as Pahlen put it, the population at large were 'given access' to the mysteries of the *shari'a* through a translation into Turki.[104] Pahlen admitted that what resulted was an unofficial, non-binding collection of laws, although he claimed that it went into several editions as a guide for administrators and judges.[105] Paolo Sartori has demonstrated that the Russian colonial context did produce significant changes in the practice of Islamic law in Central Asia, but none of these can be traced to Pahlen's new code.[106]

The Pahlen Commission's recommendations on Islamic law thus ended in a fiasco, which perhaps was only to be expected. The failure of such a textbook attempt at the creation of 'colonial knowledge' tells us a good deal about the limits of Russian power in Turkestan when compared to British India or French Algeria, where the colonial regimes were able to make much more sweeping changes to the theory and practice of Islamic jurisprudence.[107] What is so striking about this episode, however, is that even when the Russian colonial administration had substantial resources of specialized knowledge close to hand, in the form of work on Islamic jurisprudence produced by the Oriental faculties of Kazan and St Petersburg Universities, not to mention observations of the actual practice of Islamic law in Turkestan, they chose instead to rely on wholesale borrowing from another (by implication more successful, experienced and prestigious) colonial power, British India. The degree to which these two powers, despite their political rivalries and cultural differences, were essentially engaged in a common colonial enterprise in Asia, could hardly be more clearly illustrated.

Notes

1 Count Konstantin Konstantinovich Pahlen, *Mission to Turkestan. Being the Memoirs of Count K. K. Pahlen 1908–1909,* trans. N.J. Couriss and ed. Richard A. Pierce (New York: Oxford UP, 1964), p. 81.

2. See Theodore von Laue, *Sergei Witte and the Industrialisation of Russia* (New York: Columbia University Press, 1963); J.N. Westwood, *A History of Russian Railways* (London: Allen & Unwin, 1964), p. 45; Peter Gatrell, *Government, Industry and Rearmament in Russia, 1900–1914* (Cambridge: Cambridge UP, 1994), pp. 234–43.
3. See the essays by S.V. Timchenko and V. Germanova on, respectively, modern Kazakh and modern Uzbek historiography, which make up appendices 1 and 2 of S. Abashin, D. Arapov and N. Bekmakhanova, *Tsentral'naya Aziya v Sostave Rossiiskoi Imperii* (Moscow: Novoe Literaturnoe Obozrenie, 2007), pp. 338–81.
4. Lowell Tillett, *The Great Friendship: Soviet Historians on the Non-Russian Nationalities* (Chapel Hill: University of North Carolina Press, 1969); G.A. Khidoyatov, *Iz istorii Anglo-Russkikh otnoshenii v Srednei Azii v kontse XIX Veka* (Tashkent: 'FAN', 1969).
5. Lauren Benton, Law and empire in global perspective: introduction, *The American Historical Review*, 117, 4 (2012), p. 1098.
6. The temporary statute drawn up in 1867 was revised in 1886 and further amended in 1900. Semirechie was regulated under the Steppe Statute of 1891. All can be found in the *Polnoe Sobranie Zakonov Rossiiskoi Imperii* (*Complete Collection of the Laws of the Russian Empire – PSZ*): *PSZ* Sob. 2, Vol. XLII Otd.1 (1867), No.44831; *PSZ* Sob. 3, Vol. VI (1886) No. 3814; *PSZ* Sob. 3, Vol. XI (1891) No. 7574.
7. Adeeb Khalid, Culture and power in colonial Turkestan, *Cahiers d'Asie Centrale* 17/18, in: S. Gorshenina and S. Abashin (eds) *Le Turkestan Russe, un colonie comme les autres?* (Tashkent-Paris: IFEAC, 2009), p. 418.
8. Willard Sunderland, The ministry of Asiatic Russia: the colonial office that never was but might have been; Peter Holquist, 'In accord with state interests and the people's wishes': The technocratic ideology of imperial Russia's resettlement administration, *Slavic Review*, 69, 1 (2010), pp. 120–50, 151–79.
9. Alexander Morrison, Metropole, colony and imperial citizenship in the Russian Empire, *Kritika: Explorations in Russian and Eurasian History*, 13, 2 (2012), pp. 327–64.
10. G.N. Curzon, *Russia in Central Asia in 1889 and the Anglo-Russian Question* (London: Longmans, Green & Co, 1889) p. 12.
11. Most famously in the account by Agriculture Minister A.V. Krivoshein of his visit to Turkestan in 1912, in which he laid out a grandiose vision for its more thorough economic exploitation: A.V. Krivoshein, *Zapiska Glavnoupravliaiushchago Zemleustroistvom i Zemledeliem o poezdke v Turkestanskii krai v 1912 godu* (St Petersburg: Gos. Tip., 1912)
12. For a perspective that incorporates insights drawn from other empires and postcolonial scholarship see in particular Virginia Martin, *Law and Custom in the Steppe: The Kazakhs of the Middle Horde and Russian Colonialism in the Nineteenth Century* (Richmond: Curzon Press, 2001); Jeff Sahadeo, *Russian Colonial Society in Tashkent, 1865–1923* (Bloomington, Ind.: Indiana UP, 2007).
13. F.H. Skrine and E. Denison Ross, *The Heart of Asia: A History of Russian Turkestan and the Central Asian Khanates from the Earliest Times* (London: Methuen & Co. 1899), p. 414.
14. Alex Marshall, *The Russian General Staff and Asia* (London: Routledge, 2006), pp. 131–62.
15. Vladimir Bobrovnikov, Russkii Kavkaz i Frantsuzskii Alzhir: sluchainoe skhodstvo ili obmen opytom kolonial'nogo stroitelstvo, in: Martin Aust, Ricarda Vulpius and Alexei Miller (eds) *Imperium inter pares: rol' transferov v istorii Rossiiskoi Imperii 1700–1917* (Moscow: Novoe Literaturnoe Obozrenie, 2010), pp. 182–209.

16 A. Kuropatkin, Alzhiriya. Voenno-Statisticheskii Obzor, *Voennyi Sbornik* (*VS*), 3 (1876), pp. 186–236; 4, pp. 391–416; 5, pp. 160–188; 6, pp. 384–406; 7, pp. 177–204; A.N. Kuropatkin, *Alzhiriya* (St Petersburg: Tip. V.A. Poletiki, 1877).
17 V. I. Yarovoi-Rabskii, Kratkii obzor sovremennogo sostoyaniya i deyatel'nosti musul'manskogo dukhovenstva; E.T. Smirnov, Dervishizm v Turkestane, and Dzhikhad i Gazavat, in V.I. Yarovoi-Rabskii (ed.), *Sbornik Materialov po Musul'manstvu*, vol. 1 (St Petersburg: Tip Turkestanskogo Voennogo Okruga, 1899), pp. 22, 39, 49–71, 101–28; Louis Rinn, *Marabouts et Khouan: Etude sur l'Islam en Algerie* (Algiers: Adolphe Jourdan, 1884). On Rinn see Jean-Louis Triaud, *La Légende Noire de la Sanûssiya. Une Confrérie Musulmane sous le regard Français (1840–1930)* (Paris: Maison des Sciences de l'Homme, 1995), Vol. I, pp. 347–61.
18 A. Gubarevich-Radobyl'skii, *Ekonomicheskii ocherk Bukhary i Tunisa. Opyt' sravnitel'nogo issledovaniya dvukh sistem protekorata* (St Petersburg: Tip. V. Kirshbaum, 1905), pp. 200–1.
19 Alexander Morrison, Russian rule in Turkestan and the example of British India, *Slavonic & East European Review* 84, 4 (2006), pp. 666–707; Martin Aust, Rossiia i Velikobritaniia: vneshniaia politika i obrazy imperii ot Krymskoi Voiny do pervoi Mirovoi Voiny, *Imperium inter pares*, pp. 244–265.
20 N.P. Ignat'ev, military attaché in London, to the war minister A.V. Dolgorukov 26 July 1857, in P.M. Shastitko (ed.), *Russko-Indiiskie Otnosheniya v XIX v.* (Moscow: Vostochnaya Literatura, 1997), pp. 105–18; K. L'vovich, Ocherk Vozmushcheniya Sipaev v Ost-Indii, *VS* (1858), No.1, pp. 107–38; Baron A. Tizengauzen, Voenno-Statisticheskii Ocherk Britanskoi Indii, *VS* (1887), No.1, pp. 152–66; No. 2, pp. 278–305.
21 A. N. Maslov, *Zavoevanie Akhal-Teke*. (St Petersburg: A. Suvorin, 1887), p. 4.
22 M. Grulev, Ocherk Vosstanii na Severo-Zapadnom Granitse Indii v 1897g., *VS* (1899), 1, pp. 180–212; 2, pp. 405–30; 3, pp. 187–210; 4, pp. 442–40; 5, pp. 210–28; G.I. Nostits, *Vosstanie Gortsev na severo-zapadnom granitse Indii* (St Petersburg: Tip. Shtaba Voisk Gvardii, 1901).
23 N. Lykoshin, O znanii tuzemnykh narechii, in I.D. Yagello (ed.), *Sbornik Materialov po voprosu ob izuchenii tuzemnykh yazykov sluzhashchimi po voenno-narodnomu upravleniyu Turkestanskogo Kraya* (Tashkent: Tip. Sht. Turk. Voen. Okrug, 1905), p. 95.
24 Alexander Morrison, Sufism, Panislamism and information panic. Nil Sergeevich Lykoshin and the aftermath of the Andijan Uprising, *Past & Present*, 214 (Feb. 2012), pp. 292–6.
25 S.F. Ostrovskii to the Russian Consul in Bombay, A.A. Polovtsvov (n.d., 1906), in P. M. Shastitko (ed.), *Russko-Indiiskie Otnosheniya v 1900–1917g.* (Moscow: Vostochnaya Literatura, 1999), p. 201.
26 Beatrice Penati, Notes on the birth of Russian Turkestan's fiscal system. A view from the Fergana oblast, *Journal of the Economic and Social History of the Orient*, 53, 5 (2010), pp. 739–69; idem, Beyond technicalities: land assessment and land tax in Russian Turkestan (ca. 1880–1917), *Jahrbücher für Geschichte Osteuropas* 59, 1 (2011), pp. 1–27.
27 Reshenie zadachi detsentrilizatsii zemskogo khozyaistva v Britanskoi Indii, 30 September 1913, Central State Archive of the Republic of Uzbekistan (TsGARUz), Fond I-1, Op. 27, D. 1526, ll. 34–6.
28 V.F. Novitskii, *Voennye Ocherki Indii* (St Petersburg: Tip. Shtaba Voisk Gvardii, 1899); A.E. Snesarev, *Indiya kak Glavnyi Faktor v Sredne-Aziatskom Voprose* (St Petersburg: A. Suvorin, 1906). Snesarev also edited a collection of articles and translations on the

regions surrounding Turkestan which was an important source of information on India for staff officers: A.E. Snesarev (ed.), *Svedeniya kasayushchiyasya Stran, sopredel'nykh s Turkestanskim Voennym Okrugom* (Tashkent: Tip. Shtaba Turk. Voennogo Okruga 1898-1900), 19 vols.

29 B.E. Nol'de, Angliia i ee avtonomnye kolonii, *Vestnik Evropy*, 9, (1906), pp. 5-67; on Nolde see Peter Holquist, Dilemmas of a progressive administrator: Baron Boris Nolde, *Kritika* 7, 2 (2006), pp. 241-73. The 'thick' journals such as *Otechestvennye Zapiski* or the War Ministry's *Voennyi Sbornik* usually appeared monthly, and carried a mixture of historical and philosophical articles, fiction and contemporary commentary. While their circulation was fairly small (between 5,000 and 10,000 subscribers) they played a vital role in Russian intellectual life. See Robert E. Belknap, Survey of Russian journals 1840-1880, in Deborah A. Martinsen (ed.), *Literary Journals in Imperial Russia* (Cambridge: Cambridge UP, 1998), pp. 91-116.

30 David Mcdonald, Whig history with a Russian accent: B.E. Nol'de, Russian liberalism, and the problem of responsible government, 1906, unpublished MS, cited with the kind permission of the author.

31 Senator Gofmeister Graf Konstantin Konstantinovitch Palen, *Otchet po Revizii Turkestanskago Kraya, proizvedennoi po VYSOCHAISHEMU Poveleniyu* (St Petersburg: Senatskaya Tipografiya, 1910-11), 21 vols; for a brief summary of some of the report's findings in English see D.S.M. Williams, Imperial Russian rule in Turkestan: the Pahlen Investigation, 1908-09, *Asian Affairs*, 2, 2 (1971), pp. 173-9.

32 On the background and findings of the Pahlen Commission's inspection see Alexander Morrison, 'Sowing the seed of national strife in this alien region': The Pahlen Report and *Pereselenie* in Turkestan, 1908-1910, *Acta Slavica Iaponica*, 31 (2012), pp. 1-29; idem, The Pahlen Commission and the re-establishment of rectitude in Transcaspia, 1908-1909, *monde(s)*, 4 (2013), pp. 45-64.

33 Kratkii Vsepoddanneishii Doklad K.K. Palena o revizii Turkestanskogo Kraya. Chernovik, 1909 Russian State Historical Archive (RGIA), F.1396, Op. 1, D. 437, ll. 31-3.

34 Staryi Stepnyak, Smeloe Predlozhenie, *Zemshchina*, 70 (1909), in: *Turkestanskii Sbornik*, 515, pp. 177-8.

35 See Bernard Cohn, Law and the colonial state in India, in: *Colonialism and its forms of Knowledge* (Princeton, N.J.: Princeton UP, 1996), pp. 57-75; I have already considered this episode briefly in A.S. Morrison, *Russian Rule in Samarkand 1868-1910. A Comparison with British India* (Oxford: Oxford UP, 2008), pp. 274-82. See further Adeeb Khalid, *The Politics of Muslim Cultural Reform. Jadidism in Central Asia* (Berkeley, Calif.: University of California Press, 1998), p. 70; Paolo Sartori, An overview of Tsarist policy on Islamic courts in Turkestan: its genealogy and its effects, in: Abashin and Gorshenina (eds), *Le Turkestan Russe*, pp. 492-4.

36 Adeeb Khalid, *Islam after Communism: Religion and Politics in Central Asia* (Berkeley, Calif.: University of California Press, 2007), pp. 71-3. There were active campaigns among Indian Muslims to revive the *qazis*' judicial role and have them appointed by the state: Robert Ivermee, Shari'at and Muslim community in colonial Punjab, 1865-1885, *Modern Asian Studies*, 48, 4 (2014), pp. 1068-95.

37 See, for instance, L.F. Kostenko, *Srednyaya Aziya i vodvorenie v nei Russkoi grazhdanstvennosti* (St Petersburg: Tip. B. Bezobrazov, 1871), p. 85; Gen.-Ad't. K. P. fon-Kaufman, *Proekt Vsepoddanneishego Otcheta Gen.-Ad'yutanta fon-Kaufmana po Grazhdanskomu Upravleniyu* (St Petersburg: Voennaya Tip., 1885), p. 10.

38 Jane Burbank, An imperial rights regime. Law and citizenship in the Russian Empire, *Kritika* 7, 3 (2006), pp. 397-431.

39 An interesting contemporary assessment of Russian motivations is to be found in Eugene Schuyler, *Turkistan. Notes on a Journey in Russian Turkestan, Khokand, Bukhara and Kuldja* (London: Sampson, Lowe & Marston, 1876), vol. I, p. 168. On the 'institutionalization of difference' through the Islamic courts see Khalid, 'Culture and power', p. 423.

40 On the supervision of the courts see Sartori, An overview of Tsarist policy, pp. 488–92; in some cases (where Tatar officers who understood the local language were employed) such supervision was more than merely nominal.

41 And not, as Robert Crews asserts, because the military authorities had any desire to extend the structures of the 'confessional state' which existed in the Volga region, or envisaged using Islam as a tool of government. Robert D. Crews, *For Prophet & Tsar: Islam and Empire in Russia and Central Asia* (Cambridge, Mass.: Harvard UP, 2006), pp. 254–60.

42 Khalid, *Politics of Muslim Cultural Reform*, p. 69; the title of *panjahbosh* existed before the Russian conquest, but it is not clear whether they had a similar electoral role.

43 See Martin, *Law and Custom in the Steppe*, pp. 1–14; Sergey N. Abashin, *Qalim* und *Mahr* in Mittelasien. Die moderne Praxis und die Debatten über Scharia und Adat, in: Michael Kemper and Maurus Reinkowski (eds), *Rechtspluralismus in der Islamischen Welt. Gewohnheitsrecht zwischen Staat und Gesellschaft* (Berlin: De Gruyter, 2005), pp. 195–207; Pahlen noted that *'Adat* was increasingly influenced by *Shari'a*, but like most Russian officials considered this to be a recent and undesirable phenomenon. Palen, *Pravovoi Byt*, p. 85.

44 Polozhenie ob upravlenii Turkestanskogo Kraya, *PSZ*, Sob. 3, Tom VI (1886), No. 3814, 12 June 1886, pp. 318–46.

45 S.M. Dukhovskoi, *Vsepoddanneishii doklad Turkestanskogo general-gubernatora general ot infanterii Dukhovskogo 'Islam v Turkestane'* (Tashkent, 1899), reprinted in D. Yu Arapov (ed.), *Imperatorskaya Rossiya i Musul'manskii Mir* (Moscow: Natalis, 2006), pp. 142–63.

46 Paolo Sartori, Constructing colonial legality in Central Asia: on guardianship, *Comparative Studies in Society & History*, 56, 2 (2014), pp. 419–47. See further idem, Colonial Legislation Meets Shari'a: Muslims' Land Rights in Russian Turkestan, *Central Asian Survey*, special issue 'The land question in colonial Central Asia', ed. P. Sartori, 29, 1 (2010), pp. 43–60; idem, Behind a petition: why Muslims' appeals increased in Turkestan under Russian rule, *Asiatische Studien*, LXIII, 2 (2009), pp. 401–34; idem, Judicial elections as a colonial reform: the Qadis and Biys in Tashkent, 1868–1883, *Cahiers du Monde Russe* 49, 1 (2008), pp. 79–100.

47 Thomas Welsford and Nuryaghdi Tashev (eds), *A Catalogue of Arabic-Script Documents from the Samarkand Museum* (Samarkand: International Institute for Central Asian Studies, 2012), pp. 11–12, 294–479.

48 Pahlen, *Otchet*, vol. 14: *Narodnye Sudy Turkestanskago Kraya*, and vol. 19: *Pravovoi Byt Tuzemnago Naseleniya*.

49 One of the most influential critics of the existing system, whose conclusions are often echoed in the Pahlen Report, was I.I. Kraft, *Sudebnaya chast' v Turkestanskom krae i Stepnykh Oblastyakh* (Orenburg: Tip. I.N. Zharinova, 1898).

50 Morrison, *Russian Rule in Samarkand*, pp. 187, 259–67.

51 Palen, *Narodnye Sudy*, pp. 8–9.

52 Vsepodanneishaya Zapiska K.K. Palena ob administrativnogo ustroistva i narodnom sude Turkestanskogo Kraya, RGIA F.1396, Op. 1, D. 440, l. 79, this paragraph printed in Palen, *Narodnye Sudy*, pp. 11–12.

53 Five roubles for 1,000 roubles, then one more rouble for each subsequent 1,000 roubles, and 50 kopecks for each 1,000 roubles over 5,000.
54 Palen, *Narodnye Sudy*, pp. 84–6.
55 Pahlen, *Mission to Turkestan,* pp. 76–7.
56 See in particular the notorious case of Nizamuddin Khoja, who was found to have smuggled opium and to be involved in prostitution: commandant of the Samarkand District to the head of the Zarafshan *Okrug* 15 December 1883, TsGARUz F.I-5, Op. 1, D. 1305, ll. 1–6ob; Morrison, *Russian Rule in Samarkand*, pp. 261–2; bizarrely he was still in office as late as 1895, so either the accusations did not stick, or he subsequently managed to get himself re-elected: Welsford and Tashev, *A Catalogue of Arabic-Script Documents:* Docs.445 & 459b, pp. 299, 314–15.
57 RGIA F.1396, Op. 1, D. 264, ll. 223–226, ot nizhepodpisavshikh i prilozhivshikh pechati tuzemtsev g. Samarkanda in uezda, October 1908; ll. 230–237ob, Proshenie Musul'man g. Samarkanda, 10 October 1908, http://zerrspiegel.orientphil.uni-halle.de/t895.html; ll. 257–263ob, Proshenie Musul'man g. Samarkanda (n.d.). http://zerrspiegel.orientphil.uni-halle.de/t907.html. The Russian translations of these petitions seem to be severely abbreviated from the Turki originals.
58 RGIA F.1396, Op.1, D. 264, l. 203–204ob, Proshenie Zhitelei Chimbaiskogo Uchastka, http://zerrspiegel.orientphil.uni-halle.de/t905.html.
59 RGIA F.1396, Op. 1, D. 264, ll. 213–213ob, Proshenie uchenykh Musul'man i zhitelei Amu-Dar'inskogo otdela, http://zerrspiegel.orientphil.uni-halle.de/t908.html (all accessed 4 October 2013).
60 Sartori, An overview of Tsarist policy on Islamic courts, pp. 488, 495–9; in 1893/4 someone in Samarkand solicited a legal opinion as to whether the demanding of bribes was a sin which invalidated the judgement of a *qazi*, to which the answer, unsurprisingly, was 'Yes': Welsford and Tashev, *A Catalogue of Arabic-Script Documents*, Doc. 537, pp. 383–4.
61 Pahlen, *Mission to Turkestan*, p. 51.
62 Kraft, *Sudebnaya Chast'*, p. 90.
63 Vsepodanneishaya Zapiska K. K. Palena ob administrativnogo ustroistva i narodnom sude Turkestanskogo Kraya, RGIA F. 1396, Op. 1, D. 440, ll. 91–92ob.
64 'Her administrative needs are most unlike those which are desirable in the core regions of the empire', K.K. Palen, *Vsepoddanneishaya Zapiska, soderzhashchiya glavneishie vyvody Otcheta* (St Petersburg: Senatskaya Tipografiya, 1910), p. 12.
65 F.K. Girs, *Otchet, revizuyushchago, po Vysochashemu Poveleniyu, Turkestanskogo Kraya, Tainogo Sovetnika Girsa* (St. Petersburg: n.p., 1884), p. 340; N.P. Ignat'ev, *Ob"yasnitel'naya Zapiska k proektu polozheniya ob upravlenii Turkestanskim Kraem* (St Petersburg: n.p., 1884), pp. 75–7.
66 Kratkii Vsepoddanneishii Doklad K.K. Palena o revizii Turkestanskogo Kraya. Chernovik, 1909, RGIA F. 1396, Op. 1, D. 437, l. 33ob.
67 Palen, *Narodnye Sudy*, pp. 206–9, 211, 214.
68 Palen, *Narodnye Sudy*, p. 46.
69 Lawrence Rosen, *The Justice of Islam* (Oxford: Oxford UP, 2000), pp. 32, 182–3; Michael Kemper (ed.), *Rechtspluralismus in der Islamischen Welt. Gewohnheitsrecht zwischen Staat und Gesellschaft* (Berlin: De Gruyter, 2005), pp. 1–17.
70 Shari'a, *The Encyclopaedia of Islam* 1st ed., vol. IV S–Z (Leiden: Brill, 1934), p. 321.
71 Palen, *Narodnye Sudy*, p. 21.
72 Palen, *Narodnye Sudy*, pp. 4–6.
73 Palen, *Narodnye Sudy*, p. 6.

74 Palen, *Pravovoi Byt*, pp. 5–6.
75 This is something argued at greater length in Alexander Morrison, 'Applied Orientalism' in British India and Tsarist Turkestan, *Comparative Studies in Society and History*, 51, 3 (2009), pp. 619–47.
76 David Schimmelpenninck van der Oye, *Russian Orientalism: Asia in the Russian Mind from Peter the Great to the Emigration* (New Haven, Conn.: Yale UP, 2010), pp. 101–9; Crews, *For Prophet and Tsar*, pp. 178–89.
77 N.I. Grodekov (ed.), *Khidaya. Kommentarii musul'manskogo prava: Perevedena s Angliiskogo pod redaktsiei N.I. Grodekova* (Tashkent: Tip. S. I. Lakhtina, 1893), 4 vols; it has recently been re-edited and reprinted by Prof. A.Kh. Saidov as *Khidoya. Kommentarii musul'manskogo prava* (Moscow: Volters Kluver, 2008).
78 N.P. Ostroumov, *Islamovedenie 4. Shariat po shkolu Abu-Khanify* (Tashkent: Izd. 'Turkestanskikh Vedomostei', 1912), p. 4; on Ostroumov and his peculiarly rigid view of Islam and *Shari'a* see Bakhtiyar Babajanov, How will we appear in the eyes of *inovertsy and inorodtsy*? N. P. Ostroumov on the image and function of Russian Power, *Central Asian Survey*, 33, 2 (2014), pp. 270–88.
79 O sovremennom polozhenie musulmanskogo naseleniya kraya v dukhovnom otnoshenii, 10 September 1898, TsGARUz F.21, Upravlenie Nachal'nika Dzhizakskogo Uezda, Op. 1, D. 515, ll. 4–11.
80 Rosen was Professor of Arabic in the Oriental Faculty of St Petersburg University and the founder of the most influential 'school' of Russian Oriental studies. Barthold's invocation of him here, and the nature of his critique, are entirely characteristic. See Vera Tolz, *Russia's own Orient: The Politics of Identity and Oriental Studies in the Late Imperial and Early Soviet Periods* (Oxford: Oxford UP, 2011), pp. 9–19.
81 V. Bartol'd k voprosu ob izuchenii tuzemnykh yazykov, in Yagello (ed.), *Sbornik Materialov po voprosu ob izuchenii Tuzemnykh yazykov*, pp. 108–9, 111.
82 V.V. Bartol'd, Istoriya kul'turnoi zhizni Turkestan (1927), *Sochineniya* (Moscow: Izd. Vostochnoi Literatury, 1963), vol. II, pt. I, pp. 385–7.
83 On the Russian origins of some of Said's ideas see Vera Tolz, 'European, national and (anti-) imperial: the formation of academic Oriental studies in late Tsarist and early Soviet Russia', *Kritika*, 9, 1 (2008), pp. 78–80.
84 Bartol'd k voprosu ob izuchenii tuzemnykh yazykov, p. 109.
85 N.S. Lykoshin, Avtor Khidai, *Turkestanskie Vedomosti* (1907), no.106, in: *Turkestanskii Sbornik*, vol. 436, pp. 90–1; see the introduction to Burhan al-Din al-Marghinani, *Al-Hidayah: The Guidance*, vol. 1, trans. and ed. Imran Ahsan Khan Nyazee (London: Amal Press, 2006), pp. ix–xxxii; the canonical colonial edition (which is still in print throughout South Asia) is Charles Hamilton (trans.), *The Hidaya: Commentary on the Islamic Laws* (Delhi: Kitab Bhavan, 1994) (2nd ed. 1870).
86 Ken'ichi Isogai, *Yasa* and *Shari'a* in Early 16th century Central Asia, *Cahiers d' Asie Centrale*, no. 3/4: *L'Heritage timouride. Iran – Asie Centrale – Inde XVe-XVIIIe siècles* (Tachkent-Aix-en-Provence, 1997), p. 98; N.I. Veselovskii (ed.), *Samariya – Sochinenie Abu Takhir Khodzhi: Tadzhitsskii Tekst* (St Petersburg: Tip. Boraganskii, 1904), p. 32.
87 This was first translated by Sir William Jones as *Al-Sirajiyyah; Or, the Muhammadan Law of Inheritance* (Calcutta, 1792) and was later edited by Almeric Rumsey in 1869. The latter edition is still widely in print. The Arabic original was composed by Siraj-ud-din Muhammad Ben 'Abd ur-Rashid as-Sujawandi (d. 1411).

88 S.A. Kugle, Framed, blamed and renamed: the recasting of Islamic jurisprudence in colonial South Asia, *Modern Asian Studies*, 35, 2 (2001), pp. 260, 272-4, 286; see also Elisa Giunchi, The reinvention of *Sharī'a* under the British Raj: in search of authenticity and certainty, *Journal of Asian Studies*, 69, 4 (2010), pp. 1119-42.
89 Cohn, Law and the colonial state, pp. 71-2.
90 Ashraf Ghani, Disputes in a court of *Sharia*. Kunar Valley Afghanistan, 1885-1890, *International Journal of Middle-East Studies*, 15, 3 (1983), pp. 353-7, 364.
91 Michael Kemper, 'Adat against *Shari'a*: Russian Approaches towards Daghestani 'Customary Law' in the 19th Century, *Ab Imperio*, 3 (2005), pp. 147-74. Kemper however notes that the Russians struggled to contain what they saw as a creeping 'Islamisation' of customary law in Daghestan, one of the legacies of Imam Shamil's 'Shari'a State'.
92 N.P. Ostroumov, *Islamovedenie 4. Shariat po shkolu Abu-Khanify* (Tashkent: Izd. 'Turkestanskikh Vedomostei', 1912), p. 24; the original articles can be found in *Turkestanskie Vedomosti*, 1909, nos. 29, 35, 36, 38, 48, 52, 54, 58, 61, 64, 70, 74, 76, 78, 80, 81, 84, collected in *Turkestanskii Sbornik*, vols 501, pp. 61-70; 503, pp. 130-41; 506, pp. 91-104.
93 Pahlen, *Mission to Turkestan*, p. 82.
94 Palen, *Pravovoi Byt*, p. 9.
95 Palen, *Pravovoi Byt*, pp. 10-11.
96 Sir Roland Knyvett Wilson, *Anglo-Muhammadan law: a digest preceded by a historical and descriptive introduction of the special rules now applicable to Muhammadans as such by the civil courts of British India: with full references to modern and ancient authorities* (London: Thacker, Spink & Co., 1903); Sbornik Anglo-Magometanskogo prava, sostavlenii professorom Kembridzhskogo Universiteta R. Uil'sonom, polozheny v osnovu rabot Tashkentskogo s"ezda po vyyasneniu norm mestnogo material'nogo prava Turkestana, RGIA F.1396, Op. 1, D. 362, ll. 1-100.
97 Ronald Robinson, Non-European foundations of European imperialism: sketch for a theory of collaboration, in: Roger Owen and Bob Sutcliffe (eds), *Studies in the Theory of Imperialism* (London: Longman, 1972), pp. 117-42.
98 The report lists the *qazi*s of Samarkand (Niyaz Husseinbai Sufiev and Isa Khoja Khojaev), Andijan, Marghelan (Maksur Khojaev), Kokand (Hakim Jan Rahimjanov), together with *qazi*s Muhammad Rasul Khojaev, Muhammad Sharif Khojaev, Imam Khoja Ishanov, Ibrahim Bek Yusufbekov and Ashrabkhan Shirin Khojaev; *Mudarise*s Ishan Khoja Mahmud Khojaev, Sayyid Ikram Khan Ghanikhanov and Mahmud Khoja Ishan Qaziev; 'Mullahs' Muhammad Sadykov, Muhammad Tashmadov, Zahir Sheikhov, Mir-'Azam Akhundaev, Mir Sayyid Akhundaev, Mahmud Khojaev, Khoja Ishanov, Shah Murad Ishanov, Niyaz Khojaev and Ishankhan Ma'zumov (the spellings in the original are rather less consistent). Palen, *Pravovoi Byt*, pp. 11-12.
99 Pahlen, *Mission to Turkestan*, pp. 82-3.
100 M. Antonovich, Po povodu s"ezda po voprosam pravovogo byta musul'man, *Turkestanskii Kur'er*, nos. 113-17, 119 in: *Turkestanskii Sbornik*, vol. 508, p. 92.
101 Ibid., p. 98.
102 Ibid.
103 Rezul'taty proizvedennogo pod blizhaishim rukovodstvom revizuiushchago po VYSOCHAISHEMU poveleniu Turkestanskii Krai Senatora Gofmeistera grafa K. K. Palena obsledovaniya pravovoiu byta tuzemnago naseleniya trekh korennykh oblastei Turkestanskogo General-Gubernatorstva, 3 June 1909, RGIA F.1396, Op. 1, D. 363, l. 9ob-10.

104 This was made by Mullah Ishan Khoja, the former *qazi* of the Shaikhantaur district of Tashkent, while two Samarkand *qazi*s, Niyaz Husseinbai Sufiev and Isa-Khoja Khojaev, together with two from Ferghana Province – Maksur Khojaev from Skobelev and Aziz Khojinov from Marghelan – made further additions and corrections. RGIA F.1396, Op. 1, D. 264, 'Sbornik musul'manskogo prava na uzbekskim i russkom yazykakh, zamechaniya Samarkandskogo kaziya Isa-Khoja-Shirin Khojaeva i drugikh kaziev na etom sbornik'; Palen, *Pravovoi Byt*, pp. 11–12.
105 Pahlen, *Mission to Turkestan*, p. 83.
106 Sartori, Constructing colonial legality in Central Asia, p. 429.
107 See David Powers, Orientalism, colonialism and legal history: the attack on Muslim family endowments in Algeria and India, *Comparative Studies in Society & History*, 31, 3 (1989), pp. 535–71.

Part Four

Adaptation and Counterbalance

6

Same Race, Same Fate? Theories of Asian Commonality and the Shift of Regional Hegemony in East Asia After the First Sino-Japanese War (1894/5)

Torsten Weber

I. Introduction

This chapter studies the encounter of two unequal empires whose relationship, at first glance, may more resemble that of colonizer and colony than that of two empires: the young and rapidly Westernizing Empire of Japan and the old and declining Chinese Empire of the Qing (Manchu).[1] Despite obvious imbalances, at the end of the nineteenth century, China and Japan shared many characteristics that qualified both countries as empires.[2] First of all, China and Japan were self-declared empires with emperors as head of state. Although neither country possessed formal colonies (before 1895), both entertained quasi-colonial hegemonic relations with neighbouring regions or countries, parts of which had successively been incorporated into the respective imperial spheres. Through the hegemonic tributary system, China had maintained its long-standing influence in Korea and Southeast Asia as well as Tibet and Mongolia. Japan, on the other hand, had begun to incorporate Ezo (Hokkaidō) and the Ryūkyū Kingdom (Okinawa) into the country's administration after the Meiji Restoration of 1868. Moreover, both China and Japan built their expansionist moves and imperial self-perceptions on a 'manifest destiny' – or 'civilizing missions' – that has been typical of empires since ancient Rome.[3] In the case of China it was Sinocentric civilizationalism, while Japan's rationale was modernization, later supplemented by emperor-centred mythology.[4] The temporal focus of this chapter, the year 1895, is of particular interest in the study of the encounters between China and Japan because as neighbours with increasingly conflicting zones of interests and influence, one empire emerged to replace the other as the military, cultural and mercantile hegemon that set the rules for the era's regional political economies.[5] What was the deeper significance of the military encounter between Japan and China in the late nineteenth century? To what extent did it engender inter-imperial exchange and transfers that lastingly altered the relation between both empires and its peoples? Which new discourses did it generate and how did inter-imperial contacts and personal bonds translate into specific knowledge repertoires that oscillated between collaboration and competition? And how were transfers of specific knowledge orders used to reproduce differentiation and inequality that could easily be linked to imperial power practices?

The transfer of regional leadership was a gradual process stretching over some decades starting in the mid-nineteenth century when both countries reacted differently to their individual encounters with Western imperialism. While China was forced into warfare with Britain, France, Russia and the United States (the Opium Wars, 1839–42/1856–60), Japan yielded to the authority of the Western powers and started a programme of rapid 'Europeanization'. These different experiences of encounters with the 'West' also mediated the encounters between China and Japan during these decades of increasing mutual estrangement. The reversion of the regional order was completed in 1895 when Japan, empire by name (*Dai Nihon Teikoku*, lit. Great Empire of Japan) from 1889 onwards, defeated Qing China in the First Sino-Japanese War of 1894/5. The larger historical significance of this war does not only lie in the fact that it marked the beginning of outright Japanese claims for leadership – in China and in East Asia. The war had also terminated a period of around 300 years of peaceful coexistence between the peoples on both sides of the Sea of Japan. After 1895, war became a permanent threat (and often a reality) whose legacies and political instrumentalization continue to overshadow Sino-Japanese relations to this day.[6] Moreover, the war also marked a huge step towards the globalization of political affairs in East Asia. Diplomatically it directly involved France, Russia and Germany through the so-called Triple Intervention (1895) which forbade Japan larger colonial possessions on the Chinese mainland.[7] Economically, it tied European, American and Asian finance, industries and trade ever closer together as Japan's massive economic 'modernization' programme only really took off after the victorious war against the Qing.[8] And with regard to political and social discourse, it introduced to East Asia imitations of Western imperial rhetoric ('Monroe Doctrine', 'Yellow Peril') and established self-serving typologies of 'West' versus 'East' and 'Asia' versus 'Europe' which raised the level of alert at both ends of the geographical binary.

Not all of these developments occurred as direct consequences of the First Sino-Japanese War. However, the war – if seen in a larger temporal and spatial context – was far more significant than has been acknowledged by most scholarship, which typically emphasizes either the Boxer Rebellion and Boxer Expedition (1898–1900)[9] or the subsequent Russo-Japanese War (1904/5)[10] as turning points in this period. Focusing on attempts made by Japanese and Chinese thinkers and activists to find a common meta-discursive ground for post-war dealings with each other, this chapter examines how 'Asia' and Asian commonality were debated as a potential common narrative for China and Japan. At times, this Asia discourse could serve as a means to overcome new imbalances resulting from the shift in the centre of imperial gravity after 1895. At other times, however, it merely garmented expansionist and hegemonic ambitions in Asianist rhetoric while in reality it established new or reaffirmed old intra-Asian categories of inequality. From a Japanese perspective, this discussion took the form of a balancing act between outright Asianist anti-Westernism and an anti-Asianist pursuit of modernization along 'Western' lines. For China, this balancing act was complicated by

Sinocentric traditionalism and conservative forces that remained reluctant to accept or implement reforms, regardless of their origin or content. In addition, any conception of Asian commonality discussed in this discourse was suspicious either of reinforcing the imperialist ambitions of Japan as the new potential hegemon in the region or of aiming at preserving China's dominant role as the central empire in East Asia. In these negotiations of imperial hierarchies the Asianist garment often only served to mitigate the dispute and to conceal hegemonic zeal.

II. 'Asia' and the encounter of Japan and China in 1895

The First Sino-Japanese War in 1894/5 was fought – as had been the previous war between the Chinese and the Japanese at the end of the sixteenth century – over Korea. This brief but bloody encounter between the two East Asian empires marked the beginning of the reversion of the balance of power in that part of the world which had traditionally been maintained through the Sinocentric tributary system.[11] The Shimonoseki Peace Treaty of 1895 left China humiliated with a huge economic burden of indemnity payments, in addition to suffering the secession of parts of its territory and the loss of its presence in Korea. The psychological humiliation of being defeated by a small island country, a former tributary state and cultural borrower, contributed to a full scale attack on Chinese self-perception and on Sinocentrism. Japan, on the other hand, seized Taiwan as its first 'real' colony and increased its militarization in preparation for the next war(s). But Japan also had to pay a price for its victory in the 'Japan-Qing War', as it is known in Japan. Russia, France and Germany joined forces to refuse Japan substantial territorial gains on the Chinese mainland ('Triple Intervention') because those countries saw their own strategic interests in the region threatened. This interference had an almost traumatic impact on Japan and significantly contributed to the rise of nationalism and anti-Westernism there.[12] After the war, both *isms* started to fraternize with politicized conceptions of 'Asia' which had originated in the 'West' as denigrations or exoticisms of the peoples and cultures in the so-called Far East. Later known as 'Greater Asianism' (Jp. *Dai Ajiashugi*), 'Pan-Asianism' (Jp. *han Ajiashugi*) or simply 'Asianism' (Jp. *Ajiashugi*),[13] affirmations of Asian commonality based on the assumed common culture, race, interests and fate of Asians started to appear in Japanese public discourse just before the turn of the century.[14] Many of these Asianist notions centred on Japan and China and saw an alliance of some sort between the two countries or peoples as the core of any Asianist enterprise. On the one hand, Asianist ideas were easy to reconcile with anti-Westernism, as they were based on an essential strategic and racialist-culturalist opposition between the hegemonic 'West' and the subdued 'East'. On the other hand, they did not necessarily contradict nationalist notions, as many Asianist conceptions argued for the leadership role of one nation. Given the size and historical role of China in the region – and consequently its potential role as leader – it should be obvious why such ideas had not been very popular in Japan before Japan's victory over China in 1895. Until then, affirmations of 'Asia' denoting more than a certain, albeit loosely defined, geographical area had not played any role in political discourse in Japan, mainly because Asianity tended to be identified with political and cultural Sinocentrism; to be 'Asian', above all, meant to be Confucian and to use the Chinese script. In other words, it reaffirmed the centrality of China. Occasional exceptions among Japanese writings on contemporary 'Asia' usually dealt with differences between Japan, on the one hand, and Korea and China on the other hand. As opposed to Asianist ideas that affirmed Asian commonality, they usually denied Japan's belonging to Asia. In these contexts, 'Asia' denoted the 'backwardness' of Japan's neighbours in comparison to Japan's 'progress' measured by the degree of the latter country's Westernization. The most famous example of this kind of Asia consciousness is expressed in Fukuzawa Yukichi's 'Leaving Asia Thesis' (*Datsu A Ron*) of 1885. It was written in reaction to the failed Japan-sponsored reform movement in Korea and argued for Japan's political and psychological departure from Asia. Fukuzawa (1835–1901),[15] known as a leading Meiji educator and pro-Western publicist, concluded his essay with the following advice:

> [M]y country does not have time to wait for the enlightenment of our neighbours so that we can together revive Asia. On the contrary, we must leave their company and proceed together with the civilized nations of the West, without treating China and Korea in a special way because they are our neighbours but only approach them in the same way as the Westerners do. Because those who are intimate with bad friends are also regarded as bad I will from my heart decline the bad friends of East Asia.[16]

Although other views of China and Korea existed,[17] Fukuzawa's attitude may be seen as representative of the politico-intellectual mood in Japan during the 1880s and 1890s. Japan's future lay with the West, not the East, many believed, and the Japanese government continued its Western-oriented reforms in education, administration, law, the military and other fields. As we will see below, positive views of its Asian neighbours remained scarce, marginalized and short-lived in Japan. In order to appeal to the 'West' as a civilized country different from the rest of Asia, Japanese historiography and public discourse established categories that Stefan Tanaka has termed 'Japanese Orientalism'.[18] China, representing Asia, functioned as 'Japan's Orient', through which Japan could reaffirm its assumed superiority by constructing and spreading 'Orientalist' images of the 'East' as backward, exotic, and inferior.[19] The failure of Korea's reform movement prior to the Sino-Japanese War and then Japan's victory over China in 1895 only reconfirmed this widespread Orientalist view of Asia and, in particular, of China in Japan. However, in 1895 'Asia' made an unexpected return to the stage of diplomacy and public debate. It was Li Hongzhang (1823–1901), the Chinese plenipotentiary at the peace negotiations, who referred to shared racial, cultural and strategic interests of China and Japan as a potential starting point for a new relationship between the two empires. In his conversation with the two Japanese plenipotentiaries, Prime Minister Itō Hirobumi (1841–1909) and Foreign Minister Mutsu Munemitsu (1844–97), Li argued:

> In Asia, our two countries, China and Japan, are the closest neighbours, and moreover have the same language. How could we be enemies? Now for the time

being we are fighting each other, but eventually we should work for permanent friendship. If we are enemies endlessly, then what is harmful to China will not necessarily be beneficial to Japan. [...] we ought vigorously to maintain the general stability of Asia, and establish perpetual peace and harmony between ourselves, so that our Asiatic yellow race will not be encroached upon by the white race of Europe.[20]

Although this remark – made in March 1895 when the two countries were still at war but China's impending defeat was more than obvious – was surely made in the strategic interest of appealing to Japanese mercy, its content is nevertheless remarkable. As far as we know, this is the first Asianist statement ever made by a Chinese statesman. In the following years and decades the three categories of Asian commonality that Li referred to became the cornerstones of any Asianist proposal: common cultural heritage, common racial origins and common interests vis-à-vis the West. While the former two points were difficult to disagree over from the Japanese perspective, the latter was not in conformance with the official Japanese diplomatic stance. Towards the West it carefully maintained an accomodationist position which forbade any expression of commitment to a common cause of Asia or China and Japan. Although Itō did not use the word 'Asia' even once, his reply to Li's plea provides a telling insight into Japan's official position towards China and the underlying Asia consciousness during this era: 'I am very much pleased with the idea of the grand secretary [Li Hongzhang]. Ten years ago when I was at Tientsin [Tianjin], I talked about reform with the grand secretary. Why is it that up to now not a single thing has been changed or reformed? This I deeply regret.' Referring to the Sino-Japanese Treaty of 1884, negotiated in the north-eastern Chinese city of Tianjin between Itō and Li a decade earlier, Itō made clear that Japan was little interested in Asianist rhetoric. Instead, Japan's aim was to catch up with the 'West' and to join the club of Western powers, in diplomatic terms and as a civilizational peer. From a mainstream Japanese perspective, it was therefore counterproductive to evoke notions of Sino-Japanese commonality or to emphasize common Asian heritage or neighbourly proximity. In view of China's lack of reforms, being different from China – meaning: being superior to China – was seen as a means of proving Japan's modernity and civilization. Intellectually, this position closely resembled Fukuzawa's 1885 recommendation to Japan's leadership to 'decline the bad friends of East Asia', that is, to leave Asia behind and to turn to the 'West' instead.

III. New 'Asia' discourse and Sino-Japanese rapprochement after 1895

As Matthias Zachmann has demonstrated in his study of late Meiji Japanese China discourse, little changed regarding Japan's official denial of 'Asia' in the following decade.[21] On the contrary, with Japan's victory over Russia in the Russo-Japanese War of 1904/5[22] Japanese politicians became even more careful not to provoke any fear in the 'West' of a pan-Asian union under Japanese leadership.[23] In Chinese diplomacy, too, the idea of 'Asia' was soon shelved. Only one year after the Shimonoseki Peace Treaty was concluded, Li Hongzhang travelled to Germany and Russia to seek an alliance *against* Japan. Eventually, China concluded a treaty with Russia, whose political centre lay in Europe (not Asia) and whose cultural-racial heritage was rather distant from Chinese and Japanese commonality. The idea of Asian solidarity based on assumed cultural, racial and strategic commonality, as advanced by Li in 1895, was rather quickly unmasked as pure rhetoric.

On the civic level, however, ideas of Asian commonality started to gain momentum in both China and Japan from the late 1890s onwards. In fact, Sino-Japanese interactions began to flourish to such an extent that the last years of the nineteenth century and the first years of the twentieth have come to be referred to as a 'Golden Decade' of Chinese-Japanese relations.[24] A new understanding of 'Asia' on the civic level mediated this rapprochement and facilitated the Sino-Japanese 'honeymoon decade'.[25] The increased contacts between people and knowledge from both countries, which were promoted by and resulted in intensified ideas of Asian commonality, also became an important factor in the 1898 Reform Movement in China.[26] The so-called Hundred Days' Reform was initiated by reform-minded Chinese thinkers, many of whom had studied in Japan and held positive views of Japan's modernization. Rather than feeling humiliated as Chinese by defeat in the war, these intellectuals regarded Japan as a model for China to follow. Simultaneously, some Sinophile and pro-Asian thinkers and activists in Japan started to call for Japanese moderation towards its defeated neighbour.[27] The starting point for this new era of Sino-Japanese interaction was transfers of ideas and people between the two empires. The Sino-Japanese War of 1894/5 played a key role in stimulating these transfers in various ways. The biggest impact is usually attributed to the study abroad programme, partly financed by the Chinese government, which brought thousands of Chinese students to Japan to 'learn from Japan', but also to 'learn about the West through Japan'.[28] It is estimated that up to 15,000 Chinese students came to study in Japan during the period of 1895 to 1905 alone, or a minimum of 25,000 Chinese students between 1898 and 1911.[29] To cater to their demands, special schools and programmes were set up in Japan, including the Tokyo Dōbun Shoin (Tokyo Common Culture Academy),[30] founded by the Tōa Dōbunkai (East Asia Common Culture Society)[31] in 1902 and modelled after the Tōa Dōbun Shoin (East Asia Common Culture Academy), a language and culture institute founded by the same society in Shanghai in 1901. Although the East Asia Common Culture Society and its institutes remained private and non-official until the late 1930s, they secretly received substantial financial support through the Japanese government.[32] The society's leadership included high-profile Japanese political figures, above all its founder and head, Konoe Atsumaro (1863–1904). Konoe was president of the House of Peers and in 1898 merged his Dōbunkai (Common Culture Society)[33] with another proto-Asianist group, the Tōa Kai (East Asia Society), to form the Tōa Dōbunkai. In 1900, yet another early Asianist group, the Ajia Kyōkai (Asia Association), joined Konoe's society.[34] The aim of the society was to foster the exchange of knowledge between China and Japan. In practice this meant to encourage Chinese to learn from Japan – a reversal of the traditional 'Chinese teacher, Japanese student' relationship. As is obvious from the names of the societies and their institutions, they based their agenda on the significance of the region (Asia, East Asia) and its shared cultural heritage (Jp. *dōbun*/Ch. *tongwen*, lit. same script/culture).[35] This prominence of both references is rather remarkable, given the official anti-Asianist and general Sino-sceptic mood in Japan. The choice of these names can only partly be explained by rhetorical concessions to the Japanese historical indebtedness to Chinese culture. The institutions established under this rationale served to generate knowledge for Japan's imperial expansion but they also provided a forum for the unfolding of Asianist discourse and for a new understanding of Japan among Chinese, and vice versa.

IV. Japan in Chinese reform proposals

Early post-war writings by Chinese intellectuals and activists reveal that they did not follow the strategy chosen by the Chinese leadership to deal with Japan's regional rise. Rather than turning to Japan's rival, the Russian Empire, many Chinese now turned to Japan itself. It is particularly noteworthy that one of the leading figures in the post-war reform movement, the classical scholar Zhang Taiyan (also known as Zhang Binglin, 1868–1936),[36] explicitly proposed an alliance between China and Japan directed against China's new ally, Russia. The aim of this alliance was to 'revive Asia'.[37] In his Asia consciousness, Zhang displayed exactly the same elements that Li Hongzhang had referred to in 1895: racialist-culturalist commonality and shared interests due to geopolitical proximity. Zhang was one of the first Chinese to supplement the slogan '*tongwen*' (same culture) with its racialist equivalent '*tongzhong*', denoting same race.Ced Zhang also introduced the regionalist concept of 'lips and teeth, cheekbones and gums', denoting close relations of interdependency between China and Japan, to his Chinese readership. Both terms suggested an anti-Western conception of Asian commonality since they were formulated *ex negativo* against the threat posed by the 'West' and Western imperialism. These concepts became widely used in China and Japan after 1895.[38]

The two leading figures in the 1898 Reform Movement, Liang Qichao (1873–1929) and his teacher Kang Youwei (1858–1927), emphasized the practical implementation of 'learning from Japan'. In January 1898, Kang Youwei had submitted a reform proposal to the throne in which he recommended that China should 'take the Meiji Reform of Japan as the model for our reform' based on the similarity between the two empires[39]: 'The time and place of Japan's reform are not remote and her religion and customs are somewhat similar to ours, her success is manifest; her example can be easily followed.' As Peter Zarrow has pointed out, Kang's (and also Liang's) view of Japan suffered from a lack of information about the real events that led to Japan's modernization and the role of the emperor therein.[40] However, Kang's open embrace of Japan as a model for reform was almost revolutionary and, in addition to rumours of the direct involvement of the Japanese government in the 1898 movement, contributed to the refusal by the Empress Dowager Cixi – the real agent of power in Beijing since the death of the Xianfeng Emperor in 1861 – to implement these proposals. Aiming at reforms in the political, social, economic and administrative realms under the influence of liberalism, democracy and science, they would have transformed the country into a constitutional monarchy resembling Japan. Previously, Cixi had already been critical of the so-called 'Self-strengthening Movement', a moderate pro-Western reform movement, which had lasted for three decades prior to the outbreak of the First Sino-Japanese War but had proven insufficient to prevent China's defeat to the Japanese in 1895. If learning from the 'West' had failed, why should China now learn from its long-despised neighbour? After the suppression of the Hundred Days' Reform Movement, both Kang and Liang went into exile in Japan, while all their fellow activists were executed in Beijing in September 1898.[41] In Japan, Liang wrote an essay outlining the benefits for Chinese of studying the Japanese language in which he also addressed the question above.[42] Liang's text reads like an encouragement to study what had been ignored by most Chinese for too long: the language and writings of a neighbouring people with whom the Chinese shared more in common than with Europeans. As opposed to English, Liang argued, studying Japanese was relatively easy. Scientific writings on a variety of topics such as sociology, philosophy, politics, finance and economy were easier for Chinese to comprehend when written by Japanese and in Japanese, he continued. Liang did not conclude his practical advice without stressing the racialist, culturalist and geopolitical linkages between both countries and peoples[43]:

> To us, Japan is a country like lips are to teeth, like elder and younger brothers. Only by removing boundaries and lending a hand can we preserve the independence of the Yellow race and halt the Eastern advance of the European powers. One day, when a union between the two countries of China and Japan comes into existence, understanding each other's languages will become the most important issue. Therefore, just as the Japanese give priority to studying the Chinese script and spoken language, the Chinese too must prioritize the study of written and spoken Japanese.

Studying Japanese and learning from Japan, therefore, was portrayed as being not only beneficial to the internal development and modernization of China, but also as being essential for the survival of China and of East Asia in the face of the continuing threat posed by Western imperialism. It is interesting to note that the menace of Japanese imperialism played no significant role in discussions of Japan among Chinese reformers.

V. Proposals of an Asian Monroe Doctrine

The political situation in East Asia after the end of the war made political alliances between East Asian countries against the 'West' appear more urgent than ever. After the German-French-Russian Triple Intervention of 1895, Germany utilized the murder of two German missionaries to occupy the Kiautschou (Jiaozhou) Bay while Russia took parts of the Liaodong Peninsula, both in 1897. The following year Britain forced a lease of the Kowloon Peninsula (Hong Kong) upon China and the USA began to occupy the Philippines. In this context, political anti-Westernism was not difficult to spread in East Asia and became a natural companion to, if not driving force of, calls for Sino-Japanese co-operation.⁴⁴ Voices that demanded a retreat of all Western powers from East Asia grew louder among Chinese and Japanese, although officially Japan remained anti-Asianist. In the last years of the nineteenth century, the phrase 'Asia for the Asians' started to popularize a political doctrine that had been invented in the USA in the early nineteenth century to block the European influence in the 'New World', namely the Monroe Doctrine. As the 'Asian Monroe Doctrine' this principle now represented attempts to rationalize Asian demands for self-determination. It was in fact none other than Konoe Atsumaro, the founder and leader of the above-mentioned East Asia Common Culture Society, who met Kang Youwei shortly after he went into exile in Japan in 1898 and proposed to him the idea of a Monroe Doctrine for the East.⁴⁵

> Today's matters of the East are not solely the matters of the East. They are the matters of the whole world. The European Powers all compete for their own profits in the East. The East is the East of the East. Only the peoples of the East must have the right to decide the matters of the East. The American Monroe Doctrine denotes exactly this. It is the duty of our two peoples [Chinese and Japanese] to implement an Asian Monroe Doctrine in the East.

According to Konoe's diary, Kang Youwei replied affirmatively to Konoe's suggestion. But Kang must have been aware of the implications of such a doctrine. Although the Western presence and influence in East Asian affairs rendered a realization of an Asian Monroe Doctrine unlikely, if not impossible, the larger significance of Konoe's proposal lies in his formulation of a claim for Japanese leadership in East Asia, as an imitation of an American policy. Just as the American Monroe Doctrine was no democratic principle in the interest of the weak nations in the Americas but an imperialist instrument that secured the United States' hegemony in the region, similar ideas in East Asia were likely to aim at securing the dominance of the strongest power there. After 1895, there was no doubt that this was no longer China but Japan.

In a sense, Konoe's geopolitical proposal of late 1898 may be seen as a modification of his previous, strongly racialist, argument for Sino-Japanese co-operation. In fact, a few months before his conversation with Kang, Konoe had written a famous essay in the widely read Japanese journal *Taiyō* (*The Sun*) which had explicitly assumed a future confrontation of the yellow and the white races.⁴⁶ In preparation for this clash of races, Konoe had proposed an 'Alliance of the Same Races', based on close co-operation between China and Japan:

> As I see it, East Asia in the future inevitably will become the stage for a contest between the races. Even if momentary considerations of foreign policy should produce a different setting, this will be but of fleeting existence. The final destiny will be a contest between the yellow and the white race, and in this contest the Chinese people and the Japanese people will be placed in the same position, being both considered as the sworn enemy of the white race. Those who are considering a long-term strategy do well to consider these facts.⁴⁷

Similar to Liang, Konoe based his view on the inevitably common fate of Chinese and Japanese, on the one hand, and the enmity of the White 'West' towards the Yellow 'East', on the other hand. As a way out of this threat scenario, Konoe – and later Liang – suggested the imitation of the Western diplomacy of alliances or declarations of exclusive spheres of interest. Of course, from a Western perspective, an Asian Monroe Doctrine was seen as a threat to the vested interests of the established powers in the region. In response, the US secretary of state, John Hay, proposed the open door policy in China in September 1899. Eventually, this policy became the leading instrument that secured Western economic and political influence in East Asia until the 1930s when Japan began to pursue an open and aggressive anti-Western policy on the Asian mainland and, eventually, left the League of Nations in protest against the League's reluctance to acknowledge Japan's special interests in Manchuria.[48] But in the late nineteenth century, Japan's diplomatic orientation forbade such anti-Western and pro-Asianist statements. After the publication of Konoe's essay, he immediately came under pressure to withdraw his proposal. In December 1898, some weeks after his meeting with Kang, Konoe recanted his statement:

> Certainly the most urgent task today is to swiftly determine our national policy and unite public opinion. However, the most urgent task of all must be seen in defining our policy towards China. Today, I do not claim anymore that, because our empire and China share a common culture and a common race, our empire should volunteer to shoulder China's fate itself. I say that we merely should consider our own empire's future fate, decide upon an urgent policy suitable to it, respond to the opportunities and watch the changes, act with swift determination and thereby secure today's advantages.[49]

Konoe now gave priority to 'opportunities' and 'advantages' over racialist-culturalist commonality and pro-Asian geopolitical considerations. As an official representative of Japan, Konoe therefore returned to the realm of diplomatic guidelines that remained, as mentioned above, despite all disappointments with the 'West', pro-Western. But 'uniting public opinion' in this direction, as Konoe had demanded, was no longer possible. Instead, Konoe had captured the Japanese zeitgeist around the turn of the nineteenth century, at least as it was observable below the level of diplomatic realism, rather well in his essay on an 'Alliance of the Same Races' and in his conversation with Kang Youwei. Subsequently, more voices emerged that challenged the official position and advanced conceptions of an East Asian union with Japan and China at its core.[50]

The idea of an Asian Monroe Doctrine remained part of the political discourse in Japan until the end of World War II. This idea did not only represent the diplomatic strategy of a certain stream of Japanese foreign policy which viewed East Asia as Japan's vital backyard ('Greater East Asian Co-Prosperity Sphere') or 'lifeline'.[51] It also served as a reminder of the double standard of 'Western' imperialism which – to some degree at least – was tolerant of the imperialism of other European powers but was intolerant of the imperialist latecomer Japan. Eventually, the transfer of the idea of a Monroe Doctrine to East Asia and its implementation under Japanese leadership ended in utter failure and in Japan's complete defeat in 1945.

VI. Yellow Peril and White Peril

The hypocritical and self-serving character of 'Western' dealings with Asia around the turn of the nineteenth to the twentieth century is probably best represented by the employment of racial policies and discourse. An important example is the racial exclusion legislation in the USA and its accompanying discourse.[52] The so-called Chinese Exclusion Act had been inaugurated in 1882, then extended in 1892 and made permanent in 1902. Already since 1790, various Naturalization Acts had defined Chinese, Japanese and Koreans as ineligible for citizenship, which subsequently also affected other rights, such as lease and land ownership.[53] At least for a time, this foreign-attributed and indiscriminate denigration on racial grounds was a factor that reinforced notions of racial commonality between China and Japan. It also promoted the spread of the concept of '*tongzhong*' (same race) in China and Japan during the last decade of the nineteenth century, as addressed above. While the exclusionist immigration policy de facto only affected a small portion of Chinese (and later Japanese), the accompanying rhetorical insult did more damage. As 'Yellow Peril' discourse, driven by – but not limited to – white supremacists, it dehumanized almost three-fourths of the entire population of this planet.[54] Yellow Peril discourse had been thriving in the USA and Europe since the later 1880s but as a key concept entered political discourse only in the context of the First Sino-Japanese War.[55] It reached its symbolic peak shortly after the war when Kaiser Wilhelm II commissioned a painting that portrayed the scenario of an Oriental threat against which Europeans needed to prepare by resorting to arms. The painting was produced by the German painter Hermann Knackfuss (1848–1915) and was later simply referred to as the 'Knackfuss painting'.[56] It portrays Asia in the form of a sitting Buddha while Europe is depicted as a group of personifications of nations, such as France's Marianne, Great Britain's Britannia and Germany's Germania. Whereas Europe appears as a collective of strong and upright, yet individual, humans united under the cross of Christianity, Asia is visualized as mysterious, obscure, potentially dangerous and homogeneous. The official title – and hypocritical programme – of the painting was *Peoples of Europe, Protect your Holiest Goods*, falsely implying that the peoples of East Asia posed an imminent threat to Europe. The painting was later presented to Wilhelm's cousin, Tsar Nicholas II of Russia, as a supplementary visual attempt to persuade Russia's leader of the impending danger of East Asia.[57] In autumn 1900, two months after Kaiser Wilhelm II had delivered his infamous 'Hun Speech', the Japanese daily *Yomiuri Shinbun* published a parody of the Knackfuss painting which displayed a reversed discourse of racial and cultural threat.[58]

In place of the assembly of Europeans led by Saint Michael it showed armed Asian warriors, led by Confucius, who warns of Christian missionaries represented by a large ship and a cross (see Figure 6.1). In a satirical allusion to the original title of the Knackfuss painting, Confucius is portrayed as saying: 'Peoples of Asia, protect your holiest Gods!' From a Japanese and Chinese perspective, Yellow Peril rhetoric was in fact difficult to take seriously. Had the Japanese or Chinese ever sailed to Europe to invade the continent and colonize its peoples? Was not the opposite more appropriately representative of the history of European-Asian relations? It was not until the next war, the Russo-Japanese War (1904/5), that the Japanese fully realized that Yellow Peril

Figure 6.1 White Peril cartoon. Reproduced by kind permission of *Yomiuri Shinbun*

discourse was no joke. The war perfectly lent itself to Yellow Peril propaganda that readily interpreted the confrontation of the Russian and Japanese Empires as a clash of the white versus the yellow race.[59] Still, official Japanese diplomacy hurried to renew its commitment to the 'West' and to dispel Western fears of the growing strength of a potentially Japan-led Asia.[60] Pro-Asianist Japanese, however, started to actively confront the 'West' with a counterattack; in place of Yellow Peril they began using the term 'White Peril' to refer to the historical reality of modern European-Asian encounters.[61] The concept itself was another example of a transfer of political ideas and of the far-ranging intellectual entanglement of East Asian and 'Western' political discourse. The expression was probably coined by Sidney Gulick (1860–1945), a pro-Japanese American writer and missionary. Gulick can at least be credited for having popularized the term 'White Peril' following the publication of his book *The White Peril in the Far East*[62] in 1905. In short, Gulick argued what should have been plain to see for every observer, that the real danger in East Asia, namely the cause of instability and war, was the presence and activities of the Western powers there. Above all Gulick criticized Germany, France and Russia. Japan, by contrast, was a stabilizing factor in East Asia which also served as a model for China and other Asian countries to follow in their attempts at modernization and stabilization, he argued.[63] Gulick therefore welcomed a Japanese victory over Russia in the Russo-Japanese War, while Yellow Peril theorists interpreted Japan's triumph as a sure sign of the imminent threat to Europe and the 'West'.[64] The emergence in Japan of the new concept of a 'White Peril' empowered Asian-minded debaters to emphasize Asian commonality more indirectly, namely by negating the 'Western' Other. Also, it shifted the focus from the geopolitical dimension of the Asian Monroe Doctrine to a civilizational perspective, similar to the older and more widely used concepts of 'same race' and 'same culture'.

In 1905, when 'White Peril' was introduced to the wider Japanese public through speeches, newspaper and journal articles, it was rarely used as a warning.[65] Rather, it was introduced as a concept from the West that could be seen as an encouragement to trust the 'West'; after all, the Western origin of 'White Peril' theory proved that there were also reasonable voices that acknowledged that the Yellow Peril was but an illusion whereas the White Peril was reality. In a speech on Gulick's *White Peril* book, for example, Hiroi Tatsutarō, a Unitarian activist and professor at Tokyo's Tōyō University, thanked Gulick for admitting Western racial prejudice and for agreeing that Japan's war against Russia was not an expression of a 'militaristic experiment, imperialist ambition or Japanese expansionism'. Instead, it had to be seen as a struggle of 'self-existence' against Russia, the 'King of the White Peril'.[66]

As Akira Iriye argued, Japanese leaders' awareness of 'talk of the Yellow Peril' in Europe and America did not preclude them from, but rather encouraged them to co-operate with the Western powers to prevent the growth of such fears.[67] The same may be said about the official reaction to 'talk of the White Peril'. The conclusion in 1907/8 of the so-called 'Gentlemen's Agreement' between Japan and the USA, through which Japan imposed a self-restriction on Japanese emigration to the US, is exemplary of this official Japanese approach.[68] Nevertheless, 'White Peril' remained on the agenda of political debate. The Japanese journal *Taiyō* in February 1908 dedicated a special issue to the clash of races and argued that, next to conflicting economic interests, the competition of different races constituted the origin of all global conflicts.[69] It also claimed that 'all change to history occurs as a result of racial competition' and that 'the Russo-Japanese War was only the prelude to fierce competition between the yellow and white races'.[70] The *Taiyō*, however, was no Asianist mouthpiece but tried to take an analytical approach to the question of whether the 'future problem was the White or the Yellow Peril'.[71] Nevertheless, it simply presumed that not only in the 'White West' but also in the 'Yellow East' there was a common agenda or at least willingness to fight on behalf of each other. This view of course mainly rested on the experience and interpretation of the Russo-Japanese War as the proto-war of White versus Yellow. However, a precondition of the underlying assumption was the emergence of a strong Asian power as produced by the Sino-Japanese War; it had reshuffled the order in East Asia and established Japan as a regional imperial power. A decade later, World War I would prove wrong any assumptions of White or Yellow commonality; rather than fighting heathen Asians, Christian Europeans killed each other by the million. Similarly, rather than scheming an Asian union, Japan further estranged China. Its occupation of further Chinese territory and its harsh conditions (the 'Twenty-One Demands', 1915) did everything to antagonize the Chinese away from the Japanese. In this way, the 'Golden Decade' of Sino-Japanese interactions ended without a lasting positive effect on the relations and the mutual perceptions of the Chinese and the Japanese. The new conceptual vocabulary established, however, returned to the forefront of political debate and propaganda in the context of the Immigration Act of 1924 and Japan's war against China from 1931 onwards.[72] Ironically, what had served as a potential *common* agenda after 1895 became part of the rhetorical justification for Japan's aggression in China and elsewhere in Asia during the 1930s and 1940s.

VII. Conclusion

This chapter has analysed how the transfer of regional hegemony in East Asia from the Chinese to the Japanese Empire as a result of the First Sino-Japanese War of 1894/5 facilitated the emergence of a discourse on Sino-Japanese and Asian commonality. This discourse, together with increased personal interactions, formed the background to the so-called 'Golden Decade' of Sino-Japanese relations after the war. The ideational transfer and exchange regarding Asianist ideas and concepts of this era, however, not only occurred between China and Japan, but was also strongly influenced by the reception of Western political debate and diplomatic activities. As the examples of White Peril discourse and the Asian Monroe Doctrine demonstrate, (quasi-)imperialist instruments of the 'West' were easily appropriated to serve Japanese or Chinese interests. In this way, global imperial hierarchies could not only be turned upside down but could also create new, intra-regional hierarchies. Before the turn of the nineteenth century it was far from clear that the new discourse of racialist, culturalist and strategic collaboration-cum-competition produced by the inter-imperial encounter between China and Japan in 1894/5 would become the ideological framework for bilateral and international interactions during the following decades.

As a result of their increasing and changing awareness of one another around the turn of the century, Japanese and Chinese thinkers and activists contributed to the establishment and spread of new political concepts that expressed a sense of Asian self-affirmation – in opposition to the 'West' that had established negative categories of Asian commonality in the first place. Anti-Westernism, directed against political, economic and discursive denigration of Asians, served as a catalyst to racialist-culturalist and geopolitical notions of commonality ('same race, same culture', 'Asian Monroe Doctrine', 'White Peril'). Eventually, the defeat of reform-minded Chinese in 1898, the vicissitudes of the following revolution in China, Japanese imperial ambitions and pro-Western inclinations, as well as the constellation of World War I rendered projects – and eventually also ideas – of Asian commonality based on close Sino-Japanese co-operation void. While Japan continued, in imitation of Western imperialist strategies, its venture of imperial expansion, China was subsequently de-imperialized; the turmoil following the Republican Revolution of 1911/12 and the brief resurrection of imperial rule under General Yuan Shikai (1915–16) contributed to the accelerated colonization of ever larger parts of China's territory.

The year 1895 bears historical significance as a starting point for many of these developments which, for the most part, lasted half a century until Japan lost its role as regional hegemon in 1945. The accompanying anti-Western and Asianist rhetoric, coined and propagated since the mid-1890s, became defunct at the same time, although the Bandung movement since the 1950s, the Asian Values debate of the 1990s, and recent discourse on East Asian integration since the 2000s have inherited some of its logic and prose.

Notes

1 In the interest of wider accessibility, references in this chapter to sources and scholarship in languages other than English have been kept to a minimum. As the research for this article, however, is largely based on sources and scholarship in Japanese and, to a lesser extent, in Chinese, occasional references to these materials have been unavoidable. Following the original order, Japanese and Chinese family names precede first names. For a general overview of the history and historical context of the First Sino-Japanese War, with a focus on political and diplomatic history, see S.C.M. Paine, *The Sino-Japanese War of 1894–1895: Perceptions, Power, and Primacy* (Cambridge: Cambridge UP, 2003).
2 On the debate over whether or not China can be regarded as an empire see Kirk W. Larsen, *Tradition, Treaties, and Trade: Qing Imperialism and Choson Korea, 1850–1910* (Cambridge: Harvard UP, 2008), pp. 2–4.
3 See Jane Burbank and Frederick Cooper, *Empires in World History: Power and the Politics of Difference* (Princeton: Princeton UP, 2010), pp. 11–13, 42.
4 On the role of civilization in the tributary system see David Kang, East Asia when China was at the centre. The tribute system in early modern East Asia, in: Mark Beeson and Richard Stubbs (eds), *Routledge Handbook of Asian Regionalism* (London: Routledge, 2012), pp. 58–73 and on Japan's modernization and imperial myths, Carol Gluck, *Japan's Modern Myths: Ideology in the Late Meiji Period* (Princeton: Princeton UP, 1985) and Kenneth J. Ruoff, *Imperial Japan at its Zenith: The Wartime Celebration of the Empire's 2600th Anniversary* (Ithaca: Cornell UP, 2010), Introduction.
5 This is an adaptation of Pomeranz's definition of empires as 'military-mercantile hegemons that set the rules for their eras' global political economies'; see Kenneth Pomeranz, Empire & 'civilizing' missions, past & present, *Daedalus* (Spring 2005), p. 34.
6 See Zheng Wang, *Never Forget National Humiliation: Historical Memory in Chinese Politics and Foreign Relations* (New York: Columbia UP, 2012) and Caroline Rose, *Interpreting History in Sino-Japanese Relations: A Case Study in Political Decision-making* (London: Routledge, 1998).
7 On the Triple Intervention see Frank W. Ikle, The Triple Intervention: Japan's lesson in the diplomacy of imperialism, *Monumenta Nipponica*, 22, 1–2 (1967), pp. 122–30 and Urs Matthias Zachmann, Imperialism in a nutshell: conflict and the 'Concert of Powers' in the Tripartite Intervention, 1895, *Japanstudien*, 17 (2006), pp. 57–82.
8 See Gluck, *Myths*, pp. 30–1.
9 See Paul A. Cohen, *History in Three Keys: The Boxers as Event, Experience, and Myth* (New York: Columbia UP, 1997) and Susanne Kuss's essay in this volume.
10 See John W. Steinberg et al. (eds), *The Russo-Japanese War in Global Perspective: World War Zero* (Leiden: Brill, 2005) and Maik Hendrik Sprotte, Wolfgang Seifert and Heinz-Dietrich Löwe (eds), *Der Russisch-Japanische Krieg 1904/05: Anbruch einer neuen Zeit?* (Wiesbaden: Harrassowitz, 2007).
11 See Kang, East Asia, and Zhang Yongjin, *China in the International System, 1918–20: The Middle Kingdom at the Periphery* (London: Macmillan, 1991).
12 See Ikle, Triple.
13 For the inception of Asianism as a political concept in public discourse in Japan and China during the early 1910s, see Torsten Weber, Unter dem Banner des Asianismus: Transnationale Dimensionen des japanischen Asianismus-Diskurses der Taishō-Zeit (1912–26), *Comparativ*, 18, 6 (2008), pp. 34–52.

14 See Sven Saaler and C.W.A. Szpilman (eds), *Pan-Asianism: A Documentary History 1860–2010. Vol. 1: 1850–1920* (Boulder: Rowman & Littlefield, 2011).
15 On Fukuzawa's life and thought see his acclaimed autobiography in English translation; *The Autobiography of Fukuzawa Yukichi: With Preface to the Collected Works of Fukuzawa*, transl. Eiichi Kiyooka (Tokyo: Hokuseido, 1981).
16 Fukuzawa's original essay is reprinted in translation in David J. Lu (ed.), *Japan: A Documentary History* (Armonk: M.E. Sharpe, 1997). For an English summary of a classical early post-war Japanese evaluation of Fukuzawa see Sannosuke Matsumoto, Profile of Asian minded man V: Yukichi Fukuzawa, *The Developing Economies*, 5,1 (March 1967), pp. 156–72 and, with a focus on Asianism, Urs Matthias Zachmann, Blowing up a double portrait in black and white: the concept of Asia in the writings of Fukuzawa Yukichi and Okakura Tenshin, *Positions: East Asia Cultures Critique*, 15, 2 (Fall 2007), pp. 345–68.
17 See for example Kyu Hyun Kim, Tarui Tōkichi's arguments on behalf of the Union of the Great East, 1893, in: Saaler/Szpilman, *Pan-Asianism*, pp. 73–84 and Bunsō Hashikawa, Japanese perspectives on Asia: from dissociation to coprosperity, in: Akira Iriye (ed.), *The Chinese and the Japanese: Essays in Political and Cultural Interactions* (Princeton: Princeton UP, 1980), pp. 328–55.
18 See Stefan Tanaka, *Japan's Orient: Rendering Pasts into History* (Berkeley: University of California Press, 1993).
19 See Edward W. Said, *Orientalism* (New York: Vintage, 1978).
20 Li's quote and Itō's reply (see below) are taken from: Doc. 35. Li Hung-chang's Conversation with Itō Hirobumi, 1895, in: Ssu-yu Teng and John K. Fairbank (eds), *China's Response to the West. A Documentary Survey 1839–1923* (New York: Atheneum, 1966), p. 126.
21 See Urs Matthias Zachmann, *China and Japan in the late Meiji Period: China Policy and the Japanese Discourse on National Identity, 1895–1904* (London: Routledge, 2009).
22 On different aspects of the war regarding Japan's relations with and mutual perceptions of its neighbours and Western countries see Sprotte, Seifert and Löwe, *Russisch-Japanische Krieg*.
23 For example, see Baron Suematsu's rejection of Western Asianist claims in Baron Suyematsu (Suematsu Kenchō), *The Risen Sun* (London: Archibald Constable, 1905).
24 See Douglas R. Reynolds, *China 1898–1912: The Xinzheng Revolution and Japan* (Cambridge: Harvard UP, 1993), especially Chapters 1 and 2.
25 Reynolds, *China*, p. xviii. As Reynolds explains, he first used this term but upon criticism from Japanese scholars later changed it to 'Golden Decade'. It should be clear that neither term denotes selfless idealism, but rather 'mutual self-interest', as Japanese historian Hirano Kenichirō commented.
26 See Reynolds, *China*, pp. 34–6.
27 A well-known example is the autobiography of Katsu Kaishū (1823–99), a famous Meiji statesman, who called for Japanese respect towards Korea and China after the First Sino-Japanese War; see Katsu Kaishū, Hikawa Seiwa (excerpts), in: Itō Teruo (ed.), *Ajia to Kindai Nihon: han shinryaku no shisō to undō (Asia and modern Japan: Anti-invasionist thought and movement)* (Tokyo: Shakai Hyōronsha, 1990), pp. 13–15.
28 See Paula Harrell, *Sowing the Seeds of Change: Chinese Students, Japanese Teachers, 1895–1905* (Stanford: Stanford UP, 1992), p. 6.
29 See Harrell, *Sowing*, p. 209 and Reynolds, *China*, p. 42.
30 See Harrell, *Sowing*, p. 33 and Reynolds, *China*, pp. 52–3.

31 On this society see Urs Matthias Zachmann, The foundation manifesto of the Tōa Dōbunkai (East Asian Common Culture Society), 1898, in: Saaler and Szpilman, *Pan-Asianism*, pp. 115–19.
32 See Zachmann, Tōa Dōbunkai, p. 117.
33 See Urs Matthias Zachmann, Konoe Atsumaro and the idea of an alliance of the yellow race, 1898, in: Saaler and Szpilman, *Pan-Asianism*, pp. 85–92.
34 See Urs Matthias Zachmann, The foundation manifesto of the Kōakai (Raising Asia Society) and the Ajia Kyōkai (Asia Association), 1880–1883, in: Saaler and Szpilman, *Pan-Asianism*, pp. 53–60.
35 See Reynolds, *China*, pp. 141–7 on the significance of *tongwen*.
36 On Zhang's life and political thought see Viren Murthy, *The Political Philosophy of Zhang Taiyan: The Resistance of Consciousness* (Leiden: Brill, 2011).
37 See Zhang Taiyan, Lun Yazhou yize wei chunchi [It is best for Asia to stand together firmly], in: *Shiwu Bao* (China Progress), (18 February 1897) quoted after Rebecca Karl, Creating Asia: China in the world at the beginning of the twentieth century, *The American Historical Review*, 103, 4 (October 1998), p. 1104.
38 See Karl, Creating Asia, p. 1104. Sven Saaler, Pan-Asianism in modern Japanese history: overcoming the nation, creating a region, forging an empire, in: Sven Saaler and J. Victor Koschmann (eds), *Pan-Asianism in Modern Japanese History. Colonialism, Regionalism and Borders* (London: Routledge, 2007), pp. 1–18.
39 For an excerpt of the text see Kang Youwei, The need for reforming institutions, in: Wm. Theodore de Bary and Richard Lufrano (eds), *Sources of Chinese Tradition*, vol. 2 (New York: Columbia University Press, 2000), pp. 269–70 (quotes from p. 270).
40 See Peter Zarrow, Late-Qing reformism and the Meiji model: Kang Youwei, Liang Qichao, and the Japanese emperor, in: Joshua A. Fogel (ed.), *The Role of Japan in Liang Qichao's Introduction of Modern Western Civilization to China* (Berkeley: University of California Press, 2004), pp. 40–67, here pp. 43–4.
41 For the background of their flight see Zachmann, Tōa Dōbunkai, p. 115.
42 See Liang Qichao, Lun Xue Ribenwen zhi yi [On the benefits of studying Japanese], in: Kojima Shinji et al. (eds), *Chūgokujin no Nihonjinkan 100nen shi* (A History of one-hundred years of Chinese views of the Japanese) (Tokyo: Jiyū Kokuminsha, 1974), pp. 66–7 and Reynolds, *China*, p. 44.
43 Liang, Ribenwen, p. 67.
44 See Cemil Aydin, *The Politics of Anti-Westernism in Asia: Visions of World Order in Pan-Islamic and Pan-Asian Thought* (New York: Columbia University Press, 2007), pp. 54–9.
45 See Eri Hotta, *Pan-Asianism and Japan's War 1931–1945* (New York: Palgrave Macmillan, 2007), pp. 95–6; quote taken from Konoe Atsumaro, Konoe Atsumaro Nikki (Konoe Atsumaro Diary), vol. 2 (Tokyo: Kashima Kenkyū Shuppankai, 1968), p. 195.
46 Zachmann, Konoe, pp. 85–92.
47 Zachmann, Konoe, pp. 89–90.
48 See Hotta, *Pan-Asianism*, Chapter 3.
49 Quoted after Zachmann, *China and Japan*, p. 73.
50 See Chapters 7, 8, 10, and 16 in Saaler and Szpilman, *Pan-Asianism*.
51 See Hotta, *Pan-Asianism*, Chapter 3.
52 See Marilyn Lake and Henry Reynolds, *Drawing the Global Colour Line: White Men's Countries and the International Challenge of Racial Equality* (Cambridge: Cambridge UP, 2008), Chapter 11.
53 See Lake and Reynolds, *Drawing*, p. 266.

54 Estimate based on figures given for the year 1900 by Colin McEvedy and Richard Jones, *Atlas of World Population History* (New York: Penguin, 1978): Asia: 970 million, Europe: 100 million, Africa: 110 million, Americas: 145 million, Oceania: 6.75 million.
55 See Philipp Gassert, 'Völker Europas, wahrt Eure heiligsten Güter': Die Alte Welt und die japanische Herausforderung, in: Sprotte, Seifert and Löwe, *Russisch-Japanische Krieg*, pp. 278–93, here p. 281.
56 The painting is reproduced on the webpages of the German Historical Museum, www.dhm.de/archiv/ausstellungen/tsingtau/katalog/fotos/aus2_1.htm and in Gassert, Völker, p. 283.
57 See Heinz Gollwitzer, *Die gelbe Gefahr: Geschichte eines Schlagworts* (Göttingen: Vandenhoeck & Ruprecht, 1962), pp. 206–18 and Gassert, Völker.
58 Doitsu Kōtei no manako ni eijitaru Kōjinshu Dōmei [The Alliance of Yellow Peoples as reflected in the eyes of the German Emperor], in: *Yomiuri Shinbun*, 1 October 1900, p. 1.
59 See Rotem Kowner, The war as a turning point in modern Japanese history, in: Rotem Kowner (ed.), *The Impact of the Russo-Japanese War* (London: Routledge, 2007), pp. 29–46.
60 See Sven Saaler, Pan-Asianism, the 'Yellow Peril', and Suematsu Kenchō, 1905, in: Saaler and Szpilman, *Pan-Asianism*, pp. 141–8.
61 See Sven Saaler and C.W.A. Szpilman, Introduction, in: Saaler and Szpilman, *Pan-Asianism*, pp. 1–41, 15.
62 The full title of the book is *The White Peril in the Far East: An Interpretation of the Significance of the Russo-Japanese War* (New York: Fleming H. Revell Company, 1905).
63 See Gulick, *White Peril*, Chapter 6.
64 See Rotem Kowner, Between a colonial clash and world war zero. The impact of the Russo-Japanese War in a global perspective, in: *Impact*, pp. 1–25.
65 For example, Hiroi Tatsutarō, Kyokutō ni okeru hakka [The White Peril in the Far East], *Rikugo Zasshi*, 299 (1 November 1905); Kawakami Kiyoshi, Raddo hakushi no kōwaron [Dr Rudd's Theory on Reconciliation], *Asahi Shinbun*, 13 July 1905, p. 4, and Hakkaron [White Peril Theory], *Yomiuri Shinbun*, 26 August 1905, p. 2.
66 Hiroi, Kyokutō.
67 See Lake and Reynolds, *Drawing*, p. 177.
68 See Roger Daniels, *Politics of Prejudice: The Anti-Japanese Movement in California and the Struggle for Japanese Exclusion* (New York: Atheneum, 1974), Chapter 6.
69 See: Kō-Hakujin jōtotsu [The Clash of the Yellows and Whites], *Taiyō*, 14, 3 (15 February 1908), p. 9. On this issue see also Sven Saaler, The Russo-Japanese war and the emergence of the notion of the 'clash of races' in Japanese foreign policy, in: John W.M. Chapman and Inaba Chiharu (eds), *Rethinking the Russo-Japanese War, 1904–05*, vol. 2 (Folkestone: Global Oriental, 2007), pp. 274–89: 279–80.
70 Kō-Hakujin jōtotsu [The Clash of the Yellows and Whites], *Taiyō*, 14, 3 (15 February 1908), p. 231.
71 Kō-Hakujin jōtotsu [The Clash of the Yellows and Whites], *Taiyō*, 14, 3 (15 February 1908), p. 231.
72 See Aydin, *Politics*, pp. 151–60, and Hotta, *Pan-Asianism*, Chapter 4.

7

The Origins of Trans-imperial Policing: British-French Government Co-operation in the Surveillance of Anti-colonialists in Europe, 1905–25

Daniel Brückenhaus

In recent years, there has been a distinct trend among historians to extend their research beyond national borders. Numerous works on transnational movements and on connections between individual European countries have invigorated the study of modern history.[1] At the same time, historians writing in the context of the 'New Imperial History' have shown the myriad ways in which European metropoles and their colonies influenced each other.[2]

The present chapter combines these two approaches. Focusing on the period between 1905 and 1925, it traces the ways in which the emergence of transnational networks of anti-colonialists in Europe led to co-operation between the British and the French authorities. Faced with increasing numbers of activists from the British colonies who were working in France against the British Empire, British police and government officials asked their French counterparts for help. This led to transfers of strategy and information between the two countries.

As these transfers were shaped by the roles of France and Britain as the centres of the world's two largest colonial empires, they can be described not only as transnational, but also as *trans-imperial*. I have chosen this notion over the related term *inter-imperial* because it puts an emphasis on the fact that such encounters of empires did not simply occur in a space 'in between' them. Rather, the internal structures of these empires were frequently transformed through such exchanges. Instead of regarding empires as closed entities, the chapter therefore argues that in the first half of the twentieth century, the borders between them were surprisingly porous.[3]

Meanwhile, the chapter also shows that when it came to information exchange and co-operation between the French and the British authorities, this porousness was frequently called into question. Among the French population, there was much public resistance to their government acting according to British demands. Many in France, especially among liberals and left-wing groups, saw such co-operation as a sign of losing their national independence and their civil liberties. Anti-colonialists from the British colonies who were hiding in France could sometimes make use of such sentiments to protect themselves from potential expulsion or extradition at the bidding of the British government.

After first giving a short introduction to colonial policing in Europe, the chapter then follows the themes outlined above through time, focusing on four instances of attempted trans-imperial government co-operation against anti-colonialists. Comparing these case studies will allow us to determine the factors influencing the extent of trans-imperial communication and information exchange at various points in early twentieth-century history.

I. The historical context: colonial surveillance in Europe

In the years after 1905, more and more non-European anti-colonialists became politically active in Britain. Initially, the majority of them arrived from India, but soon these pioneers were joined by others who came from a large number of different British colonies. These activists were inspired by a number of recent developments that seemed to show the limited legitimacy of colonialism, as well as the chances of success of a potential rebellion against imperial rule. For instance, in India, the partition of Bengal in 1905 had led to a violent resistance campaign; and the Japanese victory over Russia in the same year provided proof that it was possible for non-Westerners to defeat a major European power.[4]

In carrying out their political work in Britain, these anti-colonialists made use of the curious split within the Western empires that combined a liberal political system in the metropole with authoritarian rule in the colonies. As – at least on paper – inner-European laws did not distinguish systematically between Europeans and non-Europeans, activists could feel considerably safer in the very centre of 'their' colonial empire than at home in the colonies, where even small acts of subversion were often punished with long prison terms.[5]

Soon, however, the British authorities began to react against the suspected 'infection' of their home country with anti-colonial sedition. The Special Branch, a political policing institution that was originally created in 1883 as part of the London metropolitan police forces,[6] began to put the local anti-colonialists under close surveillance. Moreover, the British authorities increased their control of the postal routes between Britain and India in order to prevent the sending of subversive literature and explosives.[7] The level of attempted government control increased even further after, in 1909, an anti-colonialist assassinated a British colonial official in London. A new section of the Branch, specifically devoted to Indians, was formed,[8] which would soon develop into the Indian Political Intelligence Service (IPI).[9]

Faced with this new level of government surveillance, many anti-colonialists decided to make a second move across borders; this time within Europe. Many of them relocated across the Channel to France, where they were joined by others arriving directly from the British colonies. Thereby, Paris became one of the world's most important centres of anti-colonial activity.[10]

It was this situation that motivated British officials not only to send informants to France,[11] but also to approach the French authorities, trying to convince them to co-operate against the anti-colonial threat. From 1908 onwards, the British authorities, often working through the British Embassy in Paris, were in close contact with the French Sûreté Générale (which was responsible for all kinds of 'politically motivated crimes').[12] For instance, British officials asked their French counterparts to observe the meeting places of anti-colonialists in and around Paris;[13] and French officials began to report to the British on anti-colonialists who were suspected of trying to learn bomb-making.[14]

Such co-operation broke new ground in a number of ways. In the second half of the nineteenth century Britain had been the most important destination for radical political refugees from the Continent, including socialists and anarchists. The British government had granted these activists asylum, based on an implicit pact according to which they would not cause any trouble in Britain, but instead would direct their activities outwards, back towards their original home countries. On those grounds, numerous conflicts between European governments had developed. Members of Continental administrations often had attacked the tolerant attitude of the British, and sometimes had tried to take things into their own hands, as was reflected in early examples of the British spy novel, such as Joseph Conrad's *The Secret Agent*. Meanwhile, in stark contrast to the demands for help that Continental countries had directed at Britain, the British authorities almost never had had to ask such favours in the opposite direction. This was one reason why the British government had remained sceptical about calls by Continental powers for a more extended, institutionalized international police co-operation, as had been proposed, for instance, during the anti-anarchist congress at Rome in 1898.[15]

However, this pattern changed completely at the moment when anti-colonialists began to move to the Continent. Suddenly, it was now the British who were asking Continental authorities for help against their 'own' subversives, leading to many heated discussions across Europe.

Many of these debates took place in the context of the emerging British-French alliance, the Entente Cordiale, whose constituting treaties had been signed in 1904. Increasingly, the British-French conflicts in the colonial realm of the late nineteenth century were overcome, while tensions with Germany were on the rise. Inspired, in part, by evocative accounts written by early pioneers of spy fiction, British and French officials worried about a potential German invasion of Britain.[16] What was more, they increasingly became fearful about German officials and anti-colonialists working together on schemes against the Western empires.[17] These anxieties were a crucial reason for many among the British and French authorities to propose closer co-operation. At the same time, critical voices in France warned of the danger that such pro-colonial police co-operation might undermine the very ideological foundations of the new Western alliance, whose proponents prided themselves on their liberalism that supposedly set France and Britain apart from Germany.

II. Case study 1: the *Affaire Savarkar* (1910)

One of the first instances in which British-French government co-operation against anti-colonialists came to the forefront of European debates about empire and civil liberties concerned the Indian activist Vinayak Damodar Savarkar. Savarkar was a member of the wave of politicized immigrants who arrived in Britain after 1905. For several years he was active in London, where he was busy translating the autobiography of his personal hero Giuseppe Mazzini into Marathi, and writing a well-known account of the 1857 Indian rebellion.[18] When in January 1910 the Indian police caught a number of his allies, and suspected them of being involved in the killing of a British government collector in India, the British authorities began to build a case against Savarkar. He was accused of having prepared the murder by founding secret societies, by giving anti-government speeches in India and Britain, and by helping to smuggle in from Europe the weapons that were used for the assassination.[19]

Savarkar had already anticipated this development and had left Britain for France, out of the reach of the British authorities;[20] however, for reasons that are still not entirely clear,[21] in April of that year he decided to return to England. This led to his immediate arrest, based on a warrant given out by the government of India 'for offences of sedition and abetment of murder in India'.[22] In spite of Savarkar's protests that he should be tried in Britain according to the more liberal laws of the metropole, the British authorities decided to take him back by ship to India, where he would face his charges.[23]

However, Savarkar immediately made plans to use inner-European national divides for his own purposes. Knowing that his ship was scheduled to stop in the French port city of Marseille, he hoped to escape there; possibly inspired by the example of Mazzini, who in 1831 had successfully fled to that city from Austrian persecution when fighting for Italy's national independence.[24] Savarkar knew that there was a sizable contingent of Indian fugitives in Paris. If they could aid his escape from the ship, and if he was then granted political asylum in France – similarly to how French anarchists had been granted asylum in Britain in the past – he would be safe.

But the British authorities anticipated this possibility and built on their newly established, close transnational contacts with the French police in order to prevent such an event from occurring. In June of 1910, the head of New Scotland Yard contacted the director of the French political police. In return, the heads of the French Sûreté Générale assured the British that they would 'avoid any incident' in Marseille, and promised that they would prevent any Indian without a valid ticket from entering the ship.[25]

Savarkar, aware that it was therefore impossible for the Paris Indians to reach him, took his fate into his own hands. On 8 July 1910, he asked his guards to take him to the bathroom. After entering, he locked the door, slipped through the window, jumped into the water, and swam to the quay. Once ashore he approached a French policeman and addressed him directly, hoping to be taken into French custody where he could have applied for asylum. However, as Savarkar did not speak French and the policeman did not understand English, communication could not be established. The policeman arrested Savarkar, and, with the aid of the British guards who had followed him ashore, brought him back to the ship. The boat then went on to India where Savarkar was put on trial.[26]

The Savarkar story up to this point shows how police authorities of both countries were in favour of close co-operation. However, it soon became clear that not everyone in Western Europe agreed. And as we will see, anti-colonialists in Europe quickly tried to take advantage of that fact, using inner-European pride in civil liberties and national sovereignty as a means to maintain their own transnational networks.

As soon as Savarkar was forced to continue his involuntary voyage to India, critical French voices began to make themselves heard in the public sphere. It is worthwhile examining their arguments in some detail, one of which concerned the identity of the Entente Cordiale. Many in France were sceptical of arguments justifying closer police co-operation in reference to that treaty, and instead chose to see it as an agreement directed solely at countering military threats. They also pointed out the apparent contradictions in the British demands for co-operation. Earlier, the British had protected groups like the Russian nihilists in Britain, but now they were apparently unwilling to apply the same principles to Indian fugitives to France.[27] These sentiments soon led to widespread protests in France that raised pointed questions. Were the British willing to give up their own liberal traditions as soon as these traditions went against their imperial interests? Did the British have the right to enter French territory to take back a prisoner who had escaped to French soil? And had the French policeman been authorized to return Savarkar to the ship?

The Indian anti-colonialists in France were very aware of such French discontent, and attempted to 'dock onto' the emerging French critical discourse. They were helped in that endeavour by their contacts with French journalists, and with members of the French left-wing political parties, including Jean Longuet, a grandson of Karl Marx, and the socialist leader Jean Jaurès, who voiced their protests in political meetings and in the press. It was seemingly this public pressure that eventually led the French ambassador in London to demand the return of Savarkar to French territory.[28]

Meanwhile, the press campaign initiated by the Indians spread across the Channel to Britain. The implications of the Savarkar case soon became clear to members of the international European Left more generally. The British left-wing activist Guy Aldred appealed to the 'English proletariat' in the name of a newly founded 'Committee of Savarkar's Liberation' and announced a 'Savarkar Release Tour' throughout Britain. As the Labour leader Keir Hardie pointed out, while the British had harboured radical activists such as Garibaldi, Mazzini, Kossuth and Marx in the past, now Britain was turning away from its liberal traditions, as soon as it became in its imperial interest to do so. There was a danger that a precedent would be set that might lead to the re-importation of imperial, autocratic methods of governance into the metropole, and thereby to the undermining not only of anti-colonial, but of any revolutionary work throughout Europe.[29]

As the conflict between Britain and France over Savarkar's fate continued, the governments of both countries agreed in October of 1910 to bring the case before a tribunal at the Court of Arbitration in The Hague.[30] While British and French officials came to a consensus on the sequence of events that had occurred in Marseille, the court case soon turned into a debate about whether or not Savarkar's arrest had constituted an instance of wilful and conscious police co-operation across national borders.

The British, in their official statements, stressed that it had not been the British guards who had made the arrest but that they had only assisted the French policeman in bringing Savarkar back on board. They also argued that the handing over of Savarkar by the French police had happened simply according to the earlier agreement by which the French had promised their aid against attempts to free Savarkar in Marseille. Now that the valuable prisoner was back in British hands the French authorities could not change their minds after the fact.[31]

The French brought forward a different interpretation, arguing that the French-British agreement had been much more specific, and actually did not cover what had happened in Marseille. They stressed that the British letter to the French police had only mentioned preventing the French Indians from setting Savarkar free, but had made no mention of preventing an attempt by Savarkar to free *himself*. Moreover, the French argued, the arrangement between the two police forces had not been a formal agreement between the two governments, and therefore could not have granted the British the right to escort Savarkar to (or from) French territory; such a demand would have had to be made through the official diplomatic channels. Finally, the French claimed that Savarkar's re-arrest had not even been made according to the limited British-French police agreement. They argued that the policeman had not realized the identity of the person he had arrested, thinking him merely a deserter. In capturing Savarkar the officer had acted according to an entirely different, previous French-British agreement to return deserters to their ships – an agreement which, again, was very specific and did not apply to Savarkar's case.[32]

On 24 February 1911, The Hague tribunal made public its final decision, in favour of the British pleas. The explanation focused on the fact that the British, after the exchange of letters between the two police forces, 'might well have believed that they could count on the assistance of the French police'. In their arguments the tribunal therefore embraced the British construction of reality according to which a broad, generalized agreement in favour of transnational policing had indeed been in existence. While it was admitted that 'an irregularity was committed by the arrest of Savarkar, and by his being handed over to the British Police', international law did not mandate any obligation to restore the prisoner because of a 'mistake committed by the foreign agent who delivered him up to that Power [the British]'.[33] In this last argument the tribunal also voted in favour of the British claim that the police forces could indeed be seen as 'arms' of the government.

The decision sealed Savarkar's fate for several decades. He was eventually found guilty by an Indian court and sentenced to fifty years imprisonment on the Andaman Islands. He was later moved to a number of other prisons and released in 1924 under the condition that he must not leave the district in which he was living. These restrictions were lifted only in 1937. Savarkar, taking up political work again, would go on to become one of the icons of radical Hindu nationalism.

III. Case study 2: British attacks against Indian anti-colonialists in France during World War I (1914)

As became clear in Savarkar's case, there was in 1910 a considerable amount of public resistance against British police incursions into French territory. Our next case study takes us several years forward in time, to the early months of World War I. Its main protagonists are again Indian anti-colonialists in France, and British government officials who attempted to convince their French counterparts to aid them in their fight against these activists. This example allows us to ask about the effects of the war on the chances for trans-imperial government co-operation. As will become clear, even under wartime conditions, resistance against such co-operation did not die out entirely. However, as the liberal safeguards of peacetime were weakened considerably during the fight against Germany, such critical voices lost much of their influence, allowing the British a much tighter control of French space.

We have seen above how the emerging anti-German alliance of the Entente Cordiale had structured the pre-war discussions of transnational police co-operation. After the outbreak of hostilities on 28 July 1914, this co-operation grew even closer. According to French and British wartime propaganda, the war was to be seen as a battle of Western civilization and democracy against German-Prussian autocracy and barbarism.[34]

Especially important in moving the British and French authorities closer to each other was the fact that the German government was now actively recruiting anti-colonialists from the Western empires. In co-operation with state-run organizations such as the Information Office for the Orient (Nachrichtenstelle für den Orient), these anti-colonialists worked together with German officials in sending propaganda materials to British and French colonial troops, as well as in conveying weapons and money to India. For many British and French officials, it made sense to counter this German-anti-colonial alliance not only with an extended level of surveillance but also with closer co-operation between Western European colonial and police officials.[35]

Between September 1914 and the end of 1915, large numbers of colonial soldiers were stationed on the Western Front.[36] From the very beginning, the British police were worried that Indian activists in Paris might access these troops, and subvert them with anti-colonial ideas. After an Indian revolutionary had been caught with 'seditious literature intended for dissemination amongst the Indian soldiery', the British greatly expanded their postal censorship system,[37] and they decided, once again, that they needed French police and government support to keep such radicals in check. According to a British official, the French authorities were 'all most ready and anxious' to help the British.[38] Communications from this time reveal British and French discussions about restricting the access of civilians into Indian soldiers' camps, and about increasing troop morale by making Indian soldiers see 'a good force of French troops', arranged as an 'international courtesy'.[39]

By focusing on two well-known Indian anti-colonialists of this period, namely the co-founders of the Paris Indian Society, S.R. Rana and 'Madame Cama', we can observe in more detail how government co-operation under wartime conditions played out in practice. Born in 1861 in Bombay, the Parsee revolutionary Bhikaiji Rustom Cama (called 'Madame Cama' both by her friends and by the police forces),[40] had famously unfurled the first Indian national flag of independence at the Stuttgart Socialist Congress in 1907. In 1909, she relocated her centre of activities to France,[41] where she edited the anti-colonialist journal *Bande Mataram*.[42] In 1910, British spies suspected her of sending revolvers to India, concealed in toys that were sent supposedly as Christmas presents.[43]

At the outbreak of the war, British spies in Paris observed Cama making hurried enquiries and preparations to move, as she knew that the new level of transnational government co-operation meant a much more direct British access to her and other Indians in France. A lawyer warned her against going to the northern French port town of Boulogne as this was too proximal to the Channel.[44] She eventually moved to Marseille in the south of the country, believing that there she could evade surveillance. It soon became clear, however, that British influence had reached even that part of France. When Cama attempted to establish contact with some Punjabi clerks who were serving with the Indian Expeditionary Force in Marseille, the British authorities collaborated with their French counterparts in forcing her to leave that city.[45]

This was a clear departure from pre-war policy. The British themselves acknowledged that 'under ordinary circumstances' – namely before the war – such a request would have had few chances of success. Before 1914, Cama's influential socialist friends would have raised a strong public outcry against such a removal, as Savarkar's allies had done in 1910, and French officials would have been too fearful of being seen as mere British agents. Now, however, the situation had changed. In the words of one British official, 'as military law now prevailed, there could be no pretext for [the French] not acting'.[46] These arguments prevailed. On 25 October, Cama was ordered to leave Marseille. On 1 November, after reaching Bordeaux, she was told to remain there and to report herself once a week. She had to promise to 'cease her seditious activities during the war' if she did not want to face unpleasant consequences. This ended at least her open political activity; she could not continue her publishing work.[47] While France had been before the war a safe haven for anti-British activism, this was clearly no longer the case.

While Madame Cama was at least allowed to remain in France, the British authorities went even further in their attempt to control S.R. Rana. Born in India in 1878, Rana was one of Cama's closest collaborators and had been living in Paris since the pre-war period. One British official thought him to be 'the centre of all Indian schemes'.[48] After war broke out, Rana first got into trouble with the British government over questions of citizenship. He lived with a woman of German origin who he claimed to have married secretly in London, and applied in 1914 to have his status as a British subject extended to her. The French authorities, under pressure from the British, rejected this application and then went on to keep her under 'strict supervision' as an enemy alien, not allowed to leave the south-western port town of Arcachon.[49]

Soon after, the British prevented Rana's attempt to become an interpreter for the Indian troops in France, which they saw as yet another anti-colonialist campaign to infect loyal troops with seditious thoughts. Under British influence, the French authorities promised to keep subversives away from the Indian soldiers, and the British supplied them with a list of such 'undesirables'.[50] British pressure also prevented Rana from succeeding in his attempt to be naturalized, through his military service, as a French citizen – an act that would have entirely immunized him, while on French territory, from any action the British might try to take against him.[51]

Moreover, in addition to restraining Rana's influence and radius of action within France, the British went one step further and tried to have him deported as an 'undesirable foreigner'. Comparing the public reaction to this attempt with that resulting from Savarkar's re-arrest can help us determine where the boundaries of the British ability to influence the French lay under wartime conditions.

As soon became clear, these boundaries had been expanded considerably since the war began; however, they still had not been dissolved entirely. While the French measures against Rana described so far seem to have been generally accepted under wartime conditions, even after 1914 there remained strong political pressure in France against directly handing over an anti-colonialist to the British. British officials were told by the French foreign minister that the matter was a 'very delicate one', a response that the British interpreted as driven by the French prime minister's 'socialist scruples'. The inclusion of socialists in the French wartime cabinet 'to keep the party quiet during the war' added to the suspected left-wing influence. The British hope that Mr Rana might be deported through a 'simple', non-political 'measure of police' was thereby destroyed.[52]

Meanwhile, from the further developments of the case it also becomes clear how, under wartime conditions, such resistance against government co-operation had been weakened. While in 1910 the French government had yielded to public pressure demanding Savarkar's return to France, in 1914 they decided to forge a compromise that achieved the British goal of keeping Rana out of France, while still avoiding the embarrassing measure of handing a refugee directly to his imperial masters. In October of 1914, Rana was arrested by French police. The government in Paris then proposed that Rana be brought to the French island of Martinique, where he was to stay for the rest of the war.[53]

Rana, for obvious reasons, was not content with this compromise. Attempting to repeat the pre-war strategy of creating a public outcry against French politicians who carried out the bidding of the British, he protested with letters to the French Cabinet, professing his 'love for France' and his desire to 'become a French citizen and be permitted to join the army'.[54] Several of Rana's socialist allies also protested, through the interior minister, against his deportation. However, in the end the government could not be convinced to change course and rebuke the British request.[55] Part of the reason was that under wartime conditions the government was able to stifle the outcry against Rana's release by threatening his Indian allies with internment and arrest if they continued to protest.[56] Rana himself was removed to the state prison at Bordeaux when it was discovered that he was 'still corresponding surreptitiously with his friends'.[57]

Rana's ship to Martinique left on 7 January. Continued efforts by his allies to have his deportation revoked on the grounds of 'dirty English influence' remained unsuccessful.[58] The change in French government attitudes is clear. While five years earlier the French government had tried with all means at its disposal to undo Savarkar's return to the British, now it was the French government itself that, in accordance with British wishes, made the decision to exile an Indian activist from Europe.

IV. Case study 3: the surveillance of Saad Zaghloul's delegation (1919)

After more than four years of brutal fighting, the armistice of November 1918 ended open hostilities in Europe. Soon after, a great number of negotiators came to Paris to decide on the terms of the peace treaty. Historians have recently pointed out how people from various colonial territories attempted to participate in the conference in order to influence its outcome in their favour. Many argued that the Wilsonian promise of self-determination must be applied to the colonized as well.[59]

Of course, the British authorities had little interest in anti-colonialists having a say in the new global order. To silence such unwelcome voices, the British police attempted to continue their wartime project of controlling French space even after 1918. On the following pages, we will focus on British efforts to restrain the activities of an Egyptian delegation to the conference, led by the future Egyptian prime minister, Saad Zaghloul (1859–1927), and compare them to earlier instances of attempted government co-operation.

At every stage in the story of this delegation, we can see the British authorities' efforts to restrict the Egyptians' mobility. After the conclusion of the Armistice, the delegates attempted to leave Egypt for France and Britain to agitate against the current draft of the peace treaty, which made permanent Egypt's status as a British Protectorate. The British authorities, who feared the Egyptians' influence over other members of the peace conference, not only rejected their applications for travel visas to Europe, but in March 1919 removed Saad Zaghloul, and his closest followers, from Egypt to the island of Malta.[60]

However, in the following months, the British authorities realized that they had underestimated the reaction among the Egyptian populace. Widespread riots erupted, aimed at forcing the British to allow the delegation to make their case in France.[61] When the situation was getting out of their control, the British reversed their decision. On 6 April 1919, they revoked the internment of Zaghloul and his compatriots, and granted the members of the delegation the right to travel to Europe.[62] The delegation arrived in Paris within the same month.[63]

Now that they supposed themselves out of the direct reach of the British, the delegation tried to make the most of their new-found freedom. For instance, they attempted to contact the conference participants in order to provide them with manifestos, and they sent a plea to members of the French Parliament.[64] In addition, the Egyptians also made use of a number of anti-colonialist press connections dating from the pre-war era to try to influence French public opinion. Such connections included the French editor Jean Longuet, who had repeatedly supported Indian anti-colonialists in the past.[65] The arguments the Egyptians brought forward often built on well-established templates. One of their central strategies was to stress the traditional cultural and political connections between Egypt and France, calling Egypt the 'beloved daughter of France'.[66] The delegates therefore put forward an alternative to the British notion of a unity of interest between the world's two most important colonial empires.

Even though the members of the delegation were now active outside of the borders of the British Empire, it did not take the British long to react. They instituted a secret surveillance apparatus in France, specifically aimed at the delegation. All of the delegation's propaganda material was to be sent to the British authorities in order to allow British officials to respond to Egyptian descriptions of the British as 'harsh', 'tyrannical', 'brutal' and prone to atrocities. In addition, the contacts between the Egyptian delegation and Continental communists were to be monitored,[67] as well as possible movements of Egyptians between France and Egypt.[68]

While this kind of colonial surveillance by now had almost a fifteen-year tradition, the British in 1919 also developed an additional strategy, namely to adopt the established anti-colonial method of appealing to the press and French public opinion. In what they called 'counterblast propaganda',[69] the British authorities began to supply leading newspapers in France, Italy and Switzerland with what the British saw as 'full and accurate information as to events in Egypt'.[70] French newspapers were provided with a pro-British interpretation of the Egyptian developments, which was supposed to work like an antibody against infection with 'seditious' Egyptian thoughts.[71]

In terms of the press campaign's content, the central strategy was to counter the Egyptians' arguments about a unity of interest between the Egyptian population and the French. British officials tried to argue that the Egyptians' efforts were not a specific threat to British rule alone but constituted a much more general anti-imperial danger. The British authorities stressed, first of all, that the Egyptians' activities were undermining the standing of *all* colonial powers in Northern Africa. Secondly, the agitation in Egypt would contribute to the growth of a Bolshevist campaign, which would travel across imperial borders equally easily and would challenge any capitalist country's economic interests. Finally, the British authorities portrayed the Egyptian movement as generally xenophobic. Thereby they created a stark dichotomy between all Europeans on the one hand and all Africans on the other.[72] On those grounds, the British tried to convince the French to continue their earlier co-operation based on the idea that French and British interests were identical.[73]

However, now that the war had ended, co-operation was a more difficult undertaking. The emergency laws of the period between 1914 and 1918 had now been taken back. Therefore, a straightforward repression or imprisonment of the Egyptian delegation according to British wishes was out of the question.

Under these circumstances, we can observe the emergence of yet another new British approach that would gain increasing importance in future years. As there were strong limitations to the level of *open* co-operation that French officials were willing and able to offer, the British increasingly attempted to influence the French behind the scenes only, in order to protect them from embarrassing attacks in the French public sphere. The British thereby developed what can be called a 'hidden transcript from above'.[74]

It seems that these secret British efforts to entice the French to co-operate were relatively successful, partly maintaining the heightened level of French-British co-operation during the war. Following British confidential requests, French officials gave no support to the delegation.[75] The French authorities also agreed to give directions to the press to stop printing information that had been received from the delegation. While the French authorities had no legal means to outlaw such publications, their influence over most newspapers was strong enough to enforce observation of this demand. Only the socialist press, which prided itself on its independence from government intrusion, continued to publish what the authorities saw as subversive articles.[76] The French authorities also agreed to send a notification to the press, reminding them of the fact that the French government had already recognized in principle, in 1914, the British protectorate over Egypt.[77]

French-British secret co-operation against 'subversive' journalists can be observed in more detail in the case of the French journalist Georges Vayssié, who had been working in Egypt as the editor of the *Journal du Caire* but had recently come to France. British authorities suspected him of being bribed by the Egyptians to work for their press campaign.[78] In reaction to British calls to put pressure on the journalist,[79] French officials adopted the British argument that the Egyptians were threatening *all* colonial powers in North Africa and therefore that Vayssié was also conducting 'an anti-French campaign'.[80] British and French authorities also discussed the possibility of countering the supposed Egyptian bribes to Vayssié with their own payments.[81] In May 1919, French officials requested him to 'ensure' that nothing published in his journal 'can give the impression that he encourages the nationalist movement'.[82] Vayssié apparently agreed to these demands,[83] and British informants reported soon after that the members of the Egyptian delegation were now 'being avoided by M. Vayssié'.[84]

In the end, the French indeed seem to have conceptualized their position towards the Egyptians in the trans-imperial sense that the British wished to instil in them. In May 1919, French officials told the British that their censor had been 'instructed to prevent [the] publication of information inspired by nationalists or having the character of anti-French or anti-British propaganda in Asia Minor or North Africa'.[85] In France itself, the inter-imperial co-operation was seen as equally successful. In June 1919, an informant told British officials that the members of the delegation in Paris were 'making no progress at all' and that they realized now 'that there was nothing to be hoped for from either the French or the Italians'.[86]

The case of Zaghloul's delegation provides one example of a pattern which would continue throughout much of the inter-war period. There was little co-operation on paper, and French officials never broke any of their own country's laws. When they co-operated with the British they did so in instances where they could make a convincing case that they were acting according to *French* interests, rather than just following British demands. These same arguments, however, had often been supplied by the British authorities, who tried to make them fit into the inner-French discourse. Under the surface, there were indeed considerable chances for the emergence of a Franco-British 'anti-anti-colonial holy alliance'.[87]

British-French police co-operation played an important role, among others, in making sure that in the end, the Versailles Treaty did very little to improve the situation of the colonized populations. Calls for greater equality in the colonies, in return for the colonized having fought a European war, were not heard. Instead, the treaty even increased the reach of the French and British colonial empires, as most of the former German colonies, as well as other areas, were given over to Western European control. While these new territories were officially called 'mandates' and not 'colonies', and were supposed to gradually be moved towards more autonomy, in practice, British and French rule in those regions remained autocratic.[88]

V. Case study 4: the surveillance of M.N. Roy's networks of activists (1923)

A final case study moves us again several years into the future, to the early 1920s, and focuses on the Indian anti-colonialist M.N. Roy. The British and French authorities' reaction to his activities allow us to analyse trans-imperial government co-operation in yet another political and ideological context. The years between 1919 and 1925 were characterized by economic crises and political conflict. Relations between Germany and the Western allies (especially France) remained tense, with continued occupation of the Rhineland by Western troops. At the same time, after the Bolshevik Revolution in Russia, and the founding of the Communist International (Comintern) in 1919, global communism was on the rise. Anti-colonialists, some of whom continued to reside in Germany, made use of those developments for their own purposes. Many tried to obtain communist resources for their work, while others retained their contacts with German government officials and right-wing groups. Throughout Europe, anti-colonial organizations grew in complexity and sophistication.

M.N. Roy's network provides one example of an anti-colonialist who was active in various European countries simultaneously; a situation that had a strong influence on the structures of British-French government co-operation. The British saw Roy as especially threatening; in part because of the ways in which he used various spaces outside of his 'own' empire to fight the colonial authorities.[89]

Born in 1887 in West Bengal, Roy had begun his political career as part of the revolutionary movement in Calcutta. However, in 1915 he left India and travelled to different parts of Asia, working together with German agents on anti-British schemes. After being active for several years in the USA and Mexico, from 1920 onwards he began to travel back and forth between Russia and Germany. He gained considerable influence as a specialist for 'Oriental' questions in the newly-founded Comintern, arguing against Lenin for a mass-based left-wing revolution in the colonies. In 1921, he went to Tashkent to found the Communist Party of India together with a number of other Indians in exile, but in 1922 he was again to be found in Berlin, which at this point became his main headquarters.[90]

Over the next years, the French Empire would become an equally important space for him, as he tried to find a way to smuggle his political writings, including his newspaper, the *Vanguard of Indian Independence,* into British India. While those writings were printed in Germany, from 1923 onwards, Roy took advantage of a number of small French enclaves on the Indian mainland (above all Pondicherry), which allowed easy access to British territory.[91] Roy first had the literature sent from Germany to Marseille.[92] From there it could travel the whole distance to the Indian subcontinent without leaving the French Empire, thereby remaining outside of the reach of the British censorship authorities. Once the literature arrived in Pondicherry it could be smuggled relatively easily into British India.[93] Roy's protected status in Germany allowed him to plan his activities in safety, while he used his contacts in the French Communist Party to secure employment certificates that allowed his agents to get visas for France.[94]

The British reacted by increasing their mail censorship, and calculated that they were able to confiscate about half of the propagandist materials that Roy sent to India.[95] They sentenced those collaborators in India that they could get a hold of to long prison terms,[96] and sent many additional spies to France and Germany.[97] However, for the purposes of this chapter, the most interesting question is to what extent, and in what ways, trans-imperial co-operation between the French and British authorities occurred in Roy's case.

From the beginning, the trans-national and trans-imperial nature of Roy's network convinced the British authorities that they could only succeed against him with the help of other governments. In securing this help, the British expanded upon the strategy that they had used in Zaghloul's case, namely to maintain a secret, hidden realm of communication, in addition to their official statements.

The first target of the British authorities were German officials. As in their communications with the French in 1919, the British did not make any public pleas for help. Instead, they convinced the Germans, in secret, to incriminate Roy. They informed the Germans of infractions that Roy had committed in their country, which German officials could then punish according to their own criminal laws. Thereby British influence remained invisible. After Roy and his wife had been harassed repeatedly by German police officers who likely were acting upon information provided by British sources, Roy decided to go beyond using France as a transfer route to India, and to relocate his headquarters to that country.[98] While in France, he led a (short-lived) communist International Colonial Office, and continued to send literature to India.[99]

From a British point of view, the record therefore was somewhat mixed. British pressure certainly had dislocated Roy's network. On the other hand, Roy was still out of their direct reach. However, the British authorities could now build on their numerous precedents of working together with French police forces and authorities. They soon began to put pressure on the French government to act against Roy and his followers.

At this point it is important, once again, to ask about the factors involved in French officials' decisions to comply with British demands or to reject them. Roy, in the tradition of earlier Indians active in France, had influential allies in the public sphere. He was in direct contact with members of French left-wing and left-liberal organizations, such as the French Communist Party, the Ligue des Droits de l'Homme or the left-wing newspaper *L'Humanité*, which would see any instance of police co-operation as part of a capitalist conspiracy and/or as threatening French liberal traditions.

On the other hand, working in favour of co-operation were foreign policy considerations that made some politicians willing to help their most important wartime ally. Moreover, while Roy continued to focus most of his activity on challenging colonialism in India, French politicians might well have felt threatened by Roy's Colonial Office, which was targeting not only the British but also the French colonies.[100]

In the end, the case for co-operation won out once more, and French officials agreed to support the British against Roy. After first working closely with the French in silencing Roy's supporters in Pondicherry,[101] the British then began to target Roy's centre of operations in France. However, given Roy's influential inner-European allies, the British authorities once again had to keep their influence hidden. As in Zaghloul's case, the British made sure to give the French the opportunity to act against Roy according to their own laws. After continued British pressure,[102] Roy was eventually located and arrested through the hidden co-operation of French police and British secret service agents. In January of 1925, he was expelled from French territory, after British sources had informed the French that he was living in their country using a forged Mexican passport.[103]

By enforcing their own laws against Roy, the French authorities could deny having acted according to British wishes. Of course, Roy's allies again tried to convince the French population otherwise. While they could not necessarily prove French-British co-operation, they could still try to make the case that such co-operation was likely to have occurred. Roy's wife started a large-scale media campaign that included well-known French writers and intellectuals such as Henri Barbusse. In a circular sent out to French newspapers, Evelyn Roy attacked the 'violation of the right of asylum on French soil' which was a threatening sign of how the 'closer Franco-British Entente' of recent years was undermining both national sovereignty, and Western European liberal values.[104] French writers quickly picked up these arguments. The playwright and poet Charles Vildrac described how Roy, 'pursued, spied upon by the British Police wherever he goes [...] came to France expecting to find asylum in this country, the traditional home of political liberty and the rights of men'. Pointing to the growing power of political police forces in Europe, he argued that the expulsion seemed to be 'less of an affair between the Government of France and England [sic] than a case of simple collusion between the police of both countries. The International Police has adopted the habit of "working" together, and there is nothing which they refuse each other'.[105]

When the French and British had co-operated earlier in Pondicherry, liberal critics had had relatively little influence. Now, however, when co-operation was carried out within Europe, the British authorities feared that a liberal and left-wing attack campaign might be successful and would convince the French government to allow Roy's return to France.[106] French officials who tried to defend Roy's removal even asked their British equivalents to provide them with 'information to be of assistance in resisting such pressure' from the Left.[107]

In the end, however, the protests did not prove strong enough to force the government to revoke Roy's expulsion. Roy apparently went back to the Soviet Union where he would be safe from British extradition requests. He would return to Germany a few years later; but for the time being was disconnected from the valuable routes of human and information transfer that he had been able to use while in Germany and France.[108]

However, while his example shows the great extent of police co-operation in this period, the fact that he was only expelled, rather than extradited to Britain, also shows the continuing limits under which the authorities had to act. It was still not possible for French officials to hand over a refugee on their territory directly to the British; in part because by doing so, they would have had to acknowledge, in public, that they prioritized their shared imperial interests with Britain over cherished liberal traditions at home.

VI. Conclusion

This chapter has demonstrated the complexity of the gate-keeping mechanisms that worked in favour of, or against, information exchange and co-operation between the authorities of different empires. As has become clear, such co-operation constantly had to be negotiated with a number of critical groups, including European left-wing and liberal writers. These negotiations were closely connected to inner-European debates about democracy, liberalism and government transparency, as well as about the relationship between the metropolitan/democratic element, and the colonial/autocratic element in the Western model of governance.

We have seen how French government and police officials were often quite willing to co-operate with the British authorities against the anti-colonialist threat. From their point of view, it frequently seemed natural that the Western countries, with their similarities in political ideology and interests worldwide, should stick together. In contrast, Frenchmen of left-wing and liberal persuasions (as well as the British Left) were often opposed to such co-operation; in part because it usually went together with an import of colonial methods of rule and policing into Europe. As these critics pointed out, it was ironic to justify the undermining of liberal traditions by pointing to the German threat, while simultaneously referring to these very liberal traditions to prove the superiority of the 'Western model' over Prussian authoritarianism. Given this discontent, anti-colonialists who worked south of the Channel could form temporary alliances with a critical metropolitan French public against the French colonial milieu.

For non-European activists using this strategy, their ability to protect themselves from British-French pro-colonial co-operation depended on the strength or weakness of democratic sentiments and liberal safeguards at various points in time. For example, we have seen how during World War I, when liberal norms were restricted under the prevailing state of emergency, French voices who were critical of government co-operation lost some of their influence. Thereby the British authorities were allowed more access to anti-colonialists who were hiding in France. Moreover, it also became clear how, especially after World War I, the British authorities increasingly circumvented liberal resistance against government co-operation by communicating in secret. This allowed the French government authorities to maintain the public image of metropolitan, liberal openness, while secretly supporting the import of non-democratic, colonial policing measures into Europe proper. While even under these circumstances co-operation never became total, as shown by the fact that the French authorities never willingly handed over any activists directly to the British, it did make life considerably more difficult for those opposing colonial rule.

It thus becomes clear that European history and the history of conflicts over colonialism are intertwined in complex ways. Historical developments in Europe often determined the extent to which pro-colonial government co-operation was possible, and debates over such co-operation turned into a site in which debates over inner-European political ideals could take place. The example of trans-imperial co-operation in surveillance therefore allows us to gain a more complete understanding of how the conflicts between colonial authorities and anti-colonial activists shaped the encounters of empires in early twentieth-century history.

Notes

1 For some examples among a rapidly expanding literature see Brian Nelson, David Roberts and Walter Veit (eds), *Idea of Europe: Problems of National and Transnational Identity* (Oxford, New York: Berg, 1992); Rudolf Muhs, Johannes Paulmann and

Willibald Steinmetz (eds), *Aneignung und Abwehr: Interkultureller Transfer zwischen Deutschland und Großbritannien im 19. Jahrhundert* (Bodenheim: Philo, 1998); Johannes Paulmann, Internationaler Vergleich und interkultureller Transfer: Zwei Forschungsansätze zur europäischen Geschichte des 18. bis 20. Jahrhunderts, *Historische Zeitschrift*, 267 (1998), pp. 649–85; Michel Espargne, *Les transferts culturels franco-allemands* (Paris: Presses universitaires de France, 1999).

2 For important examples see Antoinette Burton, *At the Heart of Empire: Indians and the Colonial Encounter in Late-Victorian Britain* (Berkeley: University of California Press, 1998); Catherine Hall, *Civilising Subjects: Metropole and Colony in the English Imagination, 1830–1867* (Chicago: University of Chicago Press, 2002); Antoinette Burton, Introduction: on the inadequacy and the indispensability of the nation, in: Antoinette Burton (ed.), *After the Imperial Turn: Thinking with and through the Nation* (Durham: Duke UP, 2003), pp. 4–6; Catherine Hall and Sonya O. Rose (eds), *At Home with the Empire: Metropolitan Culture and the Imperial World* (Cambridge: Cambridge UP, 2006). See also A.G. Hopkins, Back to the future: from national history to imperial history, *Past and Present*, 164 (1999), pp. 198–243.

3 Kris Manjapra argues that we should not only focus on the dichotomy between imperial centres and peripheries, but should also take 'sideways glances towards "lateral networks" that transgressed the colonial duality'. See Kris Manjapra, Introduction, in: Sugata Bose and Kris Manjapra (eds), *Cosmopolitan Thought Zones: South Asia and the Global Circulation of Ideas* (New York: Palgrave Macmillan, 2010), p. 2. Ulrike Lindner has recently studied connections between colonized regions in Africa that belonged to different empires. See Ulrike Lindner, Imperialism and globalization: entanglements and interactions between the British and German colonial empires in Africa before the First World War, *Bulletin of the German Historical Institute London*, 23 (2010), pp. 4–28; Ulrike Lindner, Transnational movements between colonial empires: migrant workers from the British Cape colony in the German diamond town of Lüderitzbucht, *European Review of History*, 16 (2009), pp. 679–95; and her contribution to this volume. See also Florian Wagner, Kolonialverbände in Deutschland, Frankreich, Spanien und Belgien: Von der kolonialpraktischen Kooperation zum 'europäischen Ideal' (1880–1914), in: Frank Bösch et al. (eds), *Europabilder im 20. Jahrhundert: Entstehung an der Peripherie* (Göttingen: Wallstein Verlag, 2012), pp. 27–53, as well as his chapter in this volume.

4 Harald Fischer-Tiné, Indian nationalism and the 'world forces': Transnational and diasporic dimensions of the Indian freedom movement on the eve of the First World War, *Journal of Global History*, 2 (2007), pp. 325–44.

5 See Nicholas Owen, The Soft Heart of the British Empire: Indian Radicals in Edwardian London, *Past and Present*, 220 (2013), pp. 143–184.

6 See Bernard Porter, *The Origins of the Vigilant State: The London Metropolitan Special Branch Before the First World War* (London: Weidenfeld & Nicolson, 1987).

7 See Tilak Raj Sareen, *Indian Revolutionary Movement Abroad (1905–1921)* (New Delhi et al.: Sterling Publishers, 1979), p. 10; B.D. Yadav, *Madame Cama: A True Nationalist* (New Delhi: Anmol Publications, 1992), p. 25.

8 On the discussions about increasing the number of Special Branch officers after the Curzon Wyllie murder see the files in British National Archive (referred to as 'NA' from here onwards), MEPO 2 1297. See also Porter, *Origins*, p. 163.

9 See Bernard Porter, *Plots and Paranoia: A History of Political Espionage in Britain, 1790–1988* (London, Boston: Unwin Hyman, 1989), pp. 130ff.

10 Harald Fischer-Tiné, *Shyamjikrishnavarma: Sanskrit, Sociology and anti-imperialism* (London et al.: Routledge, 2014), pp. 112–121.
11 Richard J. Popplewell, *Intelligence and Imperial Defence: British Intelligence and the Defence of the Indian Empire, 1904–1924* (London: Frank Cass, 1995), pp. 135–41.
12 Note dated 24 January 1909, Archives Nationales de France (referred to as 'AN' from here onwards), F 7 12900.
13 See, for instance, the notes on Mr Tata on British Embassy paper in Révolutionnaires Hindous – Dossier pour M. le Directeur de la Sûreté Générale, dated 17 May 1908, AN, F 7 12900; Note on Tata, 21 May 1908; undated note on Tata, AN, F 7 12900.
14 Weekly Report of the Director of Criminal Intelligence, 11 January, 1908, British Library, Oriental and India Office Collections (referred to as 'BL, OIOC' from here onwards), POS 3094.
15 See John Merriman, *The Dynamite Club: How a Bombing in Fin-de-siècle Paris Ignited the Age of Modern Terror* (Boston: Houghton Mifflin Harcourt, 2009), pp. 113–21; Porter, *Origins*; Joseph Conrad, *The Secret Agent: A Simple Tale* (New York: Cambridge UP, 1990 [1907]); Hsi-Huey Liang, *The Rise of the Modern Police and the European State System from Metternich to the Second World War* (Cambridge: Cambridge UP, 1992), p. 164; Pietro Di Paola, The spies who came in from the heat: the international surveillance of the anarchists in London, *European History Quarterly*, 37 (2007), pp. 189–215.
16 See David French, Spy fever in Britain, 1900–1915, *The Historical Journal*, 21 (1978); David A.T. Stafford, Spies and gentlemen: the birth of the British spy novel, 1893–1914, *Victorian Studies*, 24 (1981), pp. 489–509; Robert and Isabel Tombs, *That Secret Enemy: The French and the British from the Sun King to the Present* (New York: Alfred A. Knopf, 2007), pp. 434–36.
17 For example, Western officials pointed to Friedrich von Bernhardi's *Germany and the Next War* (1911), which argued that a potential anti-colonial uprising in the British territories would be in Germany's strategic interest. See Friedrich von Bernhardi, *Germany and the Next War* (London: Edward Arnold, 1914), pp. 95–7; A.C. Bose, *Indian Revolutionaries Abroad, 1905–1922: In the Background of International Developments* (Patna: Bharati Bhawan, 1971), p. 83.
18 Veer Savarkar, *Inside the Enemy Camp*, p. 67; English translation of the Marathi original, available at www.savarkar.org/content/pdfs/en/inside_the_enemy_camp.v001.pdf (accessed 8 July 2014); Vinayak Damodar Savarkar, *The Indian War of Independence 1857* (Bombay: Dhawale Popular, 1960 [1909]).
19 Habeas Corpus: Indian Law Student, *The Times*, 3 June 1910. On the British use of sedition law against Savarkar see Janaki Bakhle, Savarkar (1883–1966), Sedition and Surveillance: the rule of law in a colonial situation, *Social History*, 35 (2010), pp. 51–75.
20 Weekly Report of the Director of Criminal Intelligence, January 29, 1910, BL, OIOC, POS 3095.
21 On this question see, for instance, A.G. Noorani, *Savarkar and Hindutva: The Godse Connection* (New Delhi: LeftWord Books, 2002), p. 17; Dhananjay Keer, *Veer Savarkar* (Bombay: Popular Prakashan, 1966), p. 73.
22 Letter from Assistant Commissioner of Police to Under Secretary of State, 11.04.1910, NA, HO 144 1063.
23 In the High Court of Justice, Kings Bench Division, 24.05.1910, NA, HO 144 1063; Habeas Corpus: Indian Law Student, *The Times*, 21 June 1910; Habeas Corpus: Indian Law Student, *The Times*, 22 June 1910.

24 See Keer, *Savarkar*, p. 78, and Savarkar's comments on Mazzini's time in Marseille in Savarkar, *Inside the Enemy Camp*, pp. 17; 18ff.
25 Henry to Hennion, 29 June 1910; Hennion to Henry, 9 July 1910; French note on the Savarkar case, dated 18 July 1910, NA, HO 144 1063.
26 On the sequence of events see Enquiry into the conduct of the police party in charge of Vinayak Damodar Savarkar in regard to the escape of the prisoner from the P. & O. Company's S. S. 'Morea' at Marseilles, Report by Inspector E. Parker to Scotland Yard, Criminal Investigation Department, dated 8 July 1910, NA, HO 144 1063.
27 See, for instance, Le Complot Hindou, *L'Éclair*, 23 December 1908.
28 Carnegie to Sir Edward Grey Bart, 19 July 1910; Paul Cambon to Sir Edward Grey, 23 July 1910, NA, HO 144 1063.
29 Weekly Report of the Director of Criminal Intelligence, August 30, 1910; Weekly Report of the Director of Criminal Intelligence, 11 October 1910, BL, OIOC, POS 3095.
30 Award delivered 24 February 1911 by the Arbitral Tribunal appointed to the case of 'Savarkar', NA, HO 144 1063. The Tribunal was to be composed of a number of neutral statesmen from Belgium, Norway and the Netherlands, as well as a British and a French representative.
31 *Case presented on behalf of the Government of his Britannic Majesty to the Tribunal constituted under an agreement signed in London on the 25th day of October 1910, between the Government of his Britannic Majesty and the Government of the French Republic* (London: Harrison and Sons, 1910); *Reply presented on behalf of the Government of his Britannic Majesty to the Counter-Case presented on behalf of the Government of the French Republic* (London: Harrison and Sons, 1911); *Counter-Case presented on behalf of the Government of his Britannic Majesty to the Tribunal constituted under an agreement signed in London on the 25th day of October 1910, between the Government of his Britannic Majesty and the Government of the French Republic* (London: Harrison and Sons, 1911), NA, HO 144 1063.
32 *Affaire Savarkar: Mémoire présenté par le Gouvernement de la République Française* (Paris: Imprimerie Nationale, 1910); *Affaire Savarkar: Contre-Mémoire présenté par le Gouvernement de la République Française* (Paris: Imprimerie Nationale, 1911); *Affaire Savarkar: Réplique du Gouvernement de la République Française au Contre-Mémoire du Gouvernement de sa Majesté Britannique* (Paris: Imprimerie Nationale, 1911).
33 *Award delivered February 24th 1911 by the Arbitral Tribunal appointed to the case of 'Savarkar'*, NA, HO 144 1063.
34 For one example of this argument among many see Charles Chestre, *France, England and European Democracy, 1215-1915: A Historical Survey of the Principles Underlying the Entente Cordiale* (New York, London: G.P. Putnam's Sons, 1918).
35 On the work of the Nachrichtenstelle see, for instance, Tilman Lüdke, *Jihad made in Germany: Ottoman and German Propaganda and Intelligence Operations in the First World War* (Münster: LIT Verlag, 2005). On the formation and activities of the Berlin Indian Committee, which worked together closely with the German office, see K. Barooah, *Chatto: The Life and Times of an Indian Anti-Imperialist in Europe* (Oxford: Oxford UP, 2004), pp. 39-54.
36 Only the two Indian cavalry divisions stayed on in France until the spring of 1918; see David Omissi, Introduction, in: David Omissi, *Indian Voices of the Great War: Soldiers' Letters, 1914-1918* (New York: Macmillan, 1999), pp. 2-4. See also Gregory Martin,

Koloniale Truppenkontingente im Ersten Weltkrieg, in: Gerhard Höpp and Brigitte Reinwald, *Fremdeinsätze: Afrikaner und Asiaten in europäischen Kriegen* (1914–1945) (Berlin: Das Arabische Buch, 2000), pp. 16–20.

37 Indian Base Post Office, 3 December 1914, BL, OIOC, L/MIL/7/17347.
38 Annexure 2 to Enclosure No. 1: note on the possibility of seditious persons tampering with the loyalty of our Indian troops at Marseilles, 16 April 1915, BL, OIOC, L/MIL/7/17347.
39 Ibid.
40 B.D. Yadav, *Madame Cama*, p. 25.
41 Ibid., pp. 25; 34ff.
42 On the printing of the *Bande Mataram* and other anti-colonial newspapers in France and other continental countries see Weekly Report of the Director of Criminal Intelligence, October 16, 1909; Weekly Report of the Director of Criminal Intelligence, 30 October 1909, BL, OIOC, POS 3094; Weekly Report of the Director of Criminal Intelligence, 17 May 1910, BL, OIOC, POS 3095.
43 Weekly Report of the Director of Criminal Intelligence, 12 December 1910, BL, OIOC, POS 3095.
44 Weekly Report of the Director of Criminal Intelligence, 15 September 1914, BL, OIOC, POS 3095.
45 Movements of Madame Cama, NA, FO 800 56B; Weekly Report of the Director of Criminal Intelligence, 17 November 1914, BL, OIOC, POS 3095.
46 Bertie to Grey, Bordeaux, 17 October 1914, NA, FO 800 56B.
47 Weekly Report of the Director of Criminal Intelligence, 8 December 1914; Weekly Report of the Director of Criminal Intelligence, 17 August 1915, BL, OIOC, POS 3095.
48 See the notes on Mr Rana on British Embassy paper in Révolutionnaires Hindous – Dossier pour M. le Directeur de la Sûreté Générale, AN, F 7 12900.
49 Decypher of telegram from Sir F. Bertie, Bordeaux, 17 September 1914; Telegram by the Foreign Office to Sir F. Bertie, 18 September 1914; Bertie to Grey, 11 October 1914; Decypher of telegram from Sir F. Bertie (Bordeaux), 20 November 1914, NA, FO 800 56B.
50 Bertie to Grey, 3 October 1914, NA, FO 800 56B; Bertie to Grey, 17 October 1914, NA, FO 800 56B.
51 Copy of a report drawn up by the Commissaire de Police at Arcachon respecting the search which was made of Rana's lodgings, NA, FO 800 56B.
52 Decypher of a telegram from Sir F. Bertie, Bordeaux, 17 September 1914; The Case of Mr Rana. India Office, 18 September 1914; Bertie to Grey, 26 September 1914, NA, FO 800 56B.
53 Weekly Report of the Director of Criminal Intelligence, December 29, 1914, BL, OIOC, POS 3095; Decypher of telegram from Sir F. Bertie (Bordeaux), 20 November 1914; Crewe to Grey, India Office, 23 November 1914, NA, FO 800 56B.
54 Weekly Report of the Director of Criminal Intelligence, 5 January 1915, BL, OIOC, POS 3095.
55 Ibid.; Weekly Report of the Director of Criminal Intelligence, 12 January 1915, BL, OIOC, POS 3095.
56 Weekly Report of the Director of Criminal Intelligence, 5 January 1915, BL, OIOC, POS 3095.
57 Weekly Report of the Director of Criminal Intelligence, 12 January 1915, BL, OIOC, POS 3095.

58 Weekly Report of the Director of Criminal Intelligence, 1 June 1915, BL, OIOC, POS 3095.
59 See Erez Manela, *The Wilsonian Moment: Self-Determination and the International Origins of Anticolonial Nationalism* (Oxford: Oxford UP, 2007); Sophie Quinn-Judge, *Ho Chi Minh: The Missing Years, 1919–1941* (Berkeley: University of California Press, 2003), pp. 11–13.
60 A brief sketch of the career and character of Saad Pasha Zaghloul, NA, FO 141 573 5.
61 See the extensive documents on the riots in NA, FO 608 213 5.
62 Decypher of Telegram from General Allenby, Cairo, to Mr Balfour, 6 April 1919, NA, FO 608 213 5.
63 *Le Bulletin Égyptien*, Numéro 2, 22 April 1919, AN, F7 13412.
64 Délégation Égyptienne, Appel au Parlement Français, 31 July 1919, NA, FO 141 828 3. See also Noor-Aiman I. Khan, *Egyptian-Indian Nationalist Collaboration and the British Empire* (New York: Palgrave Macmillan, 2011), p. 93.
65 Peace Congress. British Policy in Egypt, 9 April 1919, NA, FO 608 213 5; Pour le peuple égyptien, *Le Populaire*, 08.04.1919.
66 Délégation Égyptienne, Appel au Parlement Français, 31 July 1919, NA, FO 141 828 3.
67 Secret. From G.H.Q. Egypt to: D.M.I., 13 April 1919, NA, FO 608 213 5.
68 Decypher. Field Marshal Lord Allenby (Ramleh), 20 August 1919, NA, FO 608 214.
69 Peace Congress. French Press & Egyptian Nationalist Claims, 28 April 1919, NA, FO 608 213 5.
70 Egypt. Cypher telegram to General Allenby (Cairo), Foreign Office, 24 April 1919, NA, FO 608 213 5.
71 Derby to Curzon of Kedleston, K.G., Paris, 25 April 1919, NA, FO 608 213 5.
72 Egypt. Decypher. General Allenby (Cairo), 17 April 1919, NA, FO 608 213 5.
73 British Delegation, Paris. Mr. Balfour to Lord Derby, 30 April 1919, NA, FO 608 213 5.
74 For the notion of 'hidden transcripts' see James C. Scott, *Domination and the Arts of Resistance: Hidden Transcripts* (New Haven and London: Yale University Press, 1990).
75 Louis Mallet to Earl Curzon of Kedleston, 5 May 1919, NA, FO 608 213 5.
76 Derby to Curzon of Kedleston, K.G., Paris, 25 April 1919, NA, FO 608 213 5.
77 No. 9, Paris, 13 May 1919, NA, FO 608 212. This last endeavour was not met with full success, however. As a French official wrote sardonically in May 1919, the news was printed only after some delay. As the official thought, 'the abundance of topics in these times had doubtlessly caused [...] [the journalists] to neglect a piece of news whose date they found a bit old'. See Ministre des Affaires Étrangères, Direction des Affaires politiques et commerciales à Monsieur Nevile Henderson, Premier Secrétaire de l'Ambassade d'Angleterre à Paris, 12 May 1919; Foreign Office to A.J. Balfour, 13.06.1919, NA, FO 608 212.
78 Memorandum, 1 May 1919, NA, FO 608 213 5.
79 British Delegation, Paris. Mr Balfour to Lord Derby, 30 April 1919, NA, FO 608 213 5.
80 British Embassy Paris, 1 May 1919, NA, FO 608 213 5.
81 Note by Nevile M. Henderson, 3 May 1919, NA, FO 608 213 5.
82 République Française. Ministère des Affaires Étrangères. Direction Politique Afrique, Paris, 10 May 1919, NA, FO 608 213 5.
83 British Delegation, Paris, May 1919, NA, FO 608 214.
84 Peace Congress, 220 May 1919, NA, FO 608 214.
85 British Delegation, Paris, May 1919, NA, FO 608 214.
86 Note on Conversation with G. N. Sarruf Bey, son of the Editor of *The Mokattan*, 27 June 1919, NA, FO 608 214. Another event that convinced the delegation's

members of the futility of their efforts was the American recognition of the British protectorate. The delegation had hoped that Wilson, based on his Fourteen Points, would support their aims. See Louis Mallet to Earl Curzon of Kedleston, 5 May 1919, NA, FO 608 213 5; Dr Woodrow Wilson, President of United States of America, London [no date], NA, FO 608 212; Peace Congress. French Attitude towards Egyptian Nationalist Delegation, 30 April 1919, NA, FO 608 213 5. On this point see also Manela, *The Wilsonian Moment*, pp. 141–57. While Manela presents a very convincing analysis of Egyptian efforts to gain the Americans' support, he seems to underplay the importance of the French as a second potential ally for the Egyptians' cause.

87 On this notion see Charles-Robert Ageron, *France coloniale ou parti colonial?* (Paris: Presses universitaires de France, 1978), pp. 230ff.

88 See Jonathan Derrick, *Africa's 'Agitators': Militant Anti-Colonialism in Africa and the West* (New York: Columbia University Press, 2008), p. 61.

89 Kris Manjapra briefly summarizes these developments in Kris Manjapra, *M.N. Roy: Marxism and Colonial Cosmopolitanism* (London, New York, New Delhi: Routledge, 2010), pp. 74–6. However, for the purposes of this study, it is worth analysing them in more detail.

90 See M.N. Roy, *M. N. Roy's Memoirs* (Bombay et al.: Allied Publishers, 1964); Manjapra, *M.N. Roy*, pp. 2, 8–9, 33, 39, 45, 52. His move to Berlin apparently had to do with the Soviet government's attempts, after the signature of the Anglo-Russian Trade Agreement of 1921, to make its 'Eastern' propaganda less conspicuous. See Indian Revolutionaries. Full statement of evidence regarding activities of Indian Communist Groups, April–November 1922, BL, OIOC, L P&J 12 117.

91 Memorandum. Case of M.N. Roy, 21 March 1925, BL, OIOC, L P&J 12 99.

92 Indian Communist Party, 26 September 1923, BL, OIOC, L P&J 12 48.

93 Memorandum. Case of M.N. Roy, 21 March 1925, BL, OIOC, L P&J 12 99; Letter from R.C.L. Sharma to M.N. Roy, dated Pondicherry, 26 September 1923, BL, OIOC, L P&J 12 48.

94 Indian Communist Party, 25 January 1924, BL, OIOC, L P&J 12 49.

95 Resumé of the Bolshevik situation prepared by the Director of the Intelligence Bureau, India [written around mid-December 1922], BL, OIOC, L P&J 12 117.

96 Deutsches Generalkonsulat für Britisch Indien und die Kolonie Ceylon an das Auswärtige Amt Berlin, Kalkutta, 10 June 1924, Politisches Archiv des Auswärtigen Amts, Berlin, R 30615. On the surveillance of left-wing activists in India itself see Suchetana Chattopadhyay, 'The Bolshevik menace: colonial surveillance and the origins of socialist politics in Calcutta', *South Asia Research*, 26 (2006), pp. 165–79.

97 Indian anti-colonialists suspected this. See Indian Communist Party, 223 August 1922, BL, OIOC, L P&J 12 46.

98 See Letter to Hose, 13 September 1923, BL, OIOC, L P&J 12 55; Minute Paper, 29 November 1923, BL, OIOC, L P&J 12 48; Indian Communist Party, 3 January 1924, BL, OIOC, L P&J 12 49; Minute Paper: Indian Communist Party, 28 May 1922, BL, OIOC, L P&J 12 46; Indian Communist Party, 23 April 1924, BL, OIOC, L P&J 12 49.

99 Le Ministre des Colonies à Monsieur le Gouverneur des Établissements Françaises de l'Inde, Pondicherry, 5 July 1924, Centre des Archives d'Outre-Mer, Aix-en-Provence, 3slotfom47; Indian Communist Party, March 1924, BL, OIOC, L P&J 12 49; Indian Communist Party, 3 December 1924, BL, OIOC, L P&J 12 49. On the International Colonial Office see Peter Martin, 'Schwarze Sowjets an Elbe und Spree?', in: Peter Martin and Christine Alonzo (eds), *Zwischen Charleston und Stechschritt: Schwarze im Nationalsozialismus* (Hamburg, Munich: Dölling und Galitz Verlag GmbH, 2004), p. 180.

The Origins of Trans-imperial Policing

100 On the International Colonial Office see Peter Martin, Schwarze Sowjets, p. 180.
101 Copy of a letter from the Secretary to the Government of Madras, to the Secretary to the Government of India, Home Department, dated Fort St George, 22 December 1923; Minute Paper [without date; stamp: 1925], BL, OIOC, L P&J 12 56. The British authorities thought the co-operation between both sides to be 'very satisfactory'. Similar agreements were made for the French colony of Chandernagore; see ibid. Among other measures, the *Vanguard* was outlawed in Pondicherry territory; see Memorandum: Case of M.N. Roy, 21 March 1925, BL, OIOC, L P&J 12 99. See also Evelyn Roy, French persecution of Indian political exiles, *International Press Correspondence*, 5, 20, 19 March 1924, p. 28, Nehru Memorial Library, Delhi, M.N. Roy Papers (3rd instalment), Speeches, Writings by others, S. No. 4.
102 Ministère des Affaires Étrangères, Paris, à l'Ambassade de Sa Majesté Britannique à Paris, 15 May 1924; British Embassy, Paris, 9 September 1924, BL, OIOC, L P&J 12 99.
103 Mr Hose, 21 January 1925; Secret. Under Secretary of State, 26 January 1925; The Under Secretary of State, 27 January 1925; Ministère des Affaires Étrangères à l'Ambassade de Grande Bretagne à Paris, 3 February 1925, BL, OIOC, L P&J 12 99.
104 Copy extracted from Weekly Report of the Director, Intelligence Bureau of the Home Department, dated Delhi, 25 March 1925, BL, OIOC, L P&J 12 99.
105 Charles Vildrac, Apropos of an Expulsion, translated from the French, dated 01 April 1925, BL, OIOC, L P&J 12 99.
106 See Notes on Minute paper, March 1925, BL, OIOC, L P&J 12 99. One official worried that 'M. Herriot's Government lives in fear of the Extreme Left.' Ibid.
107 Foreign Office to the Under Secretary of State, India Office, 1 April 1925, BL, OIOC, L P&J 12 99.
108 Roy was active in Germany again at the latest in 1929 and 1930; see Manjapra, *M.N. Roy*, pp. 83–6. He returned to India in late 1930, was arrested by the British authorities in 1931, put on trial, and, in 1932, was sentenced to twelve years in prison.

Part Five

Military and Violence

8

Co-operation Between German and French Troops During the Boxer War in China, 1900/1: The Punitive Expedition to Baoding

Susanne Kuss

The period of high imperialism – of which the Boxer War was a component – is often viewed through the prism of strict imperial competition. The proponents of this narrative have identified a situation of keen and exclusive nationalist rivalry, in which imperial governments rallied popular opinion behind a campaign of extra-European expansion. Such an interpretation often portrays imperial co-operation as not only absent from, but inherently inimical to, the logic of the imperial undertaking. Despite the widespread modern assumption of intractable colonial rivalries, France and Great Britain had already co-operated closely on Chinese soil in the pursuit of common interests in launching the Second Opium War (1860–2) as a joint undertaking. The Boxer War witnessed not only the continuation of such co-operation, but its extension to include further states, thereby according it a global dimension.

The Boxer War in China (1900/1) was a multinational war. Prosecuted as a war of intervention, it was conducted by a broad alliance between the established colonial rivals Great Britain, France and Russia; Austria-Hungary; and the imperial latecomers Germany, Italy, the USA and Japan. Not aiming to seize and hold Chinese territory, the powers sought to enforce the 'Western rules of civilized conduct' and secure the economic interests of its proponents. Although conducted by eight national contingents subject to the military precepts and command structure of the sending nation, the various actions involved in the Boxer War comprised not just the usual range of asymmetries between the imperial force and the indigenous population typical for the nineteenth century, but also unfolded on a multilateral plane. The war also provided the context for a number of cultural and military encounters between the various contingents of the nationally allied intervention force. As such, the Boxer War can be viewed as an episode of dual interaction: between the Chinese and the agents of world imperialism on the one hand, and within the imperialist setup itself.

'Interaction' is a broad concept, which does not always do justice to the range and intensity of the undertakings and encounters involved in the Boxer War. Encompassing all forms of exchange ranging from the passing encounter to close co-operation within the context of complex operations, these experiences frequently involved processes of learning and emulation, often with a long-term impact. The involvement of a total of nine different warring parties, including China, produced thirty-six mathematically possible bilateral interactions of varying form and intensity. An example of such bilateral interaction was that between the French and German contingents meeting in China as allies thirty years after fighting the Franco-German War (1870–1) and fourteen years before the outbreak of World War I. None of the contingents despatched to China were in any way prepared for the demands of a coalition war and as such an inter-imperial co-operation. Drawn from armies with a range of experience and training, the staffs of the eight intervention forces were confronted with the need to combine a range of different command structures, services, skill-sets, institutional cultures and military practices. The context of such joint exercises ranged from straightforward engagements with enemy formations to punitive expeditions and occupations.

Replicating the historiographical divides of the compartmentalized schools of national history, previous academic consideration of the Boxer War has been conducted within the framework of clearly delimited and unrelated national studies. Even a cursory reading of the literature gives the impression of eight separate campaigns. Studies by German scholars have long concentrated on establishing and explaining the nature and extent of the violence meted out by the German forces despatched to China. Rooted in the centrality of World War II to German historiography, investigations of this 'lesser' conflict have concentrated in establishing its position within long-term continuities between German colonial conflicts (including those in German South-West Africa and German East Africa during 1904–8) and the conduct of the war in the East after 1939/41. French studies of the Chinese campaign, on the other hand, tend to portray the Boxer War as but a further example of the many *campagnes coloniales* conducted by the French state within the course of the nineteenth and early twentieth centuries. Chinese studies have focused less on the intervention forces than the significance of the Boxer movement for the course of Chinese nationalism and the path to the communist revolution.[1]

This chapter seeks to investigate the genesis of the Franco-German co-operation of 1900/1 in an extra-European theatre. Developing during a multinational punitive expedition to the city of Baoding (保定) conducted with French and German participation, this co-operation was developed during the joint Franco-German administration of the city. Focusing on the interaction between the two forces and including a comparison of their treatment of the civilian population, the chapter will seek to highlight both the extent and the limits of the similarities exhibited in the approach adopted by both partners. This will facilitate an assessment of the extent and significance of Franco-German co-operation in China within the context of the wider relations between the two nations.

I. French and German troops in the Boxer War

Franco-German relations deteriorated rapidly in the aftermath of the last war of German unification in 1871; both sides now considered the other as the 'hereditary enemy.' While German policy-makers and planners feared a war of revenge, their French counterparts mistrusted the rise of an over-mighty Germany under Prussian dominance. A more immediate grievance was presented by the problem of Alsace-Lorraine. While immediate French fears of their neighbour cooled following the conclusion of the French-Russian alliance of 1894, the German military downgraded its assessment of the French threat, above all following the international humiliation of the Dreyfus affair (1895). This episode persuaded the German general staff that France was no longer a front-rank military power. The improvement of relations between the two powers in the intervening period was demonstrated by the presence of French warships at the opening of the Kiel Canal in 1895 and German participation in the Universal Exhibition of 1900 in Paris.[2]

French and German interests in the colonial sphere did not come into serious conflict until the first Moroccan Crisis of 1905/6. Although bordering French territory, the German colonies of Cameroon and Togo generated little friction; potential disagreements regarding the course of the border were defused in a process of negotiation. In China, the distance between the two powers – the German zone of influence in the North far removed from the French presence in the South – meant that the German and French involvement in the 'scramble for China' in the 1890s passed without major dispute.

On 1 November 1897, the imperial German government took the murder of two German missionaries active in Shandong province as the pretext to occupy the fishing village of Qingdao (青島). The Chinese government formalized this unilateral action in the following March by undertaking to lease a 450 km^2 area around Jiaozhou Bay to Germany for the length of ninety-nine years. The German occupation of Qingdao marked the start of the Western occupation of a number of port colonies along the Chinese east coast, and 1898 saw the occupation of the territory of Guangzhouwan (廣州灣) in the south of Guangdong province by the French; Weihaiwei (威海衛) in Shandong province; and Jiulong (九龍 Kowloon), the mainland area in front of Hong Kong, was seized by Great Britain. Russia supplemented her holdings in Dalian (大連 occupied in 1896) by seizing Port Arthur/Lüshunkou (旅順口, in Manchuria). Designed to establish a sphere of interest in the immediate hinterland and facilitate its economic exploitation, the occupation of these port towns acted as the gateway for capital investment and the export of valuable raw materials.

Charged with the occupation and administration of Qingdao, the German navy planned to transform the colony into a centre of German culture and scientific endeavour. A German-Chinese university was set up to train hand-picked Chinese students, with the aim of establishing a German-friendly elite over the long term. This concept contrasted starkly with policy in Germany's African colonies, characterized as it was by paternalism and domination rather than any attempt to establish an educated collaborator elite. As such, Qingdao was widely regarded by German colonial policy-makers as a 'model colony'.[3]

The French did not administer Guangzhouwan as a separate colony with its own governor; rather it was subject to the administration of French Indochina. Their take-over of the former Chinese tributaries of Annam and Tonkin (administered from Cochinchina) was formalized in 1895 in a treaty with the Chinese government. Planning to establish and expand its presence in southern China through domination of the Yunnan province, France also hoped to expand the port in Guangzhouwan to rival the British-held Hong Kong. Rivalling what in essence represented the hub of East Asian trade, France hoped to challenge British predominance in this highly profitable market.[4]

The foreign presence on the Chinese coast and its activities further inland provoked vehement indigenous resistance. The year 1899 saw the spread of the 'Boxer movement', a highly nationalist grouping dedicated to resisting the growing foreign presence. Originating in the German-dominated Shandong province, the Boxer movement derived its name from the traditions of a number of pugilist movements, referring to itself as *yihequan* (義和拳 The Society of Righteous and Harmonious Fists). This name was subsequently changed to *yihetuan* (義和團 The Righteous and Harmonious Militias), and this second appellation has been adopted by modern Chinese historiography, and a minority of Western scholars. Consideration of the Boxer uprising has spawned a number of controversies; a consensus has yet to be reached as to whether this movement consisted of local militias led by conservative elites or independent bands.

The grievances of the Boxer movement focused primarily on the presence and economic significance of foreign nationals, symbolized by the programme of railway-building by foreign companies, and the Jesuit missions. Established as early as the seventeenth century, the Jesuits were granted considerable freedoms, including that of land ownership. Despite its loyalist rhetoric and (perhaps even due to their) entirely nationalist bent, the Boxer movement could not be sure of the support of the Manchurian (i.e. non-Chinese) Qing dynasty. Both the imperial court around the dowager Empress Cixi (慈禧 1835–1908) and the Chinese military establishment remained divided as to the best response to the Boxers. Only recently installed at court in the place of her nephew (1898) and mindful of the power of various factions at court, Cixi was forced to steer a course between competing interpretations of the Boxer movement. For their part, the generals were divided as to the value and advisability of integrating the Boxer militias into the partially-modernized imperial army.[5]

The situation began to deteriorate in 1900, as the various Boxer groupings began a march on Peking. The killings in June 1900 of a number of missionaries, Chinese Christians and a small number of European engineers unsettled the foreign diplomats stationed in the Chinese capital; the imperialist powers responded by assembling their naval contingents in the Gulf of Zhili. Still the empress remained undecided; only the deployment of a multinational land force under the leadership of the British Admiral Edward Seymour (1840–1929) and the storming and occupation of the Dagu forts on 21 June finally persuaded Cixi to switch her full support to the Boxers.

The cities of Tianjin and Peking saw fierce fighting between Boxer and Chinese government forces and the foreign imperialist troops. In Peking, Boxer and Chinese government forces conducted a 55-day siege of the legation quarter, which provided protection for foreign diplomats, their families and a number of Chinese Christians seeking refuge from the Boxer onslaught. The relief of Peking by a multinational expeditionary force at the end of August was followed by an orgy of murder, plunder and rape, during which entire city quarters were razed to their smoking foundations. By chance, the German and French soldiers were not present at the beginning of these 'reprisals'.

The immediate German response to the crisis was to assemble the East Asian Cruiser Squadron in the Gulf of Zhili in early 1900. Despatching I and II battalions of the marine infantry from their bases in Kiel and Wilhelmshaven in the summer of the same year (III battalion was rushed to the scene from garrison duty in nearby Qingdao), a full-scale intervention force was not despatched to the region until the summer of 1900. Not a specialist colonial service, or even a regular army formation, the East Asian expeditionary force was made up of army volunteers. Plans to send active formations foundered on the resistance of the chief of the German General Staff, Alfred von Schlieffen (1833–1913), who feared that such a course could weaken the performance of the regular army in Europe, especially in the case of a war with France. Following this build-up in stages, some 23,000 German servicemen had been deployed in China by the end of 1900.[6]

The French military response was also led by the navy. Initial operations were performed by naval forces already deployed in Chinese waters and those despatched rapidly from the garrisons in Tonkin and Cochinchina. Gradually replaced by an army expeditionary force assembled in France in July 1900, these naval forces had returned to Indochina by the autumn. In January 1901, the French Expeditionary Force registered a strength of some 17,300 NCOs and other ranks, led by 700 officers.[7]

As with the German Expeditionary Corps, the French force was a heterogeneous mix of volunteers, both regulars and reservists, drawn from a number of arms and services of the French army. No regular formations or special colonial forces were despatched to China. French planners were moved by similar concerns as their German counterparts: the removal of regular units from France was ruled out so as not to weaken French defences in a possible war with Germany. In comparison to the colonial inexperience of the German army, French planners could draw on the lessons learned during the establishment and deployment of four Expeditionary Corps to Tunisia, Tonkin and Madagascar (twice) after 1881. Having lost up to a quarter of the Expeditionary Force to Madagascar in 1895 from disease, in planning the Chinese expedition, the General Staff placed considerable focus on recruitment, hygiene, nutrition and clothing.[8]

German participation in the Boxer War represented the first ever campaign undertaken by the young state. Thirsting for active service, a number of highly-motivated volunteers flocked to the colours. Looking for their lead from their commander-in-chief Kaiser Wilhelm II (1859–1941), his speech given on 27 July 1900 to troops embarking at Bremerhaven was to achieve subsequent notoriety. Later daubed the 'Hun speech', his blood-curdling summons to 'show no quarter' reverberated through the military establishment; even to the extent of being chalked in excerpt on the carriages of the troop trains taking the soldiers to war. The most striking passage drew on one of the more barbarous periods of the appropriated 'German' past:

> You are being sent to fight a well-armed foe: avenge the death of our ambassador and that of many Germans and other Europeans. Strike down the enemy wherever you encounter him! Show no quarter! Take no prisoners! Those falling into your hands are at your mercy! Just as the name of the Hun King Etzel has reverberated for a thousand years, so shall the name of Germany echo in memory; no Chinese will ever again dare so much as to look askance at a German again![9]

Emulating his German counterpart, the French President Émile Loubet (1838–1929) also chose to address his departing troops, presenting the Expeditionary Force with its colours. Speaking at Marseilles on 12 August, he echoed the imperative to exact punishment on the guilty Chinese, but his rhetoric was much more restrained. He also made an appeal for the troops to consider the good name of France in conducting their campaign:

> Treat these colours with reverence. They are to remind you of the hallowed mission with which France has entrusted you. Of a land in which the essential laws of the civilized world have been violated in such a terrible fashion. [This travesty] demands the punishment of the guilty: exact reparation for past deeds and secure the necessary guarantees for the future. They [the colours] will remind you of the honour passed on from your forebears and which now rests in your hands. The French members of this international army, formed for the defence of civilization, must present a model of discipline, endurance and courage.[10]

The military services of the interventionist powers all regarded their mission to suppress the Boxer uprising as part of the international 'civilizing mission'. The only definition of civilization applied to extra-European areas was the ability of its peoples to establish a political system which afforded sufficient protection to the white population resident there. Failure in this respect was interpreted by the European powers as sufficient grounds to justify military intervention. Moreover, the prescriptions of the Hague Convention (1899) regulating the 'humane' conduct of warfare only applied to conflicts conducted between 'civilized nations', among which China did not number. Not a signatory of this agreement, the Chinese government could not expect the protection of its precepts.

A further factor conditioning the subsequent treatment meted out to the Chinese population was the failure of the Convention to extend its protection to militias or guerrilla fighters offering armed resistance to an enemy army but not formally incorporated into the regular military structures of their state. This matter had been discussed during the conference at The Hague, but no corresponding provisions had been drafted. The imperialist powers thus expected their enemies to conform to Western military doctrine and give open battle. Any asymmetric campaigns of 'hit and run' or an organized guerrilla campaign were considered to be 'inhumane'.

This situation did not mean that the German and French troops operated in a legal vacuum. The actions of German army personnel were subject to the provisions of the *Militärstrafgesetzbuch für das deutsche Reich*; their French counterparts were bound by the *Nouveaux codes français et lois usuelles civiles et militaires*.[11] Both documents forbade violence towards the civil population and their property: the proscription of murder, rape, requisitions and plundering was familiar to all the French and German soldiers serving in the Boxer War. Despite such close legal regulation, the respective military regulations of the eight belligerent nations were rarely used to sanction the widespread violence unleashed against the Chinese civil population. The existence of sentences passed following infringement of these codes demonstrates only the expectation of certain standards of behaviour; they do not permit any inference regarding the scope and extent of the violence suffered by the Chinese at the hands of the interventionist forces.

Although the provisions of the German and French codes of military law were largely comparable in sanctioning violence towards the civilian population, the political instructions issued to the two Expeditionary Corps differed considerably. German military doctrine stressed the primacy of military necessity; as a result, the German supreme commander – Alfred Graf von Waldersee (1832–1904) – reported directly to the kaiser, bringing him greater freedoms in planning and decision-making. The French commander, General Émile Voyron (1838–1921), on the other hand, was issued with instructions from the French Foreign Ministry and the Ministry of the Navy subordinating all military action to the wider aims of French foreign policy.[12]

The commanders of the eight interventionist contingents all eyed each other with wary rivalry. However, having suffered the most high-profile loss in the form of assassination of the German ambassador, Clemens von Ketteler (1853–1900), by a Chinese soldier in Peking, Germany could hope for a greater degree of accommodation. Accordingly, it was decided to confer supreme command of the undertaking on Waldersee. Unwilling to question this majority position, the French nevertheless did not wish to see their forces degraded to the state of Germany's junior partner, and took steps to maintain the autonomy of the French force. To this end, General Voyron was issued with the instructions that: 'The full autonomy of our expedition corps is to be maintained at all times; take every necessary step to prevent the division of your force.'[13]

This level of independence was far from unique – the USA also refused to place its troops under German command; Japan and Russia only accepted Waldersee's authority with considerable restrictions. In the final analysis, German powers over 90,000 soldiers from six contingents remained nominal; the planning and prosecution of the war remained subject to a continual process of negotiation and agreement.

Despite this potential for dispute, relations between the German and French forces got off to a good start. Arriving on 31 August, Waldersee's ship *Sachsen* was welcomed in the Gulf of Aden by music and cheers from the French transport ship *La Champagne*. Answering with a rendition of the *Marseillaise*, this was countered by the *Kaiserlied*. There was much cheering on both sides.[14] Similar reports are found from meetings between the troop ships of both nations: French and German soldiers lined the railings and greeted their new allies. Other sources indicate good relations between the troops of all the eight contingents; observes noted the development of something approaching a sense of cross-national unity between the eight nations.[15]

II. The international punitive expedition to Baoding

Promoted to the rank of field marshal in May 1900, Alfred Graf von Waldersee departed Germany for China amidst considerable jubilation. Arriving in Dagu on 25 September, six weeks after the plundering of Peking, it became clear that he needed to find a suitable purpose for his command, were he not to surrender the initiative to the diplomats. It was clear to all that the war was effectively over.

Peking and Tianjin had fallen under allied occupation. The Chinese imperial court had fled to Taiyuan (the capital of Shanxi province), and was later to move to Xian (the capital of Shaanxi province). The majority of the Chinese army and the Boxer formations had been defeated, while bands of deserters and Boxers were marauding across the countryside, threatening the Chinese civilian population. With many villages abandoned, the advancing intervention forces often passed through depopulated landscapes. Writing in his memoirs, the French General Voyron asserted that those who had abandoned their villages had been Boxer supporters and had fled in fear of retribution.[16] A simplistic account, this interpretation ignores the complexity of the experiences which the Chinese population had undergone; after their recent taste of warfare, the civilian population were more likely to be suspicious of all soldiers, irrespective of their provenance and intent.

Although the war was at an end, von Waldersee began with the planning of a number of punitive expeditions, to be conducted above all in Zhili province (today: Hebei), an area in northern China in which the major cities of Peking, Tianjin and Baoding were located. He outlined his intentions as subjugating the Chinese court; expelling Chinese soldiers from the province; pacifying the land; protecting the peaceful civil population, missionaries and Chinese Christians; and pursuing and punishing 'Boxers and thieves'.[17] Despite such clear-cut aims, the troops sent to Baoding experienced considerable difficulty in determining the identity of those to be punished. 'Boxers' and members of the 'peaceful population' were almost indistinct in their outward appearance. As a result, the planning of such raids relied almost entirely on information provided by missionaries and Chinese collaborators. The latter (often Christians) frequently sought to involve the foreign armies in the advancement of their own agendas, offering their services as guides and denouncing their compatriots in order to settle old scores or gain local advantage.

Waldersee selected Baoding as a target for an expedition, as it was the only significant urban centre (with a pre-war population of some 300,000, it was secured by a defensive wall) in the province which had yet to be occupied by the allied intervention force. Moreover, he expected support for such a mission from the contingent commanders, as eleven British and American missionaries and their children had been killed in Baoding in June/July 1900. Strategic considerations also spoke in favour of this undertaking. Baoding was not only the seat of civil administration in the province, but functioned also as the co-residence (together with Tianjin) of the military governor. Waldersee had even considered the possibility of extending the allied military presence to Taiyuan, in order to increase the pressure on the nearby imperial court.

Despite such arguments, Waldersee experienced considerable difficulty in gathering support for his plans: the Russian contingent had begun its retreat into Manchuria; the Japanese forces had begun their withdrawal to avoid the winter; and the American contingent had already been scaled down to a minimum. The British contingent had recently received instructions from London to exercise restraint in the choice of its activities. Only the French, Germans and Italians remained on a war footing. Indeed, having arrived late, the contingents of these three nations reached their full strength only in the autumn of 1900. Arrived and inactive, the Germans and French were in search of a purpose. As the Austrian war reporter Eugen Binder-Krieglstein (1873–1914) remarked, in this phase of the occupation, it was principally the French and German contingents that still sought to 'take the war beyond the walls of Peking'.[18]

A number of factors conditioned French interest in Waldersee's proposal for a punitive expedition to Baoding. Established by the Treaty of Nanjing (1842) as the protector of Catholic missionaries of all nationalities in China, France also had economic interests in the area. The French-Belgian consortium, Société d'étude de Chemin de Fer en Chine, had acquired the rights to build a railway from Peking to Hankou (which ran through Baoding) in 1898. The French government did not want to see the area fall under the control of a foreign power.[19] Indeed, a French expedition had already been despatched to the region to guard these interests long before the planned punitive expedition. It is not impossible that this initiative had provoked Waldersee's proposal in the first place.

The expedition was eventually launched with British and Italian participation. While the latter was rooted in considerations of prestige, British involvement was designed to act as a counterweight to Russian moves to extend its influence into Manchuria. The British had no interests to defend (their sphere of influence was located to the south along the Yangzi river), but they hoped that a show of presence would prevent northern China from becoming a Russian sphere of influence.

The undertaking was planned as an advance on Baoding across a broad front from positions in Tianjin and Peking. Such an approach was adopted to impress both the Chinese court and the civilian population with a show of force.[20] Staged carefully by allied planners, it involved the advance of two columns: one launched from Tianjin under the command of the French general, Maurice Camille Bailloud (1847–1921), and a second despatched from Peking, led by the British general, Alfred Gaselee (1844–1918).

A veteran of Algeria and the Madagascar expedition of 1895, Bailloud had gathered considerable colonial experience. His latest command consisted of a mixed force of French and Italian infantry, Madras sappers and Bengal Lancers, the 20th Punjab Regiment, Chinese troops under British command (the Hong Kong Regiment) and a contingent of Australian marines. While the European troops (a German-Italian grouping under the command of the German general, Wilhelm von Kettler (1846–1918) and a second French unit) were sent along a northern route, Bailloud's force followed a southern path.

An officer of the Indian army, Alfred Gaselee also brought considerable colonial experience to his new command. His mixed force included the German East Asian Infantry Regiment, the 16th Bengal Lancers, a company of Sikh infantry, the 24th Punjabi Regiment, the 26th Baluchistan Regiment, a number of French marines and mountain troops and a unit of Italian naval ratings. His force was accompanied by an American military observer. With an operational strength of over 6,000 men, the two columns were also supported by an unknown number of Japanese, Chinese and Korean coolies. In addition to the men and beasts of burden employed for the task, the extensive river network in the area also enabled the transport of supplies and equipment by junk.[21]

From the outset, Bailloud gave the order to ensure strict separation in the quartering of the troops of each national contingent. In the event that units of different nationalities occupied the same village, a supplementary order established the responsibility of the senior officer commanding to ensure strict segregation of the units involved. Otherwise, the commander of each column was granted discretion in billeting their soldiers depending upon the temperature, the state of the troops and the nature of the locality. The quality of intelligence in this respect was usually insufficient for the task. Lacking the necessary cavalry, Bailloud tasked Annamite hunters with the maintenance of communications between the various units.[22]

All the participant formations experienced considerable problems of logistics and coordination. Lacking in horses (the German units were forced to import their mounts from Australia), the columns experienced transport difficulties and were forced to use a range of methods. Moreover, in the absence of comparable levels of training, it was difficult to find a uniform marching speed or order for the motley assortment of soldiers, coolies, beasts of burden, hand carts and wagons making their way to Baoding. As Waldersee's plan required that both columns arrive at their destination simultaneously, these conditions placed considerable demands on the military choreography and coordination of this entirely heterogeneous force. Both columns adopted the practice of leaving guard posts at strategic points along their route to control the surrounding area. This led to the development of an allied baseline infrastructure including dressing stations and even small shops.

The arrival of the international force in the province placed a substantial burden on the Chinese civilian population. The frequent requisitioning of food, supplies and means of transport (often ponies), for which the troops did not always pay, not only caused considerable hardship, but often descended into orgies of plunder, destruction and rape. Drawing on their considerable colonial experience, the French troops presented the village elders of the areas through which they marched with certificates of good conduct (*certificats de bien vivre*) which attested that: 'The troops under the command of General Bailloud observed the rules of military discipline throughout the entire period of their presence in this area. Moreover, they paid a fair price for all articles which they demanded and did not molest the local womenfolk in any fashion.'[23]

In addition, the American military observer in Gaselee's column saw a further difference between the approach of the German and French troops. Not only did they find themselves in direct competition with each other, but they pursued a different agenda in marching to Baoding, something expressed in their dealings with the Chinese civilian population: 'The Germans [are] going [to Baoding] to punish the Chinese, the French [...] to keep in touch with the Germans. The French policy toward[s] the Chinese is quite the opposite [to that of the Germans], it being their desire to establish themselves as having the most kindly feeling[s] for them.'[24]

The observer also noticed that the French troops despatched to Baoding before the launch of the Waldersee's punitive expedition had marked bridges, walls and official buildings with the French Tricolour. The widespread presence of the French standard was a source of constant and considerable friction between the German and French units, indicating German failure to dominate the area. This was a difficult problem to surmount, as it was forbidden to take down the flag of a foreign nation; the only option was to hoist a second national flag next to it. The issue even generated a considerable and heated correspondence between Voyron and Waldersee.[25] In the estimation of Waldersee, such and other conflicts not only made the joint task much more difficult, but gave the Chinese the impression of preponderant French influence and disunity among the nominal allies.

Both columns rejoined outside Baoding on 19 October. Gaselee was received by a delegation of senior Chinese notables from the city. Led by Ting Yong (廷雍), the treasurer (*fantai* 藩臺) of Zhili province, the delegation hoped to forestall the occupation and destruction of their city. Welcoming the expedition they made arrangements for accommodation and protection. Declining the gifts which the delegation proffered, Gaselee adopted a stance of considerable reserve towards the Chinese, and indicated that the actions of his soldiers would depend upon the circumstances he encountered. He informed the delegation that he was prepared to negotiate only with the most senior officials.

After the establishment of a guard and the flags of the four nations on all four of the city gates, the column commanders were convened to discuss the entry and occupation of the city by the powers. Hoping to guarantee the best possible exploitation of the city resources and reduce the opportunity for plunder, Gaselee argued against a full occupation of the city. The German general, Georg von Gayl (1850–1927), objected: although every effort should be taken to prevent the outbreak of plundering, he maintained that Field Marshall von Waldersee had issued direct instructions to occupy the city so as to exert pressure on the Chinese government. He argued that the physical occupation of the city and the quartering of troops within its walls was necessary to exact punishment on the population for their guilt in supporting the Boxers.[26]

On 20 October, in front of the North Gate of the city, a large group of horsemen gathered. At the head of the mounted cavalcade rode standard bearers, carrying the flags of the participant nations. Followed by the four officers commanding – the generals, Gaselee, Bailloud and von Kettler and the Italian colonel, Vincenzo Garioni (1856–1929) – they led a larger mixed group of officers through the gate. Cavalry brought up the rear: German mounted units, French *chasseurs* and Indian lancers. Entering through the North Gate, the troops rode through Baoding to the South Gate, left the city and proceeded to ride along the outside of the perimeter wall. Re-entering the city via the West Gate, they crossed through the city once more. This pageant of unrestricted entrance and re-entrance was designed to underline the impunity with which the occupiers could penetrate the city defences, and ultimately the control they wielded over the burghers of Baoding.

Holding seniority, General Gaselee assumed command of the occupation, and decided to divide the city into various quarters, which he assigned to the control of the four nations. A police officer drawn from the allied force was appointed for each district. On 21 October there was a further parade, conducted by the Germans. Set to music, they entered Baoding, occupying the eastern quarter of the city together with the Italians. The French moved into the south-western sector. Although administering a section of Baoding, the British chose to camp the majority of their Indian troops outside the city walls, as did the Chinese, Japanese and Korean coolies.

Although Baoding was spared the extent of plundering and violence suffered by Peking and Tianjin, the occupiers seized all available money and silver, designating it as 'international property'. This included the discovery in the house of the provincial treasurer of a sum amounting to some 243,000 taels (around 720,000 marks). A letter from Voyron to Bailloud indicates further episodes of theft in which he suggested that he make an inventory of all valuable objects in the city which were then to be transported to a depot in Tianjin. For his part, Waldersee thanked Bailloud in a letter for gifts sent to him by Gaselee from Baoding (although he indicated that 'he would rather have done without them').[27]

Immediately after the occupation of Baoding, General Gaselee suggested the establishment of an international committee of investigation to examine the circumstances surrounding the murder of the eleven missionaries and their children earlier in the summer. Chaired by the Bailloud, the committee came to its findings only a week later, identifying four senior Qing officials as having ordered the murder. Ting Yong (廷雍), the treasurer of the prefecture, Guiheng (奎恒), the commander of the local Manchu garrison and Wang Zhanggui (王占魁), an army colonel, were sentenced to death.

For the first time in the war, the allies decided to perform the execution according to Chinese custom (beheading), organizing it as a public spectacle. In using Chinese methods in a highly publicized setting, the allied authorities sought to demonstrate the retributive and just nature of their mission.[28] Waldersee was convinced that the application of unyielding justice against senior officials would 'exercise a lasting and healing influence' throughout the province. Voyron articulated similar sentiments, arguing that the processes should be held in Zhili, and not Peking, due to the 'moral impact' which it would exercise.[29]

Before the execution, the German contingent had already rounded up a number of suspected 'Boxers'. Marched to the city gate, they were forced to dig their own graves in full view of the city. Further retribution was exacted by the demolition of two temples in the southern area of the city and the partial slighting of the city defences: two gate towers and a section of the perimeter wall were demolished.[30] The populace was subject to a levy to cover the costs of the executions and the administration of the city. The rest of the monies gathered were divided among the troops.[31]

This marked the end of the punitive expedition to Baoding. Waldersee was entirely satisfied with the performance of General Bailloud as the commander of the Tianjin column, whom he praised as having shown skill and prudence in performing the tasks assigned to him. Writing to the French general, Waldersee also noted the good nature of the relations between the various national contingents, which he ascribed to the personal influence of Bailloud. He concluded that the expedition had improved the mutual relations between the troops and had reinforced their commitment to the joint cause.[32]

III. The Franco-German administration of Baoding

The British and Italian contingents left Baoding soon after the executions, leaving the 2nd French (4,000 strong under the command of Bailloud) and 2nd German (some 3,500 men commanded by Kettler) to administer the city. Baoding remained occupied until July 1901, shortly before the conclusion of the withdrawal settlement (the so-called 'Boxer protocol') signed by China and the occupation powers the following September. The protocol represented a considerable humiliation for the Chinese Empire.

While drawing up the plans for the expedition to Baoding, Waldersee had suggested establishing a Chinese administration under Franco-German supervision. Staffed by a French and a German officer, the remit of the committee set up to oversee the running of the city was to be established by Bailloud and Kettler. To this end, the two generals remained in almost daily contact and exercised almost unlimited joint authority.[33] Not a matter of course, French participation in this administrative set-up was eventually forthcoming and stood in direct contrast to her rejection of an international administration for Peking.

Following the establishment of the committee of administration, the two generals agreed on the creation of a number of further bilateral subcommittees. Staffed by two able to speak at least basic French or German, they were set up to address a range of specialist questions such as the activities of the Chinese courts (Commission pour la surveillance de la jurisdiction chinoise). The German representative on this body was the Lieutenant Franz Xaver Epp (1868–1947), later to head the National Socialist Colonial Political Office. Together with his French colleague Colonel Bourguignon, Epp sat on a number of courts-martial of 'Boxers' and other Chinese 'criminals'.[34] The joint administration also established a prison complex for Chinese prisoners, staffed by troops from both national contingents. After December 1900, the German military argued that the low number of inmates rendered the new prison an overly costly undertaking; any further prisoners taken by the German military police were henceforth to be quartered in a room at the back of their temporary barracks.[35]

The rising level of ill-health among the garrison troops conditioned the decision to expand the provision of healthcare services. The prevalence among both contingents of venereal disease – and the impossibility of its treatment with a bacteriological approach – led to the adoption of a prophylactic methodology in the form of a general recommendation of abstinence. The establishment by the German military authorities of a brothel reduced the impact of such entreaties; moreover, the needs of clients disappointed by its eventual closure were soon addressed by freshly-opened establishments. Reacting to this situation, the military medical authorities took the decision to treat not only their own troops, but infected Chinese prostitutes. Soon, all known brothels were subject to military medical regulation. The joint military authority decided upon the establishment of a clinic for venereal disease in which up to twelve infected Chinese women could be treated. Although staffed by members of both nations, the limited nature of the co-operation (care was restricted to the Chinese prostitutes) ruled out any lasting impact. The women were cared for by a Chinese married couple.[36]

Beyond the provision of the military infrastructure, the occupation regime provided little scope for any level of interaction between the contingents of the two nations, which remained limited in the extreme. Quartered in different areas of the town, the two zones of occupation were separated by a designated border laid down and subject to repeated alteration during negotiations between Kettler and Bailloud.[37] While the Chinese civil population was able to apply for a pass to cross these lines, the soldiers and NCOs of each contingent were restricted to movement within their own zone of occupation. According to the war diary of the German II Sea Battalion, interaction with French servicemen was conspicuous only by its absence.[38] The few contacts between the two contingents were conducted by officers invited to attend certain ceremonial events (such as a flag consecration ceremony), social occasions, stage plays and the celebration of national holidays. Sometimes, these officers were accompanied by NCOs and other ranks.[39] Both contingents adopted the practice of renaming streets and thoroughfares with German and French names such as Württembergstraße or Rue de France. Such measures of 'domestication' sought to provide points of orientation in what remained an entirely alien environment.

The first weeks of the occupation were taken up by the establishment of winter living quarters and a routine of patrols and guard duties. This was followed by a range of exercises (drill, field service, target practice, intelligence gathering etc.). Quartered in the rear section of local houses, the arrival of German soldiers in Chinese households forced the original Chinese occupants to move to the front of their houses, which often functioned as a shop. The flight of much of the city population meant however that the majority of shops remained closed.[40] Seeking to establish good relations with the local population, the German contingent was forbidden to plunder the empty shops. Although relations between the occupiers and the Chinese remained difficult, the war diary of the II Sea Battalion characterized them as 'not hostile' (*nicht feindschaftlich*).[41]

The occupation was not restricted to Baoding, but extended through its hinterland, which was divided into two spheres of influence. The result of an ongoing process of negotiation and renegotiation, the delimitation of these areas was of vital importance, as the quality of the areas which Kettler and Bailloud could secure determined the additional resources at their disposal. This division also meant that each commander was required to inform his counterpart of any police or punitive actions which crossed these newly-established borders.[42] All the credentials and passes issued by the French or German authorities were binding in the other zone.[43] United in their aim of 'pacifying' the hinterland of Baoding, the staff of the two contingents worked together closely in intelligence-gathering and sharing regarding the activities and movements of the alleged 'Boxer bands' active in the two zones. The use of the railway (under French control) in their pursuit was also subject to prior coordination.[44]

Both commanders were forced to react to mutual allegations of 'out-of-area' plundering and brutality towards the Chinese population levelled against the other force. Making such a claim against the Germans (involving the theft of a mule, an ox, a bow and arrows, furniture and assorted items of household equipment from the French sphere of influence), one French officer levelled accusations of breaking and entering. Replying that this action had been ordered by a senior officer, Kettler argued that effectuating a forcible entry to a Chinese property had been established as a common practice during the expedition to Baoding and was not a mark of plundering. He refuted the charges of plundering: any losses from empty houses could just as well have been committed by the coolies and various salesmen accompanying the expedition. For his part, Kettler complained at the number of unsubstantiated charges levelled by the French officer; he was too quick to believe Chinese allegations. Moreover, this was rendered even more bothersome by their being made at a time when the areas of jurisdiction had yet to be established.[45] Kettler sought to play down such events so as to prevent embarrassing legal processes involving his own troops, which, he feared, could undermine the authority of the occupation.[46]

A French order from April 1901 indicates the probability that such violence against the Chinese population was not a German preserve. In calling for discipline to be exercised during punitive actions, Bailloud insisted that China was not to be considered as 'enemy territory'; it was the duty of French soldiers not to punish, but to protect the resident population. All requisitioned goods should be paid for immediately, and were to be kept to an absolute minimum so as to prevent hardship. Echoing his president, the commander continued that French soldiers should pride themselves not only on their martial virtues, but also discipline and humanity. In his words, 'France has always marched at the vanguard of civilization.'[47] Violence against the Chinese population was thus not the preserve of the German contingent. Moreover, in issuing this order, the French high command revealed priorities which transcended humanitarian concerns. Wishing to establish a separate identity for his force, Bailloud intended that this measure would distinguish the French contingent from the international military force in general and the German contingent in particular.

Memoirs from French servicemen deployed in the Boxer War point to limited yet exclusively positive experiences of contact with their German counterparts. The French infantryman Léon Silbermann wrote that he had shared a table and drunk with German troops, explaining these good relations with reference to the shared challenges of a difficult campaign.[48] The appreciation of a common predicament caused soldiers from different nationalities to help each other. An explanation for the near-absence of references to the contemporary Franco-German enmity has been sought in the age of the soldiers, all of whom were born after the events of the 1870s.[49] The memoirs of the veterans all point to the special experience of facing a common challenge in forging this understanding. This development was only possible in the unique setting of an extra European war.

Some international war observers hoped that a common experience would enable Germany and France to transcend their ingrained differences and reach a new understanding. The American military periodical *Army and Navy Journal* articulated these sentiments:

> The old Kaiser is dead, gone are von Moltke and Bismarck, and a new generation both in France and Germany seems trying to forget the bitterness of the past. Perhaps they have been waiting for an occasion which would enable them to bury the old animosities without any loss of national dignity, and have found it in far-off China.[50]

Nevertheless, records made by French and German officers show the longevity of stereotypical and prejudiced forms of thinking. Arnold von Lequis (1861–1949), a German officer in a pioneer battalion, regarded 'the English' as 'reserved [and] closest to us in our attitudes thanks to our common Germanic ancestry'. His view of 'the French' was far less positive; he regarded them as 'superficial' in nature and their units, despite displaying a 'pronounced adroitness', as acutely lacking in discipline. Moreover, he ascribed to them a 'coarse attitude towards the Chinese [and a] pronounced carnality'.[51]

The tenor of these records contrasts to the matter-of-fact approach of the reports written by military observers regarding the contingents of their allies. Providing a good source of intelligence about the military practices and performances of other nations, these reports sought to provide reliable accounts of the realities which they had observed. In eschewing any evaluation of supposed character traits of the other officers and men, the authors of these reports restricted themselves to a focus on the material, equipment and arms deployed in the punitive expeditions as well as the various organizational, tactical and strategic approaches adopted by their temporary allies. Writing of the German formations despatched to Baoding, General Bailloud observed that they were staffed by fewer officers than was the case in the French army; moreover, he thought that this expedition force could well serve as the core for a new colonial army. Bailloud also criticized the poor nature of the German wagon train; a fact conditioning the recourse to wide-scale requisitions and the consequent slow progress of the German force.[52]

The semi-official publications commemorating the Boxer War published in France and Germany (from 1901), and the memoirs of the various protagonists, sought to play down the closeness of the recent alliances. The German volume commemorating the Boxer War presented the campaign as having forged common bonds of exceptionally 'comradely warmth' between the officers of the eight contingents.[53] Bailloud was described as a 'highly energetic, capable commander and an admirable soldier, excellent in his personal modesty, tenacity and [distinguished] by the high standards which he demanded both of himself and his troops'.[54] However, although he and other French commanders were singled out for praise, 'the French' were treated with mistrust for a range of sins, not least their unilateral decision to march to Baoding: 'It became necessary to ensure that the French did not draw any especial privileges from their premature occupation of Paotingfu. [As a result] it was advisable to be prepared for any later similar surprises.'[55]

In France the Paris newspaper *Le Matin* published in October 1901 (immediately after the signing of the Boxer protocol) a series of articles entitled 'Our Role in China'.[56] Including three letters from Voyron to Waldersee (written in November/December 1900), this series revealed the tensions existing between the two men and sought to demonstrate the actual independence of the French contingent in the recent war. The administration of the occupied cities and the good relations established between the Chinese population and French forces were presented as French achievements. Primarily intended as a response to internal French criticism, the publications also pointed to French insistence on their independence in foreign affairs to the exclusion of any meaningful level of co-operation with the arch-rival Germany. Voyron's memoirs (published in 1904) give little information about the international expedition to Baoding, concentrating instead on the prior French move. Good relations between the French and German contingents in the China war were to be played down.

IV. Conclusions

The French and German forces despatched to China were united in their perception of their duties as a civilizing mission: to punish the agents of disorder and restore peace to a subservient region. All the soldiers involved viewed violence against the Chinese population as a legitimate instrument with which to conduct operations both during the war and in its aftermath. This consensus was common to all the ranks and function-bearers of the sprawling and entirely heterogeneous eight-nation force. Despite this unity of purpose however, the expedition force remained divided along pre-existing national lines. France was unwilling to place her contingent under the supreme command of a German. Only four of the eight participant nations were willing to join a German-induced expedition to Baoding.

Seeking to demonstrate the power and reach of the allied intervention force, and its continued unity of purpose, Waldersee sought to establish a common front behind which no single nation could be perceived as holding the initiative or pursuing a narrow national interest.

Nevertheless, a range of evidence points to the responsive nature of Waldersee's planning, drawn up to match a prior French expedition to the area. For his part, the French commander Voyron gave his support to the new expedition to Baoding to prevent German presence in this region from subverting the French national interest. The military planners of both contingents were thus guided by entirely national precepts and sought to restrain the actions of their nominal partners. Indeed, the move to extend the duration of the occupation was reflective not of a new form of Franco-German understanding, but of rooted British and Italian reluctance to remain in Baoding over the winter.

It becomes clear that the level of Franco-German co-operation, which evolved en route to Baoding and deepened during its occupation, was borne not of volition but necessity. As a result, the commands of both contingents undertook all possible steps (separate accommodation; a clearly demarcated sector border in and around Baoding; and the restriction of international contacts) to reduce the potential for contact between the detachments of the two nations to a necessary minimum. Those few projects pursued on a joint basis – such as the provision of medical services – also brought little scope for interaction. Any form of contact – fraternization and conflict alike – was to be avoided wherever possible.

The (albeit limited) personal experience of contact between the French and German soldiers may well have been positive but remained insufficient to exercise any lasting impact on the wider relations between the two nations. Although it was now acceptable to depict individual French and German officers in a positive light, the respective national discourse regarding the 'other' remained dominated by stereotype and prejudice, mistrust and innuendo. In short, individual experiences of international inter-imperial co-operation were unable to alter the wider military and national horizon of expectations (*Reinhart Koselleck*), which continued on their late nineteenth-century trajectory. However a restricted episode of limited (forced) co-operation in an extra-European setting demonstrated that an international coordinated imperialism was feasible.

Notes

1 For Germany, see e.g.: Mechthild Leutner and Klaus Mühlhahn (eds), *Kolonialkrieg in China: Die Niederschlagung der Boxerbewegung 1900–1901* (Berlin: Links, 2007). For

France, see e.g.: Jean-François Brun, Intervention armée en Chine: l'expédition internationale de 1900–1901, *Revue historique des armées*, 258 (2010), pp. 14–45. Raymond Bourgerie and Pierre Lesouef, *La Guerre des Boxers (1900–1901). Tseu-Hi évite le pire* (Paris: Economica, 1998). For China see: Paul A. Cohen, *A History in Three Keys: The Boxers as Event, Experience and Myth* (New York: Columbia University Press, 1997); Joseph W. Esherick, *The Origins of the Boxer Uprising* (Berkeley: University of California Press, 1987); Weizhi Su and Liu Tianlu (eds), *Yihetuan yundong yibai zhounian guoji xueshu taolunhui lunwenji (Selected papers from the international symposium on the 100th anniversary of the Boxer Movement)*. Vol. 1 (Jinan: Shandong daxue chubanshe, 2001). For an international approach, see: Robert Bickers and R.G. Tiedemann (eds), *The Boxers, China, and the World* (Lanham: Rowman & Littlefield 2007); James L. Hevia, *English Lessons: The Pedagogy of Imperialism in Nineteenth-Century China* (Durham: Duke UP, 2003); Thoralf Klein, Straffeldzug im Namen der Zivilisation: Der 'Boxerkrieg' in China, in: idem and Frank Schumacher (eds), *Kolonialkriege. Militärische Gewalt im Zeichen des Imperialismus* (Hamburg: Verlag Hamburger Edition, 2006), pp. 145–81; Susanne Kuss, German, British and American Soldiers in the Boxer War 1900–1901. Multinationalism and violence, in: Zhongguo yihetuan yanjiuhui (The committee for researching the Boxer movement) (eds.), *Yihetuan yundong 110 zhounian guoji taolunhui luwenji (International Conference held on the 110th anniversary of the Boxer revolt)* (Jinan: Shandong daxue chubanshe, 2012), pp. 797–819; Victor Louzon, Les 'Huns' et les fanatiques: civilisation, barbarie et décivilisation pendant la guerre des Boxers. Lecture held on 14 November 2012 at the Sorbonne, Paris. Regarding the origins of the war: Lanxing Xiang, *The Origins of the Boxer War. A Multinational Study* (London: RoutledgeCurzon, 2003).
2 Gerd Krumeich, La puissance militaire française vue d'Allemagne autour de 1900, in: Pierre Milza and Raymond Poidevin (eds), *La puissance française à la 'Belle Époque': Mythe ou réalité?* (Bruxelles: Éditions Complexe, 1992), pp. 199–210.
3 Klaus Mühlhahn and Mechthild Leutner, *'Musterkolonie' Kiautschou: Die Expansion des Deutschen Reiches in China. Deutsch-chinesische Beziehungen 1897 bis 1914* (Berlin: Akademie Verlag, 1997), pp. 35–51.
4 Gérard Gilles Epain, *Indo-Chine: Une histoire coloniale oubliée* (Paris: L'Harmattan, 2007), pp. 109–13; Jean Bouvier, René Girault and Jacques Thobie, *La France impériale 1880–1914* (Paris: Mégrelis, 1982), p. 228.
5 Roger R. Thomson, Military dimensions of the Boxer uprising in Shanxi, 1898–1901, in: Hans van de Ven (ed.), *Warfare in Chinese History* (Leiden: Brill, 2000), pp. 288–320, pp. 290–1.
6 Susanne Kuss, *Deutsches Militär auf kolonialen Kriegsschauplätzen: Eskalation von Gewalt zu Beginn des 20. Jahrhunderts* (Berlin: Links, 2012) (3rd ed.), p. 59.
7 Jean-François Brun, Intervention armée en Chine: l'expédition internationale de 1900–1901, *Revue historique des armées*, 258 (2010), p. 27.
8 Philipp D. Curtin, *Disease and Empire: The Health of European Troops in the Conquest of Africa* (Cambridge: Cambridge UP, 1998), pp.186–90; Philippe Fouquet-Lapar (Général), Un engagement international en Chine: la guerre des Boxers (1900–1901), *Les Cahiers de mars* 144, 1 (1995), p. 89.
9 'Ihr sollt fechten gegen eine gut bewaffnete Macht, aber Ihr sollt auch rächen, nicht nur den Tod des Gesandten, sondern auch vieler Deutscher und Europäer. Kommt Ihr vor den Feind, so wird er geschlagen, Pardon wird nicht gegeben; Gefangene nicht gemacht. Wer Euch in die Hände fällt, sei in Eurer Hand. Wie vor tausend Jahren die

Hunnen unter ihrem König Etzel sich einen Namen gemacht, der sie noch jetzt in der Überlieferung gewaltig erscheinen lässt, so möge der Name Deutschland in China in einer solchen Weise bekannt werden, dass niemals wieder ein Chinese es wagt, etwa einen Deutschen auch nur scheel anzusehen, [...].' Taken from: Bernd Sösemann, Die sog. Hunnenrede Wilhelm II. Textkritische und interpretatorische Bemerkungen zur Ansprache des Kaisers vom 27. Juli 1900 in Bremerhaven, *Historische Zeitschrift* 222 (1976), pp. 342–58.

10 'Ces drapeaux vous seront dès à présent sacrés. Ils vous rappelleront la haute mission que la France a confiée à votre courage: exiger d'un pays où les lois essentielles des Etats civilisés ont été odieusement violées le châtiment des coupables; lui imposer des réparations éclatantes pour le passé, des garanties nécessaires pour l'avenir. Ils vous diront aussi que l'héritage d'honneur dont vos aînés vous ont confié le dépôt ne peut être amoindri entre vos mains et que, dans cette armée internationale formée pour la défense de la civilisation, ceux qui portent l'uniforme français ne doivent le céder à personne pour la discipline, l'endurance et le courage.' Excerpt from the speech by Émile Loubet, printed in: Émile Voyron, *Rapport sur l'expédition de Chine 1900-1901* (Paris: H. Charles-Lavauzelle, 1904), pp. 7–8.

11 *Militärstrafgesetzbuch für das Deutsche Reich*, 20 June 1872; *Nouveaux codes français et lois usuelles civiles et militaires: Recueil spécialement destiné à la Gendarmerie et à l'Armée* (Paris: Charles-Lavauzelle, 1895).

12 Telegram from the French Naval Ministry to General Émile Voyron, 19 September 1900, in: Archive Vincennes, Chine 11 H 29.

13 'La complète autonomie de notre corps expéditionnaire doit toujours être réservée, et vous devez écarter toute éventualité d'un démembrement de nos troupes.' Ibid.

14 Fedor Rauch, *Mit Graf Waldersee in China: Tagebuchaufzeichnungen von Fedor von Rauch* (Berlin: Fontane, 1907), pp. 22–3; Anon., France and Germany, *Army and Navy Journal*, XXXVIII, 2, 8 September 1900, p. 36.

15 See Gustav Paul, entry from 11 September 1900, in: Hubert Mainzer and Herward Sieberg (eds), *Der Boxerkrieg in China 1900–1901: Tagebuchaufzeichnungen des späteren Hildesheimer Polizeioffiziers Gustav Paul Hildesheim* (Hildesheim: Gerstneberg, 2001), p. 78; François Pavé, *Le journal de Jules Bedeau: Un artilleur français dans la Chine des Boxers* (1900–1) (Paris: Edition You-Feng, 2007), p. 134; idem, L'image des armées alliées à travers les journaux des diaristes français de la guerre des Boxers, *Annales de Bretagne et des Pays de l'Ouest*, 115, 4 (2008), pp. 127–44. http://abpo.revues.org/223, pp. 1–16 (accessed 15 July 2014).

16 Voyron, *Rapport sur l'expédition de Chine*, p. 181.

17 *Deutschland in China 1900–1901, bearb. von Teilnehmern an der Expedition* (Düsseldorf: Bagel, 1902), pp. 108, 110.

18 Eugen Binder-Krieglstein, *Die Kämpfe des Deutschen Expeditionskorps in China* (Berlin: Mittler, 1902), p. 21.

19 Voyron, *Rapport sur l'expédition de Chine*, p. 187.

20 Armee-Befehl von Waldersee, 8 October 1900 (Tianjin), in: *Deutschland in China 1900–1901*, pp. 113–14.

21 Regarding the various contingents, see: A.A.S. Barnes, *On Active Service with the Chinese Regiment* (London: Richards, 1902) (2nd ed., revised and enlarged); Bob Nicholls, *Bluejackets and Boxers: Australia's Naval Expedition to the Boxer Uprising* (Sydney: Allen & Unwin, 1986); and Annand Yang, (A) subaltern('s) Boxers: an Indian soldier's account of China and the world in 1900–01, in: Bickers and Tiedemann (eds), *The Boxers*, pp. 43–65.

22 Order from General Bailloud, 9 October 1900, in: *Deutschland in China 1900–1901*, pp. 115–16. See also: Voyron, *Rapport sur l'expédition de Chine 1900–1901*, pp. 177, 181.
23 'Les troupes commandées par general Bailloud ont parfaitement observé les règles de la discipline militaire à leur passage et leur séjour; elles ont payé équitablement ce quelles ont demandé et n'ont jamais importuné les femmes des habitants.' Various *certficats de bien vivre* from prefectures close to Baoding, in: Archive Vincennes, Chine 11 H 6.
24 Grote Hutchinson (captain, 6th Cavalry), Report on the Paoting Expedition and murder of American missionaries at that place, Peking, 12 November 1900, in: *Annual Reports of the War Department*. Fiscal year ended 30 June 1901. Government Publications, vol. 4274, Washington (Government Printing Office) 1901, p. 467.
25 Voyron to Waldersee, 16 November 1900, in: *Le Matin*, 27 October 1901, p. 2.
26 *Deutschland in China 1900–1901*, p. 126.
27 Voyron to Bailloud, 11 November 1900, in: Archive Vincennes, 11 H 4; Waldersee to Bailloud, 10 November 1900, in: ibid., 11 H 7.
28 James L. Hevia, Krieg als Expedition. Die alllierten Truppen unter Alfred Graf von Waldersee, in: Leutner and Mühlhahn (eds), *Kolonialkrieg in China*, p. 126.
29 Waldersee to Bailloud, 11 November 1900, in: Archive Vincennes, Chine 11 H 7; see also: *Deutschland in China 1900–1901*, p. 130; Voyron to Bailloud, 10 November 1900, in: Archive Vincennes 11 H 4.
30 *Corps expéditionnaire de Chine, 2e Brigade, Ordres de la Brigade, 1r Ordres Généraux. Baoding, 31.10.1900. Ordre de la Brigade, nr. 4, Général Bailloud*, in: Archive Vincennes, Chine 11 H 1.
31 Waldersee to Bailloud, 11 November 1900, in: Archive Vincennes, Chine 11 H 7.
32 Ibid.
33 Ibid.
34 Kettler to Bailloud, 17 January 1901, in: Archiv Vincennes, Chine 11 H 7; Kettler to Bailloud, 30 January 1901, in: ibid., 11 H 10. Regarding Epp: Katja-Maria Wächter, *Die Macht der Ohnmacht. Leben und Politik des Franz Xaver Ritter von Epp (1868–1946)* (Frankfurt, M.: Lang, 1999), pp. 28–32.
35 Kettler to Bailloud, 14 December 1900, in: Archive Vincennes, Chine 11 H 7.
36 Eugen Wolffhügel, Truppenhygienische Erfahrungen in China, *Münchner medizinische Wochenschrift* 50, 49 (8 December 1903), p. 2150.
37 Kettler to Bailloud, 30 November 1900, in: Archive Vincennes, Chine 11 H 7.
38 *Kriegs-Tagebuch des II. Seebataillons, 4. Ostasiatisches Infanterie-Regiment vom Beginn der Mobilmachung bis zum Beginn des Seetransports, speziell: vom 28. Oktober 1900 bis 10. Dezember 1900*, in: Kriegsarchiv München (War Archive Munich), B 1485.
39 Kettler to Bailloud, 2 February 1901, in: Archive Vincennes, Chine 11 H 7.
40 *Deutschland in China 1900–1901*, p. 411.
41 *Kriegs-Tagebuch des II. Seebataillons, 4. Ostasiatisches Infanterie-Regiment vom Beginn der Mobilmachung bis zum Beginn des Seetransports, speziell: vom 28. Oktober 1900 bis 10. Dezember 1900*, in: Kriegsarchiv München (War Archive Munich), B 1485.
42 *Convention relative à une délimitation entre les zones allemandes et françaises dans la région occupée entre la Grande Muraille et la voie ferrée de Pao-ting-Fou à Pékin, 29.5.1901*, in: Archive Vincennes, Chine 11 H 7.
43 *Armee-Befehl, Peking, den 12.11.1900. Armee-Ober-Kommando in Ostasien*, in: Archive Vincennes, Chine, 11 H 7.
44 Kettler to Guillet, 14 November 1900, in: Archive Vincennes, Chine, 11 H 7.
45 Kettler to Bailloud, 16 January 1901, in: Archive Vincennes, *Chine* 11 H 7.

46 Kettler to Bailloud, 22 February 1901, in: Archive Vincennes, *Chine* 11 H 7.
47 'La France a toujours marché en tête de la civilisation.' Ordre no. 13, Huai-lou, 17.4. 1901, General der 2. Brigade Bailloud, in: Archive Vincennes, Chine 11 H 1.
48 Léon Silbermann, *Souvenirs de campagne*, (Paris: Plon 1910), pp. 190, 201; also in: http://fr.wikisource.org/wiki/Souvenirs_de_campagne_par_le_Soldat_Silbermann/ Chine/; Pavé, *Le journal de Jules Bedeau*; Alain Dalotel, *De la Chine à la Guyane. Mémoires du Bagnard Victor Petit 1879–1919*, (Paris: La boutique de l'Histoire, 1996); Pavé, L'image des armées, http://abpo.revues.org/223, pp. 1–16.
49 Pavé, *Le journal de Jules Bedeau*, pp. 77–9.
50 Anon., France and Germany, p. 36.
51 Arnold von Lequis, Schlussbericht zum Kriegstagebuch, 30.8.1901, Notizen über fremde Kolonien, n.d., Militärarchiv Freiburg, N 38/31; Kuss, *Deutsches Militär auf kolonialen Kriegsschauplätzen*, p. 314.
52 *Rapport d'ensemble du Général commandant la 2e Brigade, 14.2.1900*, pp. 27–32, in: Archive Vincennes, 11 H 10.
53 *Deutschland in China 1900–1901*, p. 416 and foreword.
54 *Deutschland in China 1900–1901*, p. 114; Otto Löffler, *Die China-Expedition 1900–1901: Unter besonderer Berücksichtigung der Thätigkeit des Armee-Oberkommandos und des Deutschen Expeditionskorps* (Berlin: Mittler, 1902), p. 18.
55 *Deutschland in China 1900–1901*, p. 126.
56 Anon., Notre rôle en Chine, six parts, in: *Le Matin*, 12.10., 15.10.,17.10., 18.10., 20.10., 23.10., each pp. 1–2. The first article indicated that it had been penned by one of the 'most senior military authorities of this country'; Voyron to Waldersee, 16 November 1900/10 December 1900/30 December 1900, in: ibid., 27 October 1901, pp. 1–2.

Glossary

Baoding 保定
Cixi 慈禧
Dalian 大連
Fantai 藩臺
Guangzhouwan 廣州灣
Guiheng 奎恒
Jiulong (Kowloon) 九龍
Lüshunkou 旅順口
Qingdao 青島
Ting Yong 廷雍
Wang Zhanggui 王占魁
Weihaiwei 威海衛
Yihequan 義和拳
Yihetuan 義和團

9

Deadly Learning? Concentration Camps in Colonial Wars Around 1900

Jonas Kreienbaum

I. The new standard approach: concentration

Around 1900 the concentration of large parts of the civilian population in camps or zones became a common approach for colonial militaries facing intractable guerrilla wars in their overseas possessions. Spain first practised large scale, systematic 'reconcentration' on Cuba during the War of Independence (1895–8). Shortly after, Britain established 'concentration camps' during the South African War or Boer War (1899–1902), while simultaneously US militaries were experimenting with so called 'zones of concentration' in the Philippines. Finally, the German Empire erected '*Konzentrationslager*' in German South West Africa in order to end the war against Herero and Nama (1904–8).

How can we explain the frequent occurrence of 'concentration' in the years around the turn of the century? Or differently asked: why did all the mentioned colonial powers try to solve their military problems by interning thousands of civilians in guarded camps or zones? Was this a consequence of the encounters of empires, of the spread of techniques of colonial warfare through inter-imperial elite-networks which Volker Barth and Roland Cvetkovski stress in their introduction to this volume? And how did the local conditions of the particular colonial wars affect these possibly shared imperial tools?

Scholars working on colonial concentration policies usually give two rather contradicting answers in order to explain the frequent occurrence of 'concentration' in the years around the turn of the century. The majority of historians working on a specific case of 'concentration' assume a process of learning: following this interpretation Britain adopted 'concentration' from Spain, the United States followed the Spanish and British examples and Germany simply copied the British concentration camps from neighbouring South Africa.[1] But what is always missing is empirical evidence that could substantiate the learning hypothesis.

The second approach stresses the shared structure of the mentioned colonial wars: namely the fact that they were all guerrilla wars. According to the British military historian Ian F.W. Beckett, the forced concentration of civilians is simply to be seen as the logical answer to the main problem of guerrilla warfare.[2] Guerrillas draw their strength out of a sympathizing population that supports them with food, ammunition, shelter, new recruits, intelligence etc. Without the help of civilians, guerrillas lose their strength. Therefore, concentrating the population inhabiting areas where guerrillas operate at guarded places and thereby preventing any contact between guerrillas and supporting civilians solves the main problem for the imperial military.

This chapter focuses on the British and the German example and confronts both hypotheses with the surviving empirical evidence. Did Britain learn the 'deadly' technique of concentration – in all the cases thousands of people died at the places of internment – from Spain and, if so, in which ways and did Germany afterwards adopt it from Britain?

II. Concentration camps during the South African War

The South African War between the British Empire and the two independent Boer Republics, the Transvaal and the Orange Free State, which had started on 11 October 1899, did not turn out to be the short 'tea time war' ended by Christmas that many British had anticipated. After humiliating defeats in the initial phase of the war the British forces under Commander-in-Chief Lord Frederick Sleigh Roberts managed to invade both Boer Republics and to seize the capitals, Bloemfontein and Pretoria, by June 1900. The Boer Republics were annexed and the war seemed over, but it was really only entering its most protracted phase. The Boer forces started to split up into ever smaller groups, now avoiding pitched battles. These commandos fought as guerrillas, surprising isolated British columns and attacking their lines of communication.[3] The British response was the adoption of a 'scorched earth policy' first under Lord Roberts that was then systemized under his successor Lord Horatio Herbert Kitchener. British columns started to systematically destroy everything – from houses to food – that could help the Boer forces keep up their resistance. Part of this strategy was to drive all inhabitants – Boer and African – off the *veld* and to intern them in guarded camps. There they were under control, unable to support the guerrillas with food, ammunition, shelter, intelligence or new recruits. These so called 'refugee camps' which were erected from August 1900 also hosted a smaller number of surrendered Boers that had voluntarily come in, in order not to be forced by Boer commandos to rejoin the guerrillas. In both cases the camps served a clearly military purpose as an integral part of the British counter-guerrilla strategy.[4]

Separate camp systems were established in the Transvaal and in, what was after annexation, the Orange River Colony, and flooded by ever growing numbers of Boer women and children, but also some men who were sent in by British troops. The British camp administration, first military later civil, was unable to supply the masses of new arrivals as the number of camp inhabitants rose to over 100,000. Inadequate supply of shelters, clothes, food and medical care, along with poor sanitation and most of all a severe measles epidemic led to mass death in the concentration camps during 1901: some 25,000 to 30,000 Boers, mainly children, died in the camps.[5] The supply situation was even worse in the equally large system of 'black' camps for African internees, and the number of deaths probably reached equal heights. While the 'black' camp system was clearly also part of the British counter-guerrilla strategy, it also served a second function. The camps were a labour pool for the British military which systematically hired male camp inhabitants. Also, they were tools for a sort of social engineering. Keeping the 'natives' working and cultivating land for their own subsistence in or around the camps was seen as a means to conserve them as farming aids for white settlers after the war.[6] In the 'white' camps, social engineering took a different form. The Boers were to become modern subjects of the British Crown and the prime means to achieve this was the establishment of schools in all camps in which classes were usually given in English in order to anglicize the mass of Boer children.[7]

But despite the military's need for workers and attempts at social engineering, the counter-guerrilla function of the camps was and remained the prime motive for the British administration and military. This had also been the case during the Cuban War of Independence a few years earlier. The Spanish Captain General Valeriano Weyler y Nicolau tried to meet the guerrilla challenge posed by the 'republic in arms' fighting for an independent Cuba by 'reconcentrating' the island's rural population in existing towns and villages guarded by Spanish troops. The military rationale behind this strategy was the same as in South Africa: separating the guerrillas from the often supportive civil population in order to prevent them supplying the combatants and thereby forcing the guerrillas into submission. As later in South Africa, the most visible consequence of 'concentration' proved to be mass death among the internees. Though this was certainly not the aim of the Spanish military, but rather a consequence of poor logistics and indifference, over 150,000 *reconcentrados* died.[8]

Considering the obvious similarities between Spanish and British concentration policies and temporal proximity between the two events the question suggests itself: did British militaries get the idea of forming concentration camps in South Africa from Cuba? And how might such a process of learning have occurred?

Already contemporaries saw a connection between 'concentration' in the two places. This is obvious when Boer internees were labelled 'concentrados'[9] and camps figured as 'reconcentration camps'.[10] Emily Hobhouse felt certain: 'England, by the hands of Lord Roberts and Lord Kitchener, adopted the policy of Spain, while improving upon her methods.'[11] Especially during the early phase of concentration camps in South Africa – at the end of 1900 – several newspaper articles and letters to the editor saw a connection between the new concentration policy and Weyler's methods in Cuba. For instance, the *Pall Mall Gazette* found that with Kitchener taking over as commander-in-chief the time had come for 'stern "reconcentration" into the towns, minus the Weylerian barbarity of the starvation of the *reconcentrados*'.[12] Hereupon, one reader warned of the necessary precautions in good time that would be needed to feed the 'reconcentration towns' and expressed his fear that typhoid epidemics might break out in the 'camps'.[13]

Generally it was common to look beyond one's own national nose and to orient one's actions with a view to the practices of past wars. First of all, the Franco Prussian War of 1870/1 and the American Civil War were analysed in the Colonial Office in order to evaluate which measures were feasible in counter-guerrilla warfare. Furthermore, the contemporaneous American action in the Philippines was considered occasionally.[14] The establishment of 'concentration camps' on the archipelago was noted, but only long after the South African camp system had been put into place.[15] Likewise, Charles Callwell's *Small Wars*, the contemporary standard work on colonial wars, was consequently international in scope. Callwell drew his conclusions not only from British small wars, but considered others' experiences in colonial warfare on equal terms.[16]

The ambition to 'learn' from others' wars obviously existed. Yet, official files remain silent as to whether British militaries 'learnt' the 'concentration' of civilians on Cuba. An indication can only be found in the press. On 20 August 1900 – a month before Lord Roberts sanctioned the establishment of the first concentration camps – the *St James Gazette* discussed the latest proclamation of the commander-in-chief. The *Gazette* viewed Roberts's announcement, to detain all burghers who refused to take the oath of neutrality, or broke the oath, as an unconscious imitation of Weyler's measures in Cuba. In their opinion, though, it was a 'half-hearted' attempt as all other persons were left on their farms. The *Gazette* recommended 'copying' Weyler properly: 'If the burghers are not to be trusted, it would be far better to adopt the policy of thorough to at once, and "reconcentrate" the whole Dutch population of the Transvaal at St Helena or in Ceylon.'[17]

Whether Roberts or Kitchener took note of this article is unknown, let alone whether they were influenced by it. That they knew about Weyler's reconcentration policy is very likely given the extensive press coverage in British and even South African newspapers.[18] But whether they initiated the establishment of concentration camps in South Africa on the basis of the Cuban 'role model' is questionable. Particularly the linguistic kinship between 'concentration camp' and *'reconcentratión'* suggests a causal connection. However, it has to be borne in mind that the camps in South Africa first appeared under a different name. They were called 'refugee camps', 'refugee laager', or 'burgher camps'. The term 'concentration camp' only appeared in 1901 – soon to become widely accepted.[19]

It is equally possible that British militaries opted for the strategy of concentrating civilians independently of certain prototypes. Like the Spanish in Cuba they faced the military problem of coping with an elusive guerrilla adversary that was supported by wide sections of the civilian population. In this situation, it kind of suggested itself to withdraw the 'breeding grounds' of the guerrillas by concentrating and controlling the population and thereby effectively preventing their supportive actions. Thus, the policy of concentration in South Africa would simply be the logical consequence of a certain structural constellation as it had previously been on Cuba.[20]

After all, it remains unclear whether the establishment of the British concentration camps was inspired by the Cuban model or whether they evolved largely independently. Regarding the internal management of the camps, earlier experiences obviously mattered. These, however, were rather not to be found abroad but within the Empire. The Indian plague and famine camps served as an important illustrative model. Especially after mortality in the burgher camps peaked in the end of 1901 and panic loomed large in the Colonial Office, officials tried to apply the lessons from India. Reports on the Indian 'famine operations' of 1896/7 were analysed.[21] The India Office arranged contacts with physicians who had had experience in Indian camps and could consequently make suggestions about how to successfully manage South African concentration camps. For the Colonial Office, the surgeon general, James Cleghorn, summed up the lessons learned during his time in the Indian plague segregation camps as follows: strict discipline had to rule in the camps. In case of necessity internees should be forced to cleanliness and had to obey the rules of sanitation. Daily the inmates' shelters should be searched by the assistants of the medical officer for sick persons. These were to be brought to the hospital immediately – by compulsion if necessary. Furthermore he suggested using huts instead of tents and drastically downsizing the camps: 500 to 1,000 persons should be the maximum one physician should care for.[22]

It is interesting to note that most of these recommendations had already been implemented in the burgher camps by the end of 1901. The emphasis on personal hygiene, the enforcement of rules of sanitation, daily visits in each tent to detect sick people and the compulsory sending of them to hospital were firmly established in most of the camps.[23] These principles already seemed to be part of the Empire's 'medical culture'[24] so that they were promptly and independently implemented in different contexts. Only the demands to downsize camps and substitute huts for tents were truly novel. In addition, Thomas Holderness from the India Office stressed the importance of the supply of clear water.[25]

In any case, the suggestions were immediately passed on to South Africa. On 16 November 1901 the secretary of state for the Colonies, Joseph Chamberlain, telegraphed to Lord Alfred Milner, the South African high commissioner:

> Indian experience in famine camps indicates that [the] question of a pure water supply is paramount and that as soon as a camp becomes unhealthy and the water supply affected it must be evacuated; also that camps ought not to be too large – not over, say, 5,000. Camps of that size might be subdivided into smaller sections, with a person in subordinate charge for reporting sickness and for sanitary arrangements.[26]

A few days later, after talking to Cleghorn, Chamberlain added his interlocutor's suggestions:

> The compulsory removal of those suffering from infectious disease and of those seriously ill is essential, and for the detection of disease it would seem that great assistance would be given to the medical staff by utilizing Boer women of the right stamp as probationers in uniform, who would readily obtain access to the tents at any time of the day. As regards the observance of cleanly habits and sanitary rules some suitable and efficacious form of punishment appears to be necessary.[27]

Partly, as mentioned earlier, these proposals had already been put into practice. Otherwise they were taken seriously although they were not always implemented one-to-one. Newly-built camps in Natal and Cape Colony helped to reduce the size of some of the old laager. However, the 5,000-inmate limit was not categorically observed. Merebank camp in Natal, for instance, became the largest concentration camp with more than 8,000 inmates.[28] Milner believed that the size of camps only had a slight influence on mortality: 'A camp of 500 would have developed epidemics as much as a camp of 5,000.'²⁹ But at least the new camps stood out by their superior accommodation. The administrators used, as suggested from India, huts instead of tents.³⁰ And in the old camps, too, concrete dwellings were increasingly substituted for tents.³¹

Chamberlain concluded his telegram full of suggestions for improvements with an offer: 'If you are in any need of trained men, I am sure that I shall be able to obtain through the India Office the services of officers who have had very analogous experience in the famine camps, and you must not fail to ask for such assistance if you require it.'³² Milner accepted the offered help and in early March 1902 Lieutenant-Colonel James Thomson and Colonel James Wilkins took over the administration of the camp systems in Transvaal and the Orange River Colony respectively. Along with these 'new geniuses from India',³³ other officers with experience in Indian plague and famine camps arrived in South Africa to assume the post of superintendent of single camps. Thus, know-how from India was introduced in South African camps in two ways: first, through the evaluation of Indian lessons through the London Colonial Office and the formulation of suggestions, and second, by hiring camp experts directly from India.

Not only for 'white' camps did Indian experiences play a role. In his final report on the 'black' camps, Captain G.F. de Lotbinière, head of the Department of Native Refugees, explained: 'Having had experience in Indian Famine Camps and the advisability of keeping natives employed, a system was introduced by which the natives could earn a good wage and purchase all their requirements at very reasonable prices.'³⁴ The consequent advancement of this principle was the soon to be introduced 'agricultural scheme' which entailed that not only African men were to work – often for the military – but also women and the old were kept busy raising crops in the camps for their own supply.³⁵ This system bore significant resemblance to the Spanish attempt to name cultivation zones where Cuban *reconcentrados* could produce their own food, freeing the military from allocating rations.³⁶ However, this does not mean that the idea had necessarily been adopted from Cuba; especially as the cultivation zones hardly figured in British press reports and it is consequently questionable whether the South African authorities were at all aware of Cuban practices.³⁷

The conviction that work must be the basis for any kind of help, as a policy of cost-free provisioning, would inevitably lead to the pauperization of the needy, was deeply rooted in the British Empire.³⁸ Stowell Kessler writes in this connection:

> Further the policy forbade any assistance to the indigenous population except in the most dire circumstances, such as levels of starvation that would lead to death or endanger the British settler populations or the military. This was everywhere evident in the Empire from the black locations in the Cape Colony during famine from poor rainfall and crop destruction by locusts, to the famine and plague camps in the largest colony of the Empire, India.³⁹

Also, when during the war in German South West Africa numerous Herero fled to the British enclave of Walvisbay, women and children, who could not immediately be sent to South Africa as labourers, had to load coal and fulfil other tasks in order to get provisions.⁴⁰ Hence, it seems plausible not to understand the establishment of cultivation zones in the 'black' camps and the application of the principle that 'natives' were to work for their provisions as the consequence of a transfer of knowledge from India or Cuba, but rather as the result of a 'basic assumption'[41] of British colonial policy. One can even go further and speak of a general principle of Western colonial policy. After all, the propagation of Western work ethics was on the agenda of all European colonial powers.[42] In German South West Africa, for instance, the idea of 'educating' Herero and Nama to work, by forcing them to work, 'as they would prospectively rove around the country in idleness and after having lost all their livestock scrape a miserable living', bore close resemblance to the British doctrine.[43] In addition, for Cuba, it could be asked whether the creation of cultivation zones was understood as a means to prevent the permanent pauperization of the *concentrados*, besides the obvious wish to save costs for provisioning the internees.

Also, parallels between practices in colonial concentration sites and policies towards the poor in European metropolises can be found. 'Education through work' was also taking place in workhouses which had been established in Europe since the early modern period. As Sebastian Conrad has shown, connections between colonial and metropolitan work-education-programmes can actually be detected.[44] Furthermore, some colonial administrators perceived the compulsory enforcement of rules of hygiene in workhouses as exemplary. Lord William Onslow, under-secretary of state for the colonies, for instance, commented on the General Regulations for Natal camps as follows:

> I still think there seems to be too much inclination to 'hope' that people in the camps will be clean, decent, + sanitary, instead of making it obligatory under pain of some punishment that they should be so. When a tramp comes into an English workhouse he has to take a bath. He hates it, but it is a condition of getting a meal[.] Why not the same in a concentration camp[.][45]

On this basis it is not absurd – also in the colonial context – to understand these workhouses, with Andreas Gestrich, as a tradition from which concentration camps derived.[46]

British administrators did not only try to make experiences from other parts of the empire useful for South Africa. Simultaneously, an exchange of experiences between the camp administrations in Transvaal, the Orange River Colony and Natal existed. In February 1901 the general superintendent refugee camps of Transvaal enquired of his colleague in the neighbouring colony how the provision of inmates with clothes was regulated there as he was searching for a guideline for proceedings in his territory.[47] In November of the same year a member of the Colonial Office composed a memorandum on concentration camps that bore the title: 'Points where the camp administration seems to have been successful and deserving of imitation'.[48] And slightly later the Colonial Office recommended the reading of the monthly report of Natal camps with the words: 'I think the Natal camps may provide some useful lessons to those in charge of the T[ransvaal] and O[range] R[iver] C[olony] camps.'[49]

The administration of the 'black' camps tapped local know-how, too. Concentration camps for Africans were explicitly modelled along the 'compound system'.[50] In particular, the closed compounds, which had been introduced in 1885 in the diamond mines of Kimberley, Cape Colony, exhibit some significant similarities to the 'black' camps. Thousands of African labourers were virtually cut off from the outside world in the completely fenced-in areas for the duration of their contracts. Originally, mine managers had expected improved conditions of living for their workers through increased control. But in fact neglect, bad food provisioning and the overcrowding of compounds led to higher death rates.[51]

III. *Konzentrationslager* in German South West Africa

The Imperial Chancellor Bernhard von Bülow initiated the establishment of *Konzentrationslager* (concentration camps) in German South West Africa in December 1904. After the outbreak of war between the Herero and Imperial Germany in January 1904 it took the German colonial military months to gain the initiative in the conflict. And even after the arrival of heavy reinforcements from Germany, the battle of the Waterberg in August did not turn out to be the decisive strike General Lothar von Trotha, the German commander, had hoped for. He ordered the fleeing Herero to be pursued into the Omaheke desert and after the unsuccessful abortion of the hunt he issued his infamous *Vernichtungsbefehl* (order of destruction) which has often been interpreted as a genocidal order.[52] The decision to put up concentration camps for captured or submitting Herero, dictated from Berlin, meant a turning away from this former policy of destruction. The new camps were supposed to be measures to end the war, to function as labour pools for the colonial military and economy, and to punish the internees for revolting.[53] Besides the Herero, Nama were also interned. The Nama, living in the south of the colony, had only engaged in war in October 1904. Fighting as guerrillas they remained a military threat until the beginning of 1907, long after Herero resistance had virtually been broken (by the end of 1904).[54]

Though German decision makers in Berlin and Windhoek did not attempt to systematically kill the interned Herero and Nama, death rates were very high. As in South Africa, the main reasons for the high mortality were supply problems, indifference in the face of African suffering, and the lack of medical know-how. Officially 7,682 people or 45.2 per cent of all inmates died in the German camps.[55]

Even more than British officials must have been aware of the Cuban precedent, German decision makers must have been familiar with British concentration camps when they opted for the establishments of *Konzentrationslager* in 1904/5. The South African War had been a media event in Germany with daily press reports. One of the most prominent topics was the camps for Boer women and children.[56] On the book market, too, the 'Boer War' was a hot topic. A recent bibliography counts 358 publications in German on the war in South Africa until 1910 alone.[57] Among them were extracts from the official British 'blue books' on the camps, Emily Hobhouse's famous report on her visit to several camps in the Orange Free State and Elizabeth Neethling's account of the Boer inmates suffering in the camps.[58] Thus, it comes as no surprise that Paul Leutwein, son of the former governor in South West Africa, specified von Trotha's warfare with reference to the South African War: 'He [von Trotha] could point to the example of Kitchener who had established concentration camps for women and children of the Boers [a] few years ago in order to force this people struggling for their independence into submission.'[59]

But knowledge about British camps did not only come from the media. Some German officials, who were to play central roles in the establishment and administration of concentration camps in German South West Africa, had personally come into contact with the 'matter' in South Africa. These men may be described as part of the inter-imperial elite's intertwined epistemic community identified by Barth and Cvetkovski in the introduction. Ludwig von Estorff was one of them. He had been in South Africa in 1901 and was to take charge of the South West African *Schutztruppe* (colonial military) in April 1907. He immediately evacuated the most deadly camp on Shark Island. In South Africa he had not only accompanied the troops of Walter Kitchener, brother of the commander-in-chief, for a few weeks during the guerrilla phase of the war, but also visited a concentration camp. Taking part in the visit was another German: the German general consul in Cape Town and later governor in the neighbouring German colony, Friedrich von Lindequist.[60] It was not the first time Lindequist set foot in a camp. During the war he had repeatedly been confronted with the camps – intervening on behalf of German citizens who had been interned and supervising charitable contributions to Boer families from Germany. Decades later he recalled: 'During my visits to the largest women- and children-camps in Bloemfontein and Johannesburg I could convince myself of the correct arrival and properness of the donations which were also running through the hands of our German clergymen there.'[61]

Finally, Oskar Hintrager, vice governor in South West Africa under Lindequist, has to be mentioned, as he later unsuccessfully fought Estorff's decision to evacuate the camp on Shark Island.[62] He had participated in the South African War as a volunteer on the Boer side.[63] In fact, he never saw a British concentration camp because he had already embarked a steamer back to Germany in September 1900. But he remained interested in the fate of the Boers after his return, becoming an active member of a pro-Boer committee in Munich which also collected donations for interned women and children, and he was therefore certainly well informed about South African camps.[64]

The first proposal for the creation of concentration camps in the German colony stemmed from the Rhenish Mission Society, as far as the sources provide information, and not, as is sometimes stated, from Count Georg von Stillfried und Rattonitz.[65] On 25 November 1904 mission inspector Gottlob Haussleiter wrote to the imperial chancellor, once more offering the mission's help to mediate peace in the 'protectorate', and adding a novel suggestion: 'Finally we would like to allow ourselves to encourage the immediate designation of asylums in which those Herero who participated in the war but not in assassination could find quarter and refuge when laying down their arms. [...] To begin with individual watering places could be designated as such asylums in which proximity concentration camps would be built.'[66] Chancellor Bülow took up this suggestion and directed Trotha on 11 December, in the course of the cancellation of Trotha's order of destruction, to create concentration camps.[67] Shortly after this Bülow confirmed the order adding that Herero should be urged to work under supervision in the camps. On the margin of this document is a handwritten comment stating that this would 'entirely meet General Consul Lindequist's approval'. Thus, Lindequist, who had first-hand knowledge of South African camps, was directly involved in the decision-making process to establish concentration camps in German South West Africa. Moreover, the Rhenish Mission Society also had a special relationship with South Africa. Its area of missionary activity in Southern Africa stretched to the territory of the Cape Colony and therefore Rhenish missionaries had been directly concerned by the South African War though they had not been interned themselves – unlike their colleagues of the Hermannsburg and Berlin Missionary Societies.[68] An intensive reception of South African camps through the Rhenish Missionary Society, however, is documented in the missionary files.[69]

Of course, Lindequist's participation in the decision making alone is no proof that the concept 'concentration camp' was conveyed by a transfer of knowledge from the neighbouring British colony. Nevertheless, some further considerations make this assumption appear very likely.

First of all, it was not uncommon to perceive the experienced British Empire as a role model. Ulrike Lindner supposes in her latest study that Great Britain always served 'as point of reference for colonial considerations' as 'the role model with which the Germans engaged, imitating and demarcating'.[70] A contemporary author demanded in this spirit: 'I want to declare as a major prerequisite that every civil servant in our protectorate, who is appointed to an authoritative position, will be sent to South Africa first to study the conditions there and to see how it should and how it should not be done'.[71] And military journals concretely asked which lessons Imperial Germany could learn from the 'Boer War'.[72]

But, most notably, it has to be stressed that the word *Konzentrationslager* was only introduced into the German language in the course of the South African War. German encyclopaedias did not mention the term around the turn of the century. Only in the 1920s does it appear, usually closely connected to the Boer camps.[73] In the German language daily press the South African camps first passed as 'women's camps' or 'refugee camps' and only gradually, as in the British press, too, the term 'concentration camp' became widely accepted.[74] In 1904 Germany, the word 'concentration camp' was, without doubt, directly linked to the Boer War camps. The fact that the term *Konzentrationslager* was, from the start, officially used to denote the internment camps in South West Africa can only be interpreted as a clear sign that British concentration camps had been the point of reference. Obviously, the British Secretary of State for War St John Brodrick was right when he maintained with regard to the South African War: 'foreign troops had realized that they could learn a lot from the British Army'.[75]

In the face of the great differences regarding the function of camps in South and South West Africa it becomes very apparent that the process of knowledge transfer must necessarily be a 'creative' one: 'hardly linear, always fragmentary, quite obstinate and full of phantasy', as Birthe Kundrus describes it.[76] The system of Boer camps could not have been simply installed in the German 'protectorate' one by one. The context was too different. The prime function of South African camps, to withdraw the supply base from the guerrillas by concentrating the supporting civil population, was not transferable to South West Africa. The Herero did not fight as guerrillas and the Nama, who indeed opted for the methods of small war, did not depend on the civil population for their supplies. They rather raided German farms and isolated columns, or bartered for supply goods with tradesmen from the Cape Colony in the uncontrollable border region.[77] In the German colony the preventive separation of civilians and combatants did not make any sense and neither would have the adaptation of the policy of anglicization – the second aim of the Boer camps. Therefore, the reception of the concept 'concentration camp' in South West Africa meant only to extract fragments from the 'foreign' import, to work these and to amalgamate them with one's own, as Christiane Eisenberg formulates in her thoughts on cultural transfers, in order to get a usable concept.[78] Transferable was only the vague idea of interning a population perceived as hostile, which consisted mainly of women and children, in an enclosed place, in a camp. That was what was done in South West Africa. And that was the picture of the Boer camps which predominated in the German public mind, provided that they were not understood as places of annihilation.[79] That Boer women and children were officially 'refugees' and not prisoners and that British camps were, in part, not even fenced in, did not matter as this was hardly understood by the German public.

The approximate image of the concentration camp concept, then, amalgamated with local influences on the spot. The *pontoks* (round huts) the imprisoned Herero and Nama built for themselves as shelters in the camps were made from locally available material and constructed in the traditionally conventional fashion. The camps were in part 'fenced in' with thorn bushes which were otherwise used in the 'protectorate' for the enclosure of cattle. And forcing the interned to work was also a tested means for punishing 'rebellious' colonized. For instance, the Zwartboois, a Nama group living in the north of the colony, had been penalized in this way for their 'revolt' in 1898.[80]

Unlike the case of Boer camps, similarities between the Herero and Nama camps and South African 'black' camps are easier to discern. The similar housing and exploitation of the internees' workforce are, for example, two eye-catching characteristics which both cases share. However, the existence of camps for Africans during the South African War had hardly been noticed by German officials or the German public.[81] A process of learning in this respect seems therefore unlikely.

In this case, it is more plausible to understand the parallels – like the similarities between the administration of Indian famine camps and South African camps – as the products of shared basic assumptions of a common 'colonial culture'. Among these doctrines were the 'education' of the 'natives' to work, the understanding that the place of the colonized was solely that of a wage worker proletariat serving the Europeans, and the willingness only to intervene in a case of crisis when the well-being of the white population would otherwise be endangered. These doctrines were of great influence both in South West African prisoner camps and in South African 'black' camps. However, they did not take effect in isolation, but in combination with structural factors on the spot. The lack of labourers in both South and South West Africa has to be taken into account as a structural characteristic, if one wants to explain why internees were in both cases used on a large scale as workers for the military. And the undersupply of the interned 'natives' – but also Boers – was further aggravated by local transport problems.[82]

IV. Conclusion

In conclusion it can be stated that the establishment of concentration camps in South and South West Africa and their concrete organization were a product of different influences. International role models, indeed, spread through the encounters of empires and seemed to have played a role, but in the course of reception the imported concept had to be adjusted to the structural conditions of the respective situation of colonial war. Further, the 'import' was mixed with local traditions and shaped by 'colonial' and 'medical cultures'. Existing approaches, which either alone stress the 'adaptation' argument or the structurally similar situation in the colonial wars as an explanation for the policies of population concentration in Cuba and the Philippines, in South and South West Africa, lack complexity and cannot sufficiently explain the manifold similarities and differences of the mentioned cases. The answer to the headline question must therefore be: 'Yes', a process of 'deadly learning' took place, but for the formation of concentration camps in the wars under consideration other factors also have to be taken into account. Only part of the explanation can be found by observing encounters of empires.

Notes

1 See among others Casper W. Erichsen, *'The angel of death had descended violently among them': Concentration Camps and Prisoner-of-war in Namibia, 1904–1908* (Leiden: African Studies Centre, 2005), p. 1; Isabel V. Hull, *Absolute Destruction: Military Culture and the Practices of War in Imperial Germany* (Ithaca: Cornell UP, 2005), p. 73; Andrzej J. Kaminski, *Konzentrationslager 1896 bis heute: Geschichte, Funktion, Typologie* (Munich, Zurich: Pieper, 1990), p. 35.
2 Ian F.W. Beckett, *Modern Insurgencies and Counter-Insurgencies: Guerrillas and their Opponents since 1750* (London, New York: Routledge, 2001), p. 36.
3 On the South African War see Thomas Pakenham, *The Boer War* (London, Sydney: Futura Publications 1982); Bill Nasson, *The War for South Africa. The Anglo-Boer War 1899–1902* (Cape Town: Tafelberg, 2010); Iain R. Smith, *The Origins of the South African War, 1899–1902* (London, New York: Longman, 1996).
4 On British counter-guerrilla measures see Stephanus Burridge Spies, *Methods of Barbarism? Roberts and Kitchener and Civilians in the Boer Republics, January 1900–May 1902* (Cape Town: Human & Rousseau, 1977); Fransjohan Pretorius, The fate of the Boer women and children, in: Fransjohan Pretorius (ed.), *Scorched Earth* (Cape Town, Pretoria, Johannesburg: Human & Rousseau, 2001), pp. 36–59.
5 On the camps see Pretorius, *Scorched Earth*; Johannes C. Otto, *Die Konsentrasiekampe* (Pretoria: Protea Bookhuis, 2005) (first ed. 1954). For an overview of the literature on the camps see Elizabeth van Heyningen, The concentration camps of the South African (Anglo-Boer) War, 1900–1902, *History Compass*, 7 (2009), pp. 22–43.
6 On the 'black' camps see Stowell V. Kessler, *The Black Concentration Camps of the South African War, 1899–1902* (PhD thesis, University of Cape Town, 2003); B.E. Mongalo and Kobus du Pisani, Victims of a white man's war: blacks in concentration camps during the South African War (1899–1902), *Historia*, 44, 1 (1999), pp. 148–82. On the rationale behind the camps see Jonas Kreienbaum,

'A sad fiasco'. Koloniale Konzentrationslager um 1900 (PhD thesis, Humboldt University Berlin, 2012), pp. 81–6. 'Ein trauriges Fiasko'. Koloniale Konzentrationslager im südlichen Afrika, 1990–1908 (Hamburg: Hamburger Editionen, 2015), pp. 102–10.

7   Elizabeth van Heyningen, A tool for modernisation? The Boer concentration camps of the South African War, 1900–1902, *South African Journal of Science*, 106, 5/6 (2010), Article 242. Van Heyningen was severely criticized for describing the camps as 'tools for modernization', especially by Fransjohan Pretorius: The white concentration camps of the Anglo-Boer War: a debate without end, *Historia*, 55, 2 (2010), pp. 34–49. On the camp schools see Eliza Riedi, Teaching empire: British and dominions women teachers in the South African War concentration camps, *English Historical Review*, CXX, 489 (2005), pp. 1316–47 and Paul Zietsman, The concentration camp schools – beacons of light in the darkness, in: Pretorius, *Scorched Earth*, pp. 86–109.

8   Iain R. Smith and Andreas Stucki, The colonial development of concentration camps (1868–1902), *The Journal of Imperial and Commonwealth History*, 39, 3 (2011), pp. 417–37; Andreas Stucki, *Aufstand und Zwangsumsiedlung: Die kubanischen Unabhängigkeitskriege 1868–1898* (Hamburg: Hamburger Editionen, 2012); John Lawrence Tone, *War and Genocide in Cuba, 1895–1898* (Chapel Hill: University of North Carolina Press, 2006).

9   Rose Innes to Lord Monk Betton, Dieppe, 25 July 1901, Cadbury Research Library Birmingham (CRLB), Joseph Chamberlain Papers (JC), 13, South Africa: 1900–1902, 1/164.

10 Jean Veber, *Das Blutbuch von Transvaal* (Berlin: Dr. Eysler & Co., 1901).

11 Emily Hobhouse, *The Brunt of War and Where it Fell* (London: Methuen & Company, 1902), p. 317.

12 An old man obstinate, *Pall Mall Gazette*, 24 November 1900.

13 Reconcentration, *Pall Mall Gazette*, 28 November 1900. Further articles which contain references to Cuba are: Lord Roberts's decree, *Northern Echo*, 30 August 1900; Farm burning in the Transvaal and Orange River Colonies, *The Times*, 26 November 1900.

14 Memorandum on certain points connected with the conduct of hostilities, 24 October 1901, National Archives London (NAL), Colonial Office (CO) 417 South Africa/335 Vol. XVI. War Office, 28. Oct.–30. Dec. 1901, pp. 8–31.

15 Joseph Chamberlain to Arthur Balfour, Birmingham, 13 November 1901, JC 11 General correspondence, A-Z: 1900–1902, 5/1.

16 Charles E. Callwell, *Small Wars: Their Principles and Practice* (London: Her Majesty's Stationary Office, 1906).

17 *St James Gazette*, 20 August 1900, as cited in National Archives Pretoria (NAP), Jan Ploeger Papers (A 2030), Vol. 29 Konsentrasiekampe, 1899–1900.

18 See for example, The situation in Cuba, *The Times*, 30 November 1896; The Cuban atrocities, *Daily News*, 13 April 1898; The Cuban War, *Manchester Guardian*, 30 April 1898. In South Africa the *Cape Argus*, among others, reported on 26 Mach 1897. See A.M. Davey, The reconcentrados of Cuba, *Historia*, 5 (1960), 3, p. 194.

19 Annette Wieviorka, 'L'expression "camp de concentration" au 20e siècle', *Vingtième Siècle*, 54 (1997), pp. 4–12.

20 Ian Beckett favours this interpretation as mentioned above. Beckett, *Modern Insurgencies*, p. 36. Andreas Stucki prefers a combined approach to explain the evolving of concentration policies around the turn of the century. Stucki: *Aufbruch ins Zeitalter der Lager*, p. 339.

21 J.W. Holderness to H.W. Just, 13 November 1901, CO 417/335, pp. 201ff.

22 Memorandum, 18 November 1901, CO 417/335, pp. 218–20.

23 See, for instance, the reports by camp inspector Dr Kendal Franks from August 1901. In Barberton and Balmoral camps he had already found the mentioned principles introduced. In Middelburg, where he perceived the administration as too laissez-faire and where no system of daily tent visits existed, he encouraged corresponding changes. All reports in NAP, Private Secretary of the Governor of the Transvaal (GOV) 262.
24 This term is loosely following Isabel Hull's concept of 'military culture'. This 'culture' is characterized by certain methods of operations, routines, expectations and basic assumptions which greatly influence the actions of persons affected by it. Hull, *Absolute Destruction*, pp. 91–8. Elizabeth van Heyningen explicitly refers to a specific 'medical culture' in the British camps: Women and disease: the clash of medical cultures in the concentration camps of the South African War, in: Greg Cuthbertson, Albert Grundlingh and Mary-Lynn Suttie (eds), *Writing a Wider War. Rethinking Gender, Race, and Identity in the South African War, 1899–1902* (Athens and Cape Town: Ohio University Press, 2002), pp. 186–212.
25 Holderness to Just, 13 November 1901, CO 417/335, pp. 201ff.
26 Tel. Joseph Chamberlain to Alfred Milner, 16 November 1901, JC 14 Colonial affairs (other than South Africa): 1900–1902, 4/2/201.
27 Tel. Joseph Chamberlain to Alfred Milner, 20 November 1901, JC 14/4/2/203.
28 Monthly Report on Natal camps for February 1902, Pietermaritzburg, 12 March 1902, CO 179 Natal/222, vol. I. Despatches, Jan.–Apr. 1902, p. 453; on Merebank camp see Annette U. Wohlberg, *The Merebank Concentration Camp in Durban, 1901–1902* (masters thesis, University of Orange Free State 2000).
29 Tel. Alfred Milner to Joseph Chamberlain, 1 December 1901, JC 14/4/2/212.
30 Ibid.
31 Ibid. and Alfred Milner to Hamilton Goold-Adams, Johannesburg, 14 January 1902, Bodleian Library Oxford (BLO), Milner Papers (MP) 173 Correspondence with the Governor of the Orange River Colony, Major General Pretyman, and other officials, 1900–1904, pp. 253–7.
32 Tel. Chamberlain to Milner, 20 November 1901, JC 14/4/2/203.
33 Milner to Goold-Adams, 14 January 1902, MP 173, pp. 253–257.
34 Final Report Native Refugee Department Transvaal, NAP, Transvaal Administrative Reports (TKP) 135 Transvaal Administration Reports for 1902. Part I. Administration, Pretoria 1903, p. 1.
35 Kessler, *The Black Concentration Camps*, pp. 130–46; also Peter Warwick, *Black People in the South African War 1899–1902* (Cambridge: Cambridge UP, 1983), pp. 145–62.
36 Tone, *War and Genocide*, pp. 201ff., 206–9; Stucki, *Aufstand und Zwangsmigration*, pp. 206–12.
37 An exception is the following article which, along the way, mentions 'zones of cultivation': Spain's great offence in Cuba: 'Concentration', *Manchester Times*, 29 April 1898.
38 An example for this kind of thinking can be found in G.B. Beak, *The Aftermath of War. An Account of the Repatriation of Boers and Natives in the Orange River Colony 1902–1904* (London: Arnold, 1906), pp. 25, 29, 149.
39 Kessler, *The Black Concentration Camps*, p. 132.
40 Ulrike Lindner, *Koloniale Begegnungen. Deutschland und Großbritannien als Imperialmächte in Afrika 1880–1914* (Frankfurt, M.: Campus, 2011), p. 257.
41 Hull, *Absolute Destruction*, pp. 96ff.; also compare footnote 24.
42 Dirk van Laak, Kolonien als, Laboratorien der Moderne?, in: Sebastian Conrad and Jürgen Osterhammel (eds), *Das Kaiserreich transnational: Deutschland und die*

Welt 1871-1914 (Göttingen: Vandenhoeck & Ruprecht, 2004), pp. 261ff.; Cf. also Jürgen Osterhammel, *Kolonialismus. Geschichte – Formen – Folgen* (Munich: Beck, 2004), pp. 115ff.; and Andreas Eckert, *Kolonialismus* (Frankfurt, M.: Fischer, 2006), pp. 103, 107ff.

43 Imperial German Governorate for South West Africa to Colonial Department, 17 April 1906, Bundesarchiv Berlin (BAB), Reichskolonialamt (R 1001)/2119 Aufstand der Hereros 1904–1909, pp. 42–4.

44 Sebastian Conrad, 'Eingeborenenpolitik' in Kolonie und Metropole. 'Erziehung zur Arbeit' in Ostafrika und Ostwestfale, in: Conrad, Osterhammel, *Kaiserreich transnational*, pp. 107–28; see also John L. Comaroff and Jean Comaroff, Hausgemachte Hegemonie, in: Sebastian Conrad and Shalini Randeria (eds), *Jenseits des Eurozentrismus: Postkoloniale Perspektiven in den Geschichts- und Kulturwissenschaften* (Frankfurt, M.: Campus, 2002), pp. 247–82.

45 Memorandum, William Onslow, 23 November 1901, CO 179/220 vol. IV. Despatches, Oct.–Dec. 1901, p. 98.

46 Andreas Gestrich, Konzentrationslager: Voraussetzungen und Vorläufer vor der Moderne, in: Bettina Greiner and Alan Kramer (eds), *Die Welt der Lager: Zur 'Erfolgsgeschichte' einer Institution* (Hamburg: Hamburger Editionen, 2013), pp. 43–61; see also Jane Caplan, Political detention and the origin of the concentration camps in Nazi Germany, 1933–1935/6, in: Neil Gregor (ed.), *Nazism, War and Genocide: Essays in Honour of Jeremy Noakes* (Exeter: University of Exeter Press, 2005), pp. 22–41.

47 Tel. general superintendent refugee camps to Lieutenant Governor Bloemfontein, Pretoria, 26 February 1901, Free State Archives Bloemfontein (FAB), superintendent of the department of refugees, Orange River Colony (SRC) 2 Correspondence Files General, 1901 Feb–Mar, No. 284.

48 Memorandum on the Concentration Camps, 18 November 1901, CO 417/335, pp. 178–80.

49 Memorandum William Onslow, 3 December 1901, CO 179/220, p. 212.

50 G. F. de Lotbinière to Hamilton Goold-Adams, 18 January 1902, CO 224 Orange River Colony /7 vol. I. Despatches, Jan.–July 1902, p. 563.

51 Tilman Dedering, Compounds, camps, colonialism, *Journal of Namibian Studies*, 12 (2012), pp. 29–46; Rob Turrell, Kimberley's model compounds, *Journal of African History*, 25 (1984), pp. 59–75.

52 Jürgen Zimmerer, The Colonial War 1904–1908: War, concentration camps and genocide in South-West Africa: the first German genocide, in: Jürgen Zimmerer and Joachim Zeller (eds), *Genocide in German South-West Africa: The Colonial War of 1904–1908 and its Aftermath* (London: Merlin Press, 2008), pp. 41–63; or David Olusoga and Casper W. Erichsen, *The Kaiser's Holocaust. Germany's Forgotten Genocide and the Colonial Roots of Nazism* (London: Faber & Faber, 2010). On the German South West African War in general see Horst Drechsler, *Let Us Die Fighting: The Struggle of the Herero and Nama against German Imperialism, 1884–1915* (Berlin: Akademie-Verlag, 1986); Helmut Bley, *South-West Africa under German Rule, 1894–1914* (Evanston: Northwestern University Press, 1971); Hull, *Absolute Destruction*; Susanne Kuss, *Deutsches Militär auf kolonialen Kriegsschauplätzen: Eskalation und Gewalt zu Beginn des 20. Jahrhunderts* (Berlin: Links, 2010).

53 On the purpose behind the camps in more detail see Jonas Kreienbaum, 'Vernichtungslager' in Deutsch-Südwestafrika? Zur Funktion der Konzentrationslager im Herero- und Namakrieg (1904–1908), *Zeitschrift für Geschichtswissenschaft*, 12 (2010), pp. 1014–26.

54 Andreas Heinrich Bühler, *Der Namaaufstand gegen die deutsche Kolonialherrschaft in Namibia von 1904–1913* (Frankfurt, M., London: IKO – Verlag für interkulturelle Kommunikation, 2003); Werner Hillebrecht, The Nama and the war in the south, in: Zimmerer and Zeller (eds), *Genocide in German South-West Africa*, pp. 143–58.
55 Sterblichkeit in den Kriegsgefangenenlagern in Südwestafrika, R 1001/2140 Aufstand im Namaland (Namaqualand) und seine Bekämpfung, vol. 8, Febr. 1907–Febr. 1909, pp. 161ff.; on the reasons for mass death see Hull, *Absolute Destruction*, pp. 70–90 and Kreienbaum, *Vernichtungslager*.
56 Steffen Bender, *Der Burenkrieg und die deutschsprachige Presse: Wahrnehmungen und Deutungen zwischen Bureneuphorie und Anglophobie 1899–1902* (Paderborn: Schöningh, 2009), pp. 13–23.
57 Nicol Stassen and Ulrich van der Heyden, *German Publications on the Anglo-Boer War* (Pretoria: Protea Boekhuis, 2007).
58 *Die Concentrationslager im Transvaal und Orange River Colonie* (London: Siegle, 1902); Emily Hobhouse, *Die Zustände in den südafrikanischen Konzentrationslagern: Bericht von Miss E. Hobhouse* (Berlin: Deutscher Burenhilfsbund, 1902); Elizabeth Neethling, *Fünfzehn Monate in den Konzentrationslagern: Erinnerungen einer Burenfrau aus ihrer Gefangenschaft* (Bern: Berner Tageblatt, 1903).
59 Bundesarchiv Koblenz (BAK), N 1145 Nachlass Paul Leutwein (1882–1946), vol. 4, manuskript: Im Banne Afrikas. Romantisches Geschichtsbild des alten Wild-Südwestafrikas.
60 Ludwig von Estorff, *Wanderungen und Kämpfe in Südwestafrika, Ostafrika und Südafrika 1894–1910* (Wiesbaden: Kutscher, 1968), pp. 93ff.
61 Manuscript, Generalkonsul des Deutschen Reiches für Britisch-Südafrika in Kapstadt, BAK, N 1669 Nachlass Friedrich von Lindequist (1895–1903); see also CO 417/348 vol. VI. Miscellaneous. Despatches, January 1902, pp. 1021–4. Bloemfontein and Johannesburg were not at all the largest camps.
62 On this quarrel in detail see Kreienbaum, *A Sad Fiasco*, pp. 102–5.
63 biographical data on Hintrager, BAK, N 1037 Nachlass Oskar Hintrager.
64 J.J. Oberholster, Inleiding, *Christiaan deWet-Annale* 2 (1973), pp. 5–10, here p. 6; and Oskar Hintrager, *Steijn, de Wet und die Oranje-Freistaater: Tagebuchblätter aus dem südafrikanischen Kriege* (Tübingen: Laupp, 1902).
65 Olusoga and Erichsen, *The Kaiser's Holocaust*, pp. 159ff. In his report to the kaiser, Stillfried speaks of 'geschlossene Niederlassungen' (closed settlements) next to the workplaces where 'natives' should be accommodated in the future. That these were to be concentration camps and not villages or 'locations', which had already existed in peacetime in Southern Africa, is mere speculation. First and foremost, Stillfried's report is dated 12 December 1904, a day after the first order to build concentration camps had been issued, and it can therefore not be the 'origin' of the concentration policy. Bericht des Oberleutnants Graf von Stillfried und Rattonitz betreffend Eingeborenenfrage und militärische Verhältnisse in SWA i.d. letzten zwei Jahren, Berlin, 12 December 1904, R 1001/2117 Aufstand der Hereros 1904–7, pp. 59ff.
66 Inspector Haussleiter to Bernhard von Bülow, Barmen, 25 November 1904, Archives of the Evangelical-Lutheran Church in the Republic of Namibia (ELCRN), II. Innere Verwaltung, 5.14 Deputation. Verschiedenes, 1904–7.
67 Tel. Bernhard von Bülow to Lothar von Trotha, Berlin, 11 December 1904, R 1001/2089 Differenzen zwischen Generalleutnant Lothar v. Trotha und Gouverneur Theodor Gotthilf Leutwein über das Verhältnis von militärischen und politischen Maßnahmen zur Beendigung des Krieges, p. 54.

68 *Berichte der Rheinischen Missions-Gesellschaft* 59 (1902); Georg Haccius, *Aus der Drangsalzeit des südafrikanischen Lüneburg* (Hermannsburg: [probably 1904]); see also Ulrich van der Heyden, Der 'Burenkrieg' von 1899 bis 1902 und die deutschen Missionsgesellschaften, in: Ulrich van der Heyden and Jürgen Becher (eds), *Mission und Gewalt: Der Umgang christlicher Missionen mit Gewalt und die Ausbreitung des Christentums in Afrika und Asien in der Zeit von 1792 bis 1918/19* (Stuttgart: Steiner, 2000), p. 214.

69 Hanns Lessing refers to the respective files in the mission archives in Wuppertal. Hanns Lessing: In der Nähe dieser Wasserstelle sollen Konzentrationslager errichtet werden. Eine theologische Rekonstruktion der Rolle der Rheinischen Missionsgesellschaft während des Kolonialkrieges in Namibia (1904–1908), in: Hanns Lessing et al. (eds), *Deutsche evangelische Kirche im kolonialen südlichen Afrika. Die Rolle der Auslandsarbeit von den Anfängen bis in die 1920er Jahre* (Wiesbaden: Harrassowitz, 2011), pp. 471–95, here p. 493.

70 Lindner, *Koloniale Begegnungen*, p. 8, see also pp. 40ff., 52–59, 84–100.

71 Georg Hartmann, *Deutsch-Südwestafrika im Zusammenhang mit Südafrika* (Berlin: W. Süsserott, 1899), p. 12.

72 For instance: Was lehrt uns der Burenkrieg?, *Militär-Wochenblatt*, 42 (1902), pp. 1146–7; or Die Nutzbarmachung der Erfahrungen des Südafrikanischen Krieges, *Militär-Wochenblatt*, 85 (1902), pp. 2273ff. In these articles, questions of infantry tactics were discussed, not counter-guerrilla measures, therefore the concentration camps were of no great importance.

73 For example, Konzentrationslager, in: *Meyers Lexikon, 7th ed., Vol. VI. Hornberg-Korrektiv* (Leipzig: Bibliographisches Institut, 1927), c. 1723.

74 These quotations are taken from the *Kreuzzeitung*, which first used the term 'Konzentrations-Lagern' on 24 July 1901. *Neue Preußische Zeitung*, 21 June 1901, 22 June 1901, 24 July 1901, 13 September 1901.

75 Der Krieg zwischen England und den Buren, *Neue Preußische Zeitung*, 6 June 1901.

76 Birthe Kundrus, Kontinuitäten, Parallelen, Rezeptionen. Überlegungen zur 'Kolonialisierung' des Nationalsozialismus, *Werkstatt Geschichte*, 43 (2006), p. 61.

77 Jonas Kreienbaum, Guerrilla wars and colonial concentration camps. The exceptional case of German South West Africa (1904–1908), *Journal for Namibian Studies*, 11 (2012), pp. 85–103.

78 Christiane Eisenberg, Kulturtransfer als historischer Prozess. Ein Beitrag zur Komparatistik, in: Hartmut Kaelble and Jürgen Schriewer (eds), *Vergleich und Transfer: Komparatistik in den Sozial-, Geschichts- und Kulturwissenschaften* (Frankfurt, M.: Campus, 2003), pp. 399–417.

79 Bender, *Burenkrieg*, pp. 118ff.

80 Jürgen Zimmerer, *Deutsche Herrschaft über Afrikaner: Staatlicher Machtanspruch und Wirklichkeit im kolonialen Namibia* (Hamburg: Lit, 2001), p. 182.

81 The concentration of the African population was only mentioned as an exception. For instance in: 'Der Krieg zwischen England und den Buren', *Neue Preußische Zeitung*, 5 August 1901.

82 This model of explanation can be understood as a synthesis of Isabel Hull's 'military culture' concept, which emphasizes the importance of unquestioned basic assumptions, and Susanne Kuss's concept of the '*Kriegsschauplatz*' (theatre of war), which highlights the impact of local conditions on the development of colonial wars. However, it has to be stressed that Hull, to a certain degree, includes local constellations in her thoughts. Hull, *Absolute Destruction* and Kuss, *Deutsches Militär*, pp. 29–37.

Index

Abd el-Krim 13
abolition of slave trade 13
Afghanistan 133, 138–9
Africa 40–2, 44–6, 59–63, 65, 67–70. *See also* specific countries
agriculture 37, 43, 46
Aldred, Guy 175
Alexandria 63
Algeria 10, 129, 139, 141
Allard v. Lobbau 113
Alsace-Lorraine 199
Amboina (Ambon) massacre (1623) 48
American Civil War 221
American Empire 116, 119, 124n48
American law 110, 125n53; influence of, 112–17, 119
Amsterdam 64
Amu-Darya 134
Andaman Islands 176
Angell, Joseph 113
Angers, François-Réal 113
Annam 199
Antigua 37
Antilles 37
anti-Westernism 154–5, 159–62, 166
Arcachon 178
Argentina 44
art, artists 41, 45
Asia Association 158
'Asia for the Asians' 161
Asian Monroe Doctrine 160–2, 165–6
Asianism 154–9, 161–2, 164–6
Asmis, Robert 62
Association Internationale pour l'Exploration et la Civilisation de l'Afrique Centrale (Association Internationale Africaine) 82–3, 86–7
Australia 10, 44, 45, 48, 69, 109, 110, 119. *See also* New South Wales; Victoria
Austria-Hungary 67–8
Aylwin, Thomas 112–14, 123n21

Bailloud, Maurice Camille 205–6, 208–12
Banks, Sir Joseph 41, 43–4
Banning, Emil 91
barbarism 37
Barbusse, Henri 185
Barthold, Vasilii Vladimirovich 137–8, 147
Bashkir 128
Basutoland 45
Beauport River 113
Beckett, Ian F.W. 219
Beijing 160
Belgium, Belgian Empire 43, 57–8, 63–4, 67, 86–8, 90–1
Belich, James 44
Beneke, Max 12
Berlin 42, 44, 61, 183, 226
Berlin, Conference of (1884) 12, 40, 45
Bernhardi, Friedrich von 188
Binder-Krieglstein, Eugen 204
Bismarck, Otto von 87
Blackburn, Colin 117–18
Bloemfontein 220, 227
Boading 197–8, 203–6, 208–10, 212–13
Bombay 64, 177
Bordeaux 178–9
Bosphorus 40
Boswell v. *Denis* 114
botanical gardens 41, 46
Botswana 60
Boulogne 178
Boxer Rebellion 154, 197–217
Brandis, Dietrich 41
Braund, James 41
Bremerhaven 201
British Columbia 44
British Empire 36–8, 40–1, 43–8, 57–63, 67, 69, 107–12, 116–17, 120, 154, 160, 163, 197
British India 38–9, 41–2, 45. *See also* Indian law

British law. *See* English law; Scottish law
Brodrick, St John 228
brothels 209
Brown v. *Gugy* 112, 114
Brussels 57, 63–4, 69
Brussels Conference (1889–90) 42
Bukhara 128–9, 133, 139
bullionism 36
Bülow, Bernhard von 226–7
Burke, Edmund 37

Calcutta 63, 183
Callwell, Charles 222
Calvo, Carlos 85
Cama, Bhikaiji Rustom 177–8
Cameroon 62
Canada East. *See* Quebec
Canada 44, 47–8, 69, 110–11, 113. *See also* Ontario; Quebec
Cape Colony 44, 110, 118–20, 125n53, 223, 226, 228–9
Cape Town 227
capitalism 36, 46
Caribbean 37–8, 40, 43, 65
Caroline Islands 91
Caspian 129
Catholicism 44–5, 48
cattle diseases 42
Caucasus 127, 129–30
Central Asia 127–49
Ceylon 222
Chailley-Bert, Joseph 61, 64, 88
Chamberlain, Joseph 223–4
chartered companies 36
Chile 67
China 40, 43, 153–66, 197–8, 208, 211
Church of England 45
citizenship 11
civil law 107, 109–20
civilization 37–8
civilizing mission 202
Cixi (Empress) 159–60, 200
classical empires 37–8
Cleghorn, James 223
Code Napoléon 111, 114–15, 118
Coello, Francisco 86–7, 92
Colonial Lobby Groups 80–1
Colonial Office, British 41–2
Comité de l'Afrique Française 82

Commissioners of French Hoek v. *Hugo* 118–19
Common Culture Society 158
common law 108, 110–12, 115–19. *See also* English law
communications 39, 43, 48
Communist International (Comintern) 183
Communist Party of India 183
Confucius 156, 163
Congo Free State 80, 84, 87, 90–1
Congo 45, 64, 67
conquest 109, 111, 115, 118, 120
Conrad, Joseph 173
Cook, Capt. James 41
Coolies 205–7
Cooper, Frederick 68
co-operation, inter-imperial 120
Costa, Joaquín 82–3, 92
Court of Appeals of Lower Canada 112
Court of Arbitration in The Hague 175
Coutume de Paris 111
Crimean War 44
crossed history 111, 116
Cuba, Cuban War of Independence 92, 219, 221–2, 224–6, 230
Curzon Wyllie, William Hutt 187
Curzon, George Nathaniel 129
custom 109, 111

d'Arenberg, August 67
Daghestan 138, 148
Dagu 203
Daviron, Benoit 68
de Lorimier, Charles-Chamilly 113
decolonization 48
Denmark 67
Dépêche Coloniale 83, 93
Dernburg, Bernhard 60, 67–8, 89
Déscamps, Édouard 67, 80, 95
Deutsche Afrikanische Gesellschaft 82, 86
Deutsche Kolonialgesellschaft 82–3, 86, 90, 92
Deutsche Kolonialzeitung 80–91, 93–4, 96
Deutscher Kolonialverein 82

Index

development 94–5
Doucet, N.B. 122n13
Dreyfus affair 199
Dukhovskoi, Sergei Mikhailovich 132
Dutch colonial association 88
Dutch Empire 39, 85–6, 88, 110
Dutch law 110, 116, 118–19
Dutch Scots brigade 48

East Africa 41–2, 43, 45
East Asia Common Culture Academy 158
East Asia Common Culture Society 158, 161
East Asia Society 158
East Asia 153–66
economics 36, 37, 39
Edinburgh 37, 46
education 37, 39, 41, 45, 47
Egypt 60
Embrey v. *Owen* 116–17
emigration, colonial 85
English law 109–14, 116–20
Enlightenment 37–8, 40
Entente Cordiale 79, 173, 175, 177
environment 40–1, 43, 46, 114
epistemic communities 15
Epp, Franz Xaver 209
Estorff, Ludwig von 227
État Indépendant du Congo. *See* Congo Free State
ethnography 43, 45
Étienne, Eugène 82, 90
Europe 225
European Colonial Congress 90
Europeanization 92
Exchequer, Court of 116–17
experts, colonial 84
explorers 44–6

Far East 39, 43
Ferghana 128, 130, 138, 140, 149
Ferry, Jules 82
Fidel, Camille 93
firearms 40, 42
First Sino-Japanese War 153–8, 160, 163, 165–6
Foreign Office, British 41
forestry 41, 43, 46–7

France 36–7, 41, 45–6, 57, 59–61, 63–5, 67, 109, 154–5, 160, 163–4, 197–8. *See also* French Empire; French law
Franco-Prussian War 221
François, Curt von 87
Francophone lawyers 113
free trade 37–8, 40
Freiburg 63
French Communist Party 183–4
French Empire 39, 43–4, 60, 107, 110–11, 116, 118, 120
French law 110–20; influence of, 111, 116, 119–20
French-Russian alliance (1894) 199
Fukuzawa, Yukichi 156–7

Gale, Charles James 116–17
Garibaldi, Giuseppe 175
Garioni, Vincenzo 207
Gaselee, Alfred 205, 207–8
Gautier, Victor 93
Gayl, Georg von 207
Geneva 58
genocide 47
Gent 58
Gentlemen's Agreement (1907/8) 165
German Colonial Society 45
German East Africa 41
German Empire 39, 43–4, 198
German Legion 44
German South West Africa or the Herero and Nama War 219, 224–30
Germany 41, 43, 47, 57, 59–61, 63, 66–7, 69, 154–5, 158, 160, 163–4, 197–8
Gesellschaft für deutsche Kolonisation (Society for German Colonization) 81, 83
Gibbon, Edward 37–8
Giers, Fedor Karlovich 135
Gillman, Clement 63
Gilmour v. *Minor*. *See Minor* v. *Gilmour*
Giménez, Saturnino 91
Gippius, Alexander Ivanovich 130
Girouard, Désiré 113
Gold Coast 60, 62
Granby 107
grazhdanstvennost' (civic values) 135
Grey, Sir George 44
Grodekov, Nikolai Ivanovich 137–9

240

Grove, Richard 47
Guangzhouwan 199–200
Gugy, B.C.A. 113
Guiheng 208
Gulick, Sidney 164–5

Hague Convention 202
Hailey, Lord 46
Hamilton, Louis 62
Hardie, Keir 175
harmonization 108
Harvard University 113
Hastings, Warren 38, 138
Haussleiter, Gottlob 227
Hay, John 162
Herero 43
Hidaya 127, 137–40, 147
Hintrager, Oskar 227
Hiroi, Tatsutarō 165
historians 35–6, 40, 47–8
Hobhouse, Emily 226
Hochstetter, Ferdinand 41
Hokkaidō 153
Holderness, Thomas 223
Holzmann, Philipp 63
homogenization 108, 118
Honduras 67
Hong Kong 160, 200
Houck, Louis 113
House of Lords, Judicial Committee of the 117
Hubert, Lucien 90
humanitarianism, humanitarian colonialism 13, 86, 94
Hundred Days Reform (1898) 158–60
hunting 37, 41–2

imperial policy 120
India 10, 62–3, 65, 67, 69, 129–31, 135, 137–41, 222–5, 229. *See also* Indian law
Indian law 119, 125n53
Indian Ocean 39, 41, 43
Indian Political Intelligence Service (IPI) 172
indigenous peoples 35, 41–2, 46–48
Indochina 62, 201
Indonesia 10
industrial (societies, imperialism) 37, 39, 48

influence: distinguishing inter-imperial from transnational 110, 116, 119–20
informal imperialism 43
Information Office for the Orient (Nachrichtenstelle für den Orient) 177
inorodtsy ('aliens') 128
Inouye, Masaji 69
Institut Colonial International. *See* International Colonial Institute
Institut de Droit International 85, 89
Institutción Libre de Enseñanza 83
International Colonial Institute 80, 84, 88–96
International Colonial Office 184
International Geographical Congress Paris 1875 85–6
International Geographical Congress Brussels 1876 80, 85–7, 91, 96
Ireland 44
irrigation 89
Italian Empire 39, 44
Italy 42, 57, 59–60, 67, 69, 197
Itō, Hirobumi 156–7

Jacques-Cartier River 114
Janssen, Camille 64
Japan 39–40, 43, 68–70, 153–66, 203
Jaurès, Jean 175
Java 62
Jefferson, Thomas 113
Jesuits 200
Jiaozhou (Kiautschou) 160
Johannesburg 227
Johnston, Sir Harry 45
Jones, Sir William 38
Judicial Committee of the Privy Council 107–12, 115–20
Justinian, *Digest* of 111, 114–16, 124n39

Kang, Youwei 159–62
Kasai 87
Kaufman, Konstantin Petrovich von 132
Kazakhstan 128
Kazan University 137, 141
Kazem Bek, Alexander 137, 139
Kent, James 112–17, 124n39
Kenya 60
Ketteler, Clemens von 203, 205, 207, 209–10

Khiva 128–9
Kiel 201
Kimberley 226
King's Bench, (English) court of 116
King's Bench, District of Quebec, court of 112
Kingsdown, Lord 111, 117, 118–19
Kitchener, Lord Horatio Herbert 44, 46, 220–1, 227
Kitchener, Walter 227
Knackfuss, Hermann 163
Koch, Robert 42, 62–3
Koelle, Rev. Sigismund 45
Koenig, J.G. 41
Kolonialinstitut, Hamburg 83
Kolonialwirtschaftliches Komitee 84
Konoe, Atsumaro 158, 161–2
Korea 70, 153, 155–6, 163
Kossuth, Lajos 175
Krapf, Johan Ludwig 45
Kuropatkin, Aleksei Nikolaevich 129
Kyrgyzstan 128

labour 43, 44, 46–7, 89
Langlois, C.B. 113
language 45, 47–8
Latin America 57, 67–8
law 107–20
law, colonial 89
League of Nations 47, 48
Leiden 62
Lelièvre, Simon 113
Lenin, Vladimir Ilyich 183
Leopold II, King of Belgium 59–60, 84–5, 87, 90–1, 96
Leopoldville 88
Lequis, Arnold von 211
Leroy-Beaulieu, Paul 64
Leutwein, Paul 226
Li, Hongzhang 156–9
Liang, Qichao 159–60, 162
Ligue des Droits de l'Homme 184
Lindelfels, Baron von 42
Lindequist, Friedrich von 68, 227–8
literature, juvenile 38
Lith, Pieter van der 62, 64
Livingstone, David 46
London 66, 107, 109, 112, 115, 116, 172, 174–5, 178, 204. *See also* Privy Council

Longuet, Jean 175, 180
Louber, Émile 202
Louisiana 113–14
Louwers, Octave 64
Lower Canada. *See* Quebec
Lugard, Frederick 46, 69
Lushington, Stephen 116
Lyall, Alfred 64, 67, 93
Lyautey, Hubert 89
Lykoshin, Nil Sergeevich 130, 143
Lyon v. *Fishmongers' Company* 117

Macaulay, Thomas Lord 37
Mackay, Donald 64, 67
Madagascar 66, 201
Maine, Henry Sumner 130
malaria 23, 42
Malaya 10
Malta 180
Manchuria 205
Marchand, Jean-Baptiste 46
Marghinani, Burhan ud-Din 'Ali ibn Abu Bakr 138–9, 147
Marseille 174–6, 178, 183, 202
Martinique 179
Marx, Karl 175
Mason v. *Hill* 116
Matadi 88
Mauch, Carl 45
Mauritius 110
Mazzini, Giuseppe 174
McGranahan, Carole 68
medicine 39, 40, 42, 45, 47. *See also* tropical medicine
Mediterranean 39
Meiji Restoration 153, 159
mercantilism 36, 37–8, 48
Merebank 223
migration 44, 48
Mill, John Stuart 130
Milner, Lord Alfred 223–4
Miner v. *Gilmour* 107, 110–12, 115–20
mines 43, 46
Minor v. *Gilmour*. *See Miner* v. *Gilmour*
mise en valeur 94–5
missions, missionaries 40, 44–6, 204–5
Miyao, Shunji 69
Moloney, Alfred 67
Mongolia 153

Monroe Doctrine 40, 154, 161
Montesquieu 114
Moravians 45
Morel, E.D. 45
Morocco 90–2, 96
mufti (Islamic jurist) 132, 134, 137
Munich 227
museums 41, 43, 46–7
Mutsu, Munemitsu 156

Nachtigal, Gustav 86
Nama 43
Namibia 43
Napoleonic Code. See *Code Napoléon*
Napoleonic Wars 37, 40
Natal 223, 225
Neethling, Elizabeth 226
Netherlands 36–7, 57, 61–4, 67. See also Dutch law
networks 41, 43
New Imperialism 36, 39
New Scotland Yard 174
New South Wales 110, 125n53
New York 65
New Zealand 9, 41, 44, 69
Nicholas II (Tsar) 163
Nigeria 46, 62, 66
Nolde, Boris Emmanuelovich 130–1, 144
North Africa 44
North America 38, 45. See also Canada; United States
North Sea 39
Northern Rhodesia 45
Norway 44
Nyasaland 60

Okinawa 153
Oliva v. Boissonnault 112–13, 115
Omaheke desert 226
Onslow, Lord William 225
Ontario 110
'Open Door' (China) 40
Opium Wars 154
Orange Free State and Orange River Colony 220, 224–5
Orr Ewing v. Colquhoun 117
Ostroumov, Nikolai Petrovich 137–8, 147
Ottoman Empire 43

Pacific Ocean 41, 44
Pahlen, Konstantin Konstantinovich von der 127–41
Pamir 128
Pan-Germanism 93
Paris Evangelical Mission 45
Paris 64, 69, 172–4, 177–80, 182
Paris, *Parlement* of 111. See also Contume de Paris
Parke, James 116
Peking 200, 203–5, 207–8
Perdue, Peter 68
Persia 133, 137
Persian (language) 134, 138, 140
Peters, Carl 81, 83
Philippines, Philippine War 68, 92, 160, 219, 221–2, 230
photography and film 46
Pietsch, Tamson 41, 47
Pondicherry 183–5
Port Arthur 199
Portugal 36–7, 57, 67
Portuguese Empire 40, 43–4
Pothier, Robert Joseph 111, 114–15, 124n39
Pouvourville, Albert 79, 90, 93–6
Pretoria 220
Privy Council 108. See also Judicial Committee of the Privy Council
Protestantism 36, 45
public health 42
Putte, Isaac Fransen van der 64

qazi (Islamic judge) 131–8, 140–1, 144
Qing (dynasty) 153–5
Qingdao 199
Quebec 107, 110–20
Quebec Act of 1774 111
Queen's Bench for the Province of Quebec, Court of 113–14
Queen's Bench of Canada, court of 107
Queen's Bench of Lower Canada, court of 112
quinine 23

race, racism 11, 38, 47
railways 43, 46, 89
Rana, S.R. 177–9

Real Sociedad Geográfica de Madrid 82, 86
Reay, Lord 88
Rebman, Johannes 45
Rechenberg, Albert von 60
religion 36, 38–9, 45–7
Revolution, French 37
Revue Coloniale Internationale 80, 88
Ribbentrop, Berthold 41
Richards, Thomas 66
Richthofen, Ferdinand von 86
Rif-war 13
riparian rights 107, 111–19, 124n31
Rivière du Sud 112
Roberts, Lord Frederick Sleigh 220–2
Robertson, William 37
Rohlfs, Gerhard 86
Rohrbach, Paul 61
Roman law 109–11, 114–16, 118–19
Rome 38, 42, 69, 173. *See also* Roman law
Rosen, Viktor Romanovich 137, 147
Ross, Robert 42
Rousseau, Jean-Jacques 38
Roy, Evelyn 185
Roy, Manabendra Nath 182–5, 192–3
Royal Asiatic Society 88
royal ordinances 111
Royal Society, London 41
Russia 57, 67–8, 154–5, 157–60, 163–5, 197, 203, 205. *See also* Russian Empire
Russian Empire 39, 43
Russo-Japanese War 154, 157, 163–5

Salisbury, Lord 42
Samarkand 128–9, 132–4, 138, 140, 148–9
'same culture' 159, 165–6
'same race' 153, 159, 161–3, 165–6
Sanitation 89
Savarkar, Vinayak Damodar 173–6, 178–9, 188
Say, Chailly Léon 64
Scandinavia 44
Schlick, Wilhelm 41
Schlieffen, Alfred von 201
Schutztruppe 88
Schweinfurth, Georg 86
science 37–9, 40–3, 47–8, 83–4, 93
scientific congresses 11
Scotland 41. *See also* Scottish law

Scottish law 117–18
'Scramble for Africa' 40
Second Opium War 197
settlers 42–5, 109–10
Sewell, Jonathan 112, 114–16
Seymour, Edward 200
shari'a 127–41
Shark Island 227
Shimonoseki Peace Treaty 155, 158
shipping 43–4
Siberia 127
'sick man of Europe' (Turkey) 40
Sierra Leone 45
Silbermann, Léon 211
Skobelev, Mikhail Dmitrevich 130
slavery 40, 47
Smith, Adam 37–8
Snesarev, Andrei Evgenevich 130, 143
Sociedad Española de Africanistas y Colonistas 82–3
Sociedad Española de Geografía Comercial 82, 84
Société Belge d'études coloniales 84
Société d'étude de Chemin de fer en Chine 205
Société des études coloniales et maritimes 82
'soft power' 43
Solf, Wilhelm 68
South Africa, South African War or Boer War 43–4, 219, 220–30; law 110, 118–20, 125n 53. *See also* Cape Colony
South America 39, 43–4
Southern Rhodesia 46
Spain 36–7, 67
Spanish colonialism 85–6, 90–2
Special Branch 172
Ssese Islands 62
St Helena 222
St Lawrence River 112
St Louis v. *St Louis* 112, 114–17
St Lucia 37
St Petersburg University 137–8, 141, 147
stadial theory 37
Stanley, Henry Morton 83, 87
Stillfried und Rattonitz, Count Georg von 227
Strachey, John 130

Superior Court of Quebec City 113
Superior Court of the District of
    Montreal 107
Sûreté Générale 173–4

Taiyuan 204
Tanaka, Stefan 156
Tanganyika 63
Tashkent 183
Tatar 128, 145
technology 36, 39, 43, 46
telegraph 43
Thames River 117
The Hague 69
Thomson, James 224
Thys, Albert 64, 89
Tianjin (Tientsin) 157, 200, 205, 207–8
Tibet 153
Tilley, Helen 58
Ting Yong 207–8
Tinker, Hugh 47
Togo 62
Tokyo Common Culture Academy 158
Tokyo 69, 158, 165
Tonkin 199, 201
Toullier, Charles Bonaventure Marie
    114–15
trade and commerce 36–40, 46
transport 39, 43
Transvaal 44, 220, 222, 224–5
Trenholme, Norman William 114
Triple Intervention 154–5, 160
tropical medicine 10
Trotha, Lothar von 226–7
Tunisia 129, 201
Turkestan, Russian 127–49
tuzemtsy ('natives') 128, 135
Tyler v. Wilkinson 112, 116–17

Uganda 62
Union Coloniale Française 82–3
United States 38–9, 42, 44, 47–8, 57,
    67–8, 109, 113, 154, 160–1, 163, 165,
    197. *See also* American Empire,
    American law
'*ulama* (Islamic scholars) 134
universal exhibitions 11, 199
universities 41, 43, 47
Upper Canada. *See* Ontario

Van der Lith, Piether Antoine 80, 88
Vayssié, Georges 181–2
Victoria, Australia 125n53
Vienna, Conference of (1814–15) 40
Vildrac, Charles 185
Vinnius, Arnold 116
Voet, Johannes 118
Voyron, Émile 203–4, 206, 208, 212–13

Wakefield, Edward Gibbon 9
Waldersee, Alfred Graf von 203, 206–9,
    212–13
Walvisbay 224
Wang Zhanggui 208
Wanner, Theodor 45
waqf (Islamic endowment) 133
water 107, 110–20
Waterberg 226
Watson, Alan 114
Wealth of Nations, The 38
West Africa 59
Weyler y Nicolau, Valeriano 221–2
White Peril 163–6
Wilhelm II (German Emperor) 90, 163,
    201
Wilhelmshaven 201
Wilkins, James 224
Wilson, Roland Knyvet 139–40
Windhoek 226
Wissmann, Hermann von 41–2, 87
Woermann, Adolf 87
Wood v. Waud 116–17
Wordsworth, William 37
World War I 35, 40, 43–4, 46, 48, 165–6,
    198
World War II 46, 48, 162
Württemberg Geographical Society 45

Yamaska River 107
Yanagida, Kunio 70
Yellow Peril 154, 163–5
Young Turk movement 11
Yuan, Shikai 166

Zachmann, Matthias 157
Zaghloul, Saad 179–80, 182, 184
Zarrow, Peter 159
Zhang, Taiyan 159
Zimbabwe Ruins 45
Zürich 63